# Lecture Notes of the Institute for Computer Sciences, Social Informatics and Telecommunications Engineering 543

The LNICST series publishes ICST's conferences, symposia and workshops.

LNICST reports state-of-the-art results in areas related to the scope of the Institute.

The type of material published includes

- Proceedings (published in time for the respective event)
- Other edited monographs (such as project reports or invited volumes)

LNICST topics span the following areas:

- General Computer Science
- E-Economy
- E-Medicine
- Knowledge Management
- Multimedia
- Operations, Management and Policy
- Social Informatics
- Systems

Guan Gui · Ying Li · Yun Lin
Editors

# e-Learning, e-Education, and Online Training

## 9th EAI International Conference, eLEOT 2023
## Yantai, China, August 17–18, 2023
## Proceedings, Part I

Springer

*Editors*
Guan Gui
Nanjing University of Posts
and Telecommunications
Nanjing, China

Ying Li
Yantai University
Yantai, China

Yun Lin
Institute of High Performance Computing
Fusionopolis, Singapore

ISSN 1867-8211 ISSN 1867-822X (electronic)
Lecture Notes of the Institute for Computer Sciences, Social Informatics
and Telecommunications Engineering
ISBN 978-3-031-51464-7 ISBN 978-3-031-51465-4 (eBook)
https://doi.org/10.1007/978-3-031-51465-4



This Springer imprint is published by the registered company Springer Nature Switzerland AG
The registered company address is: Gewerbestrasse 11, 6330 Cham, Switzerland

Paper in this product is recyclable.

# Preface

Welcome to the International Conference on e-Learning, e-Education, and Online Training in the picturesque city of Yantai! It's a privilege to have such a distinguished gathering of experts and scholars in the field of digital education.

Our conference title, "International Conference on e-Learning, e-Education, and Online Training," reflects the evolving landscape of education in the digital age. As we navigate a world increasingly defined by technology, the exploration of e-learning methodologies, e-education platforms, and online training mechanisms becomes paramount.

The significance of this conference was amplified by the locale. As a coastal city, Yantai's rich history and dynamic spirit offered an inspiring setting to explore groundbreaking ideas that can shape the future of education. Yantai University, one of the nearest universities to the coast, hosted this conference in support of educational development. Through insightful discussions, sharing of research findings, and collaborative networking, we aimed to harness the power of digital tools to democratize education, bridge learning gaps, and foster lifelong learning opportunities for diverse global communities.

Looking ahead, we envision a future where geographical boundaries are no longer barriers to quality education. Personalized learning pathways, augmented-reality classrooms, and AI-driven assessment models are just a glimpse into the possibilities that lie before us.

All participants engaged wholeheartedly in exchanging ideas and seizing this opportunity to contribute to the collective advancement of e-learning and online education. We embarked on this journey of innovation and transformation together.

Thank you for being a part of this inspiring conference. Here's to meaningful conversations, insightful discoveries, and a brighter future for education worldwide.

August 2023 Ying Li

# Organization

## Steering Committee

### Chairs

| | |
|---|---|
| Ying Li | Yantai University, China |
| Guanglu Sun | Harbin University of Science and Technology, China |

## Organizing Committee

### General Chair

| | |
|---|---|
| Ying Li | Yantai University, China |

### General Co-chairs

| | |
|---|---|
| Yun Lin | Harbin Engineering University, China |
| Danda Rawat | Howard University, USA |
| Joey Tianyi Zhou | Institute of High Performance Computing, A*STAR, Singapore |
| Guan Gui | Nanjing University of Posts and Telecommunications, China |
| Shifeng Ou | Yantai University, China |

### TPC Chairs

| | |
|---|---|
| Chen Cen | Institute for Infocomm Research, Singapore |
| Ruolin Zhou | University of Massachusetts Dartmouth, USA |
| Congan Xu | Naval Aviation University, China |
| Yi Lou | Harbin Institute of Technology, China |

### Web Chairs

| | |
|---|---|
| Gang Jin | Yantai University, China |
| Zheng Ma | University of Southern Denmark, Denmark |

### Publicity and Social Media Chairs

| | |
|---|---|
| Pengfei He | Yantai University, China |
| Lei Chen | Georgia Southern University, USA |

### Workshop Chairs

| | |
|---|---|
| Zhuoran Cai | Yantai University, China |
| Ming Yan | Agency for Science, Technology and Research (A*STAR), Singapore |
| Haoran Zha | Harbin Engineering University, China |

### Sponsorship and Exhibits Chairs

| | |
|---|---|
| Jinwei Wang | Yantai University, China |
| Ali Kashif | Manchester Metropolitan University, UK |

### Publications Chairs

| | |
|---|---|
| Weina Fu | Hunan Normal University, China |
| Wenjia Li | New York Institute of Technology, USA |
| Meiyu Wang | Harbin Engineering University, China |

### Local Chair

| | |
|---|---|
| Zhuoran Cai | Yantai University, China |

## Technical Program Committee

| | |
|---|---|
| Yun Lin | Harbin Engineering University, China |
| Danda Rawat | Howard University, USA |
| Joey Tianyi Zhou | A*STAR, Singapore |
| Guan Gui | Nanjing University of Posts and Telecommunications, China |
| Shifeng Ou | Yantai University, China |
| Chen Cen | Institute for Infocomm Research, Singapore |
| Ruolin Zhou | University of Massachusetts Dartmouth, USA |
| Congan Xu | Naval Aviation University, China |
| Zheng Ma | University of Southern Denmark, Denmark |
| Lei Chen | Georgia Southern University, USA |

# Contents – Part I

# IT Promoted Teaching Platforms and Systems

# Cloud Computing-Based Sharing Platform for High-quality Teaching Resources of Higher Vocational Physical Education

Xin He(✉) and Hongjie Cao

Chongqing Vocational Institute of Engineering, Jiangjin 402260, China
17830660127@163.com

**Abstract.** In order to solve the problem of high packet loss rate during data transmission of the existing educational resource sharing platform, a sharing platform for high-quality teaching resources of higher vocational sports based on cloud computing is proposed and designed. The method first introduces blockchain technology to build a shared information hierarchy model, omits some intermediate links of shared information transmission, and establishes a trusted measurement, storage and reporting mechanism on the encrypted storage technology of physical protection. Then confirm the integrity test value of physical education quality teaching resources in higher vocational colleges, improve the trusted cloud computing mechanism, and finally calculate the matching degree of each demand corresponding to the tasks in the cloud system and the nodes of physical education quality teaching resources in higher vocational colleges, and integrate all data in the shared model into the central database to share high-quality teaching resources. The experimental results show that compared with the comparison method, the proposed method has the lowest packet loss rate in the process of data sharing and has greater application value.

**Keywords:** Cloud Computing · Teaching Resources · Sharing Platform

## 1 Introduction

As an important part of vocational education, higher vocational education is facing increasingly severe challenges and opportunities. As an important part of physical education quality, the task of higher vocational physical education is becoming more and more serious. How to improve the quality and level of physical education in higher vocational education has become a hot issue concerned by the education circle and the society. However, due to the asymmetry of teaching resources among higher vocational colleges, the uneven teaching level of teachers, the diversification of students' learning styles and the individual needs, there are some difficulties and challenges in higher vocational physical education.

With the continuous development of computer technology and network technology, most colleges and universities are using network technology to improve the teaching


G. Gui et al. (Eds.): eLEOT 2023, LNICST 543, pp. 3–16, 2024.
https://doi.org/10.1007/978-3-031-51465-4_1

quality of colleges and universities, develop their own teaching resource management system with full functions and distinctive characteristics, or set up their own electronic library. These high-quality teaching resources provide students with a learning platform for after-class review and self-study [1, 2]. In this context, the establishment of an efficient, convenient and shared teaching resource platform has become a necessary condition for the reform and improvement of physical education teaching quality in higher vocational colleges. Many scholars have conducted research on this issue. As mentioned in reference [3], in order to achieve resource integration and sharing, a study was conducted on the construction of a cloud based English digital resource library for higher education. This method first gives the Functional requirement of the higher vocational English digital resource library system from three aspects: Functional requirement, performance requirements and operational requirements, then analyzes the overall technical architecture and network topology of the education cloud platform where the higher vocational English digital resource library system is located, and finally designs and implements the core module of the higher vocational English digital resource library system based on the optimization strategy proposed in this paper, And provide some important and representative interfaces and source code. A streaming data sharing method for the Internet of Things is proposed in reference [4]. This method proposes a data stream reuse algorithm on the Storm fast data platform to identify the intersection of reusable tasks and streams from existing data streams, so as to form a combined data stream and ensure the equivalence of its output streams. Then, it proposes a de merge algorithm when the data stream is deleted and a defragmentation algorithm for partially reused data streams. Finally, it uses experiments to prove the progressiveness of the proposed method. Although the above two methods have a certain promoting effect on the integration and secure sharing of educational resources, they still cannot guarantee the accuracy of data sharing, and their packet loss rate is still high.

Based on this, the research on the sharing platform of high-quality teaching resources of higher vocational sports based on cloud computing is carried out. First, blockchain technology is introduced to establish a shared information hierarchy model, and a trusted measurement, storage and reporting mechanism of physical protection encryption storage technology is established. Then determine the integrity test value of physical education quality teaching resources in higher vocational colleges, improve the trusted cloud computing mechanism, and finally calculate the matching degree of each demand corresponding to the tasks of the cloud system and physical education quality teaching resources nodes in higher vocational colleges, incorporate all data into the central database, and share high-quality teaching resources. It is hoped that the sharing effect of educational resources can be improved through this study.

## 2 Sharing Platform of High-quality Teaching Resources for Higher Vocational Sports

The characteristics and necessity of high-quality physical education teaching in vocational colleges include the following points:

(1) Reasonable curriculum: The curriculum of physical education in vocational colleges should be based on students' learning characteristics and needs. It should not only meet the requirements of students' basic physical fitness and professional knowledge, but also take into account the development of students' personalities and the improvement of their comprehensive qualities.
(2) Diversified teaching methods: High quality physical education teaching in vocational colleges should adopt various teaching methods, such as explanations, demonstrations, etc., combined with practical operations and interactive exchanges, to stimulate students' interest in learning, promote students' independent learning and innovative thinking, and achieve the effect of applying what is learned.
(3) Strengthening practical operation: Vocational physical education teaching should focus on practical aspects, practicality oriented, and consolidate students' physical fitness through practice, cultivating professional skills and innovative abilities.
(4) High quality teachers: PE teaching in higher vocational colleges needs high-level professional teachers who not only have solid professional knowledge and rich practical experience, but also have good teaching ability and interpersonal communication communication ability, which can stimulate students' enthusiasm and interest in learning and lead students to success.
(5) Complete professional facilities: Vocational physical education teaching requires comprehensive professional facilities and laboratories, including experimental equipment, venue facilities, laboratories, multimedia classrooms, etc., to provide students with a good learning environment and promote the improvement of teaching effectiveness.

The necessity of high-quality physical education teaching in vocational colleges lies in that physical education is the foundation for students' physical and mental health development. Vocational physical education teaching can improve students' comprehensive literacy and professional competitiveness, and help them better adapt to future career requirements and social development needs. At the same time, high-quality physical education teaching in vocational colleges can also promote the development and promotion of sports, and cultivate more sports talents with professional qualities and a sense of social responsibility for society.

In the process of handling specific business logic, access to the underlying database is required. However, the following problems exist in the higher-level physical education quality teaching system:

(1) It is not user-friendly. Users may have to log in to multiple websites in order to get the resources they want, requiring multiple access rights, or even being unable to use the resources that exist.
(2) The backend services require costly maintenance.
(3) The capacity of the system cannot be dynamically changed according to the demand of access. It is easy to overload the system or to run the system empty.
(4) Repetitive use of resources is not possible, and an ideal balance between expenses and revenues cannot be found. Since this is the case, can there be a way to access all the servers and find the needed resources on those servers by just one access terminal and sending one access request? The answer is yes, and using cloud technology, all of the above requirements can be achieved.

Based on the characteristics of cloud computing, the following idea can be realized by introducing it into the platform for sharing high-quality teaching resources in higher education sports: higher education institutions in a certain region, specifically a city, a province or a country, can join together to build a unified cloud platform, integrate the computing resources of each institution into a public pool of computing resources, establish a unified interface through the cloud computing network, and deliver it to the "cloud committee". The cloud platform can be managed by the "cloud committee". The teachers and students of joint higher education institutions can access the resource pool through such a unified interface and get the required teaching information. The resource management centers of these institutions can also upload their own special resources to this public resource pool [3, 4] for students and faculty members of each higher education institution to share. It is only necessary to pay a small fee according to the usage, and do not need to care about the construction of these hardware servers. Thus, the sharing of teaching resources is realized and the "information silo" is eliminated. Students can get more learning resources, and education units can realize online publishing and online interactive teaching more quickly. Education units do not need to consider the construction investment of basic platform and software, and just concentrate on the development of courseware and production of learning resources, and leave everything else to the cloud platform.

## 2.1 Hierarchical Model of Shared Information

Since the shared information is randomly distributed in the network environment, it makes the information sharing process more complicated and cumbersome, which affects the security of information sharing. This study introduces blockchain technology to build a shared information hierarchy model in order to improve the security of information sharing [2, 5], which lays a solid foundation for the subsequent encryption of shared information attributes.

The hierarchical model of shared information based on blockchain technology is shown in Fig. 1.

As shown in Fig. 1, the application of blockchain technology divides the shared information into five layers- physical layer, blockchain definition layer, network layer, collaboration layer and application layer, and the definition of each layer and its specific functions are shown below:

(1) Physical layer

This layer refers to the physical environment of the demand side of the shared information, which informs the demand side requirements and sends them to the blockchain definition layer [6–8];

(2) Blockchain definition layer

This layer takes the responsibility of defining the tasks of the collaborative layer, such as block structure, digital signature, information transmission, and consensus mechanism. Information sharing needs to involve multiple aspects of information data, and there are large differences between the information and the needs for security are very different. The normalization of different information can be achieved through the processing of the blockchain definition layer, which is the necessary level

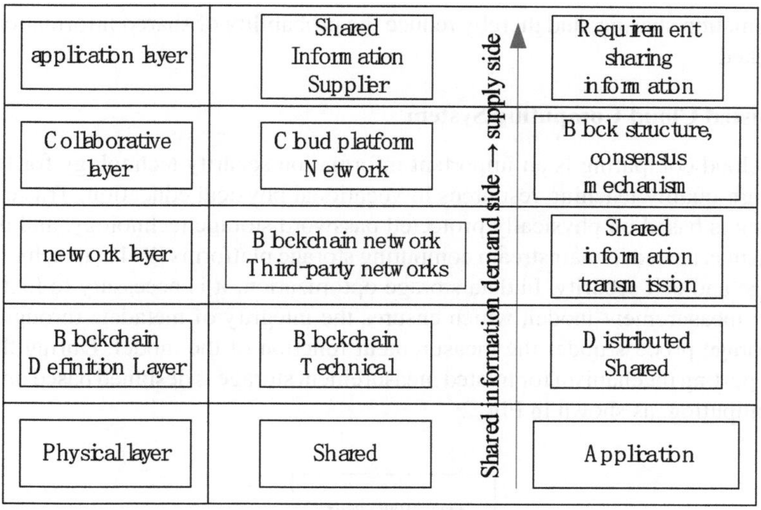


**Fig. 1.** Shared information hierarchy model

for the shared information to enter the network layer. The formula for normalization of shared information is

$$Y_i = \frac{X_i - X_{\min}}{X_{\max} - X_{\min}} \tag{1}$$

In Eq. (1), $X_i$ and $Y_i$ respectively represent the shared information before and after normalization processing; $X_{\min}$ and $X_{\max}$ represent the minimum and maximum values of shared information, respectively.

(3) Network layer

This level bears the task of sharing information transmission and is a key level of information sharing. In information sharing, this level requires certain authentication of information sharing demanders, suppliers, and shared information to ensure the security of information sharing behavior;

(4) Collaborative layer

This level undertakes tasks such as shared information storage, management, coordination, and decision-making, and records shared information sources, abstracts, security requirements, and other information in the blockchain. It operates and stores shared information through network platforms;

(5) Application layer

After receiving the requirements from the demand side, this level confirms and analyzes the shared information requirements, extracts corresponding shared information based on the requirements, integrates it, and provides feedback to the physical layer.

In the hierarchical model of shared information, shared information is not defined according to information related business processes. This approach can omit some intermediate links in the transmission of shared information, simplify the process of information sharing, and thereby reduce the probability of shared information being attacked.

## 2.2 Trusted Cloud Computing System

Trusted cloud computing is an important information security technology for the storage of high-quality teaching resources in vocational physical education. Trusted cloud computing is based on physically protected password storage technology, and the trust mechanism is nested in mainstream computing storage platforms [9–11] to achieve overall storage and call security. In data storage optimization, it is necessary to first design a storage measurement model, which ensures the integrity of metadata throughout the entire storage process under the measurement function of the model. During this process, a reporting mechanism for trusted measurement storage is designed based on trusted cloud computing, as shown in Fig. 2:

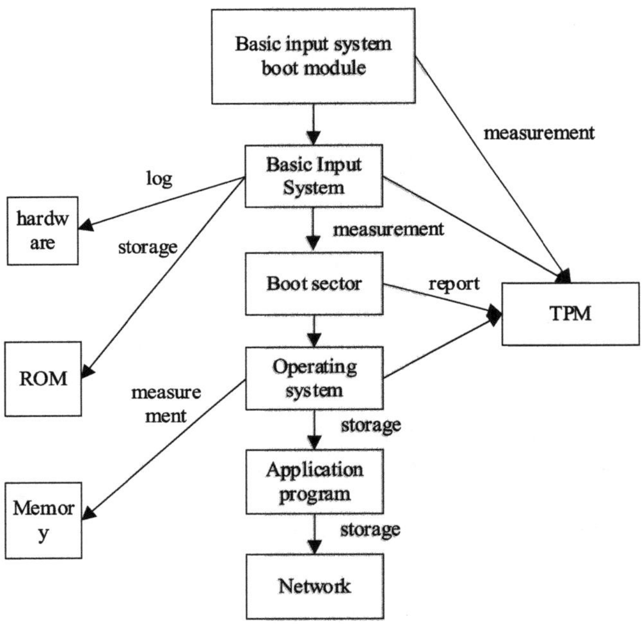


**Fig. 2.** Trusted metric storage reporting mechanism

In Fig. 2, it is mainly based on the integrity of high-quality physical education teaching resources in vocational colleges as a reference, and it is necessary to calculate the hash value and store it in the internal structure [12], and complete the storage on the storage platform. In order to save space, it is necessary to extend the calculation method of hash values and store the extended values in the configured registers to complete mutual correlation verification. During this process, an element needs to be inserted to obtain the ideal hash and offset. The situation of inserting the element is shown in Table 1:

**Table 1.** Insert Elements

| Hash bucket | Hash value | Address | Optimal bucket | Shifting |
|---|---|---|---|---|
| Hash bucket 1 | J (h1) | 112 | 3 | 2 |
| Hash bucket 2 | – | – | – | – |
| Hash bucket 3 | – | – | – | – |
| Hash bucket 4 | J (h2) | 111 | 5 | 2 |
| Hash bucket 5 | J (h1) | 102 | 2 | 1 |
| Hash bucket 6 | J (h4) | 113 | 3 | 0 |
| Hash bucket 7 | J (h3) | 105 | 2 | 2 |

In Table 1, the specific hash bucket numbers are selected for searching and shifted backward in order until the search is achieved and the integrity test values of meta-high school physical education quality teaching resources are obtained.

### 2.3 Cloud-Based System

The cloud-based system is mainly the time utilized from awareness to end, i.e., the time span. The optimal span mainly refers to the minimization of the running time to achieve the optimal span, and also to be able to enhance the quality of service in the cloud.

(1) Resource sharing: Cloud systems fully utilize existing computing resources and achieve resource sharing through virtualization technology, improving the efficiency and utilization of computing resources.
(2) Elastic scaling: Cloud systems can automatically scale computing resources according to business needs, improving the efficiency and elasticity of computing resource utilization.
(3) High reliability: The cloud system adopts multiple nodes and backup mechanisms, improving the reliability and availability of the application system.
(4) High security: The cloud system adopts professional security mechanisms and encryption technology to protect the security of user data, effectively preventing the risk of network attacks and data leakage.
(5) Easy to manage: The cloud system adopts automated management technology, which can achieve automated management and monitoring of computing resources, improving resource utilization efficiency and management efficiency.

The necessity of cloud based systems lies in the fact that with the rapid development of information technology and the continuous increase in information volume, the computing and storage capabilities of traditional single computers can no longer meet business needs. Cloud based systems provide enterprises and individuals with an efficient, convenient, reliable, secure, and economical mode of using computing resources. Cloud based systems can help enterprises achieve low-cost IT resource management and operation, improve business competitiveness and innovation capabilities; At the same time, cloud systems can also promote information circulation, optimize resource allocation, and provide strong support for the sustainable development of the economy and society.

(1) Economic principles:
As users are billed for computing services, there is a very significant gap in the cost to be paid for various types of services. In order to ensure that the interests of both users as well as cloud services are maximized, an optimal allocation of limited higher-level sports quality teaching resources is required.
(2) Load balancing:
In the context of cloud computing, there are obvious differences in the computing efficiency and performance of virtual machines, and there are also differences in the index preferences for tasks and higher-level physical education quality teaching resources. The main purpose of carrying out load balancing is to comprehensively improve the utilization rate of high quality teaching resources of senior sports in the system.
(3) Minimum sharing time:
Set the research objective as the minimum sharing time of higher-level physical education quality teaching resources, and introduce the corresponding matching factors as well as load balancing degrees in different tasks and higher-level physical education quality teaching resources, respectively.

Set the non-negative objective function that represents the solution objective. Among them, the solid annealing process and the combinatorial optimization problem have certain similarities, and the main advantages are as follows:

(1) Performing complex region search:
The algorithm is more suitable for searching in complex regions and obtaining regions with higher region values in them.
(2) Good parallelism:
Through the good parallelism of the algorithm to effectively solve a variety of nonlinear problems.
(3) Use of object function for search:
The objective function is directly converted into the fitness value to determine the scope and direction of the next search step.

Since the physical states slowly progress to low-energy states, in order to obtain better results, the simulated annealing algorithm mainly selects the states containing important contribution rates in the process of sampling.

Set the randomly generated small displacement changes and the resulting brand new state to $j$, mark it as an important state, and set the particle solid to first represent the position of state $i$ as the initial state with energy of $E_i$. The next state of the solid is $i$ and $j$, and the factor ratio corresponding to the probability ratio of the two states can be expressed as:

$$p(t) = \begin{cases} (E_i - E_j) \\ \frac{1}{Z(t)} \exp\left(-\frac{E_j - E_i}{k_B(t)}\right) \end{cases} \tag{2}$$

Set random number $A$ as a numerical value formed by a random number generator, with a value range of [0, 1]. Since $p$ represents a value less than 1, assuming $p \geq A$, it means that $i$ remains in its current state.

According to Formula (8), it can be seen that at low temperatures, the state with a small probability of acceptance and a large difference in current energy is mainly set as an important state; Under high temperature conditions, a new state with a high probability of accepting a significant energy difference from the current state is set as an important state.

Calculate the matching degree between the tasks corresponding to each requirement and the nodes of high-quality teaching resources in vocational sports, analyze the needs of different users, and add matching factors, then:

$$Match_{ij} = \frac{1}{\sqrt{\sum_{i=1}^{5} \left(Tm_i - Vm_j\right)^2}} \tag{3}$$

In order to obtain the load balancing degree, a mapping sequence of $X$ representative tasks and high-quality teaching resources for vocational physical education is set. At this time, the load balancing degree can be expressed as:

$$Load(X) = \sqrt{\sum_{i=1}^{n} \left(1 - C_1 \frac{Y_i}{Lv_i}\right)^2} \tag{4}$$

Calculate the computing ability of each high-quality teaching resource node of vocational physical education through weighted calculation, namely:

$$Lv_i = w_1 \times n(v_i) + w_2 \times p(v_i) + w_3 \times r(v_i) \tag{5}$$

In the context of cloud computing, in order to achieve high-precision and efficient sharing, a central database is established to integrate all data from the shared model into the central database, and to share high-quality teaching resources for vocational physical education according to certain classification standards. The composition of the high-quality teaching resource sharing platform for higher vocational physical education is shown in Fig. 3.

In Fig. 3, the logic of teaching senior sports quality teaching resources sharing platform is built on the basis of physical senior sports quality teaching resources, which provides additional services and functions such as common middleware, research database, teaching database, management database, database administrator and workflow manager on the physical grid by virtualizing various actual senior sports quality teaching resources on the physical layer, with servers, storage and actual network to provide abstract services for the sharing process, such as teaching resource exchange and cooperation, and the latest material mining for Civic Science and Technology, etc. Meanwhile, all grid resources above the physical resources are for modeling services and ensure that they are not integrated and invoked by other applications. The functions realized by each layer are described as follows:

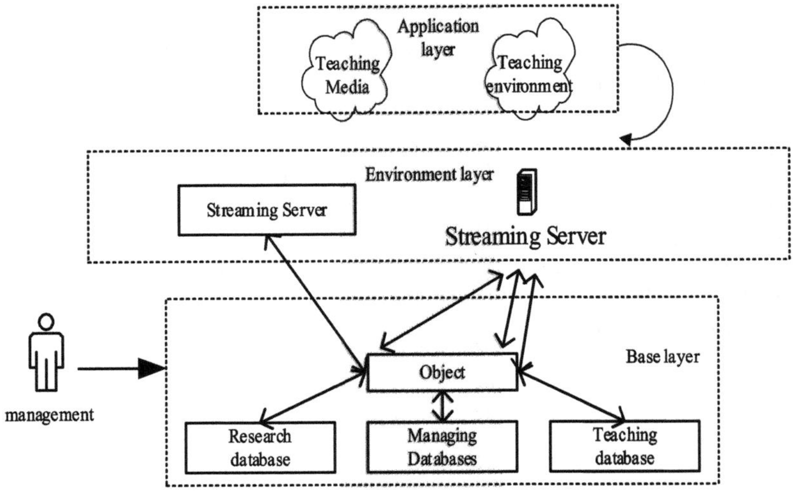


**Fig. 3.** High quality teaching resource sharing platform for higher vocational physical education

(1) Foundation layer

The foundation layer is mainly composed of the shared high quality teaching resources of higher education sports and the data of each system that provides data for the shared high quality teaching resources of higher education sports.

(2) Environment layer

It implements the specific application of the model and executes the operation command after receiving the search demand from the user.

(3) Application layer

It consists of two parts, teaching media and teaching environment, and is the interface part that feeds the results to the users.

In the case that the complexity and variation degree of shared requirements are not very large, the reuse of database is used, and the reuse number is large, and the reuse cost is larger; in the case that the complexity and variation degree of shared requirements are large, the reuse of knowledge is used, and the reuse number is small or unpredictable, and the reuse cost is unchanged. In general, the teaching and learning high quality teaching resources sharing platform developed by the structure can promote the effective use of high quality teaching resources in high level sports, and it makes the management of the model easy.

After users log in successfully, they enter the user space. In this module, users can manage the high quality teaching resources of higher vocational sports and upload and download the high quality teaching resources of higher vocational sports. When the user requests the uploading of higher-level physical education quality teaching resources, the system will check whether the user has the right to upload, for example, the visitor can't do the uploading operation. Then through the setting of user uploading high quality teaching resources for higher level physical education, the system will match the uploaded high quality teaching resources for that user according to keywords in the system in order to prevent the duplication of high quality teaching resources for higher level physical education, and check whether similar files exist.

## 3 Experiment

This experiment was conducted on a computer with a Windows 10 operating system and 2GB of memory. The computer has enough computing power and resources to carry out the research on distance education data sharing of physical education courses. Select the teaching data of a certain university's physical education course for research, obtain the educational data of its physical education course progress, and complete the acquisition of data samples. The specific situation of the experiment is as follows:

(1) Collection of high-quality teaching resources for English courses in higher vocational institutions for higher-level sports:

Multiple maintenance points are set in the platform to collect information on abnormal behavior of the platform, so as to lay a solid foundation for the later maintenance work of the platform.

(2) Platform data processing:

In order to better identify the abnormal behavior accurately in the massive data, it is necessary to carry out numerical as well as normalization operations for all the higher-level physical education quality teaching resources collected from the platform.

(3) Platform data analysis:

Data analysis is an important process of automatic platform maintenance, mainly using some specific rules analysis to realize the analysis work of platform data and determine whether the platform needs to be maintained according to the analysis results.

(4) Platform response processing:

Through the data analysis results of the platform, it can obtain the usage status of different users in the platform, and if abnormal behaviors are found in the platform, the platform needs to take corresponding response measures in time to ensure the stable operation of the platform.

With the above content set, the corresponding version and data manager can be selected and assigned to different network transmission nodes, and the version and data manager are assigned the number of nodes. Each working machine will be tested 100 times to analyze the aggregated bandwidth of different data storage structures under high load read and write. The test results are shown in Fig. 4:

In Fig. 4, tested under high load conditions, the metadata without storage structure optimization limits the amount of global aggregation bandwidth, and all of the aggregation bandwidth of customized courses, online teaching courses, and intelligent recommendation courses data storage structure is improved, which verifies the effectiveness of the method in this paper.

In order to further verify the advanced nature of the proposed method, reference [3] method and reference [4] method were selected as comparison methods to carry out comparative experiments. Test the packet loss rate of data transmission under the background of data transmission of different sizes, and get the comparison results as shown in Fig. 5.

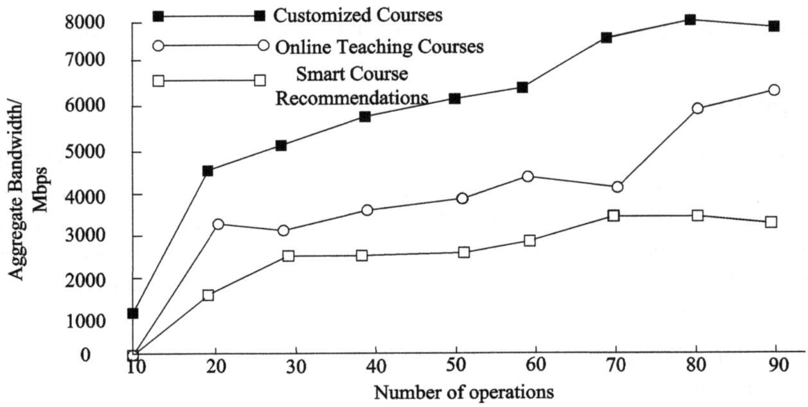


**Fig. 4.** Aggregation bandwidth of different data storage structures under high load read and write

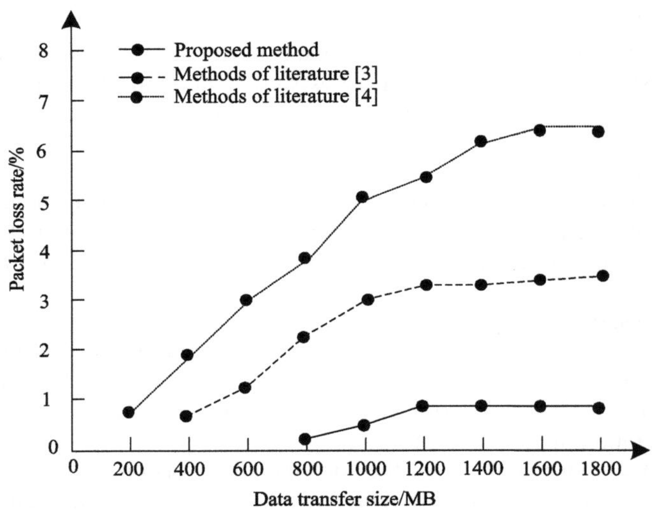


**Fig. 5.** Cloud platform cloud data transmission packet loss rate comparison knot

As shown in Fig. 5, with the application of the proposed method, the data packet loss rate is all less than 0.55%, while with the application of the two comparison methods, the data packet loss rate increases first and then becomes stable with the increase of the amount of transmitted data, and the packet loss rate is higher than 0.78%, which proves that the proposed platform has better data sharing effect.

## 4 Conclusion

The cloud-based platform for sharing high-quality teaching resources of higher-level physical education can provide a centralized, efficient and convenient information resource sharing platform for higher-level physical education teachers, help teachers achieve interoperability of teaching resources and innovation of teaching methods, and improve the quality of classroom teaching and the cultivation of students' comprehensive quality.

In the future, the construction and improvement of this platform requires the joint efforts of educational institutions, technology enterprises and government departments to adopt an open, cooperative and win-win model to actively promote the sharing and optimization of teaching resources and the overall development of higher education physical education. At the same time, it is also necessary to further improve the security and reliability of the technical platform, strengthen teachers' training and technical support, and improve teachers' digital literacy and innovation ability, so that the platform can really become an effective means to promote the reform of higher vocational physical education and improve teaching quality. It is believed that through joint efforts, the cloud computing-based higher vocational physical education quality teaching resources sharing platform will play an active role in supporting and helping to promote the development and progress of higher vocational physical education, as well as to achieve the goals of educational equity and quality education.

## References


1. Feng, J., Zhang, W., Tsai, S.-B.: Construction of a multimedia-based university ideological and political big data cloud service teaching resource sharing model. Math. Prob. Eng. **2021**(Pt.52), 9907630.1–9907630.12 (2021)
2. Cao, Q.: Study on resource sharing strategy of E-commerce innovation and entrepreneurship education based on cloud computing. Sci. Program. **2021**(Pt.10), 8268000.1–8268000.8 (2021)
3. Wang, J., Li, W.: The Construction of a digital resource library of English for higher education based on a cloud platform. Sci. Program. **2021**(Pt.10), 4591780.1–4591780.12 (2021)
4. Chaturvedi, S., Tyagi, S., Simmhan, Y.: Cost-effective sharing of streaming dataflows for IoT applications. IEEE Trans. Cloud Comput. **9**(4), 1391–1407 (2021)
5. Zu, C.: Hadoop-based painting resource storage and retrieval platform construction and testing. Complexity, **2021**(Pt.16), 9933330–1–9933330–11 (2021)
6. Li, S., Zhu, J., Chen, Z., et al.: Double-layer energy management system based on energy sharing cloud for virtual residential microgrid. Appl. Energy **282**(Pt.A), 116089.1–116089.13 (2021)
7. Liu, S., Dai, Y., Cai, Z., et al.: Construction of double-precision wisdom teaching framework based on blockchain technology in cloud platform. **2021**, 911823–911834 (2021)
8. Shekhar, C.A., Sharvani, G.S.: MTLBP: a novel framework to assess multi-tenant load balance in cloud computing for cost-effective resource allocation. Wirel. Pers. Commun. Int. J. **120**(2), 1873–1893 (2021)
9. Yang, Q.: Cloud music teaching database based on opencl design and neural network. Microprocess. Microsyst. **82**, 103897.1–103897.5 (2021)
10. Wang, F.: Enlightenment of physical education teaching experiment based on cloud computing to the current physical education reform. Sci. Program. **2021**(Pt.9), 6607539.1–6607539.11 (2021)
11. Gharehpasha, S., Masdari, M.: A discrete chaotic multi-objective SCA-ALO optimization algorithm for an optimal virtual machine placement in cloud data center. **12**(10), 9323–9339 (2021)

12. Liu, S., Li, Y., Fu, W.: Human-centered attention-aware networks for action recognition. Int. J. Intell. Syst. **37**(12), 10968–10987 (2022)
13. She, X.-B., Huang, S., Liu, C.-Q.: Web resource priority collaborative filtering recommendation based on deep learning. Comput. Simulat. **39**(002), 431–435 (2022)

# Prediction Method of Online Teaching Effect of Career Guidance Course Based on Multi Task Learning

Wei Han(✉) and Mingsheng Li

Baotou Teachers' College, Baotou 014030, China
coolhanwei@163.com

**Abstract.** There are issues with intermittent and lagging schedules in the teaching of employment guidance courses, as well as a lack of professional teachers. Online teaching can solve these problems. Therefore, in order to better analyze the learning effectiveness of online teaching in employment guidance courses, a multi task learning based prediction method for the learning effectiveness of online teaching in employment guidance courses is designed to determine whether learners have mastered the knowledge content of the employment guidance courses they are learning. Design a Chinese word segmentation sequence annotation method based on multitasking learning, implement preprocessing of online teaching data for employment guidance courses, and improve the generalization ability and effectiveness of the model. For the data after Chinese word segmentation, an improved K-means algorithm is used to mine the learning behavior information of students, thereby discovering potential patterns and patterns hidden in the data. Propose the EduHawkes model, which adds various types of feature information to predict learning outcomes based on analyzing student behavior patterns, achieving online teaching of employment guidance courses and improving the accuracy and interpretability of learning outcomes prediction. The test method shows that the accuracy of the method and the Matthews correlation coefficient are both high.

**Keywords:** Multi Task Learning · Online Teaching of Career Guidance Courses · K-Means Algorithm · Chinese Word Segmentation · Learning Effect Prediction

## 1 Introduction

If colleges and universities want to ensure their overall sustainable development, they must solve the employment problem of graduates. Only when the school successfully sends millions of graduates to jobs can it build the cornerstone of a harmonious and stable society [1]. Therefore, all colleges and universities should regard employment guidance as a major event. In terms of the current situation of employment guidance courses in China, there are still the following problems:

There are discontinuities and delays in the time arrangement of career guidance courses. Employment guidance courses in colleges and universities are generally offered


G. Gui et al. (Eds.): eLEOT 2023, LNICST 543, pp. 17–32, 2024.
https://doi.org/10.1007/978-3-031-51465-4_2

in the form of public elective courses. Although the courses involve the teaching arrangement of career planning, employment skills, employment policies and other contents, due to the lack of attention to employment guidance courses in colleges and universities, students do not have a deep understanding of the course. In addition, students are under great pressure to learn professional courses, and often only choose employment skills employment policy and other courses, while career planning and other knowledge are often ignored. The teaching effect of employment guidance can not be shown in students' career development, and guidance only stays on the surface. Although the Ministry of Education of the People's Republic of China requires that career guidance and career development courses be offered in the form of compulsory courses, until now, most colleges and universities have changed their career guidance courses to compulsory courses, but they are still optional. In addition, the career guidance courses of many colleges and universities only carry out several career lectures in the graduating students, without systematic and complete career guidance teaching training.

The teaching content of employment guidance lacks professional pertinence and the teaching form is single.

On the one hand, the content of textbooks is universal; On the other hand, the content of employment is mostly theoretical and has little practical significance, such as employment information, employment skills, employment system, etc. At present, the career guidance courses in many colleges and universities are still dominated by classroom teaching, lacking diversified teaching methods, which tend to ignore the different needs of students for the courses, and it is difficult to mobilize learning interests, which is not practical.

Employment guidance teachers lack professional teachers.

Teachers of employment guidance and career planning should not only have basic knowledge of employment, occupation, psychology, law, etc., but also have professional knowledge, be familiar with the characteristics of different majors, and master various policies and regulations in related fields. At present, the main teachers of employment guidance courses in most colleges and universities are counselors or staff of employment guidance centers. The lack of career guidance instructors and professional field instructors can not accurately grasp the employment situation of various industries, and the guidance ability is limited, so the employment guidance effect of colleges and universities is not significant [2].

In order to solve the above problems, online teaching methods of career guidance courses have emerged. In online teaching of career guidance courses, we need to pay attention to an important issue, that is, how to judge whether a learner has mastered the knowledge he is learning. Based on this background, this paper studies the prediction of online teaching learning effect of career guidance courses.

For the research on the prediction of learning effect, the current research results have been relatively rich. Some scholars have proposed a prediction method of students' online learning effect based on rank correlation analysis: for the problem that students have many online learning behavior characteristics and the accuracy of learning effect prediction is not high. A feature selection method based on rank correlation is proposed. By calculating the rank between each behavior feature and learning effect, the correlation degree of each feature and learning effect is obtained. On this basis, multiple features with the highest correlation degree are selected to form a new data set, and then normalization and one pot coding are completed, and machine learning methods and neural network models are used for training respectively. Finally, the online learning effect prediction of students is realized. On the publicly published learning data set, the rank correlation is used for feature selection combined with the multi-layer perceptron model, and the learning effect of students can be correctly classified, and the F value is higher than the traditional linear correlation selection method. Other scholars have proposed a learning process analysis and learning effect prediction method based on behavior sequence: learning process data reflects the state of learners in the learning process. Currently, many researches have been conducted on data mining and analysis of learners' learning process. Most of these coarse-grained data are based on the energy and time invested by learners in a certain learning behavior, which can not reflect the level of learners' cognitive investment in detail, and some learning behavior data have low accuracy in predicting learning effects. Compared with learner participation, the learning behavior sequence in the learning process can better reflect the learning behavior trajectory, willingness and cognitive process of learners. The lag sequence analysis method is used to analyze the learning process data on the DEEDS platform. It is found that the lag sequence analysis method can clearly reveal the important learning behavior sequence; Compared with support vector machine, logistic regression, decision tree and other data mining methods, naive Bayesian method has good prediction performance, with an average accuracy of more than 70%. The research results prove that learners' learning behavior sequence can provide teachers with a more comprehensive online learning picture to help teachers discover learners' learning habits, preferences and cognitive processes, assist teachers to reflect on the teaching process, and accurately predict learners' learning achievements through behavior sequence data, and then analyze the key attributes in the prediction model. To provide suggestions for teachers to take targeted intervention measures in the follow-up teaching process, so as to improve the educational and teaching performance. The above methods exist.

This paper designs a method to predict the learning effect of online teaching of career guidance courses based on multi task learning.

## 2 Design of Online Teaching Learning Effect Prediction Method for Career Guidance Course

### 2.1 Chinese Word Segmentation Sequence Labeling

Based on multi task learning, a Chinese word segmentation sequence labeling method is designed to implement online teaching data preprocessing of career guidance courses. This method uses tag consistency mechanism based on multi task learning to conduct in-depth training and learning, which is divided into three modules, namely, pre tagging module, multi task shared learning module, and joint training module [3].

The way of multi task learning can avoid the further spread of errors, and combine multiple tasks to learn together, making the information exchange between multiple tasks more convenient, and improving the accuracy and learning efficiency of each sub task. However, in the previous study, we mentioned that most of the existing Chinese word segmentation methods based on multi task learning are based on different data sets of different tasks, which can only ensure that multiple tasks in form learn together. In essence, each task is still relatively independent, which will inevitably lead to information conflicts, excessive noise Information sharing is limited, and very important boundary information cannot be learned, which affects the final learning effect. In order to solve the above problems and make it possible to learn tag consistency information, this study adds a pre labeling module to enhance the learning of available labeled resources and alleviate the pressure of data shortage.

First, the original named entity dataset, word segmentation dataset, and part of speech tagging dataset are recorded as:

$$M_{ner} = \left\{ m_j^{ner} \right\} \tag{1}$$

$$M_{cws} = \left\{ m_j^{cws} \right\} \tag{2}$$

$$M_{pos} = \left\{ m_j^{pos} \right\} \tag{3}$$

among $m_j^{ner}$ Represents the number of $j$ Samples; $m_j^{cws}$ Represents the No $j$ Samples; $m_j^{pos}$ Represents the number of POS data sets $j$ Samples.

Then, we use the $M_{cws}$, $M_{pos}$ Train the corresponding word segmentation device and part of speech tagging device. Next, the benchmark data set $M_{ner}$ The original samples in are de labeled and processed into plain text format. The trained word segmentation device and part of speech tagging device are used to perform word segmentation and part of speech tagging operations based on word granularity. Since the four word tagging method is used in the experiment, the four word segmentation tagging based on word granularity is required for the results obtained. Since the named entity data set uses a three word bit {B, I, O} tagging system, in order to achieve tag alignment, the four word bit word segmentation is labeled {B, M, E, S}, which is also converted into {B, I, E, S}, and the part of speech tag is also processed accordingly. For example, if the tag representing the part of speech of a noun is n, then the tag of a two word noun is {B-n I-n}, which is split and mapped to each word [4].

Finally, extract the final obtained word segmentation and part of speech tags, integrate the tags and align them to the benchmark NER dataset, and then obtain a special multi task learning dataset that neatly corresponds to the three task tags at the same time. As shown in the example in Table 8, in case of ambiguity in the pre labeling process, the label of the datum named entity identification data set shall prevail for alignment. For example, the person name entity <Wang Xiaoming> may get the segmentation of <Wang|Xiao|Ming> and the word segmentation label of <B B B> after word segmentation, which does not correspond to the original NER label <B-PER I-PER I-PER> on the border. In this case, we modify the word segmentation label to <BIE> , that is, the entity boundary shall prevail.

After the above processing, we get that the pre labeled dataset is recorded as:

$$S = \{s_i\} \tag{4}$$

One sample $s$ It is composed of character set, character named entity recognition label, word segmentation label and part of speech label.

On the basis of the pre labeling module, a multi task shared learning module is constructed, that is, joint learning for multiple tasks. The multi task shared learning module includes two parts: the shared presentation layer and the sequence decoding layer. In the following description, the input sequence is recorded as:

$$B = \{b_1, b_2, \ldots, b_n\} \tag{5}$$

among $b_n$ Representation sequence $B$ Of $n$ Words. $B$ Represents the input of a special data set D that is pre labeled.

(1) Shared presentation layer

1) BERT layer

Traditional static word vectors are usually unable to represent polysemy of a word. In this stage, a pre training language model based on BERT is selected for feature learning to represent context sensitive semantics. For the input sequence, the sequence is uniformly processed into the form that the start token is the special category embed character "[CLS]" and the end is the special separator character "[SEP]" for encoding. BERT uses the self attention mechanism to learn the dependency relationship and context semantics of each word with other words, and then uses feedforward neural networks to perform projection transformation of multiple different linear transformation pairs on the input after the Attention calculation, and finally obtains the overall information of the sequence. After the BERT layer coding calculation, the input sequence will be $B$ The conversion is recorded as:

$$F = \{f_1, f_2, \ldots, f_n\} \tag{6}$$

2) BiGRU layer

On the basis of the BERT layer, we add a two-way gating cycle unit layer (BiGRU layer) to further learn about information sharing between multiple tasks. Output sequence of BERT layer $F = \{f_1, f_2, \ldots, f_n\}$ As the input of the BiGRU layer, for the input of the time r process, the update gate zrand reset gate rrjointly determine the output of the hidden state. Record the output of two-way GRU forward and backward hidden layers as $J_{front}$, $J_{back}$, remember that the final output vector is $J$.

(2) Sequence decoding layer

On top of the shared presentation layer, we will build a sequence decoding layer according to the characteristics of the task, and decode for different tasks. In order to model the adjacency between tags, conditional random field is selected as the decoding model.

This paper proposes a tag consistency mechanism throughout the whole training process based on multi task learning Chinese word segmentation sequence tagging method. In the joint training module, the specific application of tag consistency mechanism is reflected in the loss calculation. For the problem of whether the decoding tags of different tasks are consistent, a more universal method [5] is defined.

Specifically, we first defined the loss function as shown in Formula (7):

$$loss = \omega_1 * l_{cws} + \omega_2 * l_{pos} + \omega_3 * \mathrm{l}_{ner} + \omega_4 * \mathrm{l}_{con} \tag{7}$$

In Formula (7) $l_{cws}$, $l_{pos}$, $\mathrm{l}_{ner}$ The losses of word segmentation task, named entity recognition task and part of speech tagging task are calculated respectively based on the standard (ground truth) label of their respective tasks;$\mathrm{l}_{con}$ It is the supplementary loss defined according to the tag consistency mechanism, representing the loss of cross task tag consistency; $\omega_1$, $\omega_2$, $\omega_3$, $\omega_4$ representative $l_{cws}$, $l_{pos}$, $\mathrm{l}_{ner}$, $\mathrm{l}_{con}$ Weight of.

By optimizing this loss, the model can grasp more boundary information and learn the consistent content of multi task decoding tags, such as the alignment between the boundary of word segmentation tags and the boundary of entity tags and part of speech tags, which to some extent alleviates the problem of non-standard definition of word segmentation standards. On the basis of special data sets. The network is adjusted and updated through the calculation of loss, which further emphasizes the consistency and reduces the error caused by the noise of multi task learning, so as to realize the effective sharing and fusion of multiple information under the multi task learning mode.

## 2.2 Information Mining of Students' Learning Behavior

The improved K-means algorithm is used to mine the information of students' learning behavior from the online teaching data of career guidance courses labeled with Chinese word segmentation sequence.

As a partition based clustering algorithm, K-means algorithm is widely used for its advantages of easy understanding, easy implementation, and strong interpretability. However, K-means algorithm also has some shortcomings, such as the number of clusters K value needs to be manually set, too large or too small value of K will affect the clustering effect, the initial cluster center is randomly determined, more sensitive to isolated points, etc. These shortcomings will affect the final effect of clustering, resulting in poor stability and quality of clustering results. The K-means clustering algorithm is optimized and improved from multiple factors. The main idea of the heuristic method is to solve how to deal with the next step according to the empirical rules. In the iterative calculation process of clustering, this study uses the heuristic method to reduce the calculation time required for sample point allocation and improve the operation efficiency. In each iteration process, a simple data structure is used to store the distance between each point and its nearest cluster. In the next iteration process, first calculate the distance between each point and its previous nearest cluster. If the new distance obtained by calculation is less than or equal to the previously saved distance, then the point will remain in the original cluster, and there is no need to calculate the distance between the point and other clusters. This saves the calculation time [6] of the distance between this point and other clusters.

Aiming at the problem that K-means algorithm is sensitive to outliers, this research first optimizes the iterative calculation process of K-means++ algorithm based on heuristic method, which improves the calculation speed of K-means++ algorithm, and then combines the optimized K-means++ algorithm with LOF method to improve the operation efficiency of outlier detection algorithm.

The main idea of the maximum minimum distance algorithm is to set the distance threshold, and then determine the initial cluster center. The maximum and minimum distance algorithm is used to determine the initial cluster center, as shown in Formula (8).

$$\begin{cases} h = \max\{w(i,j)\} \\ i = 1, 2, \ldots, p \\ j = 1, 2, \ldots, q \end{cases} \tag{8}$$

among $w(i,j)$ Represents a data object $x_i$ The minimum distance from the existing initial center point; $p$ Remove the number of samples selected as the initial cluster center from the dataset; $q$ The number of initial cluster centers selected for yourself.

In K-means algorithm, if a very isolated sample point is determined as the initial cluster center, poor clustering results will be obtained.

In this study, the idea of maximum and minimum distance is combined with the improved outlier detection algorithm to select the initial cluster center. First, the optimized outlier detection algorithm is used to detect outliers, and at the same time, the candidate set of outliers and the set of outliers are obtained. The set of outliers is deleted from the original dataset and stored temporarily to avoid the impact of outliers on the final clustering results. Then, based on the candidate set of outliers, select the first two initial cluster centers, calculate the distance between all the points in the candidate set of outliers, and find the two points that are farthest away as the initial cluster centers.

Based on the above improvement ideas, this paper first determines the number of clusters by combining the elbow rule and the contour coefficient method to avoid the impact of artificially specified cluster numbers on the clustering results, and then conducts outlier detection based on the improved outlier detection algorithm to avoid the adverse impact of outliers on the final clustering results. At the same time, the initial cluster center is selected step by step based on the candidate set of outliers and the idea of maximum and minimum distance, avoiding the impact of random selection of initial cluster center on the clustering results, and ensuring the stability of clustering results and the quality of clustering results. The improved clustering algorithm is as follows:

Input: set E of n data points.

Output: clustering result cluster.

1. Elbow rule and contour coefficient method determine the clustering number U of dataset E1;
2. Use the improved outlier detection algorithm to detect outliers, and obtain "outlier candidate set" E2, "outlier set" E3;
3. Obtain U initial cluster centers Centroid in E2, E3, E1 according to the improved method;
4. For each point ejin E, find the centroid cj ∈ Centroid nearest to it, and assign ejto cluster j;
5. Order:

$$\begin{cases} ClusterId[i] = j \\ NearestDist[i] = w\left(e_j, c_j\right) \end{cases} \tag{9}$$

6. While does not meet the convergence condition
7. For each cluster ClusterDict, calculate the new centroid CentroidDict;
8. Reassign each sample point to the nearest cluster;
9. End

Although the improved clustering algorithm spends extra time in selecting the initial cluster center, the number of iterations is reduced, and the calculation time of the iterative process is also reduced. In terms of running time, for small data sets, the improved algorithm is basically consistent with the original K-means algorithm, or reduced; For large data sets, it is slightly higher than the original K-means algorithm, but the optimized clustering algorithm not only has a very stable clustering result each time, but also has a better clustering effect [7].

## 2.3 Design of Learning Effect Prediction Model

The current research mostly uses exam scores as the standard to evaluate students' learning effect, but the impact of exam scores on learning effect in online learning is limited. Students obtain knowledge by watching videos on online learning platforms, resulting in a large number of learning behaviors being ignored by existing research methods. At the same time, the current research lacks the description of other characteristics, which limits the effectiveness of the prediction process. In view of these two problems, EduHawkes model is proposed. Based on the analysis of student behavior patterns, various types of characteristic information are added to predict the learning effect, so as to realize the prediction of online teaching learning effect of career guidance courses.

Firstly, the learning behavior sequence is input into the new Hawkes process to obtain the learning behavior representation vector. Secondly, the student and curriculum feature vectors are used as input, and the fusion feature vector is obtained through the counter position multiplication between the feature vectors. Finally, the fusion feature vector and the learning behavior representation vector are input into the classification model for classification after the counter position addition operation.

EduHawkes model is shown in Fig. 1. The model consists of three parts: representational learning behavior sequence, feature fusion and classification prediction [8].

At present, the commonly used sequence representation methods are based on the most basic deep learning model, which has poor interpretability and will lose the information implied in the sequence. The new Hawkes process makes up for these two shortcomings of the current representation methods. It not only inherits the high interpretability of the Hawkes process, which can represent and model online learning modes, but also has the ability of deep learning and autonomous learning implicit features, bridging the gap between sequence understanding and prediction in traditional methods.

The learning behavior sequence is constructed based on the mining data, and then the unlabeled training set (that is, all the behavior events on the sequence) is trained through the new Hawkes process. Finally, the multi-dimensional learning behavior representation vector is obtained by inputting the learning behavior sequence and outputting it.

In reality, it often happens that different students make similar learning behaviors, but their learning effects are quite different. The cognitive state of students in learning

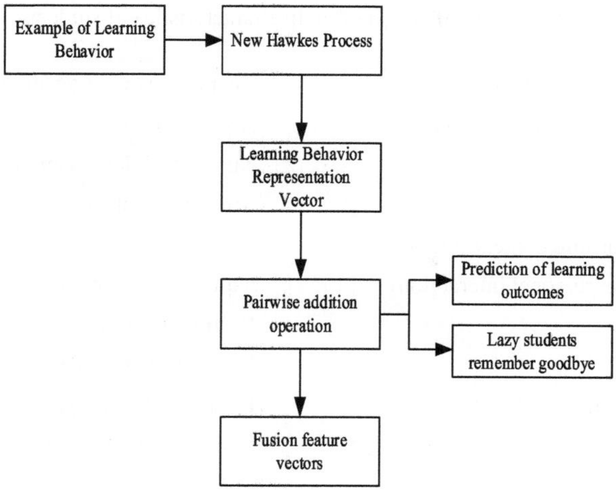


**Fig. 1.** EduHawkes Model

is restricted by many factors. Therefore, when the model is used to predict the learning effect, if it is only based on the data of students' learning behavior, the interpretability of the model will be poor. To solve this problem, this paper extracts student and curriculum features from the data set as new inputs to the model, so that the model can incorporate new features to obtain more ideal prediction results [9].

In the process of online learning, the interaction between students and online tutoring platform is the basic way of learning and the main form of student characteristics. According to the type of interaction, it can be divided into three categories: assessment interaction, learning content interaction, and interpersonal interaction. At the same time, attention is also one of the cognitive factors that affect learning. A large number of literatures have discussed the impact of the Internet environment on the attention mechanism, pointing out that attention has become a scarce resource in the Internet era full of information and information, which is easy to disperse and dissipate, thus causing cognitive problems. The impact of the Internet environment on learning attention investment has gradually attracted attention in the education field. The attention situation of online learning restricts the online learning effect of students. Therefore, when selecting students' characteristics through data sets, this paper takes into account the characteristics related to students' attention while selecting interaction type characteristics. The classification description of students' main characteristics is shown in Table 1:

Although online tutoring platform has massive teaching resources, it also brings a series of problems, such as uneven course quality, which brings some problems to students when choosing courses and affects their learning efficiency. Therefore, when selecting course features through data sets, this paper selects the features most relevant to course quality, which are mainly divided into three categories: course attributes, course popularity, and course assessment. The main features of the course are shown in Table 2:

**Table 1.** Classification of main characteristics of students

| S/N | Characteristic type | Characteristic description |
|---|---|---|
| 1 | Appraisal interaction | Number of exams |
| | | Number of classroom quizzes |
| | | Number of job submissions |
| 2 | Learning content interaction | Times of watching online video |
| 3 | Interpersonal interaction | Number of theme posts published |
| | | Number of posts viewed |
| | | Number of comment posts |
| 4 | Attention related | Preferred course type |
| | | Students' knowledge background |

**Table 2.** Classification of main characteristics of courses

| S/N | Characteristic type | Characteristic description |
|---|---|---|
| 1 | Course Properties | Course category |
| 2 | Popularity of courses | Number of liked courses |
| | | Number of course comments |
| | | Cumulative number of viewers of the course |
| 3 | Course assessment | Completion rate of course examination |
| | | Submission rate of course assignments |

After selecting specific student and course features, the features need to be extracted from the corresponding data set. Unique heat coding is a common method of feature extraction. Calculate the total number of features N, and each feature can be represented by a vector consisting of N-1 zeros and a single 1. However, there are two problems in doing so: 1. If there are many features, the transformed vector will have a huge dimension and be too sparse. The performance of deep learning for sparse input is not good. 2. Since maps are independent of each other, they cannot represent the relationship between different features. Considering these two problems, the method of feature embedding is used to express each feature in vector form with less dimensions, and to express the relationship between features, so as to better represent the feature space. Feature fusion is composed of two parts, namely, student feature vector and course feature vector. The student characteristic matrix is as follows:

$$T = \begin{bmatrix} t_{11} & t_{12} & \cdots & t_{1n} \\ t_{21} & t_{22} & \cdots & t_{2n} \\ \cdots & \cdots & \cdots & \cdots \\ t_{m1} & t_{m2} & \cdots & t_{mn} \end{bmatrix} \tag{10}$$

In Eq. (10) $m$ Indicates the number of students, $n$ Represents the dimension of student vector. Take out each row in the matrix, and the eigenvector of each student can be expressed as:

$$t = [t_{m1}, t_{m2}, \ldots, t_{mn}] \tag{11}$$

Similarly, the curriculum characteristic matrix can be expressed as:

$$D = \begin{bmatrix} d_{11} & d_{12} & \cdots & d_{1n} \\ d_{21} & d_{22} & \cdots & d_{2n} \\ \cdots & \cdots & \cdots & \cdots \\ d_{m1} & d_{m2} & \cdots & d_{mn} \end{bmatrix} \tag{12}$$

The eigenvector of each course can be expressed as:

$$d=[d_{m1}, d_{m2}, \ldots, d_{mn}] \tag{13}$$

Finally, according to the current behavior sequence, the corresponding student feature vector and course feature vector are taken out and multiplied to get the fusion feature vector, as shown below:

$$u_s = t \oplus d \tag{14}$$

As mentioned above, it is believed that the prediction results of students' learning effects will be affected by learning behavior patterns, student characteristics and curriculum characteristics. Based on this idea, after obtaining the representation vector of the learning behavior sequence using the new Hawkes process, select the fusion feature vector obtained with the above, and perform the addition operation to form a new vector as the input of the classification model. The feature operation process is shown in Fig. 2:

Before the learning effect prediction results are output through the classification model, the full connection layer needs to be used for processing. The full connection layer is a linear combination of data without considering the nonlinear nature of the activation function, which can also be called "linear layer". The formula is as follows:

$$Y = EX + g \tag{15}$$

In Eq. (15) $Y$ Refers to the function dependent variable; $X$ Refers to the function independent variable;$E$ Means a linear function; $g$ It refers to the offset vector with dimension n. This paper sets the dimension of n as 2 or 4 dimensions [10] for different classification tasks.

The output of the linear layer is sent into the softmax function for probabilistic classification, and the output of multiple neurons is mapped into the interval of (0,1), which is analyzed in the form of probability, so as to realize the classification task.

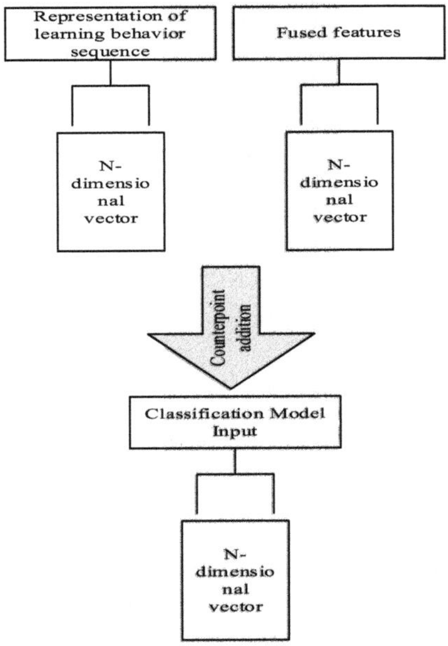


**Fig. 2.** Feature operation process

# 3 Example Application

## 3.1 Experimental Process

This paper tests the performance of the online teaching and learning effect prediction method of the career guidance course based on multi task learning.

Data preprocessing refers to a series of data processing before the experiment. At present, most of the data obtained through the teaching platform are incomplete, and there are inconsistent problems in the format, so it is impossible to directly input the model for experiments. There are many ways to preprocess: data cleaning, data reduction, data transformation, etc. The application of these processing technologies has greatly improved the quality of data and the accuracy of experimental results.

Data preprocessing has a great impact on the results of learning effect prediction, because the original dataset contains a lot of data unrelated to video viewing behavior, including the case of characters, spaces, special letters, etc. In order to reduce the impact of data on the experimental results and make the data more concise, the rules shown in Table 3 are used to process the data.

The data set is processed according to the above rules. Each behavioral data after processing is composed of the elements shown in Table 4, which are: user ID, video ID, behavioral type, timestamp, video start time and video end time.

First, the Chinese word segmentation sequence tagging method based on multi task learning is used to implement the preprocessing of Chinese word segmentation of experimental data. Then the improved K-means algorithm is used to mine the learning behavior information of students. Finally, through the designed EduHawkes model, on the basis

**Table 3.** Data Preprocessing Rules

| S/N | Data preprocessing rules | Data preprocessing method |
|---|---|---|
| 1 | Unrelated data processing | Eliminate irrelevant behavior data |
| 2 | Special letter processing | Delete special letters contained in the dataset |
| 3 | Data segmentation | Split the log data |

**Table 4.** Data Composition

| S/N | label | explain |
|---|---|---|
| 1 | v_end_t | Video end time |
| 2 | v_start_t | Video Start Time |
| 3 | t_s | time stamp |
| 4 | stu_beh_t | Video viewing behavior type |
| 5 | video_id | Video ID |
| 6 | user_id | User ID |

of the analysis of student behavior patterns, various types of feature information are added to predict the learning effect, so as to realize the prediction of the online teaching learning effect of career guidance courses.

The design method evaluates two key applications in the field of online learning:

(1) Evaluation of learning effect
(2) Slack student identification

Evaluate the performance of the model in learning effect evaluation task and slack student identification task through the following indicators:

(1) Accuracy
(2) Matthews correlation coefficient

## 3.2 Comparison Method

In the test, the online learning effect prediction method based on rank correlation analysis and the learning process analysis and learning effect prediction method based on behavior sequence are used as comparison methods, which are represented by method 1 and method 2 respectively.

## 3.3 Test Results

### 3.3.1 Accuracy Test Results

The design method and the accuracy test results of method 1 and method 2 are shown in Table 5.

**Table 5.** Accuracy Test Results

| Mining data volume (GB) | Accuracy (%) | | |
|---|---|---|---|
| | Design method | Method 1 | Method 2 |
| 50 | 92.30 | 86.20 | 82.24 |
| 55 | 92.57 | 86.31 | 82.30 |
| 55 | 92.78 | 86.40 | 82.54 |
| 60 | 92.95 | 86.65 | 82.78 |
| 65 | 93.04 | 86.74 | 82.86 |
| 70 | 93.21 | 86.88 | 82.92 |
| 75 | 93.47 | 86.96 | 83.06 |
| 80 | 93.63 | 87.08 | 83.20 |
| 85 | 93.75 | 87.25 | 83.37 |
| 90 | 93.95 | 87.45 | 83.48 |
| 95 | 94.07 | 87.50 | 83.62 |
| 100 | 94.24 | 87.61 | 83.85 |

According to the test results in the table above, the accuracy rate of the design method increases with the increase of the amount of mining data, and its accuracy rate is higher than the test results of method 1 and method 2 in the same period. The main reason is that the method proposed in this article is based on multitasking learning to design a Chinese word segmentation sequence annotation method, which implements preprocessing of online teaching data for employment guidance courses, thereby improving the generalization ability and effectiveness of the model.

### 3.3.2 Matthews Correlation Coefficient Test Results

The Mathews correlation coefficient test results of the three methods are shown in Fig. 3.

According to the test results in Fig. 3, the Mathews correlation coefficient of the design method is significantly higher than that of Method 1 and Method 2, indicating that its prediction performance is better. The main reason is that the design method uses an improved K-means algorithm to mine the learning behavior information of students in the data after Chinese word segmentation, thereby discovering potential patterns and patterns hidden in the data.

Select 10 freshmen and 10 sophomores each, extract their behaviors related to online teaching in employment guidance courses, and analyze their comprehensive scores of employment guidance courses after using online teaching methods. The results are shown in Table 6.

According to Table 6, the difference between the predicted scores of the method applied in this article and the corresponding students' historical scores is less than 1.5 points. It has been proven that the online teaching and learning effect prediction method for employment guidance courses based on multitasking learning adds multiple types of

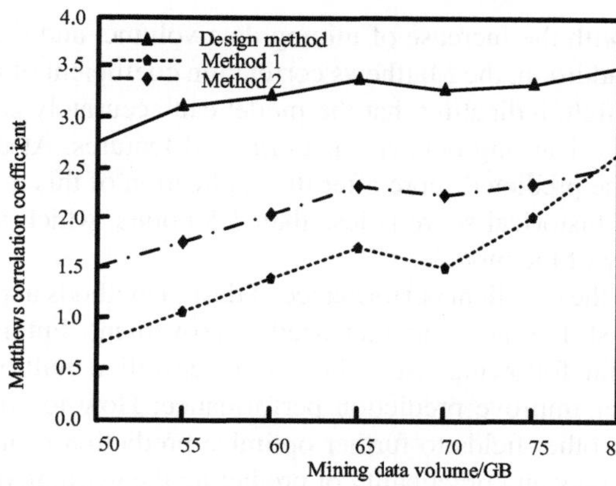


**Fig. 3.** Test Results of Matthews Correlation Coefficient

**Table 6.** Comprehensive Scoring of Employment Guidance Courses

| Freshman | Historical Score | Predicted Score | Sophomore | Historical Score | Predicted Score |
|---|---|---|---|---|---|
| 1 | 91.5 | 92.0 | 1 | 93.0 | 94.0 |
| 2 | 96.5 | 97.0 | 2 | 94.0 | 95.0 |
| 3 | 80.5 | 81.0 | 3 | 97.5 | 97.0 |
| 4 | 79.0 | 80.0 | 4 | 90.5 | 90.0 |
| 5 | 69.0 | 70.0 | 5 | 84.5 | 84.0 |
| 6 | 70.0 | 71 | 6 | 83.5 | 83.0 |
| 7 | 81.0 | 82.0 | 7 | 75.5 | 75.0 |
| 8 | 63.5 | 64.0 | 8 | 79.0 | 80.0 |
| 9 | 71.5 | 72.0 | 9 | 69.0 | 70.0 |
| 10 | 61.5 | 62.0 | 10 | 64.0 | 65.0 |

feature information to the EduHawkes model for learning effect prediction, achieving the prediction of online teaching and learning effect for employment guidance courses, improving the accuracy and interpretability of learning effect prediction, and having good prediction effects.

## 4 Conclusion

This paper takes the representation of learning behavior as the main line of the research, and takes the prediction of learning effect as the main research goal. It designs a prediction method of online teaching learning effect of career guidance courses based on multi task learning. The design method demonstrated good performance in predicting learning outcomes. The experimental results show that the accuracy of the design method gradually improves with the increase of mining data volume, and the overall accuracy is relatively high. In addition, the Matthews correlation coefficient of the design method is also significantly high, indicating that the model can accurately capture the correlation between students' learning behavior patterns and features. At the same time, the difference between the predicted score after the application of this method and the corresponding student's historical score is less than 1.5 points, which further verifies the accuracy and stability of the model.

However, despite the excellent performance of design methods in predicting learning outcomes, there are still some areas that need improvement. Future research should focus on addressing the following issues: how to better utilize multiple types of feature information to further improve prediction performance; How to combine knowledge and technology from other fields to further optimize prediction results. By addressing these issues, the accuracy and practicality of predicting the learning outcomes of online teaching in employment guidance courses can be further improved.

## References

1. Zhang, N.: A brief analysis of how online teaching can develop steadily and be far-reaching in the new era-a case study of practical course for college music programs. Psychol. Res. **12**(7), 525–529 (2022)
2. Liu, P., Wang, X., Teng, F.: Online teaching quality evaluation based on multi-granularity probabilistic linguistic term sets. J. Intell. Fuzzy Syst. **40**(2), 1–20 (2021)
3. Bulut, T., Del, T.: Technology acceptance model: the perceptions of Turkish and Kazakh English teachers in online teaching. Int. J. Lang. Acad. **37**(37), 305–315 (2021)
4. Fitriani, S.S., Weda, S., Samad, I.A., et al.: Genre-based visualization through an online teaching platform: a strategy to engage with academic texts during the Covid-19 outbreak. XLinguae **14**(1), 270–288 (2021)
5. Prabha, M.S., Dinesh, K.V.: Distance learning and community of inquiry: how webinars for postgraduates are different from undergraduate online teaching sessions? CHRISMED J. Health Res. **7**(4), 287–288 (2021)
6. Panhwar, M., Parveen, S., Baig, Q.A., et al.: Educational challenges and their influence on online teaching methods in Pakistani students during COVID 19 era. Rawal Med. J. **46**(3), 677–680 (2021)
7. Jiang, T., Cui, L., Liu, et al.: The method of ship track prediction based on cluster analysis and Att-Bi-LSTM. Comp. Integr. Manuf. Syst. 39(8), 1–5+322 (2022)
8. Khanal, P.: Lived experience of online teaching during the COVID-19 pandemic: implications for curriculum and teaching. Interdisc. Res. Educ. **5**(1–2), 89–102 (2021)
9. Lou, Z.H., Wang, H.L., Sun, C.Y.: Simulation of academic development analysis model under background of education big data. Comp. Simul. **39**(12), 306–310 (2022)
10. Sato, E., Chen, J.C.: Rise to the occasion: the trajectory of a novice Japanese teacher's first online teaching through action research. Lang. Teach. Res. **25**(2), 306–329 (2021)

# Design of a Web-Based Computer-Aided Teaching System for Fault Diagnosis

Zhenchao Lei(✉), Wei Li, and Mingfei Qu

College of Aeronautical Engineering, Beijing Polytechnic, Beijing 100176, China
leizhenchao@163.com

**Abstract.** Traditional fault diagnosis methods usually rely on the experience and knowledge of professional technical personnel, which makes fault diagnosis often difficult and complex for non professionals. The design and research of computer-aided teaching systems aims to provide a more intuitive, interactive, and visual way to assist in fault diagnosis by combining computer technology and teaching methods. In order to improve the stability, user satisfaction, and information security of computer-aided teaching systems, a web-based fault diagnosis computer-aided teaching system is designed. Build a three-tier system structure based on B/S mode, including user interface layer, business logic layer and data access layer, focus on the design of foreground function module and background management module, so that the system has foreground and background management, online communication, data download and other functions, and select SQL Server 2000 as the system database. On the basis of hardware design, traditional genetic algorithms are improved to comprehensively consider the equality of teaching resource selection and the priority selection mechanism of local teaching resources in the selection of genetic genes, improve system work efficiency, and achieve user satisfaction in practical results. The experimental results indicate that the user satisfaction of this system is higher, and the system crash rate and personal information leakage rate are lower.

**Keywords:** Web · Fault Diagnosis · Assisted Teaching · Improved Genetic Algorithm · B/S Structure

## 1 Introduction

With the rapid rise and wide application of computer technology, multimedia technology and network technology, educational technology has entered a new stage of development, from traditional blackboard, tape recorder, slide and other conventional teaching mode of media means to multimedia teaching means based on computer and network technology. It has made a qualitative leap in learning style and educational design [1]. However, the rapid popularization of the network and the development of multimedia technology only provide the basic conditions for the network teaching, and it is not an easy thing to realize the network teaching. It has become a very necessary and urgent topic to make use of existing conditions and technologies to research and develop network assisted teaching


G. Gui et al. (Eds.): eLEOT 2023, LNICST 543, pp. 33–47, 2024.
https://doi.org/10.1007/978-3-031-51465-4_3

systems that cooperate and complement each other with classroom teaching, to perfectly integrate classroom teaching and network teaching, to give full play to the auxiliary role of network in teaching, and to gradually improve online teaching technology and cultivate online teaching atmosphere [2, 3].

Reference [4] designed an embedded computer remote assisted teaching system based on web technology. The system hardware consists of memory, central processing unit, input device, and output device. The memory includes teacher side memory and student side memory. The central processing unit mainly consists of three parts: logic unit (ALU), control unit, and input/output unit. The software designs web server programs and database programs separately. To verify the effectiveness of the teaching system, a comparative experiment was designed, and the results showed that the system can effectively expand the auxiliary range and shorten the auxiliary time, but its security performance is poor and personal data information is easily leaked. Reference [5] designed a computer-aided classroom teaching system based on data mining. The data storage includes three parts: SARM storage, CD-ROM, and hard disk. An OLAP server is arranged, and a switch is used to integrate front-end tools and applications. On the basis of completing the hardware design, the massive information in the data source is classified using functions, and the hidden layer is calculated through the number of neurons to complete the design of a computer-aided classroom teaching system based on data mining. The experimental results show that the system has a higher number of concurrent users and a faster information retrieval time, but the sense of user experience is not strong, and the user satisfaction is not high. Reference [6] designed a method based on. NET platform of interactive electronic technology computer-aided teaching system, the system hardware structure by the user interface layer, business selection layer and data management layer of three layers of structure system. Teachers, students and other users enter their identity information in the user interface layer, log in to the system and enter the business selection layer, and click the corresponding program according to their application requirements. The business selection layer transmits the user selection instruction to the data management layer, and the data management layer selects the corresponding resources according to the user's requirements and feeds back to the user. The interactive mode of the system is mainly embodied in interactive teaching and information interaction. Interactive teaching is embodied in online teaching between teachers and students, and information interaction is embodied in information transmission. After testing, the system has strong anti-pressure ability and can respond to a large number of users' application instructions in real time, but the system has a high breakdown rate.

In response to the shortcomings of traditional auxiliary teaching systems, this article designs a web-based fault diagnosis computer-aided teaching system based on Web technology. The innovative points of this system design method are as follows:

(1) This system adopts a three-layer B/S architecture. Compared with the C/S architecture, the B/S structure does not increase any maintenance and upgrading workload regardless of the size of users or the number of branches, saving a lot of manpower and time.
(2) Design the front-end functional module and back-end management module of the system, and select SQL Server 2000 as the database of the computer-aided teaching system.

(3) On the basis of traditional genetic algorithms, the selection of genetic genes comprehensively considers the equality of teaching resource selection and the priority selection mechanism of local teaching resources, in order to improve work efficiency and achieve practical results that meet user satisfaction.

## 2 System Hardware Design

The computer aided instruction system designed in this paper uses modern information technology, based on a variety of media teaching resources and interactive means, to provide a good network learning environment centered on learners' independent learning. It fully embodies students' learning as the center, through providing various support services in the learning process of students, on the basis of improving the learning effect, to cultivate students' autonomous learning ability, collaborative learning ability and practical innovation ability.

### 2.1 System Mode Selection

Computers are the material foundation for designing web-based fault diagnosis computer-aided teaching systems. In the process of computer-aided teaching, computers serve as communication media between teachers and students. Web server is currently the most widely used and comprehensive type of server, based on Web technology. It refers to a computer program that provides teaching information browsing for web-based fault diagnosis computer-aided teaching systems in corresponding network environments. Students and teachers can send teaching requests, teaching files, and other data information through the server [7]. Generally speaking, a web server includes four working processes: establishing a connection, sending a request, issuing a response, and closing the connection. The working principle is shown in Fig. 1.

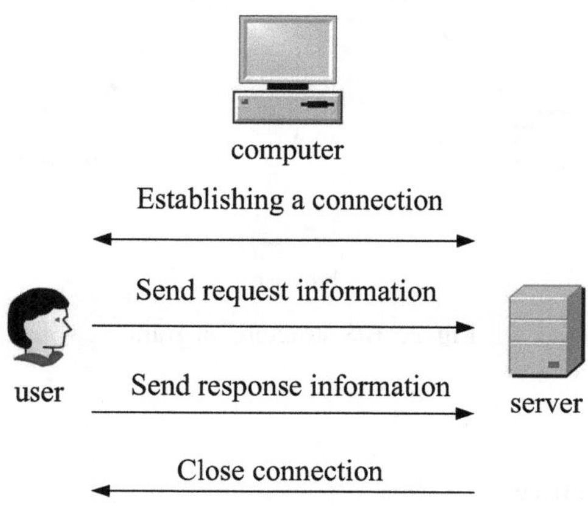


**Fig. 1.** Working Principle of Web Server

In Fig. 1, the established connection is realized by connecting the Web server and the browser through network protocol. The user can log in the browser to check whether the connection is completed. Sending requests means that users send requests to Web servers through browsers, such as login requests, access requests, teaching requests and other required requests. After receiving the request, the Web server uses related algorithms to calculate and process the request, and finally transmits the result to the browser through the network protocol, and displays the request content while displaying the result. After the response is complete, disconnect the Web server from the browser and maintain and upgrade the Web server.

Previously, web-based systems often adopted two forms of architecture: C/S mode and B/S mode. Although the traditional C/S architecture adopts an open mode, it is only a level of openness in system development. In specific applications, both the client and server sides still require specific software, which fails to provide users with the open environment they truly expect. The B/S architecture products clearly demonstrate more convenient features [8]. No matter how large the user scale is or how many branches there are, there will be no additional maintenance and upgrading workload. All operations only need to be carried out on the server. If it is in a remote location, the server can be connected to the internet for immediate maintenance and upgrading, making upgrading and maintenance easier and simpler to use, saving a lot of manpower and time. Therefore, this system adopts a B/S structure.

The typical B/S mode application system network structure is shown in Fig. 2:

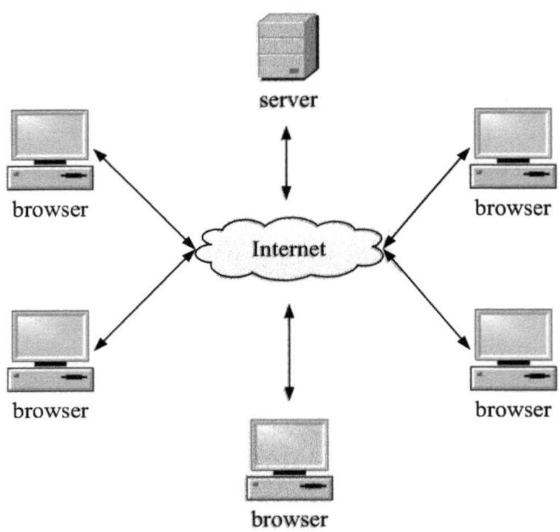


**Fig. 2.** B/S structure diagram

## 2.2 System Architecture

Based on the comparison of the advantages and disadvantages of C/S structure and B/S structure, this system adopts three layers of B/S architecture: user interface layer, business logic layer, data access layer.

(1) The user interface layer runs through Microsoft Internet Explorer or its compatible browser. Students, teachers and administrators operate on this layer.
(2) The business logic layer receives the user request input from the user interface layer, converts it into a way that the business logic process can understand, sends the data request to the data layer in an orderly manner according to the specific business logic, combines the data interpretation returned by the data layer into the information required by the user, and returns to the user interface layer. It is the core of realizing and processing business logic in the whole application software system [9]. Business logic layer is located in the Web Server and application server, in the server running Windows 2000 Server operating system, using ASP technology to develop all the system applications are placed on the server, when the user request comes, the Web server will request to the application.
(3) The data access layer is mainly the operation layer of the original data (database or text file and other forms of data storage), not the original data, that is, the operation of data, not the database. It manages data and provides a standardized open access interface to the business logic layer. The data access layer is located on the database server, where SQL Server 2000 runs. All databases of the system are placed on the server and managed by SQL Server 2000. This structure is conducive to system maintenance and load balancing, while also ensuring information security.

The system architecture diagram is shown in Fig. 3: The user interface layer receives input requests submitted by users, accesses the business logic layer, obtains access results, and sends them to users.

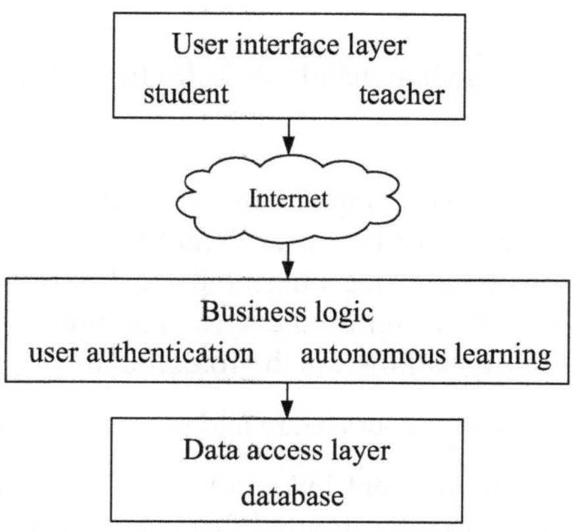


**Fig. 3.** System Architecture Diagram

## 2.3 Functional Module Design

The system is designed and developed using B/S mode, which can provide a comprehensive teaching system for teachers' auxiliary teaching and online course release; Students can query the teaching plans and video tutorials published by the teacher in the system, and complete the practical training tasks of the relevant courses [10]. As a fault diagnosis training auxiliary teaching system, this system must have the following functions: front-end and back-end management, online communication, data download, and other functions. The following is the specific process of designing system functional modules:

(1) Front desk function module

The front-end users mainly perform operations such as logging in, registering, self-testing exercises, asking questions, downloading lesson plans, and entering virtual classrooms. The functional module diagram is shown in Fig. 4.

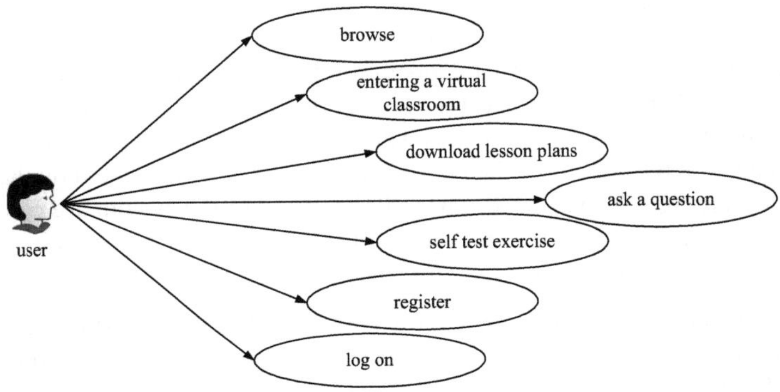


**Fig. 4.** Schematic diagram of the front-end functional module of the system

The foreground function module mainly includes the following functions:

1) Students log in

In order for the fault diagnosis computer aided instruction system to record the use of each student in detail, there must be a user login function. Specifically for the login module of the fault diagnosis training teaching auxiliary system, the addition of new users (teachers and students) is directly set by the system administrator in the background, and does not accept the user registration in the foreground.

2) Browsing function of teaching courseware and practical training tasks

Each student can click the relevant links in the system to learn the corresponding teaching courseware and browse the training tasks. On the one hand, this helps students consolidate the knowledge they have learned, on the other hand, it helps students understand the needs of fault diagnosis in work from the perspective of practical training.

3) Download function of teaching courseware and practical training materials

Each student can search for the teaching courseware or training task materials they want to download in the system, and then download them locally for offline learning.

4) Upload graphic and video tutorials

Both teachers and students can upload resources such as graphic and video tutorials through the front desk, fill in the title when logged in, and set the classification and upload type to upload. After uploading, student users need to go through the administrator's backend review before publishing, while teachers can directly upload and display teaching resources on the front desk.

5) Online communication

If students encounter questions they do not understand during the learning process, they can go to the online communication bar to send out questions and wait for answers from teachers or other classmates. They can search for questions through keywords. In the logged in state, users can easily post replies to view the content of their posts.

6) Member center management

Both teachers and students can log in to the member center to manage related matters, including memos, messages, teaching courseware, homework, training tasks, etc.

7) System Bulletin

System administrators can release, modify, delete and other operations of announcements in the background, and then the foreground user first time to understand the latest announcement content.

(2) Background management module

When the system administrator and teacher log in to the background management page, the authentication of the system administrator and teacher is added. Once the user name and password information in the session is empty, it indicates that the teacher or administrator has not logged in. At this time, a dialog box will pop up, indicating that the user has not logged in. If the login succeeds, you can enter the background to manage the system. The system administrator can recommend the top of the fine course, key training tasks, can delete expired, useless content, can batch reply to students' questions.

Background management flow chart is shown in Fig. 5.

## 2.4 Database Technology

The computer-aided teaching system, like other Web-based systems, cannot do without the support of a backend database. The backend database is mainly used to access various information and data on the website, such as using a student data table in the database to save various basic information of students, using a test question table to save various test question information, and using a message table to save message information. The database is the basic guarantee for realizing the system's dynamic interaction function. In the selection of backend databases, different requirements can be met by selecting different databases. Currently, Access and SQL Server are two commonly used database management systems.

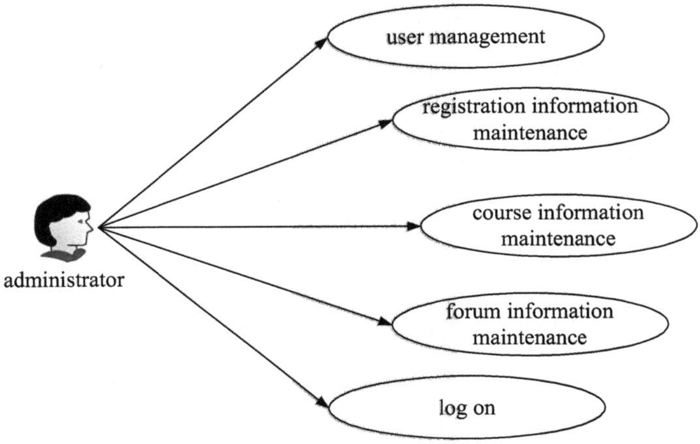


**Fig. 5.** Schematic diagram of system backend management module

Access is a desktop database management system, it is simple to operate, easy to use, the whole system only needs a "*.mdb" database file to achieve the storage and Access to the data, when the website data volume is small, the page view is small, can choose Access, but when the system data volume is large, the number of visitors, Access has certain limitations.

SQL Server 2000 is a high-end database management system and is currently one of the most popular database service systems. SQL Server itself is a member of Microsoft office components. It is organically combined with other Microsoft software (Windows Server, Internet Information Server, etc.), and makes full use of the services or functions they provide (such as security management, event log, performance monitor, memory management, asynchronous, etc.); SQL Server 2000 also provides built-in data replication capabilities, powerful management tools, and an open system architecture; The SQL Server 2000 relational database engine supports the functions required by today's demanding data processing environment. The database engine fully protects data integrity and provides more secure and reliable storage functions for relational data and structured data. It has a good set of security control mechanisms to ensure the security of databases and data in databases and prevent some problems, such as, It can prevent multiple users from attempting to update the same data at the same time; SQL Server 2000 can provide the database services required for ultra large systems, and can simultaneously manage thousands of concurrent operations to minimize the user cost of modifying the database, thus occupying the least system resources. Overall, the computer-aided teaching system designed in this article uses SQL Server 2000.

## 3 Improve the Application of Genetic Algorithm in Computer Aided Instruction System

Through the above steps, the hardware design of computer aided instruction system for fault diagnosis based on Web is completed. Then, from the point of view of algorithm design, the system of this paper is further improved. The computer aided instruction system for fault diagnosis based on Web is oriented to more users and contains more extensive resources. In the face of many users' differentiated requests for massive data, it is very difficult to design computer aided instruction system for fault diagnosis based on Web, and the main difficulty lies in how to improve user response efficiency. On the basis of traditional genetic algorithm, various kinds of teaching resources are optimized and classified respectively. In the selection of genetic genes, the equality of teaching resources selection and the selection mechanism of local teaching resources are considered comprehensively, so as to improve the work efficiency and achieve the actual effect of user satisfaction.

The Web - based fault diagnosis computer aided instruction system improves the traditional genetic algorithm in task scheduling. The key gene selection link in the genetic process increases the constraint mechanism which combines the equality of access resources and the principle of local resource preference.

(1) Chromosome coding and decoding

Based on the comprehensive analysis of the characteristics of direct chromosome coding and indirect chromosome coding, combined with the characteristics of Web-based computer-aided teaching system for fault diagnosis, the resource-task based indirect coding method is selected here: the number of subtasks is taken as the length of chromosome, and the number of genes in chromosome is taken as the number of resources allocated by corresponding subtasks. Assuming that the number of tasks facing the system is $K$, the number of processing points is $M$, and the assignment of tasks at $a$ is $TaskNum(a)$, then the total number of subtasks can be calculated by formula (1):

$$SumTaskNum(a) = \sum_{a=1}^{K} TaskNum(a) \tag{1}$$

Next, these tasks need to be renumbered, as shown in formula (2):

$$N = \sum_{a=1}^{K} TaskNum(a) + k \tag{2}$$

Finally, the completion time of each job and the total completion time of all jobs are calculated by decoding the data, ETC matrix and DTC matrix.

The calculation method of completion time of each assignment $t$ is shown in Formula (3):

$$Time(t) = \sum_{i,j=1}^{p} TaskTime(i,j) \tag{3}$$

Among them, $p$ is the location where task $i$ in task $t$ is assigned to the computing node, and $TaskTime(i,j)$ is the time when task $i$ completes sub task $j$ on the computing node $p$.

The calculation method for the completion time of the total task is shown in formula (4):

$$TotalTime = \sum_{i,j=1}^{n} NodeTime(i, j) \tag{4}$$

where, $NodeTime(i, j)$is the time it takes a compute node to complete tasks $i$ and $j$ , and $n$ is the number of tasks for a compute node.

(2) Initial population generation

Here, it is assumed that the population size is $R$, there are $m$ processing points, $z$ jobs and a total of $U$ subtasks. The first step should be to use the Max-Min algorithm to equally limit the allocation of system resources, and then randomly generate the required chromosomes. At this time, the number of chromosomes is $R$, the length is $U$, and the value interval of genes is limited to $[1, m]$.

(3) Fitness function

Genetic algorithm calculates the advantages and disadvantages of individuals through fitness function, and selects and evolves the next generation to seek the optimal solution of the problem.

The satisfaction level of users with the completion time of all assignments in individual $c$ is shown in formula (5):

$$f_1(i) = g(i)/K \quad 1 \leq i \leq R \tag{5}$$

The fitness of total task completion time is shown in Formula (6):

$$f_2(i) = 1/c(i) \quad 1 \leq i \leq R \tag{6}$$

According to formulas (5) and (6), outstanding individuals with relatively high fitness values can be selected and given to the next generation.

(4) Genetic manipulation

Genetic operations are divided into three types: selection, crossover, and mutation, which are the main ways to select and produce the next generation of individuals. Selection operation is a fundamental way to spread excellent genes in a population. When selecting an operator, use the roulette wheel selection method. Use the following formulas (7) and (8) to calculate the probability of each individual being selected one by one using the previous formulas (5) and (6):

$$P_1(i) = f_1(i) / \sum_{j=1}^{R} f_1(j) \tag{7}$$

$$P_2(i) = f_2(i) / \sum_{j=1}^{R} f_2(j) \tag{8}$$

Variations can create new search Spaces. The crossover probability function and mutation probability function are shown in Formula (9) and Formula (10) respectively:

$$P_c = \begin{cases} k_1 (f_{\max} - f') / (f_{\max} - f'), & f' \geq f_{avg} \\ k_1, & f' < f_{avg} \end{cases} \tag{9}$$

$$P_m = \begin{cases} k_3 (f_{\max} - f) / (f_{\max} - f_{avg}), & f \geq f_{avg} \\ k_4, & f < f_{avg} \end{cases} \tag{10}$$

Among them: $f$ is the individual to be mutated; $f_{\max}$ is the largest individual in the group; $f_{avg}$ is the average value of each generation of population.

The application of improved genetic algorithm in web-based fault diagnosis computer-aided teaching system lies in the allocation and scheduling of system resources for numerous remote user tasks. This article studies the architecture of web-based fault diagnosis computer-aided teaching system and improves the original adaptive genetic algorithm based on the characteristics of multi user and multi task types in web-based fault diagnosis computer-aided teaching system, Based on the traditional genetic algorithm, the genetic gene is selected by integrating data fairness and local sexual selection. Compared with the traditional algorithm, it is more efficient in responding to users' demand response.

## 4 Experimental Analysis

To verify the feasibility of a Web-based computer-aided teaching system for fault diagnosis, system performance verification was conducted.

### 4.1 System Operating Environment

According to the overall demand of the computer aided instruction system, in order to ensure the efficiency and reliability of the system operation, the server side of the system should have high hardware and software configuration. This application can run on the Internet, can also be applied to the campus network and connected to the internal LAN computer room, its operation requirements are as follows Table 1:

**Table 1.** System hardware and software environment

| Parameter | Specification |
|---|---|
| Server | CPU: P4-3.2G |
| Operating system | Windows 8 |
| WEB server | Microsoft Internet Information Server 6.0 |
| Development tool | ASP |
| Memory | 512 M |
| Network routing protocol | AODV protocol |
| Video card | NVIDIA |

In the above operating environment, system performance verification was carried out. In order to make the experimental results more reliable, a computer-assisted classroom teaching system based on data mining and an interactive electronic technology computer-assisted teaching system based on the. NET platform were used as comparative systems to compare with the system in this paper.

### 4.2 Analysis of Experimental Results

#### 4.2.1 Personal Information Leakage Rate

Computer aided instruction system is very important in the management of personal information. Therefore, the leakage rate of personal information is taken as an experimental indicator to compare the three systems, and the results are shown in Fig. 6.

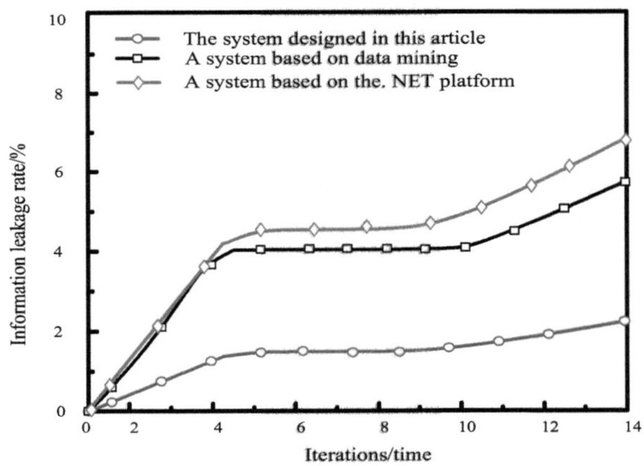


**Fig. 6.** Comparative results of personal information leakage rate

From Fig. 6, it can be seen that from the perspective of personal information leakage rate, the highest personal information leakage rate of the system in this article is only 2.3%, while the highest personal information leakage rates of the computer-aided classroom teaching system based on data mining and the interactive electronic technology computer-aided teaching system based on the. NET platform are 5.7% and 6.4%, respectively. From the above data, it can be seen that the personal information leakage rate of the system in this article is lower, which can maximize the protection of user privacy information and improve the security of user information.

### 4.2.2 Comparative Analysis of System Crash Rate

If the system crash rate is too high in the application process, the user experience will be affected. Therefore, the system crash rate is taken as the experimental index to test the system crash rate of the three systems. The comparison results are shown in Fig. 7.

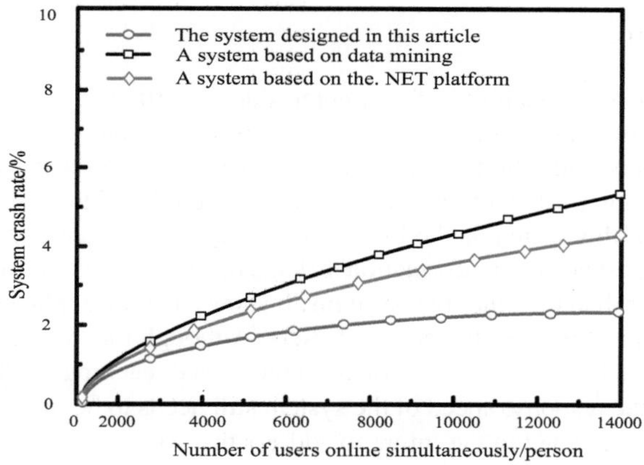


**Fig. 7.** Comparison results of system crash rates

As shown in Fig. 7, as the number of users simultaneously online increases, the crash rates of the three systems gradually increase. Relatively speaking, the crash rate of the system in this paper is the lowest and consistently lower than that of the other two systems. Through comparison, it can be seen that the system in this article can improve the stability of the system, and the probability of system failure is relatively low.

### 4.2.3 Comparative Analysis of User Satisfaction

Select students and teachers from the faulty major to evaluate the application effectiveness of the three systems through scoring. The user satisfaction comparison results of the three systems are shown in Table 2.

From the data in Table 2, it can be seen that users have higher satisfaction with the system in this article, with a maximum score of 90.6 points. However, the systems based on data mining and the. NET platform have a maximum score of 86.3 points and 79.5 points, respectively. From this, it can be seen that users are more satisfied with the effectiveness of the system in this article, indicating that the system is more in line with users' expected goals and meets their actual needs.

**Table 2.** Comparison results of user satisfaction

| Number of users/name | User rating/score | | |
|---|---|---|---|
| | The system designed in this paper | System based on data mining | System based on .NET platform |
| 100 | 90.6 | 86.3 | 79.5 |
| 200 | 89.7 | 84.0 | 75.3 |
| 300 | 88.5 | 82.1 | 74.2 |
| 400 | 87.0 | 79.5 | 73.0 |
| 500 | 86.3 | 76.3 | 72.9 |

## 5 Conclusion

In order to improve the stability of computer aided instruction system, improve user satisfaction and user information security as the research goal, design a fault diagnosis computer aided instruction system based on Web. The experimental results show that users have higher satisfaction with the system, and the highest score is 90.6. The breakdown rate of this system is the lowest and always lower than that of the other two systems. The highest personal information leakage rate of the system in this paper is only 2.3%, much lower than the other two systems. It shows that the application effect of this system is better and can meet the needs of users. Although the system designed in this article has improved the effectiveness of computer-aided teaching for fault diagnosis to a certain extent, the response speed of the system still needs to be improved, and further research will be conducted in the future to address this issue.

**Acknowledgements.** A school-level project of Beijing Polytechnic, Project Name: Research on the application of aircraft avionics fault diagnosis system in teaching (2023X021-SXZ)

## References

1. Zhang, T., Xu, M., Liu, C.: Design of physics multimedia assisted teaching system based on concept network. Mod. Electron. Tech. **43**(20), 119–121+125 (2020)
2. Wang, H.-J., Wang, Z.-F.: Design of simulation teaching system based on modular production and processing. Comp. Simul. **39**(04), 205–209 (2022)
3. Chen, J.-Y., Wang, Z., Chen, J.-Y., Chen, Z.-Q., Zhen, H.-B.: Design and research on intelligent teaching system based on deep learning. Comp. Sci. **46**(1), 550–554+576 (2019)
4. Yin, J., Yin, L.: Design of embedded computer remote auxiliary teaching system based on Web technology. Mod. Electron. Tech. **44**(16), 25–29 (2021)
5. Chen, G., Li, Y. Lv, X.: Design of computer-aided classroom teaching system based on data mining. Mod. Electron. Tech. **43**(04), 94–96 (2020)
6. Cao, L.: Interactive computer aided teaching system based on .NET platform. Mod. Electron. Tech. **43**(03), 134–137+141 (2020)
7. Wang, B., Zhao, M., Fan, Z.: Design of automatic adjustment teaching system based on network. Mach. Tool Hydraulics **50**(02), 109–113 (2022)

8. Guo, W., Wang, B., Zhao, D.-P.: Design of experimental teaching system for hydraulic control valve performance based on network. Chin. Hydraul. Pneumatics **47**(01), 122–128 (2023)
9. Sheng, W.: Design and implementation of digital holographic comprehensive experiment system for teaching. Coll. Phys. **38**(05), 45–47 (2019)
10. Qi, X., Han, L.: Design and implementation of android assistant teaching system based on web service. Microcomput. Appl. **37**(08), 6–8 (2021)

# Design of Ideological and Political Network Teaching Assistant System Based on ZigBee

Jing Luo(✉) and Yu Guan

Fuyang Normal University, Fuyang 236041, China
yyyxa123@163.com

**Abstract.** The existing teaching assistance systems mostly focus on the development of individual applications, such as roll call systems and homework systems, and few have developed a complete set of teaching assistance systems. In view of this, design a ZigBee based ideological and political network teaching assistance system. The focus is on researching wireless communication modules based on ZigBee technology. ZigBee has advantages such as low power consumption, wide network coverage, and strong self-healing ability, which can achieve efficient communication of the system. On this basis, the login function interface, teacher red pen correction module, resource learning module and Electronic assessment module are designed to achieve the functions of resource upload, homework correction and so on. The system test results show that the system pages can adjust with the screen size. When the concurrent volume of virtual users and teachers gradually increases, the system can respond to teacher operations normally, with an average response time of less than 5000ms. The failure only occurs when the pressure reaches 290, which has high security and can effectively prevent information leakage.

**Keywords:** ZigBee · Ideological and political network teaching · Coordinator · Teaching assistant system

## 1 Introduction

As a base for talent cultivation and quality education, universities have a significant responsibility in both knowledge transmission and ideological education. The ideological and political theory course is the main channel for moral education in universities, and cultivating talents with excellent moral character is one of the main goals and tasks of talent cultivation in higher education. The ideological and political theory course that highlights moral education is an important content of higher education [1]. To promote the development of ideological and political education in universities, it is necessary to actively promote the application of information technology in ideological and political courses. The teaching assistance system is able to impart knowledge more targeted, while also providing a more user-friendly way for remote communication and learning between teachers and students. In addition to fully utilizing online teaching resources


G. Gui et al. (Eds.): eLEOT 2023, LNICST 543, pp. 48–62, 2024.
https://doi.org/10.1007/978-3-031-51465-4_4

for learning, the greater advantage of teaching assistance systems is that they can guide students to learn, enable them to better grasp knowledge, transform "teaching" into "guidance", and allow students to grasp and complete more links themselves. Traditional classroom teaching can no longer meet the needs of classrooms with a large amount of information, and students need more learning resources. The emergence of teaching assistance systems in universities can allow students to independently choose teaching resources for learning, which is conducive to cultivating students' self-learning ability [2, 3].

Therefore, the research and development of ideological and political network teaching assistance systems is imperative. The current commonly used design methods for network teaching assistance systems mainly include embedded computer remote assistance teaching system design based on Web technology and physical multimedia assistance teaching system design based on concept networks. The system hardware designed by the former consists of memory, central processing unit, input device, and output device, Memory includes teacher side memory and student side memory, and the central processing unit mainly consists of three parts: logical unit (ALU), control unit, and input/output unit. The software designs web server programs and database programs separately. The experimental results show that this method can effectively expand the assistance range and shorten the assistance time, but has a higher number of response failures. The latter constructs a physics multimedia assisted teaching system architecture with the logic layer as the core, designing theoretical knowledge modules, experimental modules, and student practice modules respectively. Based on the concept network, a large number of rules in the physics teaching system are attached to concepts, forming a conceptual network knowledge system. The theoretical knowledge system design is completed, and experimental modules are designed using image and animation display methods. Based on the theoretical knowledge and experimental modules, student knowledge is modeled, comparing students' knowledge with theoretical knowledge, using computers to score students' mastery of knowledge, achieving practice and feedback on exercise results, and completing the design of a physics multimedia assisted teaching system. The experimental results show that the system has good compatibility, but its security is not good.

In response to the existing problems mentioned above, this article designs a ZigBee based ideological and political network teaching assistance system. The system has the following innovative points:

(1) Design a wireless communication module for the ideological and political network teaching assistance system based on ZigBee technology. ZigBee has advantages such as low power consumption, wide network coverage, and strong self-healing ability, which is conducive to improving the system's response speed.
(2) The login function module can enhance system security and ensure user information security.

# 2 Design of Ideological and Political Network Teaching Assistant System

## 2.1 Wireless Communication Module Design

The wireless communication module is designed based on ZigBee technology to realize the wireless communication of the system. ZigBee communication structure is the skeleton of the entire wireless network, which is directly related to the specific implementation of the wireless network. The communication structure design needs to achieve three directions of wireless communication: controller to gateway, gateway to the entire wireless network, and all nodes to gateway communication. Three types of devices are defined in ZigBee protocol: coordinator, routing node and terminal node; Only the terminal node is not a full function node and has no routing function [4]. In this system, there are two types of equipment: coordinator and routing node.

The system node needs to record the answer time, and the nodes in ZigBee network need a unified reference time, so the broadcast mechanism is used to synchronize the clock. The broadcast mechanism can avoid recording the network address of nodes in the network at the same time. Moreover, the network address of the coordinator in ZigBee network is fixed, so the coordinator can be used as a gateway, and nodes can upload data to the fixed address to facilitate the implementation of future programs. At the same time, because ZigBee single level communication distance fully meets the application of ordinary classroom space, a star communication structure of wireless network is designed as shown in Fig. 1.

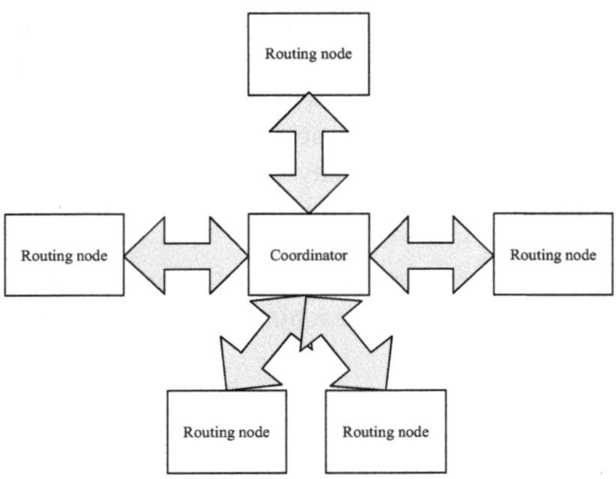


**Fig. 1.** Designed star communication structure

The coordinator is the most important part of the entire management system network. It needs to run first in the entire network. It forms a network through channels and network identifiers, and uniformly accesses and manages the added nodes, and manages all wireless networks together. In the same ZigBee communication network, there can only be one coordinator, which is indispensable hardware. A main coordinator is designed. The main coordinator consists of two parts, namely, the RF top plate and the support bottom plate. The two parts can be combined by DIP20 physical plugging to form a unified whole. Among them, the RF roof adopts CC2430 of TI Company as the transmission processing core. The chip can use ZigBee2007 protocol stack, and uses 2.4G SMA communication antenna, IEEE 802.15.4 standard. The maximum transmission distance is 100m, which is suitable for the use of reconstruction projects. The support backplane includes various serial ports and interfaces, including reset system [5].

The main coordinator consists of power supply and switch/indicator light, reset button, RS232 interface, RJ45 Ethernet interface, switching cap skipping of communication mode (serial port and RJ45), JTAG download interface, RF roof, work indicator light and antenna interface. 5V DC power supply is used to supply power for ZigBee coordinator. Turn on the power supply and toggle it to the on position, and turn off the power supply and toggle it to the off position. When powered on, the power indicator red LED lights up. Reset key is used to reset the system without power supply, and reset the program of the chip to facilitate debugging and program operation. The overall circuit framework is shown in Fig. 2.

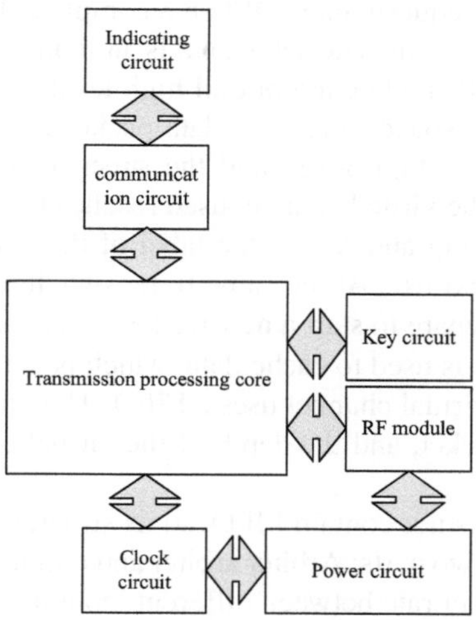


**Fig. 2.** Overall Circuit Frame

The coordinator can communicate with various universal serial devices through the standard nine pin RS232 serial port. In this design, the conversion connector of RS232 and USB is used to realize the connection management and control between the coordinator and PC computer. The coordinator exchanges data with the host computer through this interface, and transmits various monitoring information of ZigBee network to the software on PC. At the same time, the control command of the upper computer can be sent to the coordinator through this interface to control other ZigBee nodes, realizing all functions designed by the upper computer software platform and embedded terminal. The simulator interface developed by JTAG download interface system connects ZigBee emulator, which facilitates users to write, debug and simulate ZigBee protocol stack and other codes online.

The coordinator also uses the Neport Ethernet module. The coordinator can connect to the network through the Ethernet port, the jumper cap jumps to the UART position, and the coordinator communicates with the host computer through the serial port; Jump the jumper cap to the RJ45 position, and the coordinator will communicate with the upper computer through TCP/IP. The RF top plate adopts TICC2430 RF chip, which is connected to the ZigBee coordinator RF top plate through 2 * 10PIN array pins. There are two indicators: red and green. When the coordinator system is working, the RF roof panel red indicator lights up.

The distributed routing architecture is used in the routing node, and the input buffer mode is used. Of course, the structure can also be easily adjusted to the output buffer mode, depending on the specific application. Specifically, it consists of two modules. The input module includes three parts, IFC (Input Flow Controller) input flow control module, IB (Input Buffer) input buffer module and HD (Header Decoder) header decoding module.

The function of the input flow control module is to translate the handshake protocol and select the write virtual channel. in_Val: indicates that the upper level routing node has valid data coming and requests input; When a complete data packet is transmitted, the signal gives up the request. in_The ack signal is an input confirmation signal. When the Full signals from the IB module are not all high level 1, it means that at least one virtual channel has storage space to receive data packets. At this time, IFC will_The ack response signal is set to high level, and the superior routing node is notified to start data transmission; If the virtual channel used reaches full status during data packet transmission, stop responding and record the label of the current data packet and the virtual channel used for next use. At the same time, switch to the next virtual channel that is not satisfied, and prepare to start a new packet transmission.

The data cache module is used to cache data, which is mainly composed of N ($N \geq 1$) virtual channels. Each virtual channel uses a FIFO. The width of the virtual channel is the width of the data packet, and the depth of the virtual channel can be defined by the user.

The output module does not contain FIFO, so its structure is simpler than the input module, mainly including two parts: Arbiter arbiter and output flow controller OFC. The Arbiter arbiter is used to arbitrate between different input modules requesting the same output port. The RR (Round Robin) algorithm is still used here to schedule requests. Select a request and raise the corresponding x_gnt signal to notify the input port that data transmission is possible. Simultaneously notify the OFC output flow controller of the scheduling results. The output flow controller selects one channel of data as the output data based on the x_gnt allowed signal, and at the same time, pulls up the out_val signal to notify the lower routing nodes of the arrival of valid data. The ack signal feedback from the lower routing node is transmitted as a x_rd read enable signal to the input module. This way, when the input module receives both x_gnt and x_rd valid signals, the connection between the input and output modules is established, and the data packet begins to be transmitted.

The system needs to ensure that the data of all nodes can be collected reliably, and the data should be collected as soon as possible to avoid too many pauses in the teaching process and affect classroom teaching. By considering avoiding competition between nodes, it is easy to get an ideal solution: the nodes in ZigBee network upload data to ZigBee gateway in turn without gaps. In this state, data can be collected reliably and the whole data recovery process only takes data transmission time, but it is impossible to achieve this effect in the actual process. The key problem is how to let all nodes upload data without gaps. In the formulation of the actual scheme, it approaches the ideal scheme to obtain the best performance.

The following is the proposed solution: use the transmission form with return confirmation in the MAC layer of ZigBee protocol. In this mode, the gateway can completely receive data from all nodes in the network. The nodes in ZigBee network obtain the right to send data through free competition. When the node successfully uploads data each time, it will receive the ack returned by the gateway.

## 2.2 Login Function Interface and Programming Implementation

The system is object-oriented for college teachers and students, including users with three kinds of permissions, namely administrators, teachers, and students. After different users log in to the system, corresponding permissions are automatically assigned. Administrators have all the functions of the system, teachers and students correspond to different functions, and the initial password is set uniformly. After logging in to the system, users click the button on the top right, modify the avatar and password.

The user requests the system interface route app. Use ('/api/admin', admin). The server returns the admin login page, enters the login page, enters the user name and password, clicks the login button, triggers the on Submit function, uses Ajax to interact asynchronously with the background, and requests access to the login interface through post. The pool connection pool connects with the MySQL database to ensure that multiple threads work. The foreground parameters are passed to the login interface. After receiving the parameters, the login interface will query the database for the presence of the user. If the query fails, an err will be returned, and a prompt box "User name or password error" will pop up. Next, if the parameters exist, the parameters will be compared with the information in the database and cooperate with the session to determine whether the user has logged in. If the user has logged in on other devices, then a prompt box "The user has logged in, please do not log in again" pops up. Finally, the user successfully logs in and saves the login information to the session. Node.js sends a cookie with the HttpOnly attribute to the front desk. This cookie will remain for 24 h. After 24 h, clear all login information [6, 7] through the callback function.

In addition to the above, the system carries out page responsive development based on the built-in layout of Bootstrap. The responsive drive of the page comes from the screen width. By obtaining the screen width, the screen is divided into 24 grids, and then different styles are specified according to different screen widths.

## 2.3 Design of Teacher Red Pen Correction Module

The red pen correction module is mainly used for teachers to correct ideological and political workbooks and test papers. In this module, teachers can choose to correct homework books or test papers. When correcting test papers, they can choose manual correction or automatic correction. This module has two difficult parts: correction process, drawing students' and teachers' handwriting.

The correction process can be divided into two situations: one is manual correction, which means that the teacher selects the assignment book or test paper to be corrected in the system for correction, and uploads the teacher's correction handwriting to the system; One is automatic correction, which means that the system can automatically correct the objective questions in students' test papers, such as selection, judgment, etc.

a. Design and Implementation of the Perception Layer for Manual Correction

The perception layer corresponds to the bluetooth pen device used by teachers in the process of correction. The bluetooth pen device is used to collect teachers' correction handwriting dot codes. After the bluetooth pen collects the dot codes, it conducts certain processing, and then transmits the data to the system background through the BLE communication module.

b. Design and implementation of network layer for manual correction

The Bluetooth pen and the system are connected by the BLE communication module. The BLE protocol stack is mainly composed of the following parts, as shown in Table 1 [8].

The BLE protocol is used to complete the network communication between the Bluetooth pen and the teacher end system. After the connection between the Bluetooth pen and the tablet is established, the BLE communication module obtains the handwriting dot code data from the Bluetooth pen regularly and packs them, and then transmits the data through the BLE protocol. The specific process is that the Bluetooth pen calls the send method to send handwriting dot code data every 3 s or when the amount of dot code data reaches 500 or when the last time a new dot code is acquired reaches 5 s, and transmits the data to the LL layer. The LL layer first selects the physical channel for transmission, and then assigns this connection to a transmissible address, add the header and payload length fields of the LL layer. The header field identifies the packet as a data packet, and the payload length field is the length of the entire L2CAP field. Finally, add the CRC24 field to prevent data from being tampered with during transmission. LL layer packs and transmits data to L2CAP layer, which specifies the connection interval as 10ms, and specifies the logical channel number 0004 (representing ATT layer). After addition, data is transmitted to ATT layer, which uses the notify communication command to transmit data to GATT layer, which packets and packages the sent data before transmission, finally, the data is transferred to the system background for compressed storage [9].

c. Design and Implementation of Manual Correction Data

In the process of using, it is necessary to obtain various information of the Bluetooth pen, so as to display the status of the Bluetooth pen in the teacher end system. The conversion methods of dot codes in different paper sizes are different, and A4 paper is mainly used in the implementation of this system.

The flow chart of manual correction is as follows: the system page displays the list of students in the current class after the teacher selects the homework book to correct. The teacher can click the tag on the student's homework book with the smart pen. At this time, the smart pen will identify the student's name and student number. After the identification

**Table 1.** Composition of BLE protocol stack

| S/N | project | form | effect |
|---|---|---|---|
| 1 | Core layer | LL layer | Select the RF channel for communication, the method of identifying the air data packet, the time point of sending the data packet, etc |
| 2 | Assign Layer | PHY layer | Specify the radio frequency band used, modulation and demodulation methods |
| 3 | Normative layer | HCI layer | Standardize the communication protocol commands of the two chips |
| 4 | Analytic layer | GAP layer | Parse the simplest valid packet in the LL layer, and GAT simply specifies and defines this packet |
| 5 | Decisive layer | L2CAP layer | Encapsulate the data transmitted by LL layer using encrypted channel or ordinary channel and manage the connection interval |
| 6 | Security layer | SMP layer | Consider ensuring the security of the connection without affecting the user's experience |
| 7 | Define Layer | ATT layer | Define commands and operation data. BLE uses attributes to describe the data in the transmission process, including the commands that can be used for the data |
| 8 | Standardize management | GATT layer | Standardize the data content of ATT layer and manage the data of ATT layer by category |

is successful, the current student's status will be changed to being corrected on the pad, and the teacher will correct the student's homework. The teacher can also click the name of the student to be corrected on the pad, and the status of the student will be changed to being corrected. When the teacher finishes correcting a student's homework and clicks the name of the next student, the system will change the status of the current student to correct completed, select the clicked student as the current student, and change its status to being corrected. When the teacher clicks the correction completed, he will jump to the homework display page to display the students' homework. The system page displays the list of students in the current class after the teacher selects the test paper to be corrected and selects the test paper to be corrected. The following process is consistent with the homework book correction. The difference is that when the teacher clicks the correction completion, it will first judge whether the teacher has corrected the current test papers of all students in the current class. If all the corrections are completed, it will jump to the test paper statistics and analysis page, including the answer overview, answer details, high-frequency wrong questions, analysis of knowledge points in the test paper, so that teachers can understand students' mastery of these knowledge points. If the teacher has not finished correcting all the test papers, a pop-up window will prompt that the teacher has not finished correcting all the test papers, please continue to correct.

Unlike subjective questions, objective questions need to consider whether students' answers contain scoring points. Just compare them with correct answers. If they are correct, scores will be given. If they are incorrect, scores will not be given. The implementation of automatic correction function can reduce the pressure of teachers' correction. Teachers only need to correct the subjective questions of an examination paper.

The technical architecture of automatic correction function is composed of teacher side, HTTP, MQ message queue, rule engine, fault alarm, HTTPMQ message queue, good rule engine fault alarm, multi-threaded asynchronous processing, and database. The key to realize the automatic recognition function is model training. In this paper, the KNN algorithm of machine learning is used to train handwritten data and produce a handwritten data recognition model. The main steps of the algorithm are: a. Calculate the distance between test data and training data; b. Sort according to the increasing relationship of distance; c. Select K points with the smallest distance; d. Determine the occurrence frequency of the category of the first K points; e. The category with the highest frequency among the first K points is returned as the prediction classification of test data.

### 2.4 Design of Resource Learning Module

The resource learning module is a function that both teachers and students have. The premise for students to learn teaching resources is that teachers upload relevant teaching resources. After creating relevant courses, teachers enter the resource management page, where they can upload courseware, experiments, videos and other relevant resources to the server. Before uploading, they need to select the courses corresponding to the resources. After uploading, they can view the uploaded resources. Students can learn relevant teaching resources uploaded by teachers, including courseware, experiments and videos.

According to the specific analysis of this module, create a resource database table. The exname field represents the resource extension, the url field is the address used to store learning resources, the type field represents the resource type, including courseware, experiment, and video, and the status field represents the resource upload status. The resource data table is shown in Table 2.

So the design of resource learning module is completed.

### 2.5 Design of Online Examination Module

In the online examination module, intelligent test paper generation is realized through genetic algorithm. The specific process is as follows:

Step 1: Set the initial conditions for generating the test paper, the difficulty of the test questions, the score of the test questions, the question type, the order of the question number, etc.

**Table 2.** Resource Data Table

| S/N | Field Name | Chinese field name | data type |
|---|---|---|---|
| 1 | id | Resource id | Varchar |
| 2 | name | Resource name | Int |
| 3 | exname | Resource suffix | Tinyint |
| 4 | size | Resource size | Tinyint |
| 5 | author | Uploader | Varchar |
| 6 | url | Upload Path | Varchar |
| 7 | type | Resource Type | Int |
| 8 | status | state | Int |

Step 2: generate different test papers according to the set initial conditions, and these initial test papers form the initial population.

Step 3: Calculate individual fitness value according to fitness function.

The fitness function affects the performance of the test paper to judge the quality of the test paper. There are many attributes that affect the performance of the test paper, such as the difficulty of the test question, the score of the test question, the score of passing the test question, the question type, the order of the question number, etc. Each attribute has different constraints on the test question, and its weight is also different. In this system, the proportion of the difficulty of the test question and the score of different question types in the total score of the test question is used as the independent variable of the function.

A knowledge point contains many questions. Can first work out the average difficulty of all the questions contained in the knowledge point. The formula for calculating the average difficulty is:

$$R_E = \frac{\sum_{j=1}^{t} U_j}{H} \tag{1}$$

In Eq. (1), $R_E$ refers to the average difficulty of the test questions covering the knowledge point; $U_j$ refers to the difficulty of each question; $H$ refers to the number of questions; $t$ refers to the number of questions [10].

The average difficulty formula of all questions in the whole question bank is:

$$Y_E = \frac{\sum_{j=1}^{t} Q_j}{H} \tag{2}$$

In formula (2), $Q_j$ refers to the difficulty of each question; $Y_E$ refers to the average difficulty.

The constraint formula for whether the proportion of scores of different question types in the total score of the test questions is reasonable is:

$$V = \frac{\sum_{j=1}^{y} q_{j1}}{L} \tag{3}$$

In Eq. (3), $L$ refers to the total score of the test questions; $q_{j1}$ refers to the question type in the examination paper; $y$ refers to the number of different types of questions; $V$ refers to the proportion of the scores of different question types in the total scores of the test questions.

The calculation formula of fitness function is:

$$fit(y_i) = 1 - (|Y_E - W_E| \times r_1 + V \times r_2) \tag{4}$$

In Eq. (4), $r_1$ and $r_2$ refer to the weights. Assign $r_1$ a value of 0.6 and $r_2$ a value of 0.4.

Step 4: According to the roulette wheel strategy, judge the individual fitness. The ones with high fitness will remain, and those with low fitness will remain to the next generation for crossover and mutation operations to form a new generation of population.

Step 5: Repeat steps 3 and 4 to determine whether the maximum number of iterations is reached.

Step 6: Generate the test paper.

# 3 System Non Functional Test

## 3.1 Compatibility Test

Test the designed ideological and political network teaching assistant system based on ZigBee, and first test the compatibility. Since the system will operate on pads of different screen sizes during actual use, in order to test whether the system can display normally on screens of different sizes, different panels are used to test the compatibility of the system. The test results are shown in Table 3.

**Table 3.** Compatibility Test Results

| S/N | Plate model | operating system | Whether the display is normal |
|---|---|---|---|
| 1 | Glory tablet V6 | Android | normal |
| 2 | Lenovo TB3-X70 | Android | normal |
| 3 | ipad2 | IOS | normal |
| 4 | iPadmini6 | IOS | normal |

By running the system on different tablets, can find that the system runs well under the system with Android $\geq$ 4.4.4 and IOS $\geq$ 9.0.2, and the page display is normal. Because the page adopts a responsive system layout, it can ensure that the system page can be adjusted with the screen size.

## 3.2 Performance Test

A system should not only meet user needs in function, but also in performance. Therefore, in addition to testing system compatibility, non functional testing also needs to test system performance. Performance testing is to test the performance of the system on the basis of meeting the functional requirements of users. Good performance of the system can also greatly improve the user experience.

The LoadRunner test tool is used to test the performance of the main interfaces of the system. LoadRunner is a load testing tool that predicts system behavior and performance. It tests system performance by simulating real-time concurrent load of tens of millions of users and real-time performance monitoring, and quickly locates problems. Run the script generated by the LoadRunner test tool in the system to monitor the script running in real time. After the test results are generated, analyze the test results, find out the problems in the system, and judge whether the system performance can meet the expectations.

The specific test method is to test the performance of the system through the phased increase of the number of users, test the average response time of the system, the number of successful and failed accesses, and the concurrency range of the system. The standard for passing the performance test is: when the number of concurrent users is 200, the system performance is stable. The test scenario here is for the teacher to log in to the system and select the in class mode to start the class. Set the initial teacher concurrency to 10, increase 40 teachers every 5 s, and the maximum value is 450, so as to simulate 490 teachers starting the class at the same time. Set the teacher concurrency in LoadRunner, and set 10, 50, 90, 130, 170, 210, 250, 290, 330, 370, 410, 450 teachers respectively. Run the test script in the test scenario to get the test results, and collate the test results to get the system performance test results table (Table 4).

**Table 4.** System Performance Test Results

| S/N | Virtual teacher concurrency | Respond or not | Number of response failures | Average response time (ms) |
|---|---|---|---|---|
| 1 | 10 | Normal response | 0 | 586 |
| 2 | 50 | Normal response | 0 | 852 |
| 3 | 90 | Normal response | 0 | 1269 |
| 4 | 130 | Normal response | 0 | 1695 |
| 5 | 170 | Normal response | 0 | 2158 |
| 6 | 210 | Normal response | 0 | 2698 |
| 7 | 250 | Normal response | 0 | 3365 |
| 8 | 290 | Normal response | 15 | 3965 |
| 9 | 330 | Normal response | 36 | 4587 |

The system performance test results are shown in the table above. It can be seen from the test results that when the number of concurrent virtual teachers increases gradually, the system can respond to teacher operations normally, and the average response time is less than 5000ms. Failure occurs only when 290 is measured. On the whole, all data meet the expected performance test objectives. This pressure test is only carried out for a single server. The number of 200 concurrent servers can meet the demand. Clusters will be used on the system input line. The cluster's high scalability, high availability, and high manageability can effectively improve the system performance, improve the system error tolerance, and meet high concurrent user requests. To sum up, the system meets the performance requirements of users through performance testing.

### 3.3 Safety Comparison Test

The security of a system is an important way to protect the privacy of users, and security testing can eliminate the security risks of the system. First, perform the SQL injection test. The second place to strengthen security protection is permissions. The system should ensure that each user can only see the data within his/her own permissions. For this, the user name verification should be bypassed for testing. The third place to strengthen security protection is to modify and submit data information. For this, the system should test by capturing and modifying data. The fourth place that needs to be strengthened is the security risk of cross site scripting. For this, will test the system for XSS attacks. In the test, the traditional ideological and political network teaching assistant system is used as a comparison method to jointly conduct security test. The comparison test results are shown in Fig. 3.

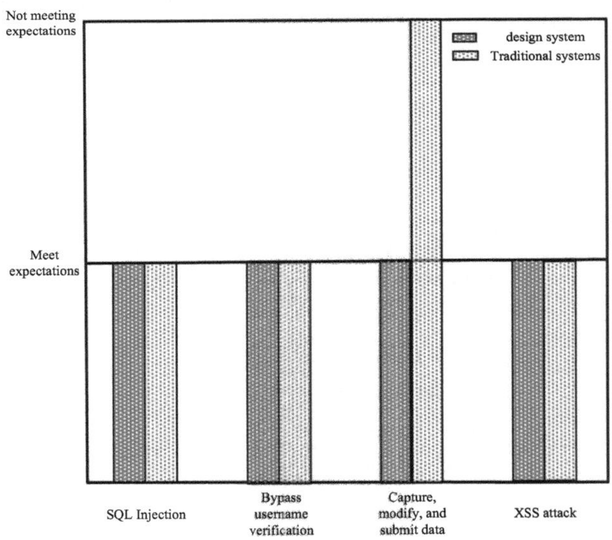


**Fig. 3.** Comparison Test Results

The expected result of XSS attack is that the statement entered in the input box will not be executed; The expected result of packet capturing modification of submitted data is that the system fails to pass the modified data and meets the expectation; The expected result of bypassing the user name verification is that the system prompts the user name or password error, instead of entering the home page as expected; The expected result of SQL injection is that the system prompts user name or password errors, rather than system errors. It can be seen from the above test results that the security of the designed system is higher than that of the traditional system, which can effectively prevent information leakage.

In order to further verify the application effectiveness of the system designed in this article, user satisfaction was used as a testing indicator. The results were compared between the embedded computer remote assisted teaching system based on Web technology, the physical multimedia assisted teaching system based on concept networks, and the system designed in this article. The results are shown in Table 5.

**Table 5.** User Satisfaction Test Results

| Number of users/person | This article designs a system | Embedded Computer Remote Assisted Teaching System Based on Web Technology | Concept network-based multimedia assisted teaching system for physics |
|---|---|---|---|
| 10 | 95.3 | 85.6 | 90.7 |
| 20 | 94.2 | 84.2 | 87.6 |
| 30 | 93.6 | 80.3 | 85.2 |
| 40 | 91.8 | 79.9 | 83.0 |
| 50 | 90.3 | 76.6 | 81.5 |

From the data in Table 5, it can be seen that the user satisfaction of the system designed in this article is higher, indicating that it can meet user needs and has better application effects in practical applications.

## 4 Conclusion

To address the issues of long response time and poor security in existing systems, a ZigBee based ideological and political network teaching assistance system is designed. The system is based on ZigBee technology to design a wireless communication module for the ideological and political network teaching assistance system, effectively improving the system's response speed. The security login function of the login function module effectively improves the security of the system. The experimental results show that the designed system has a shorter response time and can effectively ensure user information security, achieving higher user satisfaction, indicating that its application value is higher.

**Aknowledgement.** 1.Anhui Province first-class course "Introduction to Mao Zedong Thought and Theoretical System of Socialism with Chinese Characteristics" social practice course (2020xsxxkc331).

2.Quality Engineering Project of Department of Education, Anhui Province: Research on the Teaching Model of Bisection Class in the Intelligent Classroom Environment take financial management section for example (2021jyxm1120);

## References

1. Artyukhova, N.S., Saykina, O.S., Solovyeva, A.A.: Gender stereotypes in teaching aids on Russian as a foreign language for beginners. RUDN J. Lang. Stud. Semiot. Seman. **12**(4), 1236–1246 (2021)
2. Huajian, W., Zhifeng, W.: Design of simulation teaching system based on modular production and processing. Comput. Simul. **39**(04), 205–209 (2022)
3. Tabler, T.: Application of computer-based tools for mathematics teaching at various types of lessons in gymnasiums. Polonia Univ. Sci. J. **42**(5), 117–125 (2021)
4. Samorodova, E.A., Belyaeva, I.G., Bakaeva, S.A.: Analysis of communicative methods effectiveness in teaching foreign languages during the coronavirus epidemic: distance format. XLinguae **14**(1), 131–140 (2021)
5. Zahrotin, A.: Development of integrated science learning instruments using a humanistic approach with economic drawings. Jurnal Pena Sains **8**(1), 8–14 (2021)
6. Allen, H.W., Paesani, K.: Genre instruction, textual borrowing, and foreign language writing: Graduate teaching assistant perspectives and practices. Lang. Teach. Res. **26**(4), 755–776 (2022)
7. Yarosh, J.H.: The syllabus reconstructed: an analysis of traditional and visual syllabi for information retention and inclusiveness. Teach. Sociol. **49**(2), 173–183 (2021)
8. Cheng, X., Liu, K.: Application of multimedia networks in business English teaching in vocational college. J. Healthc. Eng. **2021**(4), 1–9 (2021)
9. Qi, S., Li, S., Zhang, J.: Designing a teaching assistant system for physical education using web technology. Mob. Inf. Syst. **2021**(6), 1–11 (2021)
10. Wu, X.: Research on the reform of ideological and political teaching evaluation method of college English course based on "online and offline" teaching. J. High. Educ. Res. **3**(1), 87–90 (2022)

# Web Service Based Oral English Teaching Assistant Training System

Minchen Wang(✉) and Juanjuan Ye

Wanjiang University of Technology, Ma'anshan 243000, China
jaomiye@163.com

**Abstract.** In order to solve the problem of the low fault tolerance rate of the teaching and training system and improve the auxiliary teaching ability of oral English education, an auxiliary training system for oral English teaching based on Web services is designed. Through the design of hybrid training architecture, user management module and online examination module, the hardware design of application structure of auxiliary training system is realized. According to the generation conditions of Web services that can replace adapters, the sensitive call function is defined, and the fuzzy training engine is combined to train the auxiliary teaching behavior, and the relevant application components are combined to complete the design of the auxiliary teaching training system. The experimental results show that the compatibility degree of the test program under the function of Web services is more than 90%, which can meet the practical application requirements.

**Keywords:** Web services · Teaching oral English · Auxiliary training · Alternative adapter · Training engine

## 1 Introduction

A Web service is a platform-independent, low-coupling, self-contained, programmatically based application for developing distributed interactions that can be described, published, discovered, coordinated, and configured using open XML (a subset of the Standard General Markup Language) standards. Using Web services technology enables different applications running on different machines to exchange data or integrate with each other without the need for additional, specialized third-party software or hardware. According to Web services, data can be exchanged regardless of the language, platform, or internal protocol used by the application [1]. Web Service is a self describing and self-contained available network module that can perform specific business functions. Web services are also easy to deploy, because they are based on some common industry standards and some existing technologies, such as subset XML and HTTP under the standard general markup language. Web services reduce the cost of application interfaces. Web Service provides a common mechanism for the integration of business processes between the entire enterprise and even multiple organizations. The Web Service platform requires a set of protocols to create distributed applications. Any platform has its data


G. Gui et al. (Eds.): eLEOT 2023, LNICST 543, pp. 63–77, 2024.
https://doi.org/10.1007/978-3-031-51465-4_5

representation method and type system. To achieve interoperability, the Web Service platform must provide a set of standard type systems for communicating different types of systems in different platforms, programming languages, and component models.

Tian et al. [2] interactive semantic recognition analysis based on deep learning algorithm, feature fusion of translation vocabulary and sentence output based on deep learning, automatic. Zheng et al. [3] interactive output of translation data under deep learning, and global optimization design of system software layer parameters around deep learning algorithm. However, the above systems cannot realize the mutual call and data transmission between different platforms and languages, and only by using specific middleware or transit server can the data interaction channel be established between the client and the server, so the application has limitations.

Aiming at the above problems, a new type of oral English teaching assistant training system is designed based on Web service theory. On the basis of designing the hardware of the system, the Web service is introduced to replace the adapter, reset the fuzzy training engine, and realize the smooth application of the oral English teaching auxiliary training system based on Web services. The practical value of the system is verified by case analysis, which provides students with flexible and convenient learning methods, and is no longer limited to traditional classrooms or learning centers, and provides convenience for distance education and independent learning, which is an innovative and cutting-edge application in the field of educational technology.

## 2 Application Structure Design of Oral English Teaching Assistant Training System

The hardware application structure of the oral English teaching assistant training system consists of a hybrid training architecture, a user management module, and an online examination module. This chapter focuses on its specific design methods.

### 2.1 Hybrid Training Architecture

For the oral English teaching auxiliary training system, its hybrid training architecture includes B/S model and C/S model. Under the effect of the Client architecture, it can combine the SOP auxiliary training host and the Web server terminal to schedule multiple client objects, so as to improve the specific implementation process of auxiliary training education while realizing oral English teaching.

The C/S model is directly connected with the client object and responsible for collecting students' learning habits. Its network traffic is less than that of the BlS model. Generally speaking, for the same task, the C/S model has a faster running speed; Because the C/S mode installs a complete set of application programs on the client computer, it can have a strong human-computer interaction function. The computer examination system has a strong control over the examination, which makes the use of candidates very convenient.

As the subordinate load structure of the C/S model, the B/S model can provide an access environment for teaching recipient objects and student terminals [4]. The client computer uses a general Web browser, so its designed exam interface is very friendly.

The exam terminal computer can conveniently log in to the network exam with the help of a common browser; The functions of B/S mode are all completed by the Web server. In this case, the development and maintenance work only needs to be carried out around the server, and the maintenance work is simple and easy.

Therefore, the development and design of the real network examination system for different examination tasks to be realized and different examinee objects to be served can comprehensively absorb and utilize the respective advantages of C/S mode and B/S mode, and reasonably match the mixed mode, thus realizing various functions required in the network examination system.

The complete hybrid training architecture layout model is shown in Fig. 1.

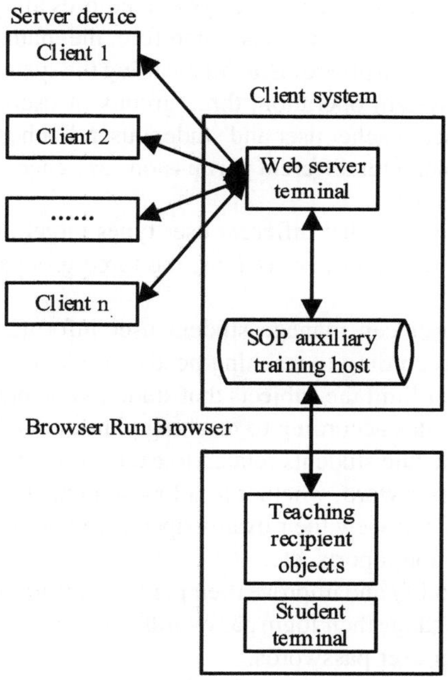


**Fig. 1.** Hybrid training architecture layout model

As can be seen from Fig. 1, the model includes server device, client system, and browser running browser. Multiple client objects can be scheduled through the Web server terminal, and SOP assists the training host to transfer customer requirements to the teaching recipient object, thus realizing various functions required in the network test system.

In addition, the C/S mode has installed a complete set of applications in the client computer, so it can achieve a more powerful human-computer interaction function.For customers, one of its greatest advantages is that it separates the program part from the database part. Even if the database structure is modified, it will not have a dramatic impact on the operation of the program. Conversely, even if the program is greatly modified, it will not affect the original structure of the data.

The advantages of B/S application lie in:

(1) Simplify the connection behavior of server components in data and data management layer;
(2) It reduces the requirements of teaching client object in hardware connection;
(3) Through centralized management of business logic, the maintainability of the system is improved.When the business logic changes, it only needs to be modified in the business logic layer, and the user layer will not be affected;
(4) The scalability of B/S mode is very strong and has strong maintainability.

## 2.2 User Management Module

The good operation and maintenance of the system requires all types of users to operate legally within their respective permissions. Therefore, the management and permission assignment of system users is a prerequisite for ensuring the system operation. According to the requirements of system operation, three groups of users are set in this system, namely administrator user, teacher user and student user. Each group of users is open to different groups of people, with different permissions assigned, and administrator users have the highest permissions.

According to the principle that different user types target different people and different user types assign different permissions, the three groups of users in the system are set as follows:

The administrator user can manage student user information, add/delete student information in batches according to teaching needs, or add, delete or modify the information of a student, set or limit the subjects that students can participate in learning and training, arrange exam dates according to teaching plans, coordinate and arrange exam subject settings, and schedule students related to exam subjects to participate in exams, Set the student's initial password, whether to allow students to view their exam scores, whether to allow students to view their exam papers, whether to allow students to view their exam paper evaluation reports, etc.

Teacher users can modify and improve their personal information. It is recommended that teacher users often change their login passwords to prevent teaching accidents caused by the leakage of teacher user passwords.

Student users have the lowest authority. In short, they log in to the system and participate in the exam.

The specific connection structure of the user management module is shown in Fig. 2.

As can be seen from Fig. 2, the user management module gives permissions to different applications for different user types, and teacher users manage login behaviors and student users, thus providing students with a lot of teaching convenience.

The user management function allows you to add or delete users in the examination system, modify user basic information, and assign user permissions. After the system administrator successfully logs in to the management system through legal means, he/she can implement the management work of creating exam administrators and examinee users, importing/exporting administrator and examinee information in batches according to work needs; After the system administrator successfully logs in legally, he/she can carry out management work [5] such as establishing examinee users, importing and exporting examinee lists in batches according to the obtained permissions. The

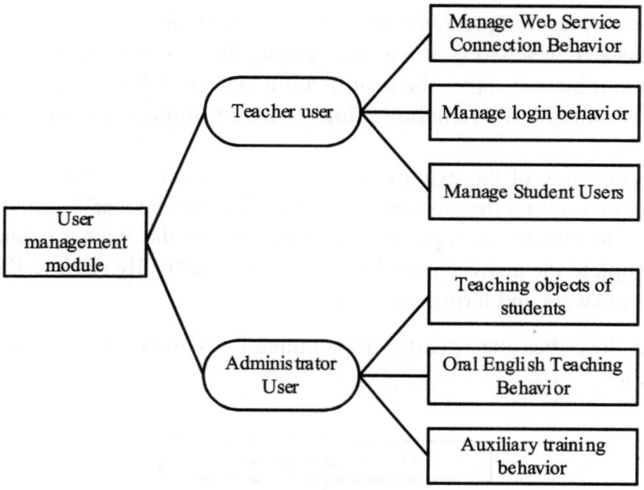


**Fig. 2.** Connection structure of user management module

system administrator has the highest authority, which can dynamically allocate or terminate the administrator's management authority over the question bank, examination papers, and examinations according to the progress of teaching and examination work, and can dynamically allocate or terminate the authority of examiners to participate in examinations and view examination results.

During the operation of the computer, it is inevitable to encounter many emergencies, such as computer disconnection, crash, automatic restart, etc., which will cause the ongoing examination to be interrupted and damaged abnormally, not only affecting the continuation of the normal examination, but also affecting the examinee's performance to a certain extent. If the terminal computer can continue to answer questions on the basis of the answers before disconnection after it resumes work, it will minimize the impact on the examination work and the examinees' scores. Therefore, whether it can continue to take the examination after disconnection has become a key problem that must be solved by the online examination system.

### 2.3 Online Examination Module

In the auxiliary training system of oral English teaching, the implementation of the online examination module needs to take into account three aspects: the examination user's test paper formation, the prevention of identical test papers, and the examinee's score query. The main task of this module is to organize and complete the examination process. It mainly includes the following contents:

(1) Open examination.The examination system is open according to the pre-set starting date and time of the oral English subject, and relevant candidates are allowed to log in to the examination system through a legal login mode to participate in the online examination of the designated subject.

(2) During the oral teaching test, the examinee can normally answer the test questions, and can check their answers at any time during the test as required.
(3) After the examination starts, the examination system will display the time that has been carried out and the remaining time of the examination to the students in real time.
(4) When the end time of the exam is not up, but the examinee has completed all his answers, he can submit the answers by himself. The system can normally retrieve the answers and terminate his exam. When the end time of the exam is up and the student fails to complete the answers, the system will automatically retrieve the examinee's completed answers and terminate the exam.

The Fig. 3 describes the specific implementation capabilities of the online exam module functions.

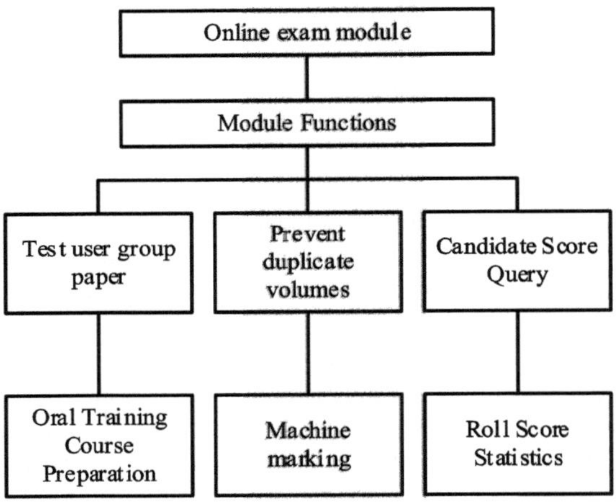


**Fig. 3.** Detailed function diagram of online examination module

According to Fig. 3, the online examination module has many functions, which can test the oral training course user group papers, has the machine marking ability, avoid drawing the same content of the paper, has the automatic scoring function, and provides the candidate score query port after the test.

In the exam preparation stage, the teacher user assigns each test paper generation parameter to the system for test paper generation according to the needs of oral English teaching tasks and test investigation requirements. The parameters that can be set by the teacher user include: exam date, exam start time, exam duration, source of question bank, difficulty of questions, type of questions, etc. After the teacher user submits the request for paper formation, The examination paper is generated by the examination system (if the automatic test paper generation operation is selected, there is no need to give so many parameters, only a small number of necessary parameters such as examination subjects, examination time, etc.), and the system will randomly form a specified number of mutually independent test papers.

In order to avoid the situation that two (or more) examinees can't take the exam normally because they have taken the exam paper with identical content, the system is designed to bind the exam paper with the IP address of the examination terminal computer where the examinee is [6] when the examinee takes the exam paper. After the exam starts, the examinee will draw a test paper. When the system receives a request for drawing a test paper, it will draw a test paper for the examinee. However, before assigning the test paper to the students, the system should first confirm the test paper to see whether there are examinees already using it. If the system detects that the test paper has been used by examinees, the system will give up the test paper and start drawing again. Only when the examination papers that are not used by other examinees are drawn can they be assigned to the examinees to take the examination.

After the examination, if the administrator has assigned the right, the examinee can view the examination answers of all subjects and courses, and can also access the standard answers of relevant examination papers for analysis and improvement. If assigned by the administrator, the examinee can query the exam scores of all subjects and courses; If assigned by the administrator, the examinee can query the test score ranking table of the relevant oral English education. In addition, with the permission of the administrator, the examinee can view the analysis report of the test paper of the individual English teaching auxiliary training courses.

## 3 Auxiliary Teaching Behavior Training

On the basis of the hardware application structure at all levels, a Web service can replace the adapter, and then the sensitive calling function is combined to reset the fuzzy training engine, so as to realize the smooth application of the Web service based oral English teaching assistant training system.

### 3.1 2Web Service Can Replace Adapter Generation

Web services generated based on the hybrid training architecture, user management module, and online examination module can replace the adapter closed-loop, and can achieve on-demand scheduling of oral English teaching resources [7]. The adjustment of Web adaptation services at all levels follows the following principles:

(1) Receive the teaching resource message sent by the sender;
(2) Store the receiver's oral English teaching and training messages;
(3) According to the mapping relationship between teaching and training messages and auxiliary parameters, the transformation or synthesis of Web services and adaptive parameters is carried out;
(4) Send the required Web service message to the receiver after the stored oral English teaching training message and parameters are converted or synthesized;
(5) Filter redundant messages or parameters.

set up $\alpha$ Real time training parameters representing spoken English teaching information, $\dot{A}$ represents the auxiliary training characteristics of teaching information parameters. The above physical quantities can be used together to schedule the authority of the Web service $S_\alpha$ Expressed as:

$$S_\alpha = \frac{\dot{A}}{\vec{a} \cdot |\Delta s|} \cdot \alpha \tag{1}$$

$\vec{a}$ represents the transmission direction vector of spoken English teaching information in the auxiliary training system, $\Delta s$ refers to the unit accumulation of spoken English teaching information.

$\Re$ represents a sample set of spoken English teaching data, $d_1, d_2, \cdots, d_n$ express $n$. The values of the unequal teaching data parameters meet the expression shown in formula (2).

$$d_1, d_2, \cdots, d_n \in \Re \tag{2}$$

In the adaptation strategy design phase, adaptation analysis can be carried out according to the substitutability principle of Web services to determine whether services can be adapted, and adaptation strategies can be designed to determine whether there are corresponding receiving or sending actions in the sending or receiving actions to determine the adaptability. However, in the case of redundant receiving action, the redundant receiving action may be followed by sending action, but since the redundant receiving action cannot be performed, any subsequent action cannot be performed.

For any Web service alternative adapter structure that has been successfully developed and can be successfully applied in practice, one of the most important research contents is the automatic generation of test papers - test paper generation operation. According to different teaching tasks and inspection purposes, the requirements for test papers are also different, and on the basis of fairness and justice, the randomness of test paper selection is required the scientific organization of the test questions and the rationality of the test paper arrangement make the test paper generation a difficult problem in the development of the computer test system [8]. When the computer test system runs in the network environment, this puts forward higher requirements, not only to continue to ensure the richness of the content and comprehensiveness of the knowledge points of the test papers obtained after the test paper generation operation, but also to complete the test paper generation operation at an extremely fast speed, and to generate the test papers in time for the candidates to answer.

Set up $\chi$ represents an alternative parameter, $\delta$ real time input vector representing spoken English teaching data, $\beta$ represents the real-time connection coefficient of Web service behavior. With the support of the above physical quantities, formula (1) and formula (2) can express the closed loop definition formula of Web service alternative adapter as:

$$D = |\chi - 1| \cdot \frac{\sum_{\delta=1}^{+\infty} \beta S_\alpha}{\left(d_1^2 + d_2^2 + \cdots + d_n^2\right)} \tag{3}$$

In the process of alternative adaptation analysis of Web services, alternative adaptation contracts will receive and cache the actions of all services, and generate new changes. Therefore, the generation process of alternative adaptation contract is a generation process of STS model, and the final result is an STS model. Finally, the feasibility of alternative adapters is verified through STS synchronous interaction.

### 3.2 Sensitive Calling Function

The function of the sensitive call function is that every time the student has finished the first online answer of the computer test system, the server side of the test system will detail the student Liu Yiyu's mastery of all knowledge of the course. The main index items recorded by the system are: exam subjects, exam chapters, types of questions, students' answers and exam time, etc. The system automatically summarizes these recorded data into a training set, and in each subsequent test, it will continue to record more data to get more training sets. After multiple test results feedback, it can control the prediction performance of sensitive calling functions under the combination of Web services that can replace the adapter closed-loop.

Regulations $g_1, g_2, \cdots, g_n$ express $n$. There are two unequal and non-zero oral English teaching data sensitivity training vectors, whose definition formula is as follows:

$$\begin{cases} g_1 = \gamma_1 \sqrt{\frac{\tilde{h}}{K_1}} \\ g_2 = \gamma_2 \sqrt{\frac{\tilde{h}}{K_2}} \\ \vdots \\ g_n = \gamma_n \sqrt{\frac{\tilde{h}}{K_n}} \end{cases} \tag{4}$$

Among them, $\gamma_1$, $\gamma_2$, $\cdots$, $\gamma_n$ respectively $n$ defining parameters of teaching and training items, $\tilde{h}$ indicates that the Web service can replace the teaching data aided training feature in the adapter closed-loop, $K_1$, $K_2$, $\cdots$, $K_n$ respectively represent the auxiliary teaching service vectors matching the parameters defined in the training item.

The input of the sensitive function call path generation technology is the interactive binary component and its corresponding data stream keywords, and the output is the sensitive function call path [9] that references the data stream keywords in the interactive binary component and may lead to security vulnerabilities. The sensitive function call path is the target of the binary code dynamic instrumentation technology, when it is applied to the interactive binary component of the device Web service. The fuzzy test method in this chapter builds an efficient anomaly monitoring mechanism for embedded Web services by monitoring the sensitive function call path.

Simultaneous formula (3) and formula (4) can define the call path of the auxiliary training object of spoken English teaching as:

$$\varphi = \left( {}^{1}/_{\phi} \right)^2 \cdot \left| \frac{D}{g_1 \times g_2 \times \cdots \times g_n} \right|^{\frac{1}{\varepsilon^2}} \tag{5}$$

$\phi$ represents the spoken English teaching data sample, $\varepsilon$ represents the transmission parameters of data flow keywords under Web service conditions.

About Parameters $\phi$, Parameters $\varepsilon$, the value condition shown in the constant formula (6) is true.

$$\begin{cases} \phi \in (-\infty, 0) \cup (0, +\infty) \\ \varepsilon \in (-\infty, +\infty) \\ \phi \neq \varepsilon \end{cases} \tag{6}$$

The binary code dynamic instrumentation technology is a mechanism to obtain the real-time execution status of the oral English teaching assistant training program. The traditional binary code dynamic instrumentation technology starts from the entry function of the target program. For interactive binary components in embedded device Web services, other functions in front of the Web business functions that actually provide functional support to the front end Web management interface are not the focus of program instrumentation.

Use formula (5) to solve the sensitive calling function. The solution result is shown in formula (7).

$$L = \frac{\lambda\sqrt{f\varphi}}{\sum\limits_{\substack{z=1\\x=1}} \hat{j}^2 - (C_z + C_x)} \tag{7}$$

where, $\lambda$ represents the binary coding parameters of teaching data based on Web services, $f$ dynamic pile insertion vector representing teaching data, $z$ and $x$ represents two unequal training program definition parameters, $C_z$ indicates parameter based $z$ call coefficient of teaching data samples, $C_x$ indicates parameter based $x$ call coefficient of teaching data samples, $\hat{j}$ represent that the Web service can replace the adapter's call feature for oral English teaching assistant training behavior.

The main purpose of generating the sensitive function call path is to find the introduction points of these keywords in the interactive binary components of the back-end Web service through the data flow keywords in the front and back ends of the Web service, and extract the sensitive function call path that takes these introduction points as the starting point and may lead to security vulnerabilities. Avoid the pointless instrumentation nodes when traditional binary code dynamic instrumentation technology is applied to embedded device Web services.

### 3.3 Fuzzy Training Engine

When designing the oral English teaching assistant training system, in order to avoid starting from the entry function of the interactive binary component and reduce the number of stub function paths, it is also necessary to first locate the introduction point of data stream keywords in the interactive binary component [10] according to the generation of sensitive function call paths. For the establishment of a fuzzy training engine, the Web service system needs to adjust the location of the introduction point according to the category of the parameter class data flow keywords: The direct reference type parameter class data flow keywords can directly find the introduction point in the interactive binary component; The introduction point of the cross process reference type parameter data stream keyword that conducts information exchange between different processes through nvram depends on the identification of the access function of nvram. The functions to be concerned about cross process reference are shown in Table 1.

Through the fuzzy training engine analysis technology and the sensitive function call path generation technology, the embedded device Web service association information

**Table 1.** Establishment conditions of fuzzy training engine

| Identify Point Objects | Engine Functions |
|---|---|
| Nvram storage | nvram.safe.set |
| Path mapping | path.bufget |
| Para input | para.setenv |
| Keyword function | Keyword.paths.api |
| Ghidra encoding | ghidra.path |
| P-code call | P-code.check.call |
| API Tuning | path.caller.chain |
| Bin service behavior | bin.keywd.doShell |

has been obtained. The specific definition is as follows:

$$X = \left(\frac{1}{V'} \times |\Delta\kappa|\right)^2 \tag{8}$$

Among them, $V'$ fuzzy definition vector representing spoken English teaching data, $\Delta\kappa$ represents the unit cumulative amount of Web service invocation code.

The data processing part of the auxiliary training system for oral English teaching for testing mainly includes two stages: Test case construction and test case compilation. In theory, test cases need to use data stream keywords as key data to construct test cases, but in actual testing, unless the sensitive calling function mentions the Web service function that needs to be "activated". The fuzzy test engine will directly use the message data captured in the dynamic simulation phase to participate in the fuzzy test, omitting the construction process of test cases.

The solution of the test case object of the oral English teaching assistant training system meets the following expression:

$$\dot{B} = \frac{|\dot{I}^2 - \eta\tilde{p}|}{\sum \vec{b}(m_1 + m_2 + \cdots + m_n)} \tag{9}$$

$\dot{I}$ indicates the scheduling characteristics of the teaching data engine, $\eta$ indicates the transmission efficiency of teaching data in the auxiliary training system, $\tilde{p}$ represents the scheduling parameters of teaching data in the training engine, $\vec{b}$ represents the teaching data sample import vector, $m_1, m_2, \cdots, m_n$ express $n$, the binary marking parameters of teaching data objects that meet the fuzzy scheduling principle.

Simultaneous formula (8) and formula (9) can express the definition conditions of fuzzy training engine as:

$$U = \sqrt{\frac{1}{\dot{y} \times |\Delta T|}} \cdot |X \cdot \dot{B}|^2 \tag{10}$$

where, $\Delta T$ indicates the unit scheduling duration of spoken English teaching training samples in the fuzzy training engine, $\dot{y}$ represents the fuzzy training processing characteristics of teaching data.

The time for the system to organize students to participate in the auxiliary teaching training can be very flexible, and can be provided to students for examination at any time within the time period specified by the school. In addition, the system can immediately grade and mark the objective questions at the end of the exam and display them to the examinees in real time. The examinees generally agree with the sense of fairness and justice that the computer system automatically produces and marks papers. In a word, this system is based on high-quality test question resources and scientific method of generating test papers, and based on students' mastery of curriculum knowledge points. Through intelligent system operation and practice, it greatly reduces the workload of teachers in exam organization, and also greatly promotes students' enthusiasm for independent learning. Finally, the quality of oral English teaching and the quality of students have been comprehensively improved.

## 4 Example Analysis

To highlight the auxiliary training system for oral English teaching based on Web servicesSpeech recognition architecture system. System based on deep learning The following contrast experiment is designed for its practical value.

### 4.1 Experimental Process

The compatibility degree of the test program can be used to describe the level of fault tolerance of the teaching and training system. Without considering other interference conditions, the stronger the compatibility ability of the Windows training host for the test program, the higher the level of fault tolerance of the teaching and training system, and the stronger the auxiliary teaching ability for oral English education.

Use the equipment components shown in Table 2 to build an online training environment for Windows teaching network.

**Table 2.** Experimental Equipment

| Item | Equipment components | Name and model |
|---|---|---|
| 1 | Online teaching host | Windows host |
| 2 | Data processor | i5-13490F |
| 3 | Data storage device | SQL Database |
| 4 | Client device | LM393 DIP8 |
| 5 | Client server | STM32F407ZGT6 |
| 6 | Online teaching terminal | DE2-115 Cyclone IV |
| 7 | Speech signal recognition element | MP802XILINX |

First, input the executive program of the Web service based oral English teaching assistant training system in the Windows host, record the actual compatibility of the examination program under the effect of the system, and the results are the experimental group values. Then, in the Windows host, enterSpeech recognition architecture system. The actual compatibility of the examination procedures under the effect of the system is recorded, and the results are compared with (1) group of values; Second, enter in the Windows host system based on deep learning, record the actual compatibility of the examination procedures under the effect of the system, and the results are the values of the control (2) groups. Finally, the obtained variable data are counted and the experimental results are summarized.

### 4.2 Data Processing

In order to verify the practical performance of the designed system, the compatibility degree is taken as the experimental index without considering other interference conditions, and the compatibility ability of the three systems at different times is compared by accessing single object and multi-object in the examination program. The higher the value, the higher the fault tolerance level of the system. Under the action of different training systems, the specific experimental values of the compatibility of the test program are shown in Fig. 4 and Fig. 5.

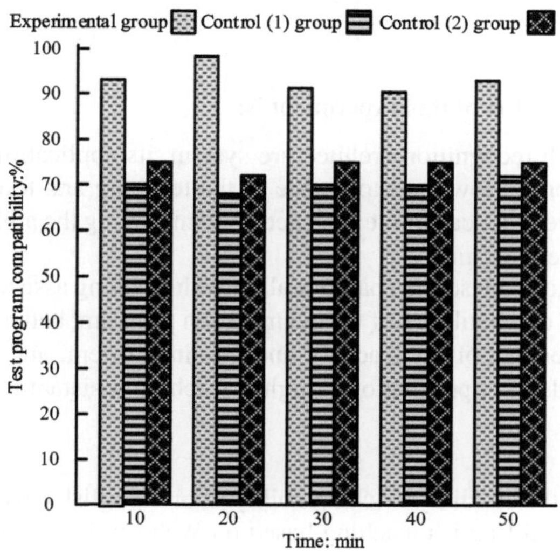


**Fig. 4.** Test program compatibility (single object access)

It can be seen from the analysis of Figs. 4 and 5 that the test program compatibility value of the experimental group is significantly different in the case of single object access and multi object access, and its average value is more than 90%. The test program compatibility of the control (1) group is relatively high in the case of multi object access, but its maximum value can only reach 68.2%, which is lower than that of the experimental

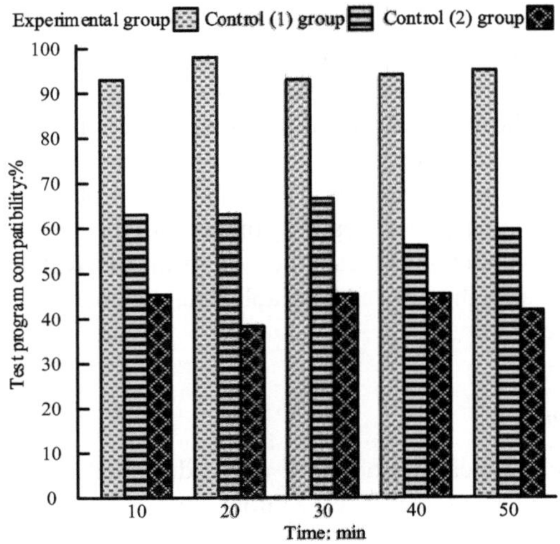


**Fig. 5.** Test program compatibility (multi object access)

group. The test program compatibility of the control (2) group is relatively high in the case of single object access, but its maximum value is only 76.2%, which is still lower than the value of the experimental group.

### 4.3 Conclusion

To sum up, the conclusion of this experiment is:

(1) Based on Speech recognition architecture system, its application is not enough to solve the problem of low fault tolerance of the teaching and training system, so it does not meet the practical application needs of improving the ability of oral English education assisted teaching.
(2) The application of Web service based oral English teaching assistant training system can improve the compatibility of the examination program, better solve the problem of low fault tolerance of the teaching and training system, and meet the practical application needs of improving oral English teaching assistant teaching ability.

## 5 Conclusion

In order to improve the auxiliary teaching ability of oral English education, an auxiliary training system of oral English teaching based on Web services is designed. Based on the advantages of C/S mode and B/S mode, the mixed training architecture is built reasonably, and the hardware components of the system are built together with user management module and online examination module. The Web service can replace the adapter, introduce the sensitive call function and reset the fuzzy training engine, so that the oral English teaching auxiliary training system can be flexibly applied. The design can be competent to complete the most important student ability test in the teaching process, complete the usual practice test and mid-term and final examination, and efficiently and quickly improve the quality of students' learning and teachers' teaching effect.

**Aknowledgement.** 1. This paper is the result of the research of "Exploration and Practice of Cultivating Speaking Ability of Non-English Majors in Applied Universities Based on "Production-oriented Approach"", a provincial-level quality project of Anhui Higher Education Institution. (Project number: 2021jyxm1596).

2. The Research Science Institute of colleges and universities in Anhui Province "Research on the validity of translation of Tourism publicity discourse based on genre analysis" (Project No. 2022AH052428).

## References

1. Laachemi, A., Boughaci, D.: Improved machine learning classifiers combined with a stochastic local search for Web services classification. Intell. Decision Technol. **14**(4), 581–609 (2021)
2. Tian, W.: English speaking test auxiliary scoring system based on speech recognition architecture. Tech. Autom. Appl. **41**(05), 168–170+179 (2022)
3. Zheng, X., Wen, L.: Design of interactive oral English automatic translation system based on deep learning. Autom. Instrum. **274**(08), 147–150+155 (2022)
4. Jaracz, J.S., Lee, Y.J.: Existence and stability of global solutions to a regularized Oldroyd-B model in its vorticity formulation. J. Differ. Equ. **327**, 259–321 (2022)
5. Pereira, T.F., Montevechi, J., Leal, F., et al.: Application of a management and storage system for knowledge generated from simulation projects as a teaching and assessment tool. Simulation **97**(12), 795–808 (2021)
6. Boté-Vericad, J.J.: Challenges for the educational system during lockdowns: a possible new framework for teaching and learning for the near future. Educ. Inf. **37**(1), 149–153 (2021)
7. Fragoso-Diaz, O.G., Caballero, V.L., Rojas-Perez, J.C., et al.: On the generation of E-learning resources using business process, natural language processing, and web services. IT Prof. **23**(2), 40–44 (2021)
8. Zhang, H.Y., Huang, H.M., Li, W.: Emotional change detection oriented speech emotion database. Comput. Simul. **38**(09), 448–455 (2021)
9. Ghasemi, R., Asli, S., Momtazi, S.: Deep Persian sentiment analysis: cross-lingual training for low-resource languages. J. Inf. Sci. **48**(4), 449–462 (2022)
10. Chigozie, M.P., Ogbo, A.I., Okoh, A., et al.: The effect of education, research and development on women entrepreneurial proclivity. Solid State Technol. **65**(5), 881–888 (2021)

# Evaluation Method of English Distance Teaching Quality in Online Education Platform

Meizhi Wu(✉)

School of Foreign Languages, Sichuan University Jinjiang College, Meishan 620010, China
wzm202303@163.com

**Abstract.** In order to improve the accuracy of English distance teaching quality evaluation in online education platform, this study proposes the design of evaluation methods for English distance teaching quality in online education platform. This method first establishes the selection principle of the quality evaluation index of English distance education, selects the appropriate quality evaluation index of English distance education, then determines the collection method of the evaluation index information, processes the collected information, and calculates the weight of the distance education quality evaluation index by using the analytic hierarchy process. Finally, the weighted average method is used to obtain the evaluation result of English distance teaching quality, which realizes the evaluation of English distance teaching quality. The experimental results show that the maximum integrity of distance teaching quality evaluation index is 96%, and the maximum information signal-to-noise ratio of distance teaching quality evaluation index is 95.46%. The results of distance teaching quality evaluation are consistent with the actual results, which fully proves that the method proposed in this paper has good application performance.

**Keywords:** English Teaching · Teaching Quality · Distance Learning · Teaching Effect · Online Education Platform · Evaluation Method

## 1 Introduction

With the development of the Internet and artificial intelligence, as well as the construction of infrastructure, live broadcast has gradually come into people's view. From the initial live broadcast of games and entertainment to the live broadcast of goods in recent years, live broadcast has opened up new scenes one after another. In East Asia, where education is emphasized, the integration of live broadcasting and education has become an inevitable trend. In particular, since the COVID-19 epidemic in 2020, teachers and students across the country have entered a new situation of "no classes and no schools", in which online education is an important support, promoting China to carry out the world's largest online education practice [1]. 2020 is also the year of online education reform. All online education companies are eager to seize the favorable terrain and win the final victory in this sudden encounter. According to the online education industry


G. Gui et al. (Eds.): eLEOT 2023, LNICST 543, pp. 78–94, 2024.
https://doi.org/10.1007/978-3-031-51465-4_6

report issued by relevant statistical institutions, the market size of the online education industry in 2020 will grow by 35.5% to 257.3 billion yuan year-on-year, with the overall online rate of 23% to 25%. Among them, the acceleration of the online process of the track of early childhood and quality education, and the K12 discipline training track is the main contributing factor to the rapid growth of the online education market. In such a hot track, online education is also in the state of "half angel, half devil", which is also controversial when it is sought after by teachers, parents and capital. However, most of the industries under the epidemic situation had no choice but to press the pause button, which led to the largest amount of financing in the education field. Science and technology also continued to make efforts in the education field. The ToB racetrack blossomed, and education OMO began to rush, of which online education was the most favored by capital. In 2020, the education industry accumulatively raised 116.4 billion yuan, including 103.4 billion yuan of online education financing, accounting for 89%. Thus, online education platform has become one of the main means of teaching.

In recent years, distance education in China has developed rapidly, but there is a serious lack of evaluation standards to ensure the quality of distance education. Some researchers have made useful attempts to evaluate the quality of distance learning, but a unified and systematic evaluation index system has not yet been formed, and the evaluation methods of distance learning are not reasonable enough. Therefore, the research on evaluating the quality of distance learning is not enough, and distance learning has the following characteristics: large scale, widely distributed regions, complex personnel background, diversified organizations. In addition, the relatively loose distance learning system, which is composed of various parts of the distance learning system, is characterized by loose structure. It increases the difficulty of collecting evaluation information. Collecting information requires a lot of time and effort, as well as long-term tracking, investigation, analysis and sorting of the information received. The teaching quality of distance learning is difficult to guarantee, which requires a complete, comprehensive and evaluation system to evaluate it.

The survey data shows that at present, a large number of domestic scholars have realized the importance of distance learning quality assessment, and have made some research achievements in distance learning quality assessment [2]. Among them, the widely used teaching quality evaluation methods are the research of teaching quality evaluation index system of modern distance higher education and the evaluation method of network education effect based on fuzzy evaluation method. The former constructs a three-level index system to evaluate the teaching quality of distance higher education. To some extent, the problem of distance teaching quality evaluation can be solved by calculating the comprehensive score, but there is still the problem of linear additivity among evaluation factors. The latter first establishes the evaluation index system of online education, and then uses the fuzzy evaluation method to evaluate the quality of distance education. Both of the above two methods have certain defects, which cannot meet the follow-up development and application of online education platform, and is not conducive to the improvement of English distance teaching quality. Therefore, the research on the evaluation methods of English distance teaching quality in online education platform is proposed to provide accurate data support for the formulation of English distance teaching quality improvement policies. In order to improve the accuracy of distance teaching quality evaluation, this study starts with the selection of appropriate evaluation indicators, first establishes the selection principles of indicators, then collects the selected indicators, uses the analytic hierarchy process to complete the weight calculation, and finally completes the final evaluation based on the weighted average method. It is hoped that this study can provide a literature reference for the related research of distance teaching quality evaluation in online education platform.

## 2 Research on the Quality Evaluation Methods of English Distance Teaching

### 2.1 Selection of Distance Learning Quality Evaluation Indicators

From the perspective of research objectives, the selection principles of English distance teaching quality assessment indicators (scientific, systematic, targeted and guiding) are formulated, and appropriate English distance teaching quality assessment indicators are selected to lay a solid foundation for the follow-up research.

Teaching is a complex systematic project, and students are the main body of learning. However, teaching methods have a key impact on students' learning quality. How to optimize these teaching methods is a comprehensive project, which needs the support of teachers, technicians and other resources of the school. Therefore, we should take these factors into full consideration when setting teaching quality assessment standards, so as to develop an effective quality assessment system [3]. After summarizing the relevant contents of the previous article and combining the survey data, this study believes that the following principles should be followed when developing the distance learning quality evaluation system, as shown in Table 1.

According to the principles shown in Table 1, appropriate selection of English distance learning quality evaluation indicators is made, and the selection results are shown in Table 2.

As shown in Table 2, the selected distance learning quality evaluation indicators are mainly divided into three layers, of which the number of first level indicators is 4, the number of second level indicators is 11, and the number of third level indicators is 33, which can comprehensively describe the actual situation of distance learning quality and provide support for the accurate evaluation of English distance learning quality [4].

### 2.2 Collection and Processing of Evaluation Indicator Information

Based on the above selected evaluation indicators of English distance learning quality, determine the information collection method of evaluation indicators, and process the collected information to provide a basis for determining the weight of subsequent evaluation indicators.

If the evaluation experts want to make a comprehensive and objective evaluation of the evaluated object, they must possess a large amount of evaluation information. Some of this information is provided by the evaluated unit, and some needs to be collected by the evaluation experts using various tools and methods. The evaluation system provides rich auxiliary functions for experts to collect evaluation information [5]. From the perspective

**Table 1.** Selection Principles of Teaching Quality Evaluation Indicators

| principle | Content description |
|---|---|
| Scientific | Combined with the characteristics of distance learning, the setting of evaluation indicators must be more scientific and reasonable, consistent with the characteristics of distance learning. The indicator design cannot be static, and can not be formulated only through historical data. It needs to use modern information technology to dynamically follow up the participants in teaching work, find new problems in time, and combine the dynamic with the static, so as to ensure that the teaching quality evaluation indicators can change with the development of the times, and ensure that the evaluation indicators are scientific and reasonable |
| systematicness | In the process of teaching quality evaluation, we should also pay attention to the relationship between various elements. Each step is an important part of teaching work, and each step is closely linked. This requires us to pay attention to the details and at the same time have an overall plan for the development of the whole project. Each evaluation indicator must be closely linked. In addition to considering the rationality of each indicator, it is also important to maximize the effectiveness of the evaluation system |
| pertinence | When selecting the evaluation indicators for the teaching quality of distance education, we should fully consider these teaching characteristics and teaching priorities, and develop a targeted evaluation system. For example, for the evaluation of teaching preparation, in addition to the content of courseware, we should also examine the applicability of questions, so that the final evaluation criteria can be more effective |
| Orientation | In order to give full play to the directional effect of teaching quality evaluation indicators, it is necessary to study the full attributes of the distance teaching process, master the key teaching environment, understand the problems existing in the current teaching process, so that the problems existing in the teaching process can be tailored to the case, develop appropriate technical indicators, and guide the development of teaching work. Improve teaching effect |

of expert evaluation, there are many ways to collect evaluation information, and the following five methods are commonly used, as shown in Table 3.

According to the contents shown in Table 3, and in combination with the research needs, it is determined that the evaluation indicator information collection method is the questionnaire method. The collection of evaluation indicator information often shows the characteristics of incomplete information, inconsistent expression of information, and being greatly affected by noise. Data cleaning smoothes noisy data by identifying or deleting outliers, and fills in missing values to "clean" data. Therefore, the main tasks of information processing are: missing value processing, smoothing noise data, redundant information removal and information standardization.

**Table 2.** Evaluation Indicators of English Distance Teaching Quality

| Primary indicators | Secondary indicators | Level III indicators |
|---|---|---|
| Distance learning preparation | Distance learning resources | resources material |
| | | Network courseware |
| | | learning resource |
| | Distance learning environment | information environment |
| | | Personal learning environment |
| | | Network virtual class or study group |
| | Student preparation | Technical support system |
| | | Online learning skills |
| | Teacher competence | Multimedia Teaching Technology |
| | | Prepare lessons for online teaching |
| Distance learning activities | Teaching guidance | Real time communication frequency |
| | | Asynchronous AC frequency |
| | | Network guidance |
| | Teaching organization | Teaching arrangement |
| | | Compilation of teaching documents |
| | | Implementation of course plan |
| | teaching activities | teaching process |
| | | Discussion arrangements |
| | | Online Teaching Practice |
| | | Operation correction requirements |
| | | Student assessment |
| Learning support | psychological support | Psychological adjustment |
| | | Complaint response |
| | | Emotional interaction between teachers and students |
| | Learning support | E-learning assessment |
| | | Learning guidance response |

(*continued*)

**Table 2.** *(continued)*

| Primary indicators | Secondary indicators | Level III indicators |
|---|---|---|
| | | Learning technology response |
| Reform and development | Teaching research | teaching activities |
| | | Scientific research activities |
| | | Further study or training |
| | reform in education | Teaching evaluation reform |
| | | Discipline teaching reform |
| | | Network teaching reform |

**Table 3.** Collection Methods of Evaluation Indicator Information

| Collection method | Evaluation information | Evaluation method |
|---|---|---|
| Observation method | Morphological information<br>Qualitative information | Site visit |
| Interview method | Morphological information<br>Qualitative information | Site visit |
| Questionnaire method | Morphological information<br>Qualitative information<br>Quantitative information | Online assessment |
| Research method | Qualitative information<br>Quantitative information | Site visit<br>Online assessment |
| Role playing | Morphological information<br>Qualitative information<br>Quantitative information | Online assessment |

Wherein, the missing values are supplemented by regression estimation method, and the expression is

$$Y_k = \alpha_0 + \sum_{i=1}^{n} \alpha_i \beta_{ik} \tag{1}$$

In Eq. (1), $Y_k$ represents the regression estimate corresponding to the missing value of evaluation indicator information $X_k$; $\alpha_0$ represents the initial regression coefficient; $\alpha_i$ represents the regression coefficient corresponding to the $i$-th evaluation indicator information; $\beta_{ik}$ represents the regression relationship between the $i$-th evaluation indicator information and the missing value $X_k$.

This study uses morphological filtering to filter noise information, and the noise filtering effect is shown in Fig. 1.

In order to facilitate the research, the evaluation index information after denoising is recorded as $\{X_1, X_2, \cdots, X_n\}$ [6]. Due to the large number of evaluation indicators

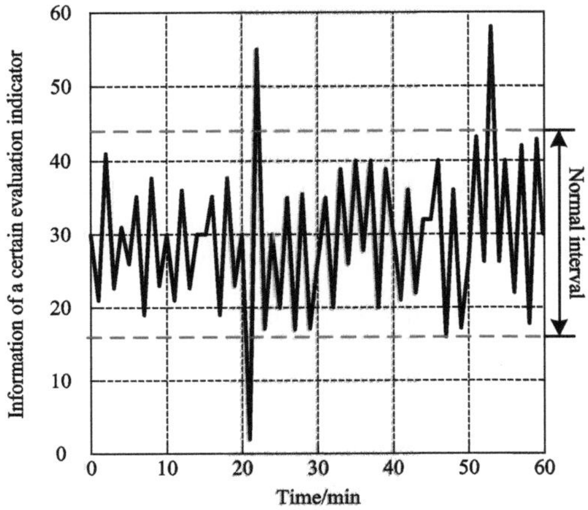


(1) Evaluation index information before denoising

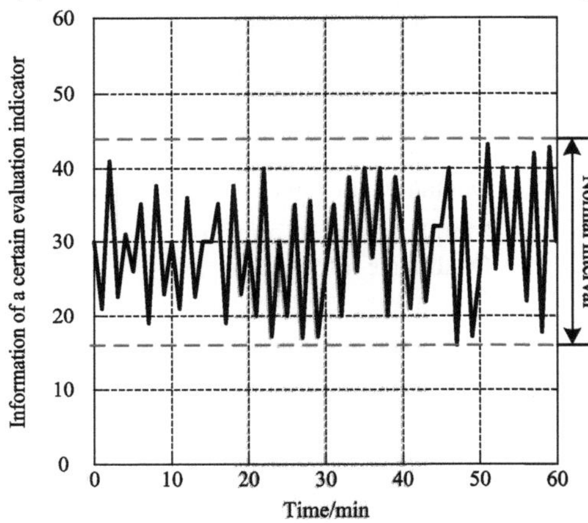


(2) Evaluation index information after noise removal

**Fig. 1.** Example of noise information filtering effect of evaluation indicators

and the impact of the collection process, the evaluation indicator information contains a lot of redundant information. Covariance is used to measure the correlation between the two evaluation indicator information. The calculation formula of covariance between the information of two evaluation indicators is

$$Cov\left(X_i, X_j\right) = \frac{\sum_{i=1}^{n} \left(X_i - \overline{X}\right)\left(X_j - \overline{X}\right)}{n - 1} \tag{2}$$

In formula (2), $Cov\left(X_i, X_j\right)$ represents the covariance difference between the evaluation indicator information $X_i$ and $X_j$; $\overline{X}$ represents the average value of evaluation indicator information; $n$ represents the total amount of evaluation indicator information.

According to the calculation result of formula (2), the redundancy information determination rules are formulated as follows:

$$\begin{cases} Cov(X_i, X_j) \geq \chi^* \text{ Redundancy} \\ Cov(X_i, X_j) < \chi^* \text{ Normal information} \end{cases} \tag{3}$$

In Eq. (3), $\chi^*$ represents the judgment threshold for redundant information, which needs to be set based on actual evaluation indicator information.

The minimum maximum normalization method is used to normalize the evaluation indicator information, and the expression is

$$Z_i = \frac{X_i - X_{i-\min}}{X_{i-\max} - X_{i-\min}} \tag{4}$$

In Eq. (4), $Z_i$ represents standardized evaluation indicator information; $X_{i-\min}$ and $X_{i-\max}$ represent the minimum and maximum values of the evaluation indicator information.

In summary, record the post-processing evaluation indicator information as $\{Z_1, Z_2, \cdots, Z_N\}$ to provide support for subsequent research.

### 2.3 Determination of Weights of Distance Learning Quality Evaluation Indicators

The weight of the evaluation index is directly related to the accuracy of the final evaluation results, so the research uses the analytic hierarchy process to calculate and determine the weight of the distance teaching quality evaluation index [7].

The calculation steps of distance learning quality evaluation index weight based on analytic hierarchy process are as follows:

Step 1: Build the analytic hierarchy process framework.

It is generally divided into three layers, the top layer is the target layer, the middle layer is the criterion layer or indicator layer, and the bottom layer is the scheme layer.

Step 2: Construction and assignment of judgment matrix.

According to the judgment matrix criteria, the proportion of each factor of a certain level to a certain criterion is determined by comparing the influence of the lower level to a certain criterion (or target) of the upper level. It is required to compare the importance of each element in pairs. The importance is assigned as 1–9. The rules are as follows:

$$a_{ij} = \begin{cases} 1 & r_i \text{ and } r_j \text{ are equally important} \\ 3 & r_i \text{ is slightly more important than } r_j \\ 5 & r_i \text{ is significantly more important than } r_j \\ 7 & r_i \text{ is more important than } r_j \\ 9 & r_i \text{ is extremely important than } r_j \\ 2/4/6/8 & \text{the median value of the above judgment} \end{cases} \tag{5}$$

In formula (5), $a_{ij}$ represents the importance of any two evaluation indicators $r_i$ and $r_j$, and there exists $a_{ji} = \frac{1}{a_{ij}}$.

The judgment matrix can be constructed according to formula (5), and the expression is

$$A = \begin{bmatrix} a_{11} & a_{12} & \cdots & a_{1n} \\ a_{21} & a_{22} & \cdots & a_{2n} \\ \vdots & \vdots & a_{ij} & \vdots \\ a_{n1} & a_{n2} & \cdots & a_{nn} \end{bmatrix} \tag{6}$$

In formula (6), $A$ represents the judgment matrix.

Step 3: Hierarchical single sorting.

Hierarchical single ranking refers to the relative weight of each factor of all judgment matrices against their criteria, and its essence is to calculate the weight vector. Apply and principle to normalize and calculate each column of the consistency judgment matrix to obtain the corresponding weight [8]. Normalize each column of the inconsistent judgment matrix to approximate its corresponding weight, and calculate the arithmetic mean of column $n$ vector as the final weight. The calculation formula is

$$\omega_i = \frac{1}{n}\sum_{j=1}^{n}\frac{a_{ij}}{\sum\limits_{k=1}^{n} a_{kj}} \tag{7}$$

In Eq. (7), $\omega_i$ represents the weight value corresponding to evaluation indicator $r_i$.

Step 4: Judge the consistency of the matrix.

In practice, consistency test is required to judge whether the matrix meets the general consistency. Only when the general consistency is met can the logical rationality of the judgment matrix be confirmed, and further analysis of the results is required. The steps of consistency inspection are as follows:

a. Calculate consistency indicators $CI$, expressed as

$$CI = \frac{\lambda_{\max} - n}{n - 1} \tag{8}$$

In Eq. (8), $\lambda_{\max}$ represents the maximum eigenvalue of the judgment matrix $A$.

b. The corresponding average random consistency index $RI$ was obtained through a lookup table, as shown in Table 4.

c. Calculate consistency ratio $CR$, the expression is

$$CR = \frac{CI}{RI} \tag{9}$$

In Eq. (9), $CR$ If the value is less than 0.1, the consistency of the judgment matrix is acceptable.

Step 5: Overall ranking and inspection of levels.

Overall ranking refers to the relative weights of all factors in the judgment matrix and target layer. This weight is calculated from top to bottom and synthesized layer by layer. If the relative weight of element $m$ in layer $k-1$ is equal to the overall goal $\omega^{k-1} = \left(\omega_1^{k-1}, \omega_2^{k-1}, \cdots, \omega_n^{k-1}\right)^T$, and the individual sorting weight of element $j$ in the upper

**Table 4.** Average random consistency index *RI* surface

| Matrix order | *RI* | Matrix order | *RI* |
|---|---|---|---|
| 1 | 0 | 9 | 1.46 |
| 2 | 0 | 10 | 1.49 |
| 3 | 0.52 | 11 | 1.52 |
| 4 | 0.89 | 12 | 1.54 |
| 5 | 1.12 | 13 | 1.56 |
| 6 | 1.26 | 14 | 1.58 |
| 7 | 1.36 | 15 | 1.59 |
| 8 | 1.41 | - | - |

level of layer $n$ in part $k$ is $\delta_j^k = \left(\delta_{1j}^k, \delta_{2j}^k, \cdots, \delta_{nj}^k\right)^T$, it is not constrained by $j$. The weight of the dominant element is zero or in order $\delta^k = \left(\delta_1^{k-1}, \delta_2^{k-1}, \cdots, \delta_n^{k-1}\right)^T$, indicating that there are no $k-1$-layer elements in the order of $k$-layer elements. Therefore, for the total target $k$, the total order of layer elements is:

$$\omega^k = \left(\omega_1^k, \omega_2^k, \cdots, \omega_n^k\right)^T = \delta^k * \omega^{k-1} \tag{10}$$

Similarly, consistency testing is conducted on the overall sorting results. Generally speaking, if the weight of factor $n$ in layer $B$ is $\omega_j (j = 1, 2, \cdots, n)$, and if one indicator $B_j$ of factor $B$ in upper layer $C$ has a consistency of $CI_j$ for a single sorting, and the corresponding average random consistency index is $RI_j$, then the consistency rate of the entire hierarchical sorting of factor $C$ is:

$$CR = \frac{\sum_{j=1}^{n} \omega_j CI_j}{\sum_{j=1}^{n} \omega_j RI_j} \tag{11}$$

When the value of $CR$ is less than 0.1, the consistency of the judgment matrix is acceptable.

Through the above process, we have completed the calculation of the weight of remote learning quality evaluation indicators and recorded it as $\{\omega_1, \omega_2, \cdots, \omega_n\}$, making sufficient preparations for the subsequent acquisition of remote learning quality evaluation results.

### 2.4 Acquisition of Distance Learning Quality Assessment Results

Based on the above results of the selection of English distance teaching quality evaluation indicators, the results of indicator information processing and the results of indicator weight calculation, the weighted average method is used to obtain the English distance teaching quality evaluation results, providing data support for the improvement of distance teaching quality.

The weighted average method can not only comprehensively consider the weight of experts in the evaluation of different indicators, but also consider the weight of each indicator itself, which can maximize the accuracy of teaching quality evaluation results [9]. The teaching quality evaluation result based on the weighted average method is

$$\xi = \frac{\sum_{i=1}^{n} r_i * Z_i * \omega_i}{\vartheta^2} + \varepsilon^o \tag{12}$$

In Eq. (12), $\xi$ refers to the evaluation result of the quality of English remote teaching; $\vartheta^2$ represents the standardization factor; $\varepsilon^o$ represents the error adjustment item of the teaching quality evaluation results, which determines the accuracy of the teaching quality evaluation results.

According to the calculation result of formula (12), set the English distance learning quality evaluation rules as follows:

When the quality evaluation result $\xi$ of English remote learning is within the range of [0, 0.2), it is considered that the quality of English remote learning is excellent.

When the quality evaluation result $\xi$ of English remote learning is within the range of [0.2, 0.5), it is considered that the quality of English remote learning is good.

When the quality evaluation result $\xi$ of English remote learning falls within the range of [0.5, 0.8), it is considered that the quality of English remote learning is average.

When the quality evaluation result $\xi$ of English remote learning falls within the range of [0.8, 1], it is considered that the quality of English remote learning is poor.

Through the above process, we completed the evaluation of the quality of English distance learning, and provided help for the development of English distance learning and online education platform [10].

## 3 Experiment and Result Analysis

### 3.1 Determination of Weights of Distance Learning Quality Evaluation Indicators

Calculate and obtain the weights of distance learning quality evaluation indicators according to the procedures shown in Sect. 2.3, so as to facilitate the follow-up experiments. The weights of distance learning quality evaluation indicators are shown in Table 5.

As shown in Table 5, the weight complies with the rules: $\sum_{i=1}^{n} \omega_i = 1$. It shows that the accuracy of obtaining the weight value of distance teaching quality evaluation index is high, and subsequent experiments can be carried out.

### 3.2 Determination of Experimental Parameters

The proposed method adds a parameter error adjustment item in the calculation of teaching quality evaluation results $\varepsilon^o$. Its value is directly related to the accuracy of

**Table 5.** Weights of Distance Teaching Quality Evaluation Indicators

| Secondary indicators | weight | Level III indicators | weight |
|---|---|---|---|
| Distance learning resources | 0.05 | resources material | 0.02 |
| | | Network courseware | 0.02 |
| | | learning resource | 0.01 |
| Distance learning environment | 0.08 | information environment | 0.04 |
| | | Personal learning environment | 0.03 |
| | | Network virtual class or study group | 0.01 |
| Student preparation | 0.06 | Technical support system | 0.04 |
| | | Online learning skills | 0.02 |
| Teacher competence | 0.12 | Multimedia Teaching Technology | 0.08 |
| | | Prepare lessons for online teaching | 0.04 |
| Teaching guidance | 0.10 | Real time communication frequency | 0.05 |
| | | Asynchronous AC frequency | 0.03 |
| | | Network guidance | 0.02 |
| Teaching organization | 0.08 | Teaching arrangement | 0.03 |
| | | Compilation of teaching documents | 0.02 |
| | | Implementation of course plan | 0.03 |
| teaching activities | 0.18 | teaching process | 0.06 |
| | | Discussion arrangements | 0.02 |
| | | Online Teaching Practice | 0.01 |
| | | Operation correction requirements | 0.07 |
| | | Student assessment | 0.02 |
| psychological support | 0.04 | Psychological adjustment | 0.01 |
| | | Complaint response | 0.02 |
| | | Emotional interaction between teachers and students | 0.01 |
| Learning support | 0.12 | E-learning assessment | 0.05 |
| | | Learning guidance response | 0.04 |
| | | Learning technology response | 0.03 |
| Teaching research | 0.10 | teaching activities | 0.06 |
| | | Scientific research activities | 0.02 |
| | | Further study or training | 0.01 |

(*continued*)

**Table 5.** (*continued*)

| Secondary indicators | weight | Level III indicators | weight |
|---|---|---|---|
| reform in education | 0.07 | Teaching evaluation reform | 0.01 |
| | | Discipline teaching reform | 0.03 |
| | | Network teaching reform | 0.03 |

teaching quality evaluation results. Therefore, before the experiment, it is necessary to $\varepsilon^o$ Determine the best value.

Obtain parameters through testing $\varepsilon^o$ The relationship with the accuracy of teaching quality assessment results is shown in Fig. 2.

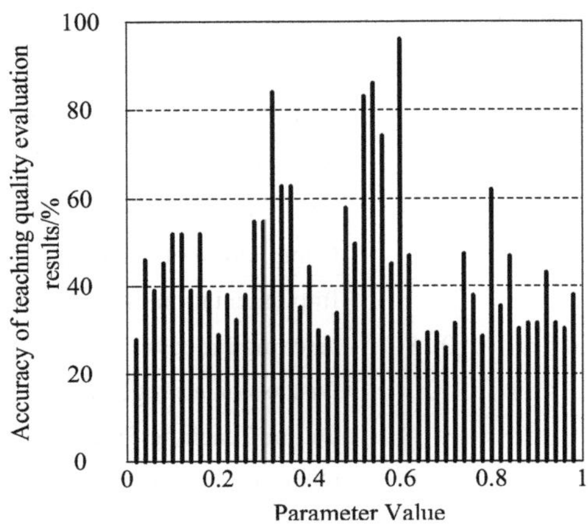


**Fig. 2.** Parameters $\varepsilon^o$ Schematic diagram of the relationship with the accuracy of teaching quality evaluation results

As shown in Fig. 2, when parameter $\varepsilon^o$ is 0.6, the accuracy rate of teaching quality evaluation results reaches the maximum of 96%. Therefore, the optimal value of parameter error adjustment item can be determined to be 0.6.

### 3.3 Analysis of Experimental Results

In order to verify the advanced nature of the proposed method, reference [5] method and reference [6] method are selected as comparison methods 1 and 2, and combined with the above experimental preparation content, a comparative experimental study on distance teaching quality evaluation is carried out. In order to prove the application effect of this method objectively, we choose the integrity of distance teaching quality evaluation indicators, information signal-to-noise ratio and result accuracy as evaluation indicators. First of all, completeness refers to whether the evaluation index can comprehensively cover all aspects of distance teaching. By selecting a complete evaluation index, we can understand the quality of distance teaching more accurately, so as to carry out targeted improvement and optimization. Secondly, the information signal-to-noise ratio refers to the proportional relationship between the information provided by the evaluation index and the noise. In the evaluation of distance teaching quality, the index with higher signal-to-noise ratio can make the evaluation result more accurate and reliable. By eliminating distractions and noise, we can get a more accurate picture of the true quality of distance teaching, and evaluate and make decisions accordingly. Finally, accuracy is an important attribute of the evaluation index, which reflects the degree of consistency between the evaluation results and the actual situation. Choosing accuracy as the evaluation index can ensure that the evaluation results of distance teaching quality are in line with the actual situation. This helps us to find the problems and shortcomings in time, and take corresponding improvement measures to improve the quality of distance teaching. To sum up, the completeness, information signal-to-noise ratio and accuracy of distance teaching quality evaluation indicators are selected as evaluation indicators, which can help objectively prove the application effect of this method and provide scientific basis for improving the quality of distance teaching. The specific analysis process of the experimental results is as follows:

### 3.3.1 Analysis of the Integrity of Distance Learning Quality Evaluation Indicators

The number of distance learning quality evaluation indicators is too small to comprehensively evaluate the quality of distance learning, and the evaluation results obtained are quite different from the actual results. It can be seen that the integrity of distance learning quality evaluation indicators plays a vital role. The integrity of distance learning quality assessment indicators obtained through experiments is shown in Fig. 3.

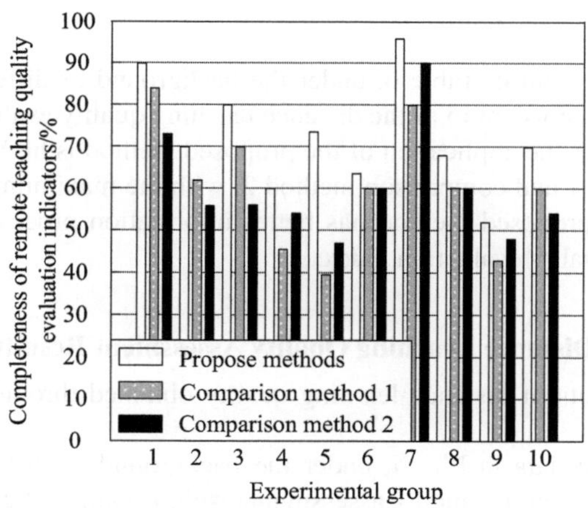


**Fig. 3.** Schematic diagram of the integrity of distance learning quality evaluation indicators

As shown in the data in Fig. 3, under the background of different experimental groups, the integrity of distance teaching quality evaluation indicators obtained after the application of the proposed method is higher than that of comparison method 1 and comparison method 2, with the maximum value of 96%, which indicates that the selection of distance teaching quality evaluation indicators of the proposed method is more accurate.

### 3.3.2 Signal to Noise Ratio Analysis of Evaluation Indicator Information

The SNR values of distance learning quality evaluation index information obtained through experiments are shown in Table 6.

**Table 6.** Information SNR of Distance Teaching Quality Evaluation Indicators

| Experimental group | Propose method | Comparison method 1 | Comparison method 2 |
|---|---|---|---|
| 1 | 89.45 | 45.12 | 52.10 |
| 2 | 90.12 | 32.00 | 41.23 |
| 3 | 82.10 | 41.02 | 42.58 |
| 4 | 95.46 | 36.59 | 44.75 |
| 5 | 90.12 | 38.45 | 52.31 |
| 6 | 84.45 | 51.20 | 40.12 |
| 7 | 71.02 | 41.29 | 48.78 |
| 8 | 85.44 | 52.78 | 42.13 |
| 9 | 86.32 | 53.64 | 32.05 |
| 10 | 85.12 | 52.18 | 36.58 |

Note: The unit is dB.

As shown in the data in Table 6, under the background of different experimental groups, the signal-to-noise ratio of the distance teaching quality evaluation index information obtained after the application of the proposed method is higher than that of the comparison method 1 and comparison method 2, with the maximum value of 95.46%, indicating that the proposed method has better information processing effect on the distance teaching quality evaluation index.

### 3.3.3 Analysis of Distance Learning Quality Assessment Results

The evaluation results of distance learning quality obtained through experiments are shown in Fig. 4.

As shown in the data in Fig. 4, under the background of different experimental groups, the distance teaching quality assessment results obtained after the application of the proposed method are consistent with the actual results, while the distance teaching quality assessment results obtained by comparison methods 1 and 2 have a large deviation from the actual results, indicating that the distance teaching quality assessment results obtained by the proposed method are more accurate.

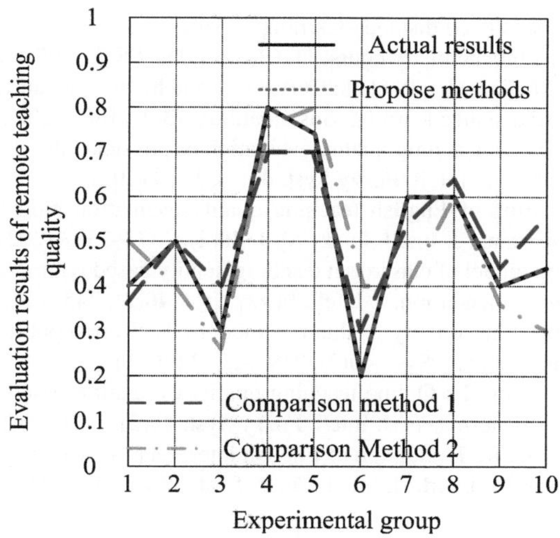


**Fig. 4.** Sketch map of distance learning quality assessment results

## 4 Conclusion

In order to improve the accuracy of English distance teaching quality evaluation on online education platform, a new method is designed in this study. First, in the process of determining the quality evaluation index of English distance education, the selection principle is clarified, and the appropriate evaluation index is screened. Secondly, the collection method of evaluation index information is developed, and the obtained information is processed. The AHP method is used to determine the weight of the evaluation index of distance education quality. Finally, the weighted average method is used to obtain the evaluation result of English distance teaching quality, so as to achieve a comprehensive evaluation of its quality. The core of this method is to ensure the accuracy and reliability of the evaluation index. The experimental results show that the evaluation results of distance teaching quality are consistent with the actual results and have a certain application effect. Modern distance education evaluation is an open and dynamic practice process. It needs to be adjusted in time according to changes in the actual situation, and constantly corrected and enriched. The content of distance education teaching quality evaluation conducted by the author is the core of distance education teaching quality evaluation, but not the whole. Although the distance education teaching quality evaluation index system established in this study has certain application value, it lacks a large-scale test of reliability and validity, which is also the goal of the next study.

## References


1. Misses, M., Jiménez, N.J.: Development of a platform with real-time performance for electrical circuits education. IEEE Latin Am. Trans. **19**(12), 2147–2155 (2021)
2. Vilchez, J., Kruse, J., Puffer, M., et al.: Teachers and school health leaders' perspectives on distance learning physical education during the COVID-19 pandemic. J. School Health **91**(7), 541–549 (2021)

3. Kamber, D.N.: Personalized distance-learning experience through virtual oral examinations in an undergraduate biochemistry course. J. Chem. Educ. **98**(2), 395–399 (2021)
4. Cicha, K., Rizun, M., Rutecka, P., et al.: COVID-19 and higher education: first-year students' expectations toward distance learning. Sustainability **13**(4), 1889 (2021)
5. Liu, S.: Research on the teaching quality evaluation of physical education with intuitionistic fuzzy TOPSIS method. J. Intell. Fuzzy Syst. **40**(5), 1–10 (2021)
6. Huang, W.: Simulation of English teaching quality evaluation model based on Gaussian process machine learning. J. Intell. Fuzzy Syst. **40**(2), 2373–2383 (2021)
7. Sun, Q.: Evaluation model of classroom teaching quality based on improved RVM algorithm and knowledge recommendation. J. Intell. Fuzzy Syst. **40**(2), 2457–2467 (2021)
8. Hou, J.: Online teaching quality evaluation model based on support vector machine and decision tree. J. Intell. Fuzzy Syst. **40**(2), 2193–2203 (2021)
9. Liu, P., Wang, X., Teng, F.: Online teaching quality evaluation based on multi-granularity probabilistic linguistic term sets. J. Intell. Fuzzy Syst. **40**(2), 1–20 (2021)
10. Lu, C., He, B., Zhang, R.: Evaluation of English interpretation teaching quality based on GA optimized RBF neural network. J. Intell. Fuzzy Syst. **40**(2), 3185–3192 (2021)

# Distance Education Platform for Mental Health Courses in Secondary Vocational Schools Based on Cloud Computing

Ning Ding[1,2(✉)], Yiwen Chen[1,2], and Shanyu Gu[3]

[1] Institute of Psychology, Chinese Academy of Sciences, Beijing 100101, China
dingningnew@163.com

[2] Department of Psychology, University of the Chinese Academy of Sciences, Beijing 100049, China

[3] Guangxi Communications Vocational and Technical College, Nanning 530023, China

**Abstract.** In order to solve the problem of the limited response ability of the remote client terminal of the distance education platform, this study proposed a cloud computation-based distance education platform for secondary vocational mental health courses. This method first establishes the hierarchical structure system of the education platform, optimizes the connection of typical functional modules and completes the design of the platform application architecture based on the established platform structure system, then completes the construction of OpenStack cloud environment based on the cloud computing service model, and finally configains the data center system based on the relevant mental health course information. Realize the application of various platform technologies. The experimental results show that the application of this platform can make the remote client terminal instantaneous response rate reach the maximum value within 20 min, which is 8.6Mb/s. The response speed and the client terminal instantaneous response rate are superior to the comparison method, which has certain application value.

**Keywords:** Cloud Computing · Mental Health Curriculum · Distance Education Platform · Hierarchy · Function Module · Openstack Environment · Data Center

## 1 Introduction

In recent years, secondary vocational school "campus events" caused by mental health problems have increased year by year, and the mental health problems of secondary vocational school students have increasingly become the focus of attention of schools, society and parents. The psychological quality of contemporary secondary vocational school students not only affects their own development, but also relates to the improvement of the quality of the whole nation, and more importantly, to the cultivation of trans century talents. For contemporary secondary vocational school students, having a positive and optimistic attitude towards life, good interpersonal skills, and healthy psychological quality are important factors to ensure their growth and success, and are also


G. Gui et al. (Eds.): eLEOT 2023, LNICST 543, pp. 95–110, 2024.
https://doi.org/10.1007/978-3-031-51465-4_7

the basic requirements of the society for high-quality talents. Therefore, it is increasingly important to set up courses for students' psychological health education in secondary vocational schools [1]. The curriculum of mental health education for secondary vocational school students generally takes scientific, systematic and focused teaching of mental health knowledge to students, and timely education and guidance of students' mental confusion and psychological problems as the main teaching task, so that students can learn to adjust their own emotions appropriately while mastering relevant knowledge and theories, and promote the development of physical and mental health.

At present, more than one hundred countries and regions have carried out distance education. Since 1998, China has successively carried out pilot work of distance education in many key universities. After more than ten years of development, distance education has trained a large number of talents for the country, and more and more people have benefited from distance education. The construction of the national network education platform has also made great achievements. Each distance education pilot unit has its own network teaching platform to provide online independent learning services for distance education students. However, China has a vast territory, and the informatization level in remote and poor areas and rural areas is limited, and the software and hardware resources are scarce. As a result, the investment in distance education in colleges and universities is uneven, and the education scale and development speed are different, which makes the country unable to establish a unified standard for distance education in colleges and universities. Although the remote education platform based on virtualization and the remote education platform based on mobile embedded terminal technology can keep the core network host running at a high speed for a long time, it is difficult to improve the instantaneous response rate of the customer terminal to a high level due to the particularity of the mental health course and the limited connection of the lower level device terminals. Therefore, it does not meet the practical application needs of strengthening the construction of the secondary vocational mental health curriculum in the education platform system.

Cloud computing is an emerging network architecture with outstanding computing and storage capabilities, which can be used to deal with various complex problems. This research combines cloud computing technology with distance education system, which can give full play to the advantages of cloud computing technology [2]. Use cloud computing technology to uniformly manage the infrastructure resources required for distance education, form a virtual resource pool, and provide cloud services for users through the network. Distance education institutions can rent infrastructure in the cloud at a lower cost, which is equivalent to having their own servers and other equipment, and can easily deploy their own applications in the cloud. The on-demand service and elastic expansion characteristics of cloud computing enable distance education institutions to use cloud infrastructure according to their actual needs. When leased equipment is not enough to support the growth of user access, it is only necessary to increase the lease of equipment in the cloud without changing the application architecture, effectively avoiding the waste of hardware resources, reducing development costs, thus significantly increasing the scalability of the development platform.

## 2 Architecture Design of Distance Education Platform

The design of distance education platform architecture needs to first solve the problem of platform demand analysis, and establish the connection relationship between typical functional modules with the help of the hierarchical structure of each platform.

### 2.1 Platform Demand Analysis

The distance education platform for mental health courses in secondary vocational schools mainly uses the advantages of cloud computing technology, which can provide powerful computing and storage capabilities with the help of ordinary devices, to develop a distance education platform on the cloud platform built by the OpenStack project. In this way, we can reduce the waste of resources and reduce the development cost of the distance education platform. In reality, physical devices are decentralized and independent of each other. Virtualization technology can say that these decentralized devices can be unified, and virtualization technology can be used to build a unified virtual resource pool. The same type of physical devices can be integrated as a whole [3]. The open source components provided by cloud computing system can uniformly manage resources and provide infrastructure resource services for distance education institutions.

The functional requirements of the platform are as follows:

(1) The platform should have the characteristics of cloud computing, which can provide IaaS functions externally, organize distributed physical resources such as computers, servers, etc. to form a hardware resource pool, and conduct unified management and configuration. At the same time, a visual management interface should be provided to simplify management operations.

(2) The platform should have a visual interface to facilitate user operation. Users can register on the cloud platform, obtain certain permissions after verification, log in to the cloud platform to rent resources in the cloud, and customize the resources they need. The platform should have the authentication function of identity and authority to ensure the security of the platform.

The solution expression of platform security application conditions is:

$$O = \sqrt{\frac{1}{\alpha\tilde{p}}[1 + (\beta\dot{I})]} \tag{1}$$

In the formula, $\tilde{p}$ represents the registration characteristics of remote education end users in the cloud platform system; $\alpha$ represents the response parameter indicating the connection behavior; $\beta$ represents the cloud resource sharing parameter; $\dot{I}$ represents a customized vector of mental health course resources.

(3) Users can rent cloud devices, customize services and deploy remote education platforms according to the actual needs of their applications.

(4) The main function of the distance education platform is to provide different functions for ordinary users of the distance education platform, such as teachers, students and administrators, respectively corresponding to the teaching, learning and management functions of the distance education platform.

The applied function expression of distance education of mental health course in secondary vocational schools is:

$$U = \chi \cdot \sum_{\substack{i=1 \\ u=1}} \left| \frac{y_i \cdot y_u}{\delta \overline{y}} \right|^2 \tag{2}$$

In the formula, $i$ and $u$ represent two randomly selected function approval vectors, $y_i$ represents the parameter $i$ based remote education platform response indicator, $y_u$ represents the parameter $u$ based remote education platform response indicator, $\overline{y}$ represents the average value of the remote education platform response indicator, $\delta$ represents the deployment permission of educational functions, and $\chi$ represents the validation coefficient of educational resources.

Formulas (1) and (2) are used to derive the demand analysis expression of distance education platform as follows:

$$Y = \left( \frac{1}{\gamma^{-\varepsilon}} \right)^3 \times \left[ \phi R^2 - (O \times U) \right] \tag{3}$$

In the formula, $\gamma$ represents the utilization parameter of educational resources, $\varepsilon$ represents the development authority of the educational platform, $\phi$ represents the Partition coefficient of mental health curriculum resources, and $R$ represents the real-time accumulation of educational resources.

For student users, they can use the distance education platform for independent learning and various learning support services, such as learning exchange services such as learning forums, homework resource download, score viewing, course selection and other functions. For teacher users, the platform should provide teaching functions and the function of communicating with students. For administrator users, it provides various management functions, such as user management, score management, student information management and other management functions, as well as related data statistics and summary.

## 2.2 Platform Hierarchy

The distance education platform for mental health courses in secondary vocational schools can be divided into two parts, one is the learning platform used by student users, and the other is the management platform used by various administrators. The learning platform mainly includes the functions of personal information management, video on demand, course evaluation, learning exchange, information retrieval, etc. The management platform mainly includes the modules of student information management, course selection management, score management, resource management, user management, etc. The specific function module diagram of the platform is shown in Fig. 1.

There are two main types of users of the learning platform: students and teachers. Students and teachers have different permissions due to their different roles in the system, but they use roughly the same functional modules. There are six major module functions: login authentication module, learning support module, course module, course selection score module, opinion feedback module, and personal center module. This structure

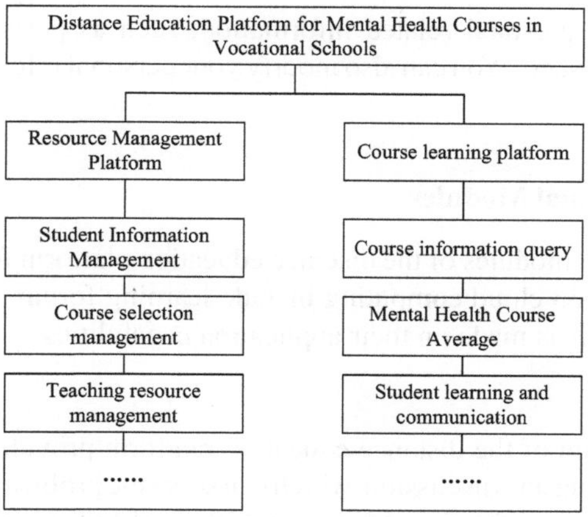


**Fig. 1.** Functional Structure of Platform

mainly provides students with relevant support for online learning, mainly including learning forums, interest groups, and online Q&A. These three parts provide students with different learning exchanges; Task reminders are mainly used to remind the recent Q&A plan and other information; The assignment resources mainly provide the upload and download services of assignments. Students can view the relevant resources and assignments of the selected courses, download the relevant assignment topics of the selected courses, and submit the assignments online [4]. After submission, you can view the status, scoring and other information of the job. Teachers can view their uploaded resources, assign homework, download student homework, and upload the corrected homework to the system after correction.

For the average application capability of the platform hierarchy, follow the expression shown in Formula (4).

$$E = \left. \frac{\sum_{\iota=1}^{+\infty} \dot{e}^2 |\Delta T|}{\varphi \cdot Y} \right|_{\varphi \neq 0} \tag{4}$$

In the formula, $\iota$ represents the upload parameters of remote education resources, $\dot{e}$ represents the functional characteristics of the remote education platform application module for secondary vocational mental health courses, $\Delta T$ represents the unit response cycle of the remote education platform, and $\varphi$ represents the user classification coefficient in the education platform system.

Course selection score mainly completes the function of course selection and score query. Within the specified time for course selection, students can select courses on the platform, view the scores of the tested courses, and view their own course selection [5]. Teachers can view the performance statistics. Opinion feedback mainly provides two functions, namely, the website letter and the dean's mailbox, to feed back the opinions or suggestions of students or teachers on using this platform. The Personal Center is mainly used to view personal related information, such as posts, messages, interest groups created by users, etc. You can also modify your personal information and platform password.

### 2.3 Typical Functional Modules

The typical functional modules of the distance education platform for vocational mental health courses based on cloud computing include learning forums and interest groups. The following analysis is made on their application capabilities.

(1) Learning Forum

The learning forum of the distance education platform provides the platform users with a space for learning and discussion, which can solve the problems students encounter at ordinary times, and is an effective supplement to the real-time question answering module. Teachers and administrators can fully communicate with students here. The learning forum adopts the real name system. The forum is mainly divided into three categories: public forum, professional forum and course forum. The public forum includes modules related to system function modules, such as enrollment module, student status module, educational administration module, etc., and information of corresponding departments of major online education institutions [6]. The columns of the professional forum correspond to the majors in the teaching plan one by one, providing professional discussions. The curriculum forum comes from the actual curriculum in teaching, and students and teachers can conduct curriculum learning exchange in the relevant curriculum forum. The functional module division of the learning forum is shown in Fig. 2.

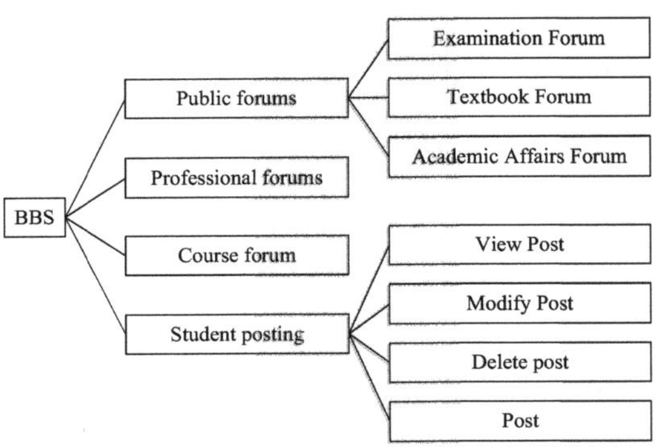


**Fig. 2.** Functional module of learning forum

(2) Interest Groups

The interest group is set up by students themselves, which attracts students with the same interest to participate in the discussion system. Users can freely create and apply for the participation of users. The number of members sharing resources among members

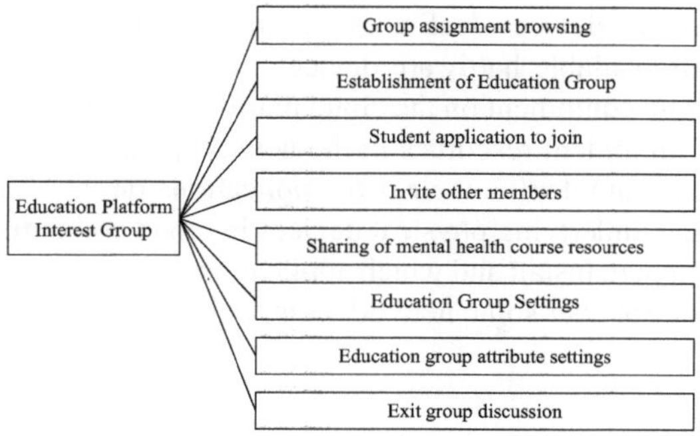


**Fig. 3.** Function module of interest group

of the same group can be up to 100, and this data can be adjusted by the administrator. The main functions are shown in Fig. 3.

Students can browse all groups under interest groups after logging in. On the interest group list page, students can view the name, founder account, founder name, creation time, theme, number of visits and other information of all interest groups, and can filter and query the interest group list by conditions. The filtering results are still returned in the same form of list. Students can browse the group or apply to join the group according to their personal interests and become members of the group only after being approved by the group leader.

Students can create their own group, view my group and related group information, and delete the group they created. Resource sharing within the same group. Group members can upload resources for use by group members, and can leave messages in the group to communicate with others [7]. Everyone can also delete their own uploaded files, and the team leader can delete all files in the group. Students can invite others to join or leave the group. The teacher's operation of interest groups is consistent with that of students. The administrator has the management function for the group, mainly including group resources, adding, deleting, modifying and checking messages, deleting groups, etc.

# 3 Platform Technology Implementation

According to the actual connection of the remote education platform architecture, build a cloud computing service model, and configure the data center with the help of OpenStack cloud environment system, so as to realize the smooth application of the remote education platform for secondary vocational mental health courses based on cloud computing.

## 3.1 Cloud Computing Service Model

Cloud computing is divided into three different service modes from the perspective of user experience, namely software services, platform services and infrastructure services.Infrastructure is provided to users as a service. Here, infrastructure refers to all available hardware resources including memory, storage devices, network devices, CPUs and other basic hardware devices. IaaS uses virtualization technology to form a unified resource pool for all available hardware devices for efficient automatic management. Ordinary users can rent equipment on the cloud platform. For educational users, "cloud" refers to unlimited equipment resources in the network, which can be rented to obtain infrastructure services and deploy their own applications on it. Although users cannot control or manage the underlying physical devices in cloud computing, they can decide which operating system to install and which applications to deploy on the leased devices, and can also gain control over some network components, such as routers and firewalls. As shown in Fig. 4.

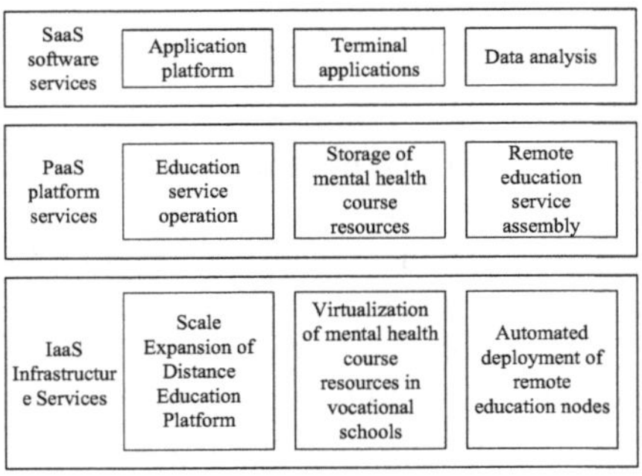


**Fig. 4.** Cloud computing service model architecture

The platform includes application development platform, deployment platform, etc.It is an abstract service based on infrastructure resources. Users do not need to care about how the underlying cloud infrastructure operates, and it effectively avoids the complexity of hardware facilities, such as the configuration and management of operating systems, servers, networks, etc. [8]. Users only need to deploy their own developed or purchased applications on the leased platform, control the hosting environment of applications, etc., and do not need to care about the underlying infrastructure and development platform. It has the advantages of convenient development, simplified deployment and maintenance.

Software services enable users to access applications through a browser on a client such as a personal PC, without installing applications on their own computers or servers. It is a new form for users to obtain software services. Users can subscribe to the software services they need according to their actual needs. There is no need for complex hardware equipment, professional developers and maintenance personnel, and software services can be rented in the form of services only through the Internet, which greatly reduces the cost of using software for users. In the software as a service layer model, it mainly provides software services for customers, and these software are running in the cloud.

### 3.2 OpenStack Cloud Environment Construction

In order to solve the problem of high concurrency existing in traditional platforms, this study builds a cloud platform for the following reasons: Through elastic resource allocation and horizontal expansion, the cloud platform can flexibly deploy computing, storage and network resources according to actual needs to cope with high concurrency pressure. During high load periods, the system dynamically increases the number of servers and allocates requests through load balancing technology to improve the throughput and concurrent processing capability. Secondly, the cloud platform also has a certain automatic scaling function, which can automatically expand and reduce resources according to preset trigger conditions, which enables the cloud platform to independently adjust the scale of resources according to the load situation, so as to achieve the purpose of efficient use of resources. Finally, cloud platforms offer a variety of flexible storage options, such as object storage, file storage, and databases, to meet the high-throughput read/write and storage needs for large-scale data. In summary, building a cloud platform provides a resilient and scalable solution for highly concurrent scenarios, ensuring that the system can maintain stability, high availability and high performance levels in response to high load stress. To build a cloud platform, you can simply install the required OpenStack components on the infrastructure, and the running ability of OpenStack components fully meets the requirements of cloud computing. Cloud computing is a computing method that provides users with dynamic, scalable, and virtualized resources in the form of services through the Internet. Users do not need to understand the infrastructure supporting cloud computing. Cloud computing can also meet the needs of different fields, such as scientific research and commercial fields. Cloud computing is not a new technology. Long before the emergence of cloud computing, various related technologies were developing and maturing, such as distributed processing technology, parallel processing technology, grid computing technology, public computing technology and software as a service technology.

The operation capability of OpenStack components is defined as:

$$w = \left( \frac{\lambda E}{q_{\max} - q_{\min}} \right)^2 + 1 \tag{5}$$

In the formula, $\lambda$ represents the access parameters of the OpenStack component, $q_{\max}$ represents the maximum value of the cloud platform response parameters, and $q_{\min}$ represents the minimum value of the cloud platform response parameters.

The OpenStack cloud environment mainly includes a control node and a computing node, which are used for testing the cloud platform. There can be multiple calculation nodes in practical application. The steps for installing a control node and a computing node are basically the same, but the main installed components are different. Before installing OpenStack components, it is necessary to analyze the existing hardware environment, select the appropriate operating system and determine the OpenStack version; Then the installation and configuration of authentication server, computing service and image service; Finally, the installation of storage service and Web control end [9]. For cloud computing tasks, choose Ubuntu Server 14.04 as the operating system, and use the Kilo version of OpenStack.

The statistics of OpenStack component computing power conform to the following expression.

$$Q = \left( \eta \cdot \vec{A} \right) \times \sqrt{s_1^2 + s_2^2 + \cdots + s_n^2} \tag{6}$$

In the formula, $\vec{A}$ represents the Kilo version running vector of the OpenStack component, $\eta$ represents the transmission efficiency of secondary vocational mental health course resources in the OpenStack cloud environment, and $s_1, s_2, \cdots, s_n$ represents $n$ randomly selected remote education service mirror response parameters.

Install the operating system, configure the network, database and other information according to the process, and install the control node and computing node. The construction of an IaaS platform has been basically successful. In the cloud platform, each user only needs to register an account, and then can configure different instances from the image to operate resources independently, reducing the management work for the platform administrator. Users can freely use resources, deploy applications, install software, etc. in the cloud in a customized way.

Simultaneous Formula (5) and Formula (6) can define the OpenStack cloud environment building expression as:

$$D = \left| \frac{\hat{d}}{w} \right|^2 \cdot Q \cdot \sum_{-\infty}^{+\infty} f \cdot \frac{1}{\dot{g}} \tag{7}$$

In the formula, $\hat{d}$ represents the educational account registration features on the IaaS platform, $f$ represents the deployment parameters of remote education resources for mental health courses in secondary vocational schools, and $\dot{g}$ represents the cloud computing response vector in the OpenStack environment.

The OpenStack cloud environment consists of three roles: client, controller, and computing node. The client has no special requirements for the machine and can be built using any physical host within the same LAN segment; The controller is composed of components such as Nova provided by OpenStack, which can be deployed on one machine or different physical hosts depending on the deployment mode. The remote education platform for secondary vocational mental health courses based on cloud computing adopts the method of deploying the controller on a single physical machine. The computing section consists of separate physical machines, which must support virtualization technology. The main function of a computing node is to run a virtualized instance and provide computing services.

### 3.3 Data Center Configuration of Education Platform

The data center has an embedded vCenter Server to deploy the vCenter Server, vCenter Server components and Platform Services Controller on one server. On the contrary, the centralized architecture separates the vCenter Server and Platform Services Controller and deploys them on different servers. The specific configuration process is as follows.

Step 1: Use VMware vSphere Client to access the vCenter Server in the browser, enter the vCenter user name and password, and log in to the vCenter Server.

Step 2: Create a data center in vCenter Server, and enter the name of the data center "Distance Education Platform Data Center".

The response capability of the distance education platform data center is defined as:

$$G = |\Delta H| \cdot \sqrt{\left(\frac{\tilde{h}}{\bar{j}}\right)^2 - \lambda D} \tag{8}$$

In the formula, $\Delta H$ represents the accumulated distance education resource courses in the secondary vocational open stack cloud environment, $\tilde{h}$ represents the response characteristics of the education resource vCenter server component, $\tilde{j}$ represents the response characteristics of the education resource of the platform service controller project, and $\lambda$ represents the discrimination vector of the education resource.

Step 3: Select the Add Host option in the data center, and add the ESXi host to the data center through the IP address. During the addition process, you need to configure several configuration items, such as name and location, connection settings, and license allocation, to complete the host addition.

In the vSphere virtualization environment, clusters are the basis for virtual machines to achieve HA (high performance) and FT (fault tolerance). By default, there is only one working network in the vSphere environment, a virtual switch vSwitch0, and a physical network card [10] connected to each ESXi host. To manage and use clusters, a virtualized environment requires network redundancy and at least two shared storage. To ensure network redundancy, you need to add another physical network card for each ESXi host to connect to vSwitch0. Also add network storage for ESXi hosts.

The virtualization operation expression of the distance education platform data center is:

$$K = \left(\frac{1}{\mu}\right)^2 \cdot \sqrt{G\left(\hat{l}^2 - 1\right)} \tag{9}$$

In the formula, $\mu$ represents the connection parameters of the physical network card in the data center, and $\hat{l}$ represents the virtualization fault tolerance vector of the data center.

Using formula (9), the data center configuration expression is derived as:

$$M = \vartheta \cdot \sqrt{K \times \frac{\left|\sum_{-\infty}^{+\infty} \xi \times \dot{X}\right|}{\sum_{c=1} V_c + V_0}} \tag{10}$$

In the formula, $\vartheta$ represents the real-time response permissions of the data center for vocational and mental health courses on the remote education platform, $\xi$ represents the remote education resource exchange parameters of the data center, $\dot{X}$ represents the real-time transmission characteristics of the remote education resources in the platform system data center, $c$ represents the calibration parameters of the education resources, $V_c$ represents the remote education resource storage vector based on parameter $c$, and $V_0$ represents the initial value of the remote education resource storage vector.

Using formula (10), the operation expression of the distance education platform for secondary vocational mental health courses based on cloud computing is derived as follows:

$$B = \frac{\omega \cdot M}{\hat{b}} \tag{11}$$

In the formula, $\omega$ represents the service parameters of the distance education platform, $\hat{b}$ represents the real-time service characteristics of distance education resources for mental health courses in secondary vocational schools.

So far, the creation and the most basic configuration of the data center have been completed, and virtual machines can be created in the data center to provide the most basic services for the remote education platform. After the basic configuration is completed, the advanced configuration of the data center can be carried out to realize the advanced features of vMotion, DRS (Distributed Resource Scheduler), HA (High Availability) and FT (Fault Tolerance).

## 4 Example Analysis

In order to verify the practical value of the distance education platform for secondary vocational mental health courses based on cloud computing, the distance education platform based on virtualization, and the distance education platform based on mobile embedded terminal technology, the following comparative experiments are designed.

### 4.1 Principle and Steps

In order to fully verify the practicability of the proposed platform, the instantaneous response rate of the remote client terminal is selected as the platform performance index for the following reasons: First, user experience is a key consideration, especially for remote access and interaction scenarios. The instantaneous response rate of remote client terminal can accurately measure the response speed of the system, so as to evaluate the performance of the platform. Secondly, the instantaneous response rate provides a real-time indicator, which can observe the performance of the system under high concurrent load in time, help to detect potential problems early and take corresponding optimization measures. In addition, it has the accuracy to directly measure the response time of user requests after they reach the system, providing a reliable measure to evaluate the system's ability to handle them in real time under different loads. At the same time, the remote client terminal instantaneous response rate is an intuitive indicator that can be widely understood and applied to various roles such as system administrators, developers, and decision makers to evaluate the performance of the platform and provide a basis for performance optimization and improvement. To sum up, choosing remote client terminal instantaneous response rate as platform performance index can comprehensively evaluate system response speed, timely find performance problems, and provide reliable data support for decision-making and performance optimization. For the education platform system, without considering other interference conditions, the faster the instantaneous response speed of the remote client terminal, the stronger the response ability of the terminal system, which is more in line with the practical application needs of strengthening the construction of secondary vocational mental health curriculum.

The specific implementation process of this experiment is as follows.

- Use the equipment elements shown in Table 1 to build the distance education environment required for the experiment.
- Input the executive program of the remote education platform for secondary vocational mental health courses based on cloud computing into the platform host, record the numerical changes of the instantaneous response rate of remote client terminals under the effect of the system, and the results are experimental group variables.

**Table 1.** Distance Education Environment

| Project | Experimental equipment | Instrument model |
|---|---|---|
| 1 | Distance education terminal | STM32F103VCT6 |
| 2 | Cloud storage server | Stc89c52RC kit |
| 3 | Teaching resource processor | STM32F407ZGT6 Development Board |
| 4 | Data sharing chip | PYNQ Linux 7010 chip |
| 5 | Terminal server | Kintex-7 FPGA |
| 6 | Data Register | EPM240 CPLD |

- Input the executive program of the virtualization based distance education platform into the platform host, record the numerical change of the instantaneous response rate of the remote client terminal under the effect of the system, and the results are the first control group variables.
- Input the remote education platform executive program based on mobile embedded terminal technology into the platform host, record the numerical changes of the instantaneous response rate of remote client terminals under the effect of the system, and the results are the second control group variables.
- According to the variable data obtained, the experimental rules are summarized.

### 4.2 Data Processing

The following figure reflects the specific numerical changes of the instantaneous response rate of remote client terminals in the experimental group, the first control group and the second control group.

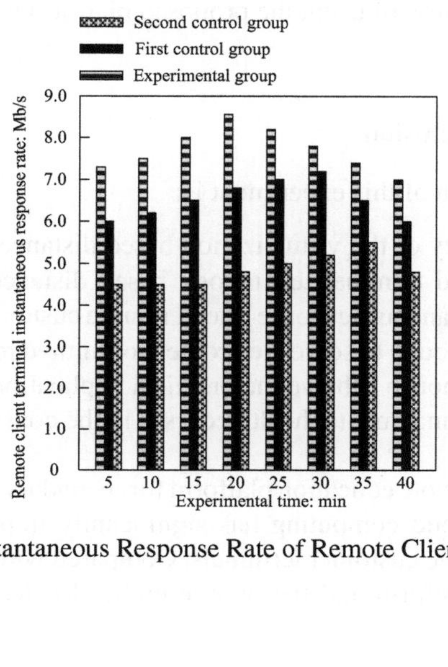


**Fig. 5.** Instantaneous Response Rate of Remote Client Terminal

Further analysis of the experimental data in Fig. 5 shows that, with the passage of time, the instantaneous response rate of the remote client in the experimental group shows a trend of first increasing and then decreasing. In the previous experimental stage, with the increase of the number of concurrent requests, the instantaneous response rate of the experimental group increased rapidly, reaching the highest value of 8.6 Mb/s. However, the instantaneous response rate of the experimental group began to gradually decline, indicating that the processing capacity of the system under high load conditions is still limited.

Compared with the experimental group, the change trend of instantaneous response rate of remote client terminal in the first control group was basically the same. At 30 min into the experiment, the instantaneous response rate of the first control group reached a peak of 7.2 Mb/s, which was slightly lower than the highest value of the experimental group. This may be because the first control group used a similar architecture and resource allocation, but the experimental group was better able to cope with high concurrency due to the elastic and scalable nature of the cloud platform.

The instantaneous response rate of the remote client in the second control group increased gradually after stabilizing in the early stage, and tended to decrease in the late stage. Compared with the experimental group and the first control group, the instantaneous response rate of the second control group was significantly lower, and only reached the highest value of 5.5 Mb/s at 35 min of the experiment. This may be because the second control group did not adopt the elastic and scalable characteristics of the cloud platform to effectively cope with high concurrent stress.

In summary, through further analysis of Fig. 5, it can be concluded that the experimental group showed better response ability and the highest instantaneous response rate in the high-concurrency scenario. The first control group, as the baseline group, performed relatively well and was close to the experimental group. The instantaneous response rate of the second control group was significantly lower because the elastic and scalable characteristics of the cloud platform were not adopted. This further validates the advantages and effectiveness of using the proposed platform to solve high concurrency problems.

## 4.3 Experimental Conclusion

To sum up, the conclusion of this experiment is:

(1) The application ability of the virtualization based distance education platform and the mobile embedded terminal technology based distance education platform in improving the instantaneous response rate of remote customer terminals is relatively weak, which is not enough to solve the problem of limited response ability of remote customer terminals, nor to achieve the practical application needs of strengthening the secondary vocational mental health courses in the construction of the education platform system.

(2) The application of remote education platform for secondary vocational mental health courses based on cloud computing has significantly improved the instantaneous response rate of remote customer terminals. Compared with the virtualization based remote education platform and the mobile embedded terminal technology based

remote education platform, it can better solve the problem of limited response capacity of remote customer terminals, so as to realize the construction of the secondary vocational mental health curriculum in the education platform system.

## 5 Conclusion

Aiming at the problem of poor response ability of the distance education platform of mental health course in secondary vocational schools, a cloud-based distance education platform of mental health course in secondary vocational schools is proposed and designed. This paper establishes the hierarchical structure system of the education platform by analyzing the platform requirements, optimizes the docking mode of typical functional modules, then completes the construction of OpenStack cloud environment based on the cloud computing service model, and finally completes the design of the distance education platform by configuring the data center system based on relevant course information. The experimental results show that the client instantaneous response rate of the proposed platform reaches 8.6 Mb/s at the 20th min, which is better than the comparison method. Thus, it can be shown that the distance education platform of the secondary vocational mental health course can give full play to the characteristics of cloud computing technology, provide distance learning services and resource storage services by using the powerful computing power of cloud computing technology, organize distributed infrastructure resources in the network by using virtualization technology, form a unified resource pool, and automatically manage these resources by software. Providing IaaS services externally can effectively solve the problem of high concurrency on traditional platforms, improve the instantaneous response ability of clients, and achieve better application results.

## References

1. Gogireddy, N.R., Singamsetty, P.K.: RWWO: an effective strategy for workflow scheduling in cloud computing with predicted energy using Deep Maxout Network. Energy Harvesting Syst. **8**(2), 87–102 (2021)
2. Alsharari, N.M.: Cloud computing and ERP assimilation in the public sector: institutional perspectives. Transforming Gov. People Process Policy **16**(1), 97–109 (2022)
3. Alkhabra, S.A.: An exploration of applicability of social constructivism approach in distance learning amid the COVID-19 pandemic; the case study of Hail University (UOH). Int. J. Inf. Learn. Technol. **39**(3), 282–304 (2022)
4. Boursinos, D., Koutsoukos, X.: Assurance monitoring of learning-enabled cyber-physical systems using inductive conformal prediction based on distance learning. Artif. Intell. Eng. Des. Anal. Manuf.. Intell. Eng. Des. Anal. Manuf. **35**(2), 251–264 (2021)
5. Weidlich, J., Kreijns, K., Bastiaens, T.J.: Individual differences in perceptions of social presence: exploring the role of personality in online distance learning. Open Educ. Stud. **3**(1), 188–201 (2021)
6. Lomakovych, V.: Boosting students' motivation in the process of studying practical course of the German language during distance learning. The Scientific Issues of Ternopil Volodymyr Hnatiuk National Pedagogical University Series pedagogy **1**(2), 113–120 (2022)
7. Levina, V., Zubanova, S., Ivanov, A.: Axiological linguistics and teaching of Russian as a foreign language in the context of distance learning against the backdrop of the pandemic. XLinguae **14**(1), 212–227 (2021)

8. Vlassopoulos, G., Karikas, G.A., Papageorgiou, E., et al.: Assessment of Greek high school students towards distance learning, during the first wave of COVID-19 pandemic. Creat. Educ.. Educ. **12**(4), 934–949 (2021)
9. Maleko, E.V., Kiva-Khamzina, Y.L., Rubanova, N.A., et al.: Peculiarities of distance learning in higher education: the teacher's functions as a chat communication organizer. Cypriot J. Educ. Sci. **16**(1), 341–357 (2021)
10. Lu, S., Hou, G.: Research on cloud computing resource prediction based on Big Data analysis technology. Comput. Simul. **39**(10), 502–505+537 (2022)

# Research on Multimedia Distance Education Resource Management System Based on Knowledge Graph

Jie Gao and Lini Wu(✉)

Department of Building Management, Chongqing College of Architecture and Technology, Chongqing 400030, China

694010668@qq.com

**Abstract.** With the rapid development of information technology, multimedia distance education plays an increasingly important role in modern education. In order to solve the problems existing in the existing teaching resource management system, a multimedia distance education resource management system based on knowledge mapping is proposed. The hardware configuration of the system is improved based on at 45db80 chip. In order to ensure the operation of the hardware configuration, the information classification management algorithm of the multimedia distance education resource management system is optimized combined with the knowledge map algorithm, and the information classification algorithm and information management process are improved according to the knowledge map algorithm, so as to realize the design of the multimedia distance education resource management system. Finally, the experiment proves that the multimedia distance education resource management system based on knowledge map is more effective than the traditional management system, and the detection results can reach more than 90%, which fully meets the research requirements.

**Keywords:** Knowledge Map · Multimedia Distance Education · Educational Resources · Resource Management System

## 1 Introduction

With the rapid development of information technology, multimedia remote education plays an increasingly important role in modern education. Multimedia remote education resources include teaching materials in the form of videos, audio, teaching documents, etc., which are transmitted to students through networks and other communication technologies, enabling them to receive high-quality educational resources at any time and place. However, with the increasing number and diversification of distance education resources, effective management and organization of these resources have become increasingly complex.

The research on multimedia remote education resource management system has important practical significance and application prospects. Firstly, effective resource


G. Gui et al. (Eds.): eLEOT 2023, LNICST 543, pp. 111–125, 2024.
https://doi.org/10.1007/978-3-031-51465-4_8

management can improve the efficiency of educational resource utilization and the sharing of high-quality educational resources. By establishing a comprehensive management system, educational institutions can better organize and manage various types of teaching resources, ensure timely updates, integration, and sharing of resources, and thereby improve teaching quality and effectiveness. Secondly, the multimedia remote education resource management system helps to meet the needs of personalized learning. Different students have different Learning styles and rhythms. Through a flexible management system, students can choose appropriate teaching resources according to their own needs to achieve the goal of personalized learning. In addition, the multimedia remote education resource management system also helps to promote the development of educational informatization. With the popularization and application of information technology, utilizing multimedia remote education resources for teaching has become a trend. An efficient resource management system can provide better technical support and services, promoting the further development of educational informatization.

Reference [1] proposed a teaching resource management system based on Big data analysis. The system structure includes application presentation layer, service middle layer, Cloud storage layer and acquisition layer. The teaching resources are collected through the teaching resources collection module and stored in the Cloud storage module. After the division of teaching resources, they are input into the distributed file system HDFS for management. Reference [2] proposed a teaching resource management system based on the recommendation of Collaborative filtering. The system hardware uses embedded framework technology, uses SN74LVC8T245 logic master as the hardware central processing core, and carries out multi-dimensional feature matching processing on resource data through embedded communication protocol. The software design adopts the collaborative filtering mechanism. According to the multi-dimensional feature processing results of the hardware on the recommended terms, collaborative filtering is carried out on the term association information, so as to obtain the resource data with the strongest correlation with the key words, and complete the resource management.

In order to improve the performance of distance education resource management, a multimedia distance education resource management system based on Knowledge graph is proposed. The overall research approach of this article system is as follows:

(1) In order to ensure the implementation of system management functions and the overall stability of operation, the hardware of the system is designed with the AT45DB80 chip as the core.
(2) The Knowledge graph is used to optimize the information classification management algorithm of the multimedia distance education resource management system.
(3) According to the Knowledge graph algorithm, improve the information classification algorithm and information management process, and realize the design of multimedia distance education resource management system.

## 2 System Hardware Configuration

The overall functional design structure of the system refers to the composition of the whole system, as well as the physical and logical relationship between various parts and elements of the system. The main task of the overall structure design is to define each functional module. The system combines the Windows XP operating system and later versions or the Mac OS X 10 operating system and later versions. System requirements for running Maya 2013 (64 bit); Windows: 7 SP1 operating system or XP x64 SP2 operating system; Mac OS X 10.7. x operating system; Red Hat Enterprise Linux 6.0 WS operating system. Windows and Linux Intel Pentium with AMD Athlon processor (or later) supported by SSE3 instruction set. Macintosh: Macintosh computer with Intel 64 bit processor. Certified hardware accelerated OpenGL graphics card. Microsoft Internet Explorer 8 Internet browser or later, Apple Safari web browser, or Mozilla Firefox web browser. Correctly handle the internal relations of the modules, as well as the call relations and data relations between them, define the internal structure of each module, and display the hardware configuration of the distance learning resource management system, as follows (Fig. 1):

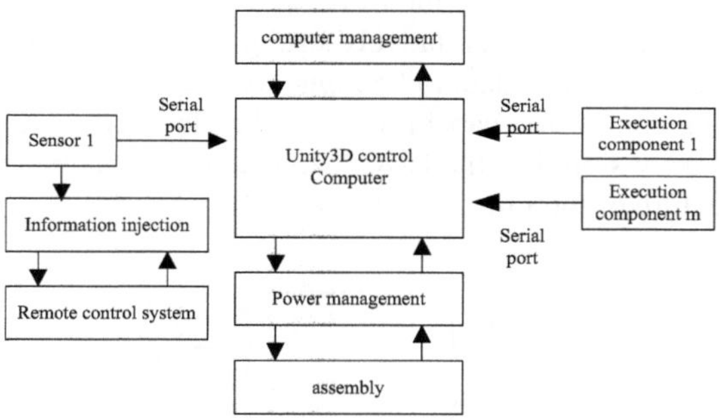


**Fig. 1.** Hardware Configuration of Remote Teaching Resource Management System

In the hardware configuration of the remote teaching resource management system, the system requirements for running Unity3D 3.5.5: Windows: XP SP2 or later; Mac OS X: Intel CPU & "Leopard" 10.5 or later. Core dual core Intel Core Duo processor or higher end model. 1GB memory and above. NVIDIA GeFore GTX_560 graphics card and higher or ATI Radeon HD_58_50 graphics card and higher configuration (desktop computer); NVIDIA GeFore GTX460 graphics card and higher configuration or AMD Radeon HD 7730M and higher configuration (notebook).

The peripheral circuit of the network chip can be connected with the external input power supply of the remote communication management system. While fully coordinating the ratio of voltage and current, the scattered electronic flow can be integrated into a bundle transmission form. Under the condition that the electronic input is maintained continuously, the GND network chip will spontaneously change from the disconnected state to the connected state, and feedback the stored electronic parameters to the lower level execution structure of the system in combination with the three types of resistance equipment components C, R, and M. The actual access resistance of type C resistance equipment is relatively high, which can occupy a large number of transmission voltage parameters in the case of high-level transmission. Then, according to the real value matching relationship between type R resistance equipment and type M resistance equipment, the subsequent electricity voltage division coordination is carried out. The

L capacitor is located in the middle of the peripheral circuit of the network chip, which serves as a link between the preceding and the following. It can properly dredge the accumulated electrons while transferring the transmission current.

The multimedia distance education resource module uses ENC28J60 components as the core to build the equipment, and the left and right ends are simultaneously equipped with equal communication transmission interfaces. The left interface is connected to the input end of the network communication data, and the right interface is connected to the output end of the network communication data [3]. In the cloud computing network environment, as the total amount of communication data to be transmitted changes, the occupation status of the input interface will gradually change. Generally, when the total amount of data to be input does not exceed 7.5×At 1015T, only the first 10 input ports can reach full occupancy status; When the total amount of data to be input reaches 9.3× At 1015T, all input interfaces can meet the rated transmission standard, but the last four interfaces can only maintain the intermittent input state. Compared with the input interface, the output interface has a relatively strong transmission and connection capability. When the total amount of data to be input keeps rising, these physical interfaces always have a strong connection capability until the cloud computing communication information temporarily stored in the ENC28J60 element is completely transferred to the application structure of the lower system (Fig. 2).

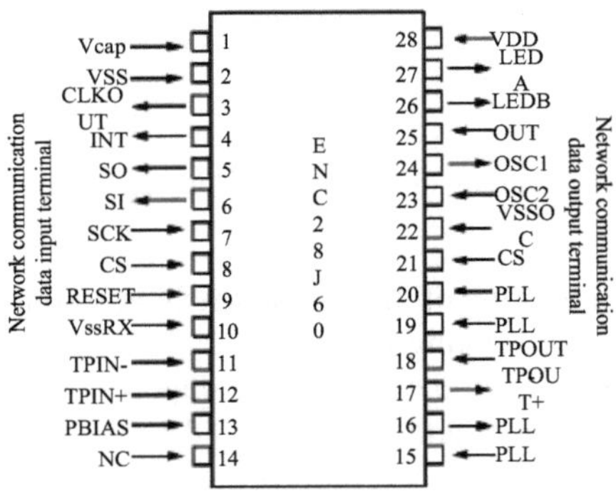


**Fig. 2.** Structure diagram of multimedia distance education resource module

Based on the above hardware structure, further optimize the system sensor interface circuit, separate the data plane and control plane forwarded by the bottom traffic switch and bottom router, and improve the traditional vertical integration state; Then the network switch is used as the device for traffic forwarding between the bottom traffic switch and the bottom router; Finally, the controller is used to control and manage the logically centralized devices, simplify the allocation strategy, and achieve reasonable allocation of shared ip resources.

# 3 Optimization of Basic Information Management Functions of Distance Education Resources

The statistical resource module is mainly used to make statistics on the actual utilization rate of different mathematical education resources. The module functions include the indicator setting statistics function, the result analysis and processing function, and the data report function.

The statistical resource module is mainly used to make statistics on the actual utilization rate of different Mathematics education resources. The module functions include the indicator setting statistics function, the result analysis and processing function, and the data report function. The specific functions of the resource management module include resource storage, maintenance of the resource library, review of resources, definition of resource permissions, and management of resource classification systems. The resource warehousing function specifically includes uploading individual resources and batch importing. Uploading a single resource refers to the user using a browser to upload a single resource in the user resource library [4]. Batch import refers to the user resource library implementing inbound processing of resource packages through this function. Defining resource permissions in the resource library includes defining the permissions of resources, administrators, and users.

In the design process of path identification in traditional systems, it is affected by the pop-up of the previous identification path, making it impossible for the new identification path to be represented by a single identifier for a route. Under the Knowledge graph, a route is represented by an identifier. Traffic will not be replaced or lost during the exchange process, and can all flow into the backbone for identification processing. Once leaving the backbone network, the pop-up logo reduces the mobility of the underlying traffic switch, thereby reducing the number of tasks executed by the switch and avoiding the occurrence of traffic packet forwarding delay. The resource identification format adopts the MPLS multi-protocol identification exchange header format, as shown in Fig. 3.

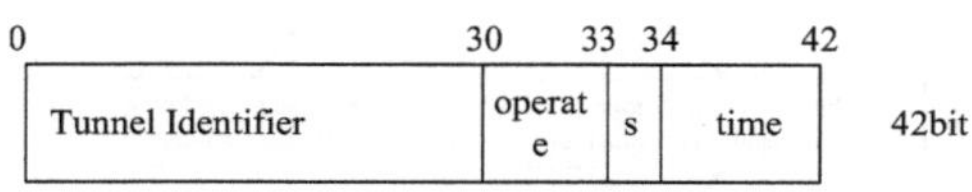


**Fig. 3.** Resource ID Format

The resource ID format shown in Fig. 3 shows that this format represents at least 500,000 tunnel ids, which can be used as the alternative path for all devices on the ip resource backbone network. Since the underlying traffic switch supports multi-protocol identity exchange header format forwarding, to solve the problem of excessive exchange information in the above contents, the classification management method of multimedia distance education resources is adopted to solve the problem of excessive information in the information controller and traffic switch of the whole network table entries, and the non-overlapping table entries in the knowledge graph are used for acute specific aggregation processing of each table entry. The network congestion problem is avoided by adjusting the convergence density.

The function of management resource classification system is mainly used to classify mathematical education resources according to metadata and manage the classification system. The function of setting statistics for classified indicators is mainly used by administrators to set statistical parameters, so as to make statistics on different types of mathematical education resources [5]. The result analysis and processing function mainly displays the statistical results in the form of data and charts. The data report function is mainly used to summarize and sort out the statistical data of educational resources in various time periods and make tables. The specific functions are as follows:

(1) Count resource visits and publish the ranking list of visited resources.
(2) Implement resource statistics according to resource categories.
(3) Make statistics on resource distribution according to media format.
(4) Statistics of mathematical education resources downloaded, uploaded and browsed by users.
(5) The statistics of mathematics education resources downloaded, uploaded and browsed by time.
(6) Mathematics education resources download, upload, browse ranking.
(7) Upload company rankings.

The collection of teaching management resource information includes two key links: link information collection and node information collection. Link information collection is a process of in-depth integration of teaching management resources. On the premise of removing redundant scheduling instructions, teaching management resource information will be rapidly transmitted in the scheduling link. Selective retention of some resource data with low correlation [6]. The collection process of teaching management resource information is shown in Fig. 4.

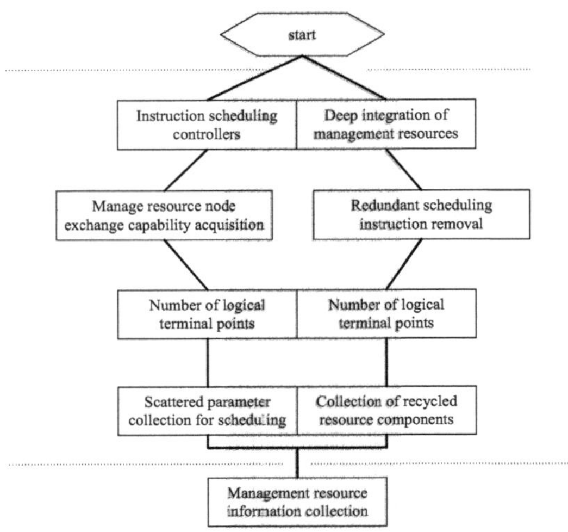


**Fig. 4.** Flow chart of information collection of teaching management resources

The resource management module mainly realizes the purpose of managing mathematics education resources by constructing and managing the resource base. The resource base constructed by resource management module includes platform resource base and user resource base. The platform resource library is mainly maintained, constructed, and managed by the administrator. The user resource library is managed by the user himself, including the resources uploaded by the user himself, which are not collected by the platform resource library and audited. The resources in the user repository that are collected and audited by the platform repository are managed by the user only after the user has collected them. On the basis of the known time series of teaching management resources to be controlled, the parameter conditions such as the membership function and fuzzy rule of knowledge graph will not change, and the fuzzy control coefficient between adjacent resource data becomes the only variable that affects the definition result of optimization parameters.

## 4 Optimization of Classified Management Function of Multimedia Education Resources

In combination with the dynamic network scenario of the knowledge map, all teaching management resources can be divided into multiple components according to the available spectrum occupancy rate. When the scheduling request disappears, the SDON architecture will fully release the original spectrum resources, thereby changing the initial location of teaching management resource data and completing a dynamic scheduling migration operation. Throughout the entire migration operation, the spectrum rate occupied by teaching management resources is always kept at $k$, and the upper limit of virtual resource migration is never exceeded $d$. Based on this, the dynamic scheduling and migration standard calculation process of teaching management resources can be expressed as:

$$G = \prod \theta - 1 \prod_{l=1}^{d} z\varepsilon^{-\frac{1}{2}} \sqrt{d}(k + s)^{\varepsilon} \tag{1}$$

Among them, $G$ represents the dynamic scheduling and transfer standard for teaching management resources, $s$ represents the minimum value condition for virtual resource transfer, $z$ represents the occupancy cycle frequency of the SDON architecture, and $\vartheta$ and $\varepsilon$ represent two different dynamic transfer coefficients, respectively. All parameter conditions related to teaching management resources are put into the formula, and then the new scheduling algorithm can run smoothly according to the above operation process. According to the multiprotocol ID exchange header format, we designed the classified management of teaching resource scheduling paths, and the results are shown in Table 1.

According to the classified management scheme of multimedia distance education resources, the task of resource classification is realized under the knowledge map. Therefore, the classified management of multimedia distance education resources is also analyzed from three aspects: network sharing structure, control platform and infrastructure. The bottom layer traffic exchange protocol interacts with the network device to realize no idle connection of the bottom layer network device. The periodic receiving behavior is used to obtain the link table item information, and the table item rules are distributed to the underlying infrastructure through the control platform. After the traffic converges,

**Table 1.** Classified Management of Multimedia Distance Education Resources

| Network sharing structure | Task scheduling database | | |
|---|---|---|---|
| | Identity management | Table Item Adjustment | Classification and Management of Multimedia Distance Education Resources |
| control platform | Topology information discovery | information acquisition | Table Item Distribution Rules |
| Underlying infrastructure | Network devices support traffic exchange protocols | | |
| | Backbone network entrance 1 | Backbone network entrance 2 | Backbone network entrance 3 |

the control platform can submit the traffic to the network structure for resource sharing [7] through an external interface. The knowledge map can be used to complete the separation of traffic forwarding and control plane from forwarding plane. On the implementation layer, the multimedia distance education resource classification management function can be used to avoid the impact of scheduling on the underlying traffic forwarding and maintain high forwarding efficiency. From the physical point of view, the design concept of overlay network structure is adopted to analyze the remote transmission of teaching resources, as shown in Fig. 5.

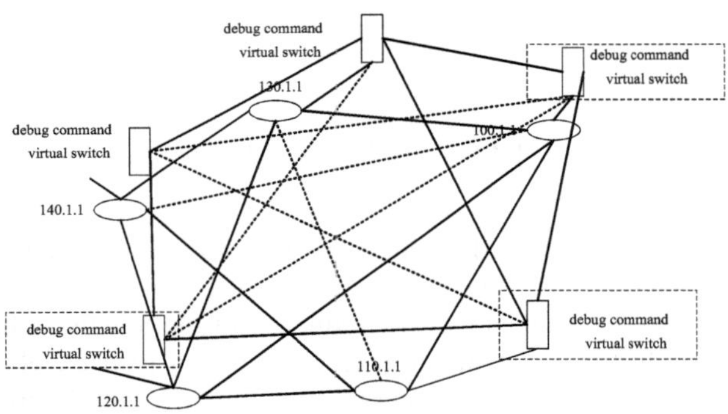


**Fig. 5.** Classification management of resources in physical state

The IP resource management and allocation scheme designed from the physical point of view needs to install a server at the traffic switch, and use the APP traffic detection software to schedule the traffic. The software can sense the network transmission quality, and feedback it to the control platform in real time for the controller in the platform to calculate, thus completing the distribution of the traffic switch table items. Use APP detection software to summarize the classified management results of multimedia distance education resources, and analyze the remote transmission of teaching resources, so as to provide a basis for the design of IP resource management and allocation scheme in a logical state [8]. The information processing algorithm is optimized by combining the information processing flow of multimedia distance education resource management. If the information set of the multimedia remote education resource management system is $H$, the information set can be divided into $F$ layers, with a common feature of $A$ and an abnormal feature of $B$, then any information feature of the dataset will be collected:

$$W^k = \begin{cases} G - H_A^k(Ea, Eb) \\ G + F_B^k(Ea, Eb) \end{cases} \tag{2}$$

In the above formula, $E$ represents the level of information feature resolution during system operation; $E$ represents the data fusion value. Further combining cloud computing and Euler algorithm to calculate the relationship value between the dependent variable $Ay(x_n)$ of the information management program and the independent variable $Bx(y_n)$ of the teaching program, the specific algorithm is as follows:

$$Q \approx \prod\prod \frac{Ay(x_n) - Bx(y_n)}{W^k - G} - 1 \tag{3}$$

On the premise that the total amount of teaching management resource data can meet the control demand, the deterministic and non deterministic relations are planned and integrated. When using the mathematics education resource management platform, users can put the resources they want to collect in their own favorites at any time for future use. At the same time, users can also add the resources in the favorites directly to the related resources to build hyperlinks and network knowledge bases of related knowledge. According to the generation mode of cloud concept, the knowledge map can be divided into two parts: forward generation and reverse generation. Among them, the knowledge map of forward generation can establish a standard normal cloud structure according to the distribution characteristics of resource data to be scheduled. The knowledge map of reverse generation uses the mapping relationship between resource data to be scheduled to build a new cloud drop unit. Let $|x|$, $x'$ and $\overline{x}$ represent the expectation, entropy and super entropy values of the Knowledge graph respectively, and use the above variable values to express the forward and reverse occurrence characteristics of the Knowledge graph as follows:

$$\widehat{z} = \prod B - Ay(x_n)^{\frac{\alpha(\overline{x}-x')^2}{2(\overline{x}-x')^2}} \tag{4}$$

$$\breve{z} = \bigcap A + Bx(y_n)^{m - \frac{y(|y|)^2}{2(|y|)^2}} \tag{5}$$

Among them, $\widehat{z}$ represents the positive occurrence characteristics of the Knowledge graph, $\breve{z}$ represents the reverse occurrence characteristics of the Knowledge graph, $y$ representing a random resource data to be scheduled, $m$ represents another random resource data to be scheduled, but $b \neq m$, $\alpha$ represents the standard scheduling coefficient of the normal cloud, if $\chi$ represents the basic operational parameters of the cloud drop unit. Construct a complete time series of teaching management resources. Let $U_{\max}$ represent the upper limit value of teaching management resource data, and $U_{\min}$ represent the lower limit value of teaching management resource data. The joint formula (4) can express the deterministic and non deterministic relationship between the controlled management resources as follows:

$$\widehat{q} = \chi \int_{U_{\min}}^{U_{\max}} \frac{\lambda_i(w_1 - w_2) + Ay(x_n)^{\frac{\alpha(\overline{x}-x')^2}{2(\overline{x}-x')^2}}}{\widehat{z}U_{\max}} \tag{6}$$

$$\breve{q} = \chi \sum_{U_{\min}}^{U_{\max}} \breve{z}U_{\min}\lambda_u - Bx(y_n)m - \frac{y(|y|)^2}{2(|y|)^2}/2(w_1 + w_2) \tag{7}$$

Where, $\widehat{q}$ and $\breve{q}$ respectively represent the deterministic and non deterministic relationship between the management resources to be controlled, $\theta_i$ and $\theta_u$ respectively represent two different variable definition standards, $i$ and $u$ respectively represent the data value results of teaching management resources when the standard is obtained, and $w_1$ and $w_2$ represent two different scheduling time nodes. $y(w)$ is artificially defined as the time series of teaching management resources to be controlled, $\beta$ represents the average value of two different scheduling time nodes, and the simultaneous formula (2) can express $y(w)$ as:

$$y(w) = \prod\prod 1 + (\widehat{q} + \breve{q})^{3\beta} - \frac{0.33e\varpi}{Q(\beta - G) - \widehat{z} + \breve{z}} \tag{8}$$

In the above formula, $\varpi$ represents the scheduling coefficient after normalization, $e$ represents the time quantitative factor of teaching management resources, and $\beta$ represents the establishment condition of sequence cycle. For the standard teaching management resource data set, the adjacent two data always maintain the same scheduling frequency, but because the storage space occupied by the data itself is different, the fluctuation peak and valley values in each frequency cycle are also different [9]. In order to better determine the control and optimization parameters of teaching management resources, $\lambda$ is defined to represent the scheduling frequency coefficient between adjacent resource data, $\overline{\varpi}$ represents the average value of the fluctuation peak value in the frequency period, and $\overline{\kappa}$ represents the average value of the fluctuation valley value in the frequency period. Using the above variables, the calculation results of the control and optimization parameters of teaching management resources can be expressed as:

$$N = \int_{\overline{\kappa}}^{\overline{\varpi}} [\lambda y(w) + \prod 1 - at \sum y(w) + \ln r]dr \tag{9}$$

Where $a$ represents the attribute function parameter of the knowledge map, $t$ represents the fuzzy scheduling rule, and $\ln r$ represents the logarithm of the maximum scheduling operator $r$ based on the natural number. Integrating all the above theoretical basis, the optimization control processing of teaching management resources based on knowledge map is completed.

Let $\alpha_0$ represent the minimum recommended quantity index of University Online Learning Resources Based on multiple intelligent algorithms, $\overline{y}$ represent the average access quantity of University Online Learning users in unit time, $\beta_1$ and $\beta_2$ represent two different search conditions of learning resources, $p_1$ and $p_2$ represent two different storage vectors of learning resources, and $W_1$ represent the application storage conditions of online learning resources in the first level host, $W_n$ indicates the application storage conditions of online learning resources on the host at the $n$ th layer. Then:

$$H_a(E) = \prod 1 - \frac{N(\alpha_0 - 1)^2\{\beta_1 - \beta_2\}}{\bar{y}} \sum_{i=1}^{m} \ln \bar{y}[p_1 W_1 - p_2 W_n] \tag{10}$$

The evaluation results are graded, converted based on the measured values of the test system, and marked with 0–100 numerical grades respectively. The benchmark image of each test system and the score of the tested system are sorted out. The consistency of the scores shall be tested. The teaching contents in different stages and the different testing contents and teaching cycles in the same testing stage shall be evaluated respectively. The two groups of scoring values shall be compared and checked. If the difference between the scoring values is more than 20 points, it shall be regarded as the system testing results and be discarded. If the effective scoring times given in the same testing stage are less than 85% of the total scoring times. Cancel all the scores, and finally calculate the average score, standard deviation and 95% confidence interval [10] of the two states of each test image. Based on the above algorithm, the B/S model is applied to the client information management scheme to standardize the running steps of the online management system software of colleges and universities, as follows:

1. Input the teaching plan of colleges and universities. Teachers of courses generally input the teaching plan of the next semester at the end of the semester in class.
2. To modify a college teaching plan, if the administrator or user finds that there is an error in the teaching information that has been entered, or wants to modify the plan, he can apply to the superior for approval, and then the relevant staff or the teacher in the classroom will re authorize the teacher to complete the second correct information entry.
3. For the statistical query of information, all users of the system have their own statistical functions and query permissions. The query methods include individual query and combined structure query.
4. The purpose of entering and exporting teaching plans and storing backups is to ensure that information is not leaked, so the system will automatically check the existing data regularly, and automatically start the backup if there is a risk of data loss. Ordinary users have no permission to back up, only the system administrator has.

Based on the above steps, we can standardize and classify the massive educational information, so as to effectively meet the research requirements of multimedia distance education resource management.

## 5 System Test

In order to verify the operation effect of multimedia distance education resource management system based on knowledge map, the operation effect of traditional online management system is compared.

In order to ensure the rationality and effectiveness of the experimental detection effect, the experimental environment and parameters are standardized.

The experimental environment selects Intel Pentium I V166MXGHz configuration, SVGA graphics card, memory of at least 168 MB, and storage space of more than 80 GB. Windows NT Information Server 4.2 and Windows 2000/xp, TCP/IP version network protocol are selected for the Web server operating system. Database: Microsoft SQL Server 2000. The browser is Internet Explore 5.2.buildSDN experimental platform of Floodlight+Mininet. The virtual switch of model 2.4.0 is used inside, which can realize the bottom switching equipment, and support path identification and table item release functions. Floodlight runs on a separate virtual switch and provides a control platform for the knowledge map. It is mainly responsible for monitoring the network link load and dynamically adjusting the table entries; Mininet is used to design the network topology and support information interaction between the network structure and the control platform on Floodlight. The protocol data packet is transmitted to the host through the programming language script language, and the traffic is poured into the backbone network. The following table reflects the details of the experimental parameter settings of the model machine in the experimental group and the control group under the same experimental environment (Table 2).

**Table 2.** Experimental Parameter Setting Table

| Parameter | experimental group | control group |
|---|---|---|
| EMT /(min) | 60 | 60 |
| CEC | 0.52 | 0.52 |
| IMD /(%) | 64.17 | 64.17 |
| IPQ | 0.63 | 0.63 |
| IDD /(T) | 71.24 | 71.24 |

In the above table, the EMT parameter represents the experimental time, the CEC parameter represents the implementation coefficient of the knowledge map, the IMD parameter represents the ideal extreme value of the matching difference, the IPQ parameter represents the ideal dispatching authority amount, and the IDD parameter represents the ideal extreme value of the fragmentation degree. To ensure that the experimental results have strong persuasiveness, the experimental parameters of the experimental group and the control group are always consistent.

In the above experimental environment, the operation stability of the traditional system and the system in this paper is recorded. For the convenience of recording, the operation and detection results of the online management system of higher education in this system are recorded as A, and the detection results of the traditional comparison system are recorded as B. The specific experimental results are shown in the following figure (Fig. 6):

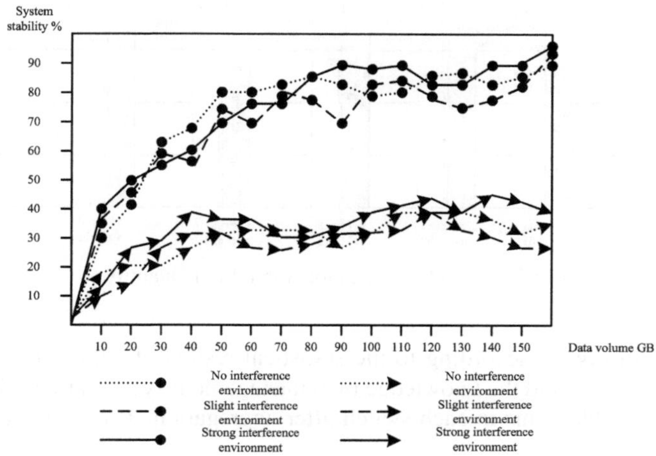


**Fig. 6.** Analysis of Experimental Results

Based on the above monitoring results, it can be seen that the multimedia remote education resource management system proposed in this paper based on the knowledge map has obvious stability effect in the application process. Because of the traditional system, it further simulates the resource congestion problem in the network, uses 60 services as the experimental object, and concentrates these 60 services between switches 1 and 2. That is, between the subnets 168.11.0.0/9 and 168.12.0.0/9, the two links are congested. The knowledge map is mainly used to represent a route by an identifier. In this process, there will be no replacement or loss, and all of them can flow into the backbone for identification processing; However, in the process of designing path identification in traditional systems, the impact of the pop-up of the previous identification path will make it impossible for the new identification path to realize that one route can be represented by one identification. In order to illustrate that the method of knowledge mapping is more effective than the traditional system for rational allocation of IP resources, it is necessary to compare the two methods, collect and report the current network information of the path, and uniformly schedule the path to the background router through the path quality detection service for path selection, so as to control the classified management of multimedia distance education resources; However, the traditional system directly schedules the traffic, which is easy to cause traffic packet delay, jitter, packet loss and other problems in the link. In order to illustrate that the knowledge mapping method is more effective than the traditional system for ip resource management and allocation, it is necessary to compare the two methods.

Select 5 virtual switches, and the table entries generated are random. Analyze the table entries of the converged virtual switches by counting the number of table entries. The actual number of aggregation table items is shown in Fig. 7.

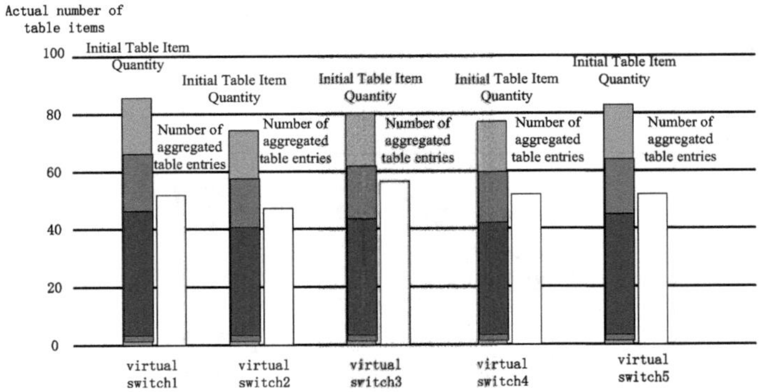


**Fig. 7.** Actual Aggregation Table Item Quantity

As shown in Fig. 7, according to the statistical results of aggregated table items, the traditional system and the knowledge map management system are used to compare and analyze the table items in each switch after aggregation. The results are shown in Table 3.

**Table 3.** Table Items of Switches with Different Methods

| Number | IP Range | Traditional system management scope | Knowledge Graph Management System Management Scope |
|---|---|---|---|
| 1 | 168.11.0.0/9—168.12.0.0/9 | 168.32.0.0/9—168.35.0.0/9 | 168.12.0.0/9 — 168.15.0.0/9 |
| | 168.11.0.0/9 —168.12.0.0/9 | 168.43.0.0/9—168.45.0.0/9 | 168.21.0.0/9 — 168.24.0.0/9 |
| | 168.30.0.0/10 —168.35.0.0/9 | 168.72.0.0/10 —168.78.0.0/9 | 168.35.0.0/10 — 168.42.0.0/9 |
| 2 | 168.48.0.0/9 —168.48.0.0/9 | 168.78.0.0/9 — 168.145.0.0/9 | 168.11.0.0/9 — 168.128.0.0/9 |
| 3 | 168.128.0.0/9 — 168.128.0.0/9 | 168.145.0.0/9 — 168.188.0.0/9 | 168.11.0.0/9 — 168.192.0.0/9 |
| 4 | 168.192.0.0/9—168.192.0.0/9 | 168.188.0.0/9 — 168.193.0.0/9 | 168.11.0.0/9 — 168.187.0.0/9 |
| 5 | 168.187.0.0/9 — 168.187.0.0/9 | 168.193.0.0/9 — 168.199.0.0/9 | 168.11.0.0/9 — 168.193.0.0/9 |

By comparing the IP range after the convergence of the traditional system and the IP range after the convergence of the knowledge map management system in the table, it can be seen that the accuracy of the resource management range can be effectively improved by using the knowledge map management system, which cannot be verified by using the traditional system. By comparing the exchange items in the classification management of multimedia distance education resources between traditional systems and knowledge map management systems, it can be seen that the knowledge map method is more reasonable for resource allocation. In conclusion, it is feasible to use knowledge mapping management system to manage and allocate ip resources.

## 6 Conclusion

Aiming at the security requirements of network teaching information in colleges and universities, a multimedia distance education resource management system based on knowledge map is proposed. The fusion of knowledge map technology has the advantages of low cost and high reliability, which can effectively solve the problem of low monitoring accuracy in traditional management systems. Although the system has good application prospects, the stability of the system needs further investigation.

## References

1. Xu, Y.: Massive teaching video resource management system based on Big Data analysis. J. Shanxi Datong Univ. (Nat. Sci. Edn.) **38**(01), 30–34+44 (2022)
2. Fan, Y., Ying, D.: Design of national defense education resource management system based on collaborative filtering recommendation. Mod. Electron. Tech. **44**(20), 22–26 (2021)
3. Tlili, A., Altinay, F., Huang, R., et al.: Are we there yet? A systematic literature review of Open Educational Resources in Africa: a combined content and bibliometric analysis. PLoS ONE **17**(1), 615–619 (2022)
4. Campbell, S.H., Bernardes, N., Tharmaratnam, T., et al.: Educational resources and curriculum on lactation for health undergraduate students: a scoping review. J. Hum. Lact. **38**(1), 89–99 (2022)
5. Conti, A., Clari, M., Luciani, M., et al.: Exploring the use and usefulness of educational resources among nurses during the first wave of the COVID-19 pandemic: a cross-sectional study. J. Contin. Educ. Nurs. **2**, 53–56 (2022)
6. Warren, J.E.: Open Educational Resources (CLIPP 45): edited by Mary Francis, Chicago, IL: Association of College and Research Libraries, A Division of the American Library Association, 2021. J. Access Serv. **18**(2), 12–16 (2021)
7. Hartley, J.M., Lobatos, S., Daniel, J.L., et al.: Empowering environmental justice decision makers: increasing educational resources for U.S. environmental protection agency's mapping tools. Environ. Justice **5**, 14–19 (2021)
8. Duran, C.G., Ramirez, C.M.: Integration of Open Educational Resources using semantic platform. IEEE Access **36**(9), 164–169 (2021)
9. Nurulpaik, I., Permana, J., Mirfani, A.M., et al.: The influence of educational resources, geographic conditions, demographic conditions, economic conditions, population capacity on junior high school gross participation rate. Jurnal Manajemen dan Supervisi Pendidikan **5**(2), 89–100 (2021)
10. Livenko, A.: Economic and organizational aspects of educational resources in the current conditions of Ukraine. Ekonomika ta Derzhava **3**, 94–97 (2021)

# Push Method of Chinese Online Education Personalized Course Content for Foreign Students

Jiaxiu Han[1(✉)] and Miao Guo[2]

[1] China West Normal University International College, Nanchong 637000, China
13458214202@163.com
[2] Shanghai Civil Aviation College, Shanghai 200232, China

**Abstract.** In order to improve the quality of Chinese online education personalized course content push service, the weighted information entropy is introduced to design and research the content push service of Chinese online education. Based on the interest preference of Chinese online learning of foreign students in colleges and universities in China, complete the construction of personalized portrait of foreign students in colleges and universities in China; extract features from the contents of personalized courses of Chinese online education; calculate the similarity between the contents and images of various courses by using weighted information entropy; and realize the push of the contents of personalized courses of Chinese online education of foreign students in colleges and universities in China by using collaborative filtering algorithm. Through comparative experiments, it is proved that this method can improve the classification and push precision of course content, shorten the execution time and recovery time.

**Keywords:** Information Entropy · College Students Studying in China · Chinese Education · Online Education · Personalization · Online Courses · Content Push

## 1 Introduction

At present, colleges and universities to study in China exist in a variety of circumstances, the need for Chinese language learning to adapt to China's higher education. Specifically, from the perspective of nationality distribution, students are mainly from Thailand, South Africa, Morocco, Bangladesh, Kazakhstan, South Korea and other countries. Students come from non-English-speaking countries and need to be assisted by a second or even a third language. From the source of students, it is divided into academic students and non-academic students, of which non-academic students accounted for the majority. At the language level, some students had taken short-term courses before they came to China, and could understand the basic classroom language and dialogue. At the age level, degree students are exchange students, while non-degree students include college preparatory students and social workers from all over the world. From the point of view of internal needs, the students with academic qualifications are the auxiliary study of


G. Gui et al. (Eds.): eLEOT 2023, LNICST 543, pp. 126–138, 2024.
https://doi.org/10.1007/978-3-031-51465-4_9

the course of this major for the completion of Chinese teaching; the students without academic qualifications are divided into the students with normal communication and exchange in life, and other students can continue to study the professional contents of the selected major only after they have systematically studied Chinese and passed the HSK examination. According to the curriculum arrangement and standards, the students studying in China not only have the knowledge and content of Chinese, but also have the cross-cultural content, such as the advanced study of Chinese culture courses [1]. The following courses are offered according to the types of teaching and students' needs: HSK training course, Chinese comprehension, Chinese reading and writing, Chinese spoken language, Chinese listening and Chinese culture. Many foreign students cannot come to China to study Chinese, they need to study Chinese and take Chinese examinations in advance. Therefore, we need to pay attention to their online learning.

Make use of the information and network platform to integrate the Internet and Chinese international education, make use of the advantages and characteristics of the network, create new opportunities for the development of Chinese international education, make Chinese international education adapt to the new development. With the increasing demand for Chinese language learning all over the world, how to provide effective Chinese language learning resources and Chinese language learning platforms for foreign students in colleges and universities will become an important task for the development of international Chinese language education. The construction of online course content resources is an important basis for promoting the development of Chinese language learning of foreign students in colleges and universities.

The motivation for researching personalized course content push methods for Chinese online education for international students is to meet their personalized learning needs, improve learning effectiveness, increase learning motivation and interest, and provide diverse learning resources. By customizing course content and adjusting it according to students' learning progress and ability level, it can better help international students understand and master Chinese language knowledge. At the same time, various types of textbooks, learning materials, and multimedia resources are provided to enrich students' learning experience. This personalized course content push method can enable international students to actively participate in learning, improve the effectiveness and efficiency of learning. In recent years, a large number of Chinese learning platforms and Chinese learning resources have been emerging, which has brought trouble to the use of Chinese learning resources by college students. Under this background, it is extremely urgent to carry on the push research to the on-line Chinese teaching curriculum. A scholar [4] has proposed a trust awareness recommendation approach based on a deep sparse automatic encoder to generate the user's potential characteristics, using reliability metrics to select implicit ratings to enhance rating profiles for users with insufficient ratings. Reliable enhanced rating profiles and trust statements can be used as input to deep sparse autoencoders to generate the user's potential characteristics. Calculates similarity between users and makes recommendations. One scholar [5] created an initial glossary of terms from the existing user learner profile and used the course ontology to determine the exact needs of users. Metadata is initially classified using the XGBoost algorithm, and core data sets are classified using rich user terms. Then, the concept similarity is calculated by genetic algorithm to calculate semantic similarity, which is recommended to users. In practical application, all kinds of push methods do not need the user to provide a clear goal, but can directly find the information that the user may be interested in. However, there are still some drawbacks in the application of push method. For example, the resources pushed for users are too similar to the content of user history query records. Based on the introduction of weighted information entropy, this paper tries to design and study the individualized push method of Chinese online education curriculum resources. The innovation of this research lies in the use of weighted information entropy to calculate the similarity between course content and image, and the combination of Collaborative filtering algorithm to achieve the construction of personalized image of foreign students in Chinese universities and the push of online education course content, so as to meet their interest in online learning in China.

## 2 Personalized Portrait Construction of Chinese Online Education for Foreign Students in Colleges and Universities

In the online Chinese education for college students studying in China, the basic information of college students studying in China and the data that can indicate the users' interests and preferences shall be obtained, and these information and data shall be cleaned and converted to generate labels through statistics and analysis, and the construction of personalized portraits of the users of the online Chinese education platform for college students studying in China shall be completed [6]. In order to improve the accuracy of the push method, a personalized portrait of Chinese online education for college students in China is constructed by integrating the interests of college students in China, and the interest of college students in China is represented by a spatial model:

$$U = \{(T_1, W_1); (T_2, W_2); \cdots ; (T_n, W_n)\} \quad (1)$$

In the formula, $U$ represents the spatial model representation of the user interest of the university students studying in China; $T_1, T_2, ..., T_n$ represents the dimension label of the user interest of the university students studying in China; $W_1, W_2, ..., W_n$ represents the weight of a dimension label of interest. When creating the personalized portrait of Chinese online education for foreign students in colleges and universities, the corresponding portrait is generated according to the classification number of the contents of the education courses read by foreign students in colleges and universities. Assuming that the number of occurrence of the classification number at the end of the users of the returned university students in China is greater than or equal to m, the label in the portrait shall be "classification number", and the weight shall be "the number of times the corresponding course content of the classification number has been borrowed by the returned university students in China", and m shall be the subsequent filter parameter condition. In addition, in the content of online Chinese education courses, there are also user message boards, comment data and other resource information of some overseas students of colleges and universities in China. For this part of content, the method of manual labeling may be adopted [7] to take the key words in the resource information as the portraits of overseas students of colleges and universities in China, and continue to assign weight to the personalized portraits of overseas students of colleges and universities in China in accordance with the specific content of messages and emotions contained in comments of overseas students of colleges and universities in China [8]. Based on the above contents, we can not only describe the users of Chinese online education, but also reduce the operation burden of Chinese online education platform and provide favorable conditions for the subsequent courses.

## 3 Feature Extraction of Chinese Online Education Courses

Firstly, it is necessary to determine the distribution of the content data of online Chinese education courses. In the environment of heterogeneous data storage of the content data of online Chinese education courses, the preference for decision-making characteristics of the content data of online Chinese education courses shall be introduced, and the integration of the personalized portrait of users of overseas Chinese students of colleges and universities in China and the content characteristics data of online Chinese education courses shall be realized [9]. In this process, the following formulas may be used:

$$Q(x) = \frac{P(x)}{\sum_{i=1} (V_i(x) - P_i(x))} \tag{2}$$

In the formula, $Q(x)$ represents the characteristic data of the content of online Chinese education courses obtained through the above operation; $P(x)$ represents the personalized portrait label of the users of overseas Chinese students of colleges and universities corresponding to the characteristic data; $V_i(x)$ represents the characteristic value of all the content of online Chinese education courses; $P_i(x)$ represents the personalized portrait label of the users of overseas Chinese students of colleges and universities corresponding to a specific content of online Chinese education courses. On the basis of the above formula, the integration of the personalized portraits of foreign students in colleges and universities and the feature data of the content of online Chinese education courses needs to be completed, and on the basis of this, the integration of the feature data of the content of online Chinese education courses itself is also required. The process can be expressed by the following formula:

$$S = \varphi^s \cdot \delta + \varphi^b \cdot A \tag{3}$$

In the formula, $S$ represents the objective function for feature extraction of the content of a Chinese online education course; $\varphi^\delta$ represents the weight coefficient for feature extraction under $\delta$ push delay condition [10]; and $\varphi^A$ represents the feature extraction weight when the consumption is $A$ in the feature extraction of a certain Chinese online education course content. Based on the above operations, the integration of various resources in the Chinese online education curriculum should be realized. After the integration, the characteristic data should be reconstructed in multi-dimensions [11]. The data can be reconstructed by the method of fusion and matching, and the reconstructed data can be imported into the Chinese online education course content push database.

# 4 Course Content Similarity Calculation Based on Weighted Information Entropy

Weighted information entropy is a measure of data uncertainty. It is the information entropy of weighted data. In information theory, entropy is a measure of uncertainty of random events. It represents the average amount of information contained in all events in a set of events. Weighted information entropy takes into account the weight of each event when calculating entropy, which can be any positive number [12]. Weighted information entropy can be used in data compression, data classification, data analysis and other fields. The implementation steps are shown in Fig. 1 below:

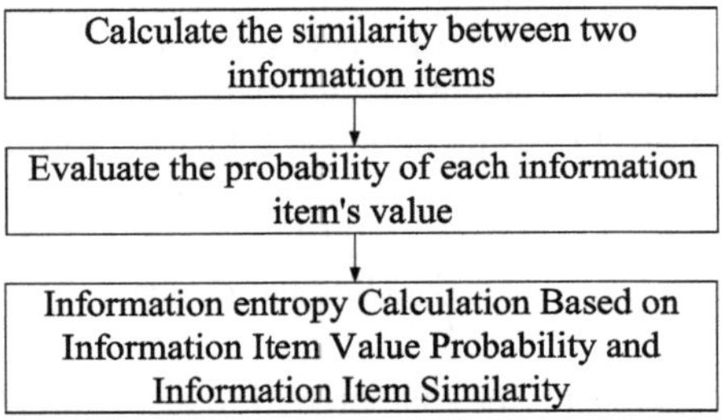


**Fig. 1.** Flow of information entropy calculation

In order to improve the efficiency of pushing and reduce the burden of pushing, weighted information entropy [13] is introduced to calculate the similarity of Chinese online education courses.

During the calculation, the information entropy is used to describe the push probability of the course content:

$$\begin{bmatrix} X \\ p \end{bmatrix} = \begin{bmatrix} X_1 & X_2 & \cdots & X_n \\ p_1 & p_2 & \cdots & p_n \end{bmatrix} \tag{4}$$

In the formula, $X$ represents a random variable for discrete course content; $p$ represents $X$ push probability distribution. The lower the information entropy is, the more orderly the curriculum content is, and the higher the information entropy is, the more chaotic the curriculum content is. Assuming that the information entropy of a certain course content in the Chinese online education course can be expressed as $H(X)$, the following formula may be used as the basis for calculation:

$$H(X) = r[y(x_i)] \tag{5}$$

In the formula, $y(x_i)$ represents the logarithmic negative value of the probability of a given course content being pushed; $r$ represents the result of the ordered degree measurement of Chinese online education content [14]. Convert formula (5) further to the following formula:

$$H(X) = \sum_{i=1}^{n} p_i \log_2 \frac{1}{p_i} \tag{6}$$

In the formula, $p_i$ represents the probability that category I of an online Chinese course is pushed. The information entropy can be used to describe the confusion degree of the content information of online Chinese education courses, and to provide a basis for judging the unity of the content information. When there is only one category in the content of a Chinese online education course, the value of $p_i$ is 1 and the value of $H(X)$ is 0. When the probability of pushing n classifications is the same, then $p_i$ turns to the reciprocal of the number of classifications, that is 1/n, $H(X)$ has the maximum value, $\log_2 n$. After the content similarity of Chinese online education courses is calculated, the basis for subsequent collaborative filtering of the course content is provided. On this basis, we can also measure the similarity between the content of Chinese online education courses and the interest of foreign students in China. Assuming a grade difference of D between one user A and another user B for the same course content, the following formula can be used to calculate the value of $g$:

$$g = |g_A - g_B| = (|d_1|, |d_2|, \cdots |d_n|) \tag{7}$$

In the formula, $g_A$ means that user A scores the content of Chinese online education courses; $g_B$ means that user B scores the content of Chinese online education courses; $d_1, d_2, \ldots, d_n$ means that user A scores the difference between user B and user A on each item of Chinese online education courses. After calculating the difference between user A and user B on the content of the same Chinese online education course, this difference is analyzed in frequency. Classify the difference value and calculate the probability of each classification. Assuming that in the process of frequency statistics, g is subdivided into M values, in extreme cases, when each value of g is different, M = N exists; when each value of g is the same, M = 1 exists. The total frequency of g occurrence can be obtained by summarizing the frequency of the occurrence of a category. The weighted information entropy of g is calculated in combination with the above formula (6). The range of information entropy is 0–+∞. When the value of information entropy is 0, the similarity between user A and user B is very similar. By using the above methods, we can not only calculate the similarity of two universities' students studying in China, but also calculate the similarity of many universities' students studying in China. For example, suppose that between user A and user B, the g value of user A is 1, and the g value of user B is 2; between user A and user C, the g value of user A is 3, and the g value of user C is 4, and if the similarity between user A and user B is 1, then the similarity between user A and user C is also 1. Based on the above logic, we determine the similarity between all the users of Chinese online education courses, and carry out subsequent collaborative filtering and push of the courses.

## 5 Collaborative Filtering Push of Chinese Online Education Course Content Resources

Through the above calculation, we can get the similarities between the contents of Chinese online education courses and those of foreign students in China, and feedback the preferences of foreign students in China. For several users of Chinese online education courses, a user rating matrix can be established according to the way shown in Fig. 2.

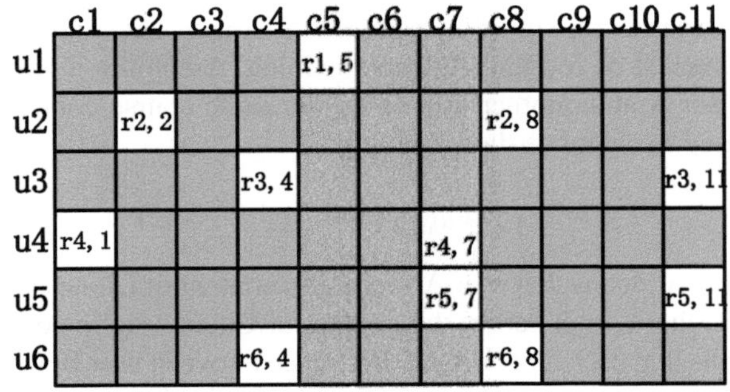


**Fig. 2.** Scoring matrix of university students studying in China for course contents

In Fig. 2, u represents foreign students from universities in China, c represents the content of the course, and rij represents the results given by users of foreign students in universities in China. The gray areas in the image indicate that university students coming to China did not receive or grade the course content. In Fig. 1, RIJ can be divided into two types: explicit feedback and implicit feedback according to the specific forms of Chinese students' behavior. Based on the feedback results given by overseas students from colleges and universities in China, the following formula is used as the threshold for collaborative filtering of resources:

$$f = r_A + \frac{Sim(A, B) * (r_A - r_B)}{\sum Sim(A, B)} \tag{8}$$

In the formula, $f$ represents the collaborative filtering threshold for resources; $r_A$ represents the scoring results given by user A for all the evaluated push course content; $Sim(A, B)$ represents the similarity of scoring results given by user A and user B for the same push course content; and $r_B$ represents the scoring results given by user B for all the evaluated push course content. Take the value of f as the basis for collaborative filtering of resources. If the threshold of collaborative filtering of resources for a given course content is calculated and the result is greater than f after calculation, the course content does not meet the push conditions and is filtered from the push results[15]; if the result is less than or equal to f, the course content meets the push conditions and is retained in the push results and displayed on the real interface for overseas students in China, so as to achieve the individualized course content of online Chinese education for overseas students in China (Fig. 3).

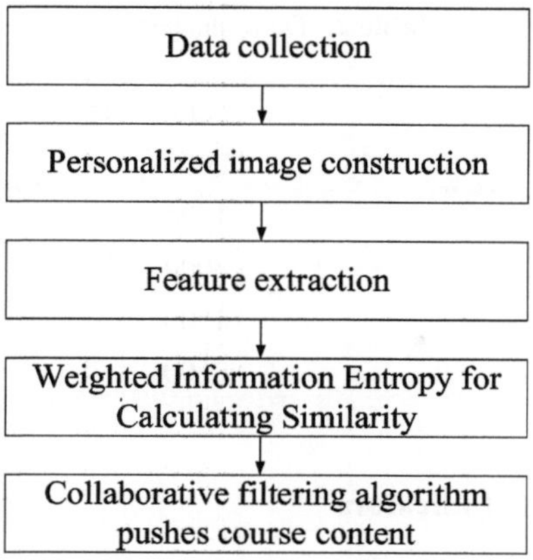


**Fig. 3.** Flow chart of the algorithm implementation

# 6 Experimental Results and Analysis

## 6.1 Experimental Preparation

But this method is still at the stage of theoretical research. In order to popularize this method and evaluate its effect, we need to design and compare experiments on the basis of existing research. Therefore, the following will take the design of comparative experiments to test the effectiveness of this method. Using literature [4] method and literature [5] method as the control group, this paper compares and analyzes the recommendation effects of three recommendation methods in the same experimental environment.

In order to test the effectiveness of the content push method of Chinese online education personalized course for foreign students in colleges and universities in China, a simulation experiment is conducted (Table 1).

**Table 1.** Test environment

| Environmental parameter | Parameter value |
|---|---|
| CPU | Intel Cy Young G4900 |
| RAM | Kingston DDR4 2400 16G |
| OS | Windows 10 |
| Programming languages | Java |
| Programming environment | Eclipse3.2 |

The resources used in the experiment are a university database, which extracts Chinese online education courses and other related contents for foreign students in China as data sets. The dataset contains 20, 000 pieces of data and is divided into five datasets, as shown in Table 2.

**Table 2.** Data sets tested

| Data set number | Sample size |
|---|---|
| 1 | 2000 |
| 2 | 1000 |
| 3 | 3000 |
| 4 | 1500 |
| 5 | 2500 |

## 6.2 Comparison of AUC Indicators

The AUC value is chosen as the evaluation index. The AUC value refers to the surrounding area under the work characteristic curve ROC. The higher the AUC value is, the better the effect of the recommendation method is, the more reasonable the subsequent recommendation is. In the course of the experiment, three recommendation methods are set up to classify the personalized course content of Chinese online education for foreign students in colleges and universities in China with the data volume of 200 Mbits to 1000 Mbits, and in the course of classification, the ROC values of each of them are calculated according to the following formulas:

$$ROC = (l - L)/L \tag{9}$$

In the formula: $l$ means the data of the correct classification of the personalized course content of online Chinese education for overseas Chinese students in colleges and universities; $L$ means the total data of the personalized course content of online Chinese education for overseas Chinese students in colleges and universities. The ROC values of the three recommended methods are calculated according to the above formulas, and the results are drawn as the experimental results shown in Fig. 4.

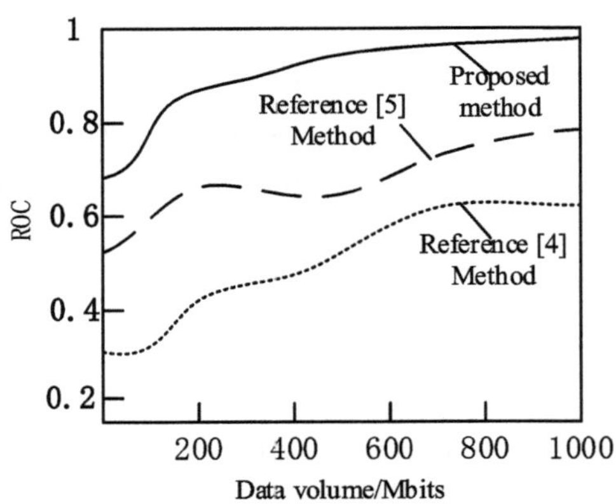


**Fig. 4.** Comparison of AUC values

As can be seen from the two curves in Fig. 4, the ROC value of this method is obviously higher than that of Reference [4] Method and Reference [5] Method. Therefore, through the above experimental results, it is proved that the proposed method can classify the content of personalized course of Chinese online education for foreign students in China accurately in practical application, and provide more favorable conditions for pushing the content of personalized course of Chinese online education for foreign students in China.

### 6.3 Comparison of Push Accuracy

Based on the comparison of the three methods, 5 international students were selected as the experimental volunteers, who were numbered A, B, C, D and E. Three push methods are used to push the corresponding Chinese online education personalized course content according to the students' preference. Compared with the click rate, the push precision is quantified. The results are recorded in Table 3.

**Table 3.** Comparison of click-through rates for push course content

| User | Click through rate of this method (times/100 Mbits) | Reference [4] Method click rate (times/100 Mbits) | Reference [5] Method click-through rate (times/100 Mbits) |
|---|---|---|---|
| User A | 23.65 | 9.22 | 15.52 |
| User B | 24.72 | 8.54 | 16.34 |
| User C | 25.86 | 6.26 | 12.76 |
| User D | 27.24 | 7.25 | 14.36 |
| User E | 29.55 | 9.62 | 15.33 |

From the experimental results in Table 3, it can be seen that the click-through rate of the proposed method is more than 22 times, the click-through rate of the reference [4] method is less than 10 times, and the reference [5] method is less than 17 times. It can be seen that the Chinese online education personalized course content pushed by this method is more welcomed by the overseas Chinese students, and more in line with the actual needs of the Chinese online education personalized course content.

### 6.4 Implementation Time Comparison

The average execution time of this method is 238 ms, the average execution time of reference [4] method is 467 ms, and the average execution time of reference [5] method is 512 ms. Compared with other methods, the implementation time of this method is significantly reduced, and the speed of content push is accelerated. The efficiency of this method is higher (Fig. 5).

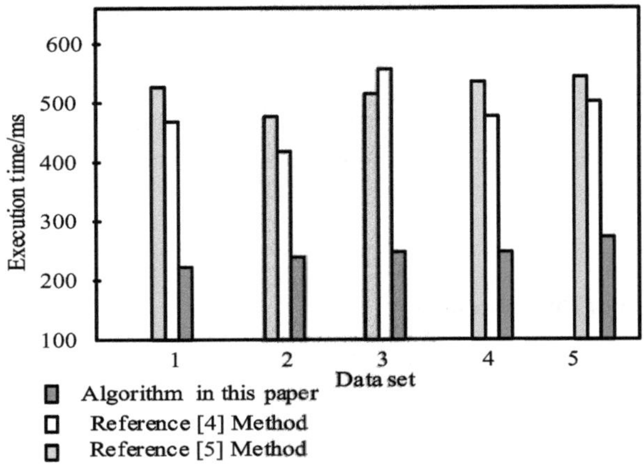


**Fig. 5.** Execution Time Comparison/ms

### 6.5 Reliability Comparison

In order to test the reliability of the method, some unstable conditions are artificially created. When the method changes in the working environment of the platform, the result is shown in Table 4. It can be found from Table 4 that the method of pushing the individualized course content of Chinese online education for foreign students in colleges and universities in China has reached a stable state in a short time, with the scope of [100.2, 184.2], while the time for the method of reference [4] method and reference [5] method to reach a stable state is obviously prolonged, with the scope of [105.6, 390.9] and [319.5, 405.6], respectively, which indicates that the method of this paper is more reliable, more able to adapt to the change of external environment, and has stronger robustness.

**Table 4.** Reliability Comparison

| Degree of change in working environment | This method achieves steady state time/ms | Reference [4] method to reach steady state time/ms | Reference [5] method to reach steady state time/ms |
|---|---|---|---|
| Very large | 184.2 | 390.9 | 405.6 |
| Big | 167.7 | 207.1 | 388.6 |
| General | 130.6 | 189.8 | 341.5 |
| Small | 114.7 | 158.2 | 327.6 |
| Very small | 100.2 | 105.6 | 319.5 |

The method proposed in this paper stands out from traditional approaches in several aspects. Firstly, it demonstrates superior application performance by providing different results tailored to different types of overseas Chinese students. The classification of course content based on personalized interests achieves higher ROC and AUC values, enabling the delivery of courses that align with the specific preferences of individual overseas Chinese students.

Furthermore, the verified method in this paper successfully pushes personalized course content for online Chinese education to overseas Chinese students over 22 times. This indicates a significant level of interest among university-level overseas Chinese students in the content recommended by the proposed method, surpassing the outcomes of alternative approaches. The average time required for content push in this method is 238, which is remarkably fast. This not only enhances user satisfaction but also facilitates regular online education activities for overseas Chinese students in universities.

It is worth noting that the method in this paper exhibits greater stability compared to other approaches when subjected to external disturbances. The recovery time from disturbance to stability is significantly shorter at 18.24 ms. This reliability contributes to the overall effectiveness and comprehensive promotion of the proposed method.

In conclusion, the distinctive features of this method, including its ability to deliver personalized course content and its superior stability and reliability, make it a valuable technical support for online Chinese education among college-level overseas Chinese students.

## 7 Closing Remarks

Based on the introduction of weighted information entropy, this paper puts forward a method of pushing the content of Chinese online education personalized course for foreign students. Based on the analysis of user portraits of foreign students in Chinese colleges and universities, this paper extracts the features of personalized course contents of Chinese online education. Through experiments, the advantages of the push method are verified from the classification accuracy and push accuracy of the course content. From the analysis of execution time and reliability index, the performance of push method is verified. In the practical application, if we can push the content of Chinese online education for the students in China according to the above ideas, we can not only provide the service, but also promote the overall operation quality of the platform. In future research work, we will build an online learning platform to provide an interactive and social learning environment for international students, encourage them to communicate, share experiences and resources with each other, and enhance the interactivity and sociality of learning.

## References


1. Ma, G., Black, K., Blenkinsopp, J., et al.: Higher education under threat: China, Malaysia, and the UK respond to the COVID-19 pandemic. Compare J. Comp. Int. Educ. **52**(5), 841–857 (2022)
2. Manegre, M., Sabiri, K.A.: Online language learning using virtual classrooms: an analysis of teacher perceptions. Comput. Assist. Lang. Learn. Assist. Lang. Learn. **35**(5–6), 973–988 (2022)

3. Agyeiwaah, E., Baiden, F.B., Gamor, E., et al.: Determining the attributes that influence students' online learning satisfaction during COVID-19 pandemic. J. Hosp. Leis. Sport Tour. Educ. **30**, 100364 (2022)
4. Ahmadian, M., Ahmadi, M., Ahmadian, S.: A reliable deep representation learning to improve trust-aware recommendation systems. Exp. Syst. Appl. **197**, 116697 (2022)
5. Agrawal, D., Deepak, G.: HSIL: hybrid semantic infused learning approach for course recommendation. In: Motahhir, S., Bossoufi, B. (eds.) Digital Technologies and Applications, ICDTA 2022. LNNS, vol. 454, pp. 417–426. Springer, Cham (2022). https://doi.org/10.1007/978-3-031-01942-5_42
6. Toro-Domínguez, D., Martorell-Marugán, J., Martinez-Bueno, M., et al.: Scoring personalized molecular portraits identify Systemic Lupus Erythematosus subtypes and predict individualized drug responses, symptomatology and disease progression. Brief. Bioinform. **23**(5), bbac332 (2022)
7. Kuang, A.: Construction of personalized advertising accuracy model based on artificial intelligence. In: 2022 International Conference on Artificial Intelligence and Autonomous Robot Systems (AIARS), pp. 395–398. IEEE (2022)
8. Shakhovska, N., Fedushko, S., Melnykova, N., et al.: Big Data analysis in development of personalized medical system. Procedia Comput. Sci. **160**, 229–234 (2019)
9. Buchaiah, S., Shakya, P.: Bearing fault diagnosis and prognosis using data fusion based feature extraction and feature selection. Measurement **188**, 110506 (2022)
10. Calvini, R., Pigani, L.: Toward the development of combined artificial sensing systems for food quality evaluation: a review on the application of data fusion of electronic noses, electronic tongues and electronic eyes. Sensors **22**(2), 577 (2022)
11. Patil, R.R., Kumar, S.: Rice-fusion: a multimodality data fusion framework for rice disease diagnosis. IEEE Access **10**, 5207–5222 (2022)
12. Sidhu, A.S., Singh, S., Kumar, R.: Bibliometric analysis of entropy weights method for multi-objective optimization in machining operations. Mater. Today Proc. **50**, 1248–1255 (2022)
13. Siddique, M.A.B., Islam, A.R.M.T., Hossain, M.S., et al.: Multivariate statistics and entropy theory for irrigation water quality and entropy-weighted index development in a subtropical urban river, Bangladesh. Environ. Sci. Pollut. Res.Pollut. Res. **29**, 8577–8596 (2022)
14. Aydoğdu, A., Gül, S.: New entropy propositions for interval-valued spherical fuzzy sets and their usage in an extension of ARAS (ARAS-IVSFS). Exp. Syst. **39**(4), e12898 (2022)
15. Li, H., Jian, W.: User big data cycle intelligent recommendation algorithm based on collaborative filtering. Comput. Simul. **40**(03), 476–479+489 (2023)

# University Innovation and Entrepreneurship Education Resource Sharing System Based on Cloud Service Platform

Yu Jia(✉)

College of Marxism, Wuhan Railway Vocational College of Technology, Wuhan 430205, China
dshfgbsegs566@163.com

**Abstract.** There may be situations of resource dispersion, information isolation, and duplicate construction among different universities, resulting in low efficiency and uneven quality of resource utilization. Therefore, studying how to establish a resource sharing system for innovation and entrepreneurship education in universities is of great significance. The conventional university innovation and entrepreneurship education resource sharing system mainly uses the Web Server system to process service requests, which is susceptible to the impact of service binding and retrieval, resulting in long system query time. Therefore, it is necessary to design a new university innovation and entrepreneurship education resource sharing system based on the cloud service platform. The hardware part is designed with FPGA chips, IDE controllers, and PIO transmitters. The software part is based on the cloud service platform to build an education resource sharing scenario, construct an education resource sharing architecture, and design an innovation and entrepreneurship education resource function module to shorten the time for education resource sharing. Integrating hardware and software to achieve resource sharing of innovation and entrepreneurship education in universities. The system testing results indicate that under the preset testing environment, the performance of the university innovation and entrepreneurship education resource sharing system designed in this article based on the cloud service platform is good, and all functional modules have passed the system testing, proving that the designed education resource sharing system has a certain degree of reliability and has made a certain contribution to promoting the development of university innovation and entrepreneurship.

**Keywords:** Cloud Service Platform · Universities · Innovation · Entrepreneurship · Sharing of Educational Resources

## 1 Introduction

The research background of the resource sharing system for innovation and entrepreneurship education in universities lies in the current problems of dispersed, isolated, and repetitive construction of innovation and entrepreneurship education resources among universities [1]. To address these challenges, establishing a resource sharing system is of


G. Gui et al. (Eds.): eLEOT 2023, LNICST 543, pp. 139–155, 2024.
https://doi.org/10.1007/978-3-031-51465-4_10

great significance. This system can integrate innovation and entrepreneurship education resources from various universities, providing comprehensive resource support, including high-quality teaching content, entrepreneurship cases, and mentor guidance [2–4]. Through resource sharing, the cultivation of innovation and entrepreneurship abilities can be promoted, and the diversity of teaching quality and methods can be improved. At the same time, resource sharing systems can also improve resource utilization efficiency, avoid duplicate construction and resource waste [5]. In addition, the system also promotes innovation and entrepreneurship research and practice, providing a broader platform for academic exchange, cooperation, and incubation and transformation of innovation and entrepreneurship projects [6]. In summary, studying the resource sharing system for innovation and entrepreneurship education in universities is of great significance for improving the quality of innovation and entrepreneurship education, promoting the cultivation of students' innovation and entrepreneurship abilities, and promoting innovation and entrepreneurship research and practice.

Reference [7] proposed a teaching resource sharing system based on Microservices architecture, and built an education resource cloud sharing architecture based on Microservices architecture. On this basis, Design education resource collection module, education resource attribute annotation module, education resource storage module and education resource retrieval module, provide users with education resource collection, upload, storage and retrieval services, and realize the operation of university education resource cloud sharing system. Reference [8] proposes an education resource sharing system based on the VEM framework, which consists of four levels: preprocessing, feature extraction, classification, and sharing of teaching resources through collaborative work. In the preprocessing stage, redundant information is removed to reduce system storage space. The feature extraction module uses the semantic Adjacency matrix to calculate the feature value of the vocabulary in the resource and select the vocabulary with larger feature value. In the classification module, the Hyponymy and hypernymy is used to build a classification framework, calculate the relationship strength between each word pair, and achieve classification according to the different strength. Store the resource numbers that have completed the classification separately, and teachers can directly search for the completed resource sharing. Although the above two systems can achieve the sharing of educational resources, they have the problem of long sharing time and are difficult to meet the user's usage needs.

A university innovation and entrepreneurship education resource sharing system based on cloud service platform is proposed to address the problems existing in the existing education resource sharing system. By combining FPGA chips, IDE controllers, and PIO transmitters, the sharing function of the system is achieved. The software part achieves rapid sharing of educational resources by building sharing scenarios and building a cloud platform sharing architecture.

## 2 Hardware Design

### 2.1 FPGA Chip

Educational resource sharing system uses FPGA chip as processing chip.In addition to the FPGA configuration chip and the memory chip necessary to run the SOPC system, peripheral interfaces related to system functions are added to the peripheral devices [9]. Most processing tasks and peripheral drivers in SOPC system can be implemented in FPGA chip, and its composition block diagram is shown in Fig. 1 below.

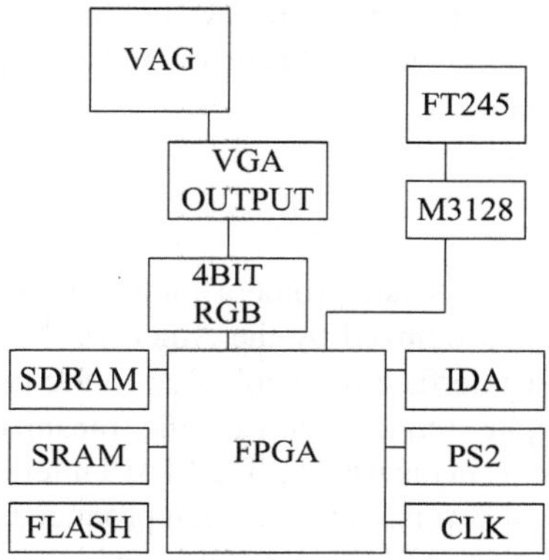


**Fig. 1.** FPGA chip composition block diagram

As shown in Fig. 1, FPGA is the core processor, and all designs in this paper are based on FPGA.EPCS4, M3128, FT245 and USB BLASTER form the configuration circuit of FPGA.EPCS4 stores the load file of FPGA. After the system is powered on, the system will transfer the load file into the FPGA to generate logical circuits. FLASH is used to store the running code of NIOS II in case of power failure. When the system is powered on, NIOS II starts from FLASH and loads the code into memory. SDRAM and SRAM are the memory of NIOSII soft core runtime. The IDE adapter cable converts the signal sequence to the sequence required by the IDE hard disk and connects it to the hard disk. VGA and PS2 are used for data display and external control of the system to complete human-computer interaction [10].

This paper uses the FPGA development board DE1 as the development platform. The DE1 development board is a multi-functional FPGA development board developed by Youjing Company. The FPGA model it uses is the EP2C20 of Cyclone II series. There are abundant peripheral interfaces on the DE1 development board, which can connect a variety of external devices, including audio interface, VGA interface, RS232 interface, SD card interface and PS/2 interface. In addition, the DE1 development board also provides two sets of 40 pin general GPIO interfaces, which enables it to expand a variety of functions. In addition, the crystal oscillator on the DE1 development board can provide 50 MHz, 27 MHz and 24 MHz clocks, which can meet the requirements of general design.

The FPGA adopts Cyclone II EP2C20 of Altera Company, which has about 18000 logic units, 240000 bit on-chip memory, four phase-locked loops and 52 9-bit hardware multiplier memories. Its logic resources are rich and cost-effective. The main modules involved in this design are NIOSII. CPU, various peripherals in SOPC system, IDE interface controller and VGA controller. After testing, the total logic resources used in these four parts account for about 50% of all FPGA resources, so the logic resources of FPGA can meet the system requirements and leave a large space for expansion.

Another important parameter of FPGA is the capacity of on-chip memory. The on-chip memory of Cyclone II series is generally insufficient. Because of the need to open up memory for two CPUs, and the implementation of NIOS II CPU also requires a lot of on-chip memory. Therefore, off chip SDRAM and SRAM are required. The SRAM used by the DE1 development board is 512 K bytes, and the SDRAM is 8M bytes, which can meet the system requirements.

## 2.2 IDE Controller

IDE interface is a hard disk interface protocol jointly defined by CDC, Compaq and Western Digital and finally recognized by the American National Standards Institute, also known as ATA/ATAPI interface protocol. Due to the continuous development of technology, people have higher requirements for the transmission speed of stored data, which leads to many problems in the use of ATA/ATAPI interface protocol. After continuous improvement, a total of 7 versions have been produced, namely ATA/ATAPI-1 to ATATAPI-7.Among them, ATATAPI-7 has not been widely used, and only Maxtor has launched a series of hard disks adopting ATA/ATAPI-7 standards. To maintain product compatibility, each new version is based on the old version and can support subsequent versions.

ATA/ATAPI - 6 is also called ATA/ATAPI 100 because it can theoretically make the transmission rate of the hard disk reach 100MB/s. It can use 40 pin and 80 pin transmission cables, and ATA/ATAPI-6 protocol still supports lower versions. Devices using ATA/ATAPI-4 and ATA/ATAPI-5 protocols do not need to update the version, but can directly use the ATA/ATAPI-6 interface. This not only makes users who have already invested no longer have to waste money to update their equipment, but also enables equipment manufacturers to update product versions without losing their original customers. In this way, their enthusiasm for using new technologies has been greatly improved. This has greatly promoted the development of ATA/ATAPI protocol ".

The minimum unit of hard disk data storage is sector, that is, at least one sector must be read or written every time data is read or written. The addressing mode of hard disk sector includes physical addressing mode (CHS addressing) and logical addressing mode (LBA addressing).Physical addressing refers to addressing using the physical storage form of hard disk. The physical address consists of "track number - head number - sector number". Logical addressing refers to numbering the sectors in the hard disk from 0, and the sector number is the logical address.

ATA/ATAPI-6 protocol adopts LBA addressing mode. The conversion of head and track in physical addressing will take a long time. LBA addressing can avoid this problem. LBA addressing speed is faster when carrying out mass data transmission. ATA/ATA-6 protocol specifies the mechanical parameters of IDE interface, and the connection interface of IDE controller is shown in Fig. 2 below.

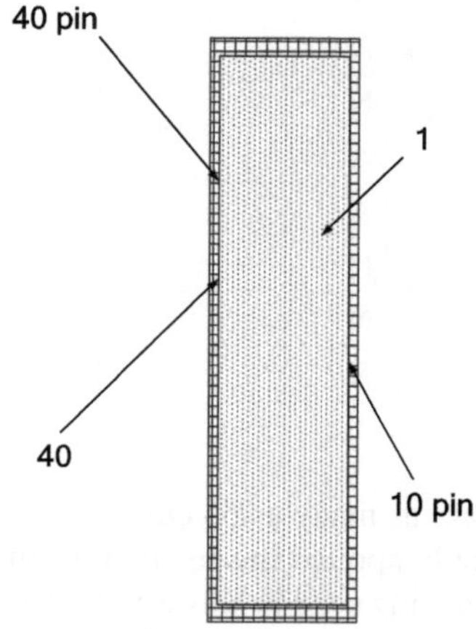


**Fig. 2.** IDE controller connection interface

It can be seen from Fig. 2 that the left part is the signal line, with a total of 40 pins, of which 20 pins are not connected. The right part is the hard disk jumper, with ten pins in total. The jumper is used to set the number of the hard disk in the PC to determine whether the hard disk is the primary hard disk or the secondary hard disk. The connection of the hard disk jumper of different manufacturers is different. Only one hard disk is used in this article, so the hard disk is set as the main hard disk. The hard disk used needs to be shorted with jumper caps for pin G and pin H to indicate that the hard disk is the main hard disk. If you want to set the hard disk as a slave hard disk, you need to use a jumper cap to short the C and D pins.

The host sends commands and relevant parameters to the disk device controller through registers, and controls the disk device controller to execute relevant commands. The host can master the command execution of the disk device controller by reading the contents of the register.CS0, CS1, DA2, DA1, DA0 are the address signals of the I/0 register, and the storage parameters are shown in Table 1 below.

**Table 1.** Deposit Parameters

| CS0 | CS1 | CS2 | CS3 | CS4 |
|---|---|---|---|---|
| N | A | N | N | A |
| A | N | A | A | A |
| A | N | N | N | N |
| A | N | A | A | N |
| A | N | N | N | A |
| A | N | A | N | A |
| A | N | A | N | N |
| A | N | N | A | A |
| A | N | N | A | N |
| N | N | X | X | X |

Table 1 shows that there are as many as 63 commands defined in ATA/TAIP-6 protocol, and some of them are only applied in specific transmission modes. Here we only introduce the four main commands used in this article: READ SECTOR (S), WRITE-SECTOR (S), READ DMA, and WRITE DMA. The command codes of the four commands are 20H, 30H, C8H, and CAH. To execute the above commands, the system needs to first write the required parameters to the relevant registers, and then write the command values to the command registers.

IDE hard disk has two transmission modes: PIO and DMA. DMA transmission mode can be divided into two types: multi word DMA transmission mode and serial DMA transmission mode. Register transmission must use PIO transmission mode, and data transmission can use both modes. Each transmission of PIO mode group data needs to achieve a complete preparation timing and end timing. The actual time of data transmission is only a small part of the whole time sequence. A small amount of data in PIO mode has little impact on the speed, but it will greatly reduce the transmission efficiency when a large amount of data is transmitted. And every transmission requires CPU participation, which will take up a lot of CPU time, reducing the overall efficiency of the system.

PIO transmission mode can be used when the amount of data is small.DMA mode only needs to realize the preparation timing and end timing once for each group of data transmission.Its preparation timing and ending timing are more complex than PIO mode.The advantages of DMA transmission are not obvious when the amount of data is small, but the efficiency and speed of transmission will be greatly improved when the amount of data is large.According to the above discussion, the system adopts the mixed use of PIO mode and DMA mode.This is because the design task is to store a large amount of data to the disk, while reading data only needs to be completed in the PC.Therefore, when storing data to the hard disk, the amount of data is large, and DMA transmission mode is adopted.When reading data from the disk, the amount of data is small, and PIO transmission mode is adopted. The structure block diagram of IDA controller is shown in Fig. 3 below.

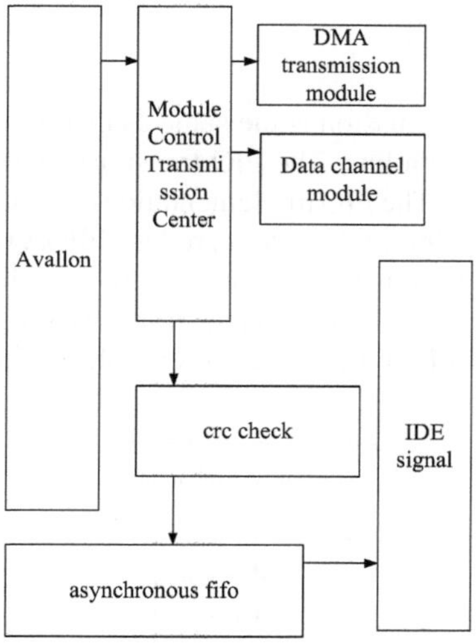


**Fig. 3.** IDA Controller Structure

It can be seen from Fig. 3 that the synchronization design makes the timing control of the whole system more simple, and it is easy to avoid many timing problems. If multiple clocks are used, the same clock source and cabling resources cannot be used for cabling during system integration. Different clock sources provide clocks at different times, which will lead to different clock delays between different modules, causing problems with data retention time and reducing data transmission speed. In this design, the whole system uses the same clock, avoiding the clock matching problem caused by using mixed clocks. In addition, the trigger resources of FPGA are very rich, while the combinational logic resources are relatively small. The synchronous design can make full use of the advantages of FPGA.

Avalon bus interface is responsible for communication with NIOS II CPU. This article uses it as an interface for custom peripherals. It is used to receive the control commands and related parameters of the CPU, respond to the read operation of the CPU, and provide the running results of the IDE controller to the CPU. The IDE controller data is converted to the Avalon bus format for transmission. The module control and PIO transmission module is responsible for interpreting CPU commands and controlling the operation of the entire IDE controller. It converts CPU commands into operations that need to be executed. For example, after receiving DMA read commands and sector addresses, it sets the registers that need to be read and written to execute DMA read commands, stores the relevant parameters in the registers, or reads the contents of the relevant registers and judges the operation of the IDE interface controller. As PIO transmission is closely related to the above contents, PIO transmission will also be realized in this module. It includes the realization of register transmission timing and PIO transmission protocol. After realizing the signal timing required for PIO transmission, it transmits the signal value to the IDE interface module, and controls the transmission outside the IDE interface module.

### 2.3 PIO Transmitter

The timing used for PIO transmission is the same as that used for register transmission except for the width of the data line. The PIO transmission data line is 16 bits, and the register transmission is 8 bits. The PIO implementation circuit and module control circuit all use register transmission timing. In order to reduce FPGA resource consumption, this design uses the method of module reuse to implement them in one module. In this way, half of the logic resources can be saved, and the transmission speed will not be affected. The module block diagram of the PIO transmitter is shown in Fig. 4 below.

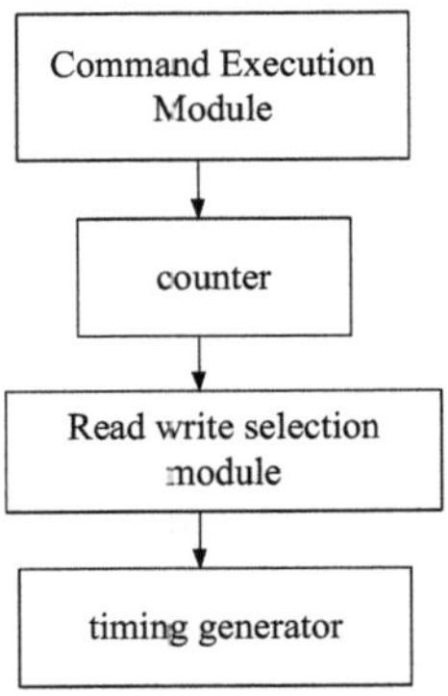


**Fig. 4.** PIO transmitter module block diagram

As shown in Fig. 4, the module receives information from the following three registers: w_r_ flag is used to receive disk device initialization, PIO read, PIO write, DMA transfer and other operation commands;file_ reg_ _addr is used to receive the address of the register to be operated: addr__reg is used to receive the sector address of the data to be read or written. The command execution module receives CPU instructions and sector address values from the Avalon bus interface, and implements the PIO read, PIO write protocol, and DMA transfer protocol command parameter writing. This module is based on the_r_The CPU command received by the fag register prepares the relevant register parameters required, and controls the timing generation module to store them in the corresponding register or read the contents of the register. The read/write selection module is used to select the data transmission direction. The transmission conversion conditions at this time are shown in Table 2 below.

**Table 2.** Command transmission conversion conditions

| Conversion conditions | Content description |
|---|---|
| 1 | The host starts PIO transmission |
| 2 | Activate the disk and write PIO transmission commands and parameters |
| 3 | Disk device is fully turned on |
| 4 | BSY = 0,DRQ = 0 |
| 5 | BSY = 1 |
| 6 | BSY = 0,DRQ = 1 |
| 7 | Interrupt enable is closed and data register reading is completed |
| 8 | Data register read incomplete |
| 9 | Data register reading completed, execute all commands |

It can be seen from Table 2 that combined with the above command transmission conversion conditions, the commands issued by the system can be executed to improve the operating reliability of the system.

# 3 Software Design

## 3.1 Building Educational Resource Sharing Scenarios Based on Cloud Service Platform

In the education resource system, it mainly includes two subjects: user group and resource group. The user group is mainly composed of students, teachers and other members of the public, while the resource group mainly refers to a large number of digital education resources existing in the education resource system, such as teaching materials, coaching materials, handout courseware, books and journals, teaching audio and video, exercise books, examination questions, etc. The cloud service platform is a large-scale virtual and extensible platform, which can use infrastructure as IaaS, platform as PaaS and software as SaaS. Therefore, according to the characteristics of the cloud service platform, this paper has built an educational resource sharing scenario, as shown in Fig. 5 below.

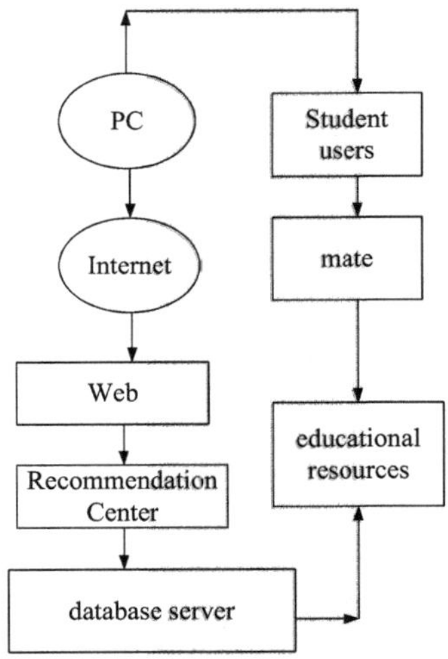


**Fig. 5.** Educational resource sharing scenario

It can be seen from Fig. 5 that student users are the main body of the education resource system, so they are also the main group using education resources. If you want to recommend resources to students more accurately, you must design a resource recommendation scheme specifically for the characteristics of student user groups. Student users are learners. It is precisely because they need to increase knowledge that they need educational resources, so there is a demand for learning. Different students have different characteristics in terms of learning background, learning style, learning ability, etc., while different educational resources have different characteristics in terms of background information, material type, difficulty, etc. Paying attention to students' personalized characteristics and selecting appropriate resources for them can more effectively improve students' learning efficiency, stimulate students' interest and improve students' learning pleasure, Make students enjoy the learning process more.

Just like the diversity of students' demand for resources, the types of educational resources are also very diverse. The resource model we have established should not only distinguish the differences of resources, but also reflect the basic characteristics of resources. The characteristics of educational resources mainly include background information, material types, difficulty, etc.

The effective information of resources to students is calculated through a series of matching algorithms. We can think that when the amount of effective information of educational resources for student users is relatively high, the student user will be more matched with the educational resources. Students can meet their needs better by learning the resources, so we can recommend the resources to the students. On the contrary, if the amount of effective information of educational resources for student users is relatively low, the matching degree between the two is also relatively low. It is considered that this resource cannot meet the needs of students, so it is unnecessary to recommend this resource. The resource matching similarity can be calculated according to the above sharing scenarios and resource allocation principles $\cos\theta$, , as shown in (1) below.

$$\cos\theta = \frac{b \cdot c}{|b| * |c|} \tag{1}$$

In formula (1), $b$ and $c$ respectively represent resource matching vectors in different Vector space. At this time, in order to measure the correlation between resources, Pearson correlation coefficient $p(x, y)$ needs to be calculated, as shown in (2) below.

$$p(x, y) = \frac{\sum x_i * y_i - n\overline{x_i y_i}}{(n-1)} \tag{2}$$

In formula (2), $x_i$ and $y_i$ respectively represent the correlation vector, $n$ represents the matching dimension, and Hamming distance refers to the total number of different bits of characters at the corresponding position of two strings of the same length. It can also be used to calculate the difference between two vectors. Formula $D$ is shown in the following (3).

$$D = \sum_{i=0}^{n} x_i \oplus y_i \tag{3}$$

In formula (3), the values of each one-dimensional feature of two vectors are character based. It is difficult to calculate the similarity between two vectors with character based values using traditional methods. Here, we introduce an encoding method that represents the strings of each dimension of the vector using the corresponding binary encoding. Therefore, we can assume a binary vector. The calculation equations $SI$ and $RI$ are shown in (4) and (5).

$$SI = \{S_0, S_1, ..., S_N\} \tag{4}$$

$$RI = \{r_0, r_1, ..., r_N\} \tag{5}$$

In formulas (4) and (5), $S_0, S_1, ..., S_N$ represents the resource matching vector before using binary encoding, and $r_0, r_1, ..., r_N$ uses the resource matching vector after using binary encoding. Based on the analysis of the similarity calculation methods of the above vectors, it can be seen that the Pearson correlation coefficient calculation requires at least two overlapping parts of the two vectors. When the overlapping parts are less than two, the Pearson correlation coefficient cannot be calculated, This is very unfavorable for calculating the correlation between two vectors; Although cosine similarity can be used to calculate the similarity of any two n-dimensional vectors, its solving process is very complex; The calculation of the Hamming distance of the two vectors is very simple, and the accuracy of the results is also very high. Therefore, this paper uses the calculation of the Hamming distance as a measure of the similarity of the basic information vector. $D(SI/RI)$ is calculated as follows (6).

$$D(SI/RI) = \sum_{i=0}^{n} S_N \oplus r_N \tag{6}$$

The above education sharing scenario can effectively improve the system throughput and make the system run more smoothly.

### 3.2 Building an Educational Resource Sharing Architecture

The overall function of the educational resource sharing platform studied in this paper is divided into two parts: the Web end and the client end. The Web end includes the educational resource sharing platform, personal real name cyberspace and the background management system of the sharing platform. Clients include PC client, Android client and IOS client. Ordinary users and administrators can upload and share various educational resources on the sharing platform. Resources can only be viewed, downloaded and displayed in the foreground and client software after being reviewed and released by the administrator.

This paper mainly studies the unified management, standardized processing, distributed storage and real-time retrieval of uploaded resources under the support of Hadoop technology, so that users can use various resources more quickly and conveniently for learning and communication. The users of the educational resource sharing platform mainly include six categories: students, teachers, parents, super administrators, ordinary administrators and tourists who have not registered with the system. The continuous expansion of the scale of educational resources, the variety of types, and the different ways of expression make the sharing of educational resources become the bottleneck of the development of distance education and online education. In order to unify and standardize the information representation and storage among educational institutions, so as to retrieve the resources needed by users more efficiently and accurately, it is necessary to design and develop a resource sharing platform suitable for massive educational resource storage and retrieval. The platform is composed of three systems: resource sharing platform, real name cyberspace and client software. Users can freely jump between the three systems to carry out personalized learning, collaborative learning and communication. The designed educational resource sharing architecture is shown in Fig. 6 below.

It can be seen from Fig. 6 that the resource sharing platform is divided into two modules: front and back. The front desk provides access for ordinary users and tourists, and the back desk is the interface for administrators to manage the system. The front desk provides users with multi-functional basic education resource services, such as curriculum resource ranking, resource retrieval, resource upload and download, resource online demonstration, resource sharing and other functions. At the same time, the platform also adopts an effective integral incentive mechanism to encourage users to actively share all kinds of high-quality teaching resources and achieve the convergence of high-quality resources. The background provides a good interface for administrators to manage the whole system. Administrators can manage users, roles, resources, logs, exams, and credits by category.

Real name cyberspace mainly provides learning, social and management services, and provides effective learning and social environment for teachers, students and parents, such as online learning, lesson preparation and office, social interaction, etc. Users can not only work and study in their own learning space, but also enrich their after-school life on the social platform. The client software is an effective expansion of resource sharing platform and network real name space, providing support for online teaching and communication of teachers, enriching teaching forms and improving the traditional teaching mode. Teachers, students and parents can also conduct instant messaging, file exchange

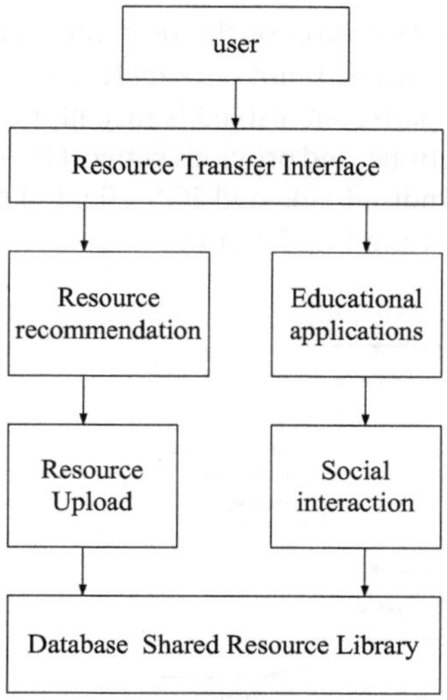


**Fig. 6.** Educational resource sharing architecture

and mutual learning through the client, which greatly promotes the communication and cooperation among users.

### 3.3 Design Innovation and Entrepreneurship Education Resource Function Module

The resource sharing platform is mainly responsible for the effective organization of basic education resources and user resources, the centralized collection and construction of basic education resource database, and the provision of educational resource sharing, resource evaluation, resource display, social interaction, online learning, mutual learning, online office and other functions for basic education authorities, teachers, students and parents. The cross platform instant messaging capability is provided through the client software to facilitate users to access the platform through multiple terminals at any time, anywhere, and provide the background management system to manage various resources and maintain the application system to ensure the stable and efficient operation of the entire platform. According to the platform architecture, the entire educational resource service platform includes three parts: the resource sharing platform Web end, personal real name cyberspace and client software. Its specific functions are as follows:

(1) Web front desk: including login, resource ranking, resource search, resource details view, resource upload, resource display, resource evaluation and resource download;
(2) Web end background: including portal management, user management, role management, space management, resource management, exam management, score management and log management;
(3) Personal real name cyberspace includes teacher space, student space, parent space and their common functions, providing users with online office, online learning, social interaction and other functions.

(4) The client software is an extension of the resource sharing platform and personal real name cyberspace functions. It not only includes the main functional interfaces provided by the first two parts, but also adds instant messaging, lesson preparation, homework and other functions, and provides support for online teaching, specifically including the PC side, Android side and IOS client. The top-level structure of the functional module is shown in Fig. 7 below.

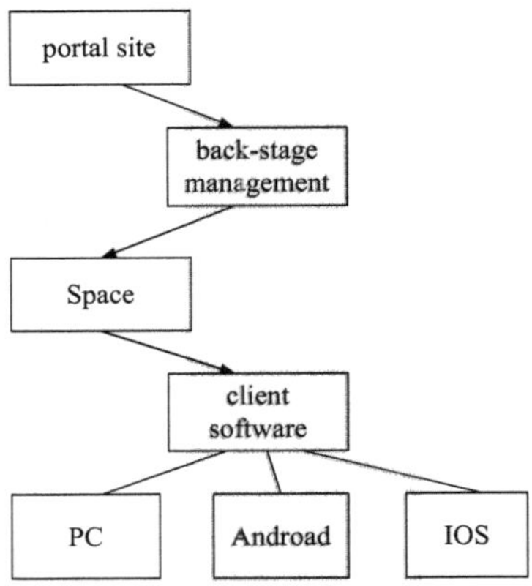


**Fig. 7.** Top structure of function module

It can be seen from Fig. 7 that the Web end is mainly divided into two modules: portal and background management system. The foreground function module is mainly the platform for ordinary users and tourists to carry out relevant operations, while the background management system provides interfaces for various administrators to monitor and manage the entire system. The super administrator is mainly responsible for the management of key functional modules, and grants various roles and permissions to corresponding ordinary administrators. It details the responsibilities of administrators, precisely controls the permissions of administrators at all levels, facilitates dynamic addition and expansion, and provides the most favorable guarantee for the good operation of the platform.

# 4 System Test

In order to verify the running performance of the designed university innovation and entrepreneurship education resource sharing system based on cloud service platform, this paper builds a test platform, runs the system designed in this paper, and conducts system testing, as follows.

## 4.1 Test Preparation

This education resource sharing system includes clusters and three types of servers. One is the database server, which installs Oracle10g database, followed by the Web server, which deploys eight Tomcat6 servers, uses load balancing strategies to improve the performance of the entire platform, and finally is the application server, which contains multiple client software servers, including the client master server, resource server, HTTP search server, file transfer server, chat server, desktop sharing and whiteboard server.

The virtual environment built by the system consists of two physical machines and four virtual machines. A management machine manages other machines through VMware Vcenter. The specific hardware configuration of the environment required for application server, database server and client software is shown in Table 3 below.

**Table 3.** Test Environment

| to configure | application server | database server |
|---|---|---|
| hardware configuration | CPU:<br>Intel(R)Core(TM)<br>90@3.6 GHz<br>i7–47<br>Memory: 16 GB (Samsung DDR3 1600 MHz)<br>Hard disk: Seagate ST1000DM003-1H162 (1TB/7200 rpm) | CPU:<br>Intel(R)Core(TM)i7–47<br>90@3.6 GHz<br>Memory: 16 GB (Samsung DDR3 1600 MHz)<br>Hard disk: Seagate ST1000DM003-1H162 (1TB/7200 rpm) |
| software configuration | Windows Server 2008 | Windows Server 2008 |
| network environment | 100M LAN | 100M LAN |

Table 3 shows that the Java EE container on the test server side uses Tomcat 6.0.23. Tomcat server is an open source web server jointly developed by Apache, Sun and other companies. It meets the test requirements. After the above test environment is configured, subsequent system tests can be carried out.

## 4.2 Test Results and Discussion

Under the above configured testing platform, system testing can be carried out by adjusting the testing instructions, importing different numbers of resource files, comparing and verifying the system with reference [7] system and reference [8] system, and recording the query time of resource files for the three systems. The test results are shown in Table 4.

From Table 4, it can be seen that the file resource query time of the system in this article is the shortest among the three types, proving that the designed system has good operational performance, reliability, and certain application value. This is because the system in this article optimizes queries from both hardware and software aspects, thereby shortening query time.

**Table 4.** Test Results

| Number of resource files | The query time of this system (s) | Query time of reference [7] system (s) | Query time of reference [8] system (s) |
|---|---|---|---|
| 20 | 1.5 | 9.6 | 7.8 |
| 40 | 1.6 | 10.2 | 9.6 |
| 60 | 1.7 | 11.4 | 10.4 |
| 80 | 1.8 | 12.3 | 11.2 |
| 100 | 1.9 | 13.2 | 13.5 |
| 120 | 2.0 | 14.2 | 14.9 |
| 140 | 2.1 | 15.1 | 15.7 |

## 5 Conclusion

The integration and collaborative sharing of innovation and entrepreneurship education resources can not only effectively avoid the idleness of internal resources and the duplication of resources among universities, but also strengthen the complementary advantages of resources among universities. Only scientific and reasonable integration of innovation and entrepreneurship resources and improvement of the utilization rate of innovation and entrepreneurship education resources can comprehensively improve the quality of innovation and entrepreneurship education and cultivate high-quality innovation and entrepreneurship talents that adapt to economic and social development. Combined with the current innovation and entrepreneurship background, this paper uses the cloud service platform to build an effective university innovation and entrepreneurship education resource sharing system, and carries out system testing. The results show that the designed innovation and entrepreneurship education resource sharing system has good operation performance, reliability, and certain application value, and has made certain contributions to promoting the development of university innovation and entrepreneurship.

The university innovation and entrepreneurship education resource sharing system based on cloud service platforms has many advantages, but there are also some limitations. Firstly, establishing such a system requires corresponding technical support and infrastructure, including requirements for cloud computing, network, and data storage. This may impose certain restrictions on some universities with limited resources or poor technical conditions. Secondly, in the process of sharing educational resources, it is an important challenge to ensure that the personal information and sensitive data of teachers and students are fully protected, and to strengthen data security and privacy control. In addition, the use and management of the system require relevant technical training and support to ensure that users can fully utilize the system's functions.

The future development direction can further expand and improve the university innovation and entrepreneurship education resource sharing system based on cloud service platforms. Firstly, it is possible to enhance the intelligence and personalization of the system, providing users with more accurate recommendations and customized teaching content through technologies such as data analysis and machine learning. Secondly, various innovation and entrepreneurship resources can be further integrated, including innovation and entrepreneurship projects, investors, and corporate partners, to build a more complete innovation and entrepreneurship ecosystem. In addition, it is possible to strengthen the connection with other universities, enterprises, and social resources, promoting deep integration of industry university research cooperation and innovation and entrepreneurship practices. Finally, through an open platform architecture, third-party developers can be encouraged to participate, enrich the system's functions and applications, and provide more diverse educational services and support.

**Aknowledgement.** The CPC Construction brand building project of "Locomotive Project in the new era" of Wuhan Railway Vocational College of Technology: On Strengthening and Improving the Work Path of CPC Construction Running ahead Construction of the Chinese Communist Youth League in Higher vocational colleges in the new era (Project number: 2022Z001).

Students ideological and political education special topic of Wuhan Railway Vocational College of Technology: An Empirical study on class culture construction in Higher Vocational Colleges in the new era (Project number: 2022SZ03).

## References

1. Jiang, T.: Simulation of network dynamic resource flexible scheduling based on pattern fusion. Comput. Simulat. **38**(6), 5–10 (2021)
2. Li, K.C., Wong, T.M.: A review of the use of open educational resources: the benefits, challenges and good practices in higher education. Inter. J. Innov. Learn. **3**, 30–35 (2021)
3. Farahian, M., Parhamnia, F.: Knowledge sharing through WhatsApp: does it promote EFL teachers' reflective practice? J. Appli. Res. Higher Educ. **14**(1), 332–346 (2022)
4. Hunnaball, M., Jones, J., Maguire, M.: Independent and state school partnerships (ISSPs) in England: systemic tensions and contemporary policy resolutions. J. Educ. Administ. History **4**, 1–15 (2021)
5. Ferreira, D.J., Melo, T., Berretta, L.O.: Case Study of a blind computer graphics student's online interactions. Inter. J. Inform. Commun. Technol. Educ. Offic Public. Inform. Resources Manag. Assoc. **17**(1), 72–87 (2021)
6. Golos, D., Moses, A., Gale, E., et al.: Building allies and sharing best practices: cultural perspectives of deaf people and ASL can benefit all. Learn Landscapes **14**(1), 97–110 (2021)
7. Li, Y.C., Chen, J.F., Cheng, P.P.: Micro-service architecture based cloud sharing system of recessive education resources in colleges and universities. Mod. Electron. Tech. **44**(20), 47–52 (2021)
8. Tang, X.J.: Design of teaching resource sharing platform based on VEM framework. J. Jilin Univ. Inform. Sci. Edn. **40**(02), 288–294 (2022)
9. Camacho, H., Coto, M., Jensen, S.P.: Participatory methods to support knowledge management systems design in educational environments. Inter. J. Knowl. Manag. Stud. **12**(1), 34–37 (2021)
10. Vonog, V.V., Kharlamenko, I.V., Kolga, V.V.: Video conference tools as an element of technogenic educational environment in the system of foreign language teaching. Inform. Educ. **1**, 57–62 (2021)

# English Literature Appreciation Teaching Resources Retrieval System Based on Mutual Information Entropy

Xiaojun Jiang[1(✉)] and Haiquan Chi[2]

[1] School of Translation Studies, Xian Fanyi University, Xi'an 710105, China
seanrain2022@163.com

[2] Liao Ning Provice Zhangwu Senior High School, Zhangwu 123200, China

**Abstract.** With the development of globalization and the increase of international communication, the appreciation of English literature has become an important part of English learning for many learners. English literature appreciation aims to help students understand and appreciate the artistic value, cultural connotation and language expression of English literary works. The imbalance of resource allocation is the main reason why the application host can not accurately retrieve teaching information. In view of the above problems, a retrieval system for English literature appreciation teaching resources based on mutual information entropy is designed. According to the calculation result of mutual information entropy, the generalized entropy function is solved, and then based on this, the processing of teaching resources is completed, so as to achieve the acquisition of teaching resources based on mutual information entropy. Improve the retrieval architecture, and through the definition of resource retrieval methods, realize the application of various technical means, and complete the design of English literature appreciation teaching resource retrieval system based on mutual information entropy. The experimental results show that the application of the above retrieval system can make the maximum balance of resource allocation reach 95%, which solves the problem that the application host cannot accurately retrieve teaching information due to the imbalance of resource allocation.

**Keywords:** Mutual Information Entropy · English Literature Appreciation · Teaching Resources · Resource Retrieval · Generalized Entropy Function · Retrieval Architecture · Ratio Balance

## 1 Introduction

English literature refers to literary works written in English. English works in American literature can be counted as part of English literature, but they are usually treated as an independent and important discipline; The same is true of Irish literature. Although there are many repetitions between English literature and English literature, they include literature from other regions and languages in Great Britain, so they are two different


G. Gui et al. (Eds.): eLEOT 2023, LNICST 543, pp. 156–171, 2024.
https://doi.org/10.1007/978-3-031-51465-4_11

concepts. In academic circles, "English literature" is often analyzed and criticized in departments or projects devoted to "English research". The reason is that the former colonies of England have developed their own English literature, and the English used in these places is different from each other [1]. So English literature has developed various branches with the changes of English in the world. Literary appreciation is to obtain aesthetic pleasure and spiritual satisfaction through the interpretation of the language symbols of the works. It is divided into three stages: perception, taste, and understanding. It has differences and consistency, certainty and uncertainty. It is the reader's psychological activities such as imagination, association, emotion, thinking, and recreation based on the understanding of literary works to meet aesthetic needs, to pursue the readability and interest of theoretical works.

The construction of educational resources is to integrate educational and teaching resources by means of information technology, and finally build an interactive and multimedia shared resource warehouse. The purpose of building an educational resource database is to serve education. Therefore, we should fully consider the needs of education in terms of both content and function, so that students, teachers and other educators can easily and timely obtain the information they need and have usability. On the basis of understanding the needs of users, we must carry out anti demand analysis, that is, combining with the actual situation, scientifically analyze and express the demand information provided by users from a more professional perspective. At present, the construction of basic education resources exists: there are many ways to construct education resources, but the two main ways are: 1. Directly purchase the existing commercial education resources products in the market; 2. Organize school teachers to develop educational resources by themselves.With the continuous expansion of data on the Internet, there are a lot of valuable education information, and online education resources have gradually become an important source of education resource database construction. At present, there are many kinds of educational resources on the Internet, which provide learners with a wide range of choices and broad space for development.

For the construction of English literature appreciation teaching project, the vertical retrieval system based on Lucene and the retrieval system based on Grassberger estimate judge the unit cumulative amount of teaching resource information according to the two parameters of browsing times and authoritative sources, and analyze and read XML documents related to teaching tasks with the help of the open source software package Dom4j. However, the above two types of systems cannot guarantee the balanced allocation of teaching resources, so it is easy to make the application host unable to retrieve accurate teaching information. In information theory, mutual information entropy is the average amount of information contained in each received message, also known as information entropy, source entropy, average self information amount [2]. Here, messages represent events, samples, or characteristics from a distribution or data flow. In the information world, the higher the entropy, the more information can be transmitted. The lower the entropy, the less information can be transmitted. Literature [3] designed a density-based clustering algorithm based on MapReduce based on weighted grid and information entropy. Based on the spatial distribution of data points, an adaptive partitioning strategy (ADG) was proposed to carry out adaptive partitioning of grids. A weighted grid construction strategy (NE) is designed, and a density computing strategy (WGIE) is designed to calculate the density of the grid based on weighted grid and information entropy. A core cluster computing algorithm based on MapReduce (COMCORE-MR) is proposed to compute the core cluster of clustering algorithm in parallel. Literature [4] Visualizes citation navigation using Litmaps, the ultimate scientific discovery platform. It provides an interface for discovering scientific literature, exploring areas of research, and discovering articles that are highly relevant to the map. Litmaps provides quick-start options to import articles from the reference manager, keyword search, ORCID ID, DOI, or using torrent articles. This paper uses the research strategies of keyword search and Open Educational Resources (OER).To solve the above problems, a new retrieval system for English literature appreciation teaching resources is designed based on the principle of mutual information entropy. Based on the principle of mutual information entropy, a complete generalized entropy function is defined, and the necessary search conditions are combined to realize the on-demand processing of teaching resources. Generalized correlation function is used as the classification feature of information entropy, and support vector machine classifier is used to realize the classification retrieval of English literature appreciation teaching resources. By improving the connection form of the search structure and combining the necessary search conditions, the design of the English literature appreciation teaching resource retrieval system is completed.

## 2 Acquisition of Teaching Resources Based on Mutual Information Entropy

Obtaining teaching resources is a necessary link to build a retrieval system for English literature appreciation teaching resources. Supported by the principle of mutual information entropy, a complete generalized entropy function is defined and necessary retrieval conditions are combined to achieve on-demand processing of teaching resources.

### 2.1 Calculation of Mutual Information Entropy

Mutual information entropy is an important concept in information theory, which can be used to describe the statistical correlation between two systems, or the extent to which one system contains information about another system. The dependence between two variables can be measured by calculating the information entropy of two variables and the gap between their joint entropy, which can be used to express the amount of information shared between two variables.

Generally speaking, mutual information entropy can represent the received random variable $\tilde{p}$ Post acquired variables about teaching resources $\dot{O}$ Information quantity of: it can measure the degree of the reduction of the uncertainty of the other when one of the two variables is known, indicating the degree of statistical constraints between two random variables. For example, if $\dot{O}$ and $\tilde{p}$ Independent of each other, then the random variable is received $\dot{O}$ Will not get any information about $\tilde{p}$ And their mutual information entropy is 0. Discuss another extreme case, if $\dot{O}$ and $\tilde{p}$ One to one correspondence, they are mutually deterministic functions, without any uncertainty, and share all the information transmitted. In this case, mutual information entropy and $\dot{O}$ (or $\tilde{p}$) The uncertainties provided separately are the same, and the mutual information entropy is equal to $\dot{O}$ Entropy of ($\tilde{p}$ Entropy).When $\dot{O}$ and $\tilde{p}$ It is also applicable to this situation when it is the same random variable.

Therefore, mutual information entropy can be used to measure the correlation between specific classes when they are divided. When the amount of information is large, it indicates that there is a large correlation between the two, and vice versa.

The calculation formula of information entropy is:

$$\tilde{p} = \sum_{\delta=1}^{+\infty} \beta \dot{O} \cdot \left[ \frac{(\chi - 1)^2}{\overline{I}} \right] \tag{1}$$

Among them, $\delta$ Represents the information transmission coefficient of teaching resources, $\beta$ It indicates the probability of the retrieval of English literature appreciation teaching resources, $\chi$ It represents the evaluation variable of teaching resource information, $\overline{I}$ It refers to the unit accumulation of English literature appreciation teaching resource information.

The amount of information contained in a random event is only related to the probability of the event. The lower the probability of an event occurring, the greater the amount of information contained in the received information when the event actually occurs. That is, when the probability of an event occurring is infinitely close to 0, the amount of information corresponding to its occurrence will be very large, otherwise the amount of information will be very small. The mutual information entropy can be obtained by calculating the mathematical expectation of the amount of information.

The calculation result of mutual information entropy is:

$$\partial_{\tilde{p}} = \log \left| \hat{i} \right| \frac{1}{\alpha \cdot \tilde{p}} \tag{2}$$

$\hat{i}$ Represents the unit expectation parameter of the information entropy index.

Mutual information entropy can not only describe the linear correlation between variables, but also effectively characterize the nonlinear correlation. The mutual information entropy feature in information theory has a high accuracy rate when retrieving English literature appreciation teaching resources in a low SNR environment, so it is feasible to use it as a classification feature.

## 2.2 Generalized Entropy Function

The teaching resource detection system based on mutual information entropy function performs Wigner bispectrum analysis on the real target echo or deception jamming signal, calculates their DSWB, and uses singular value decomposition to achieve dimensionality reduction, and then uses the equidistant algorithm to obtain the dimensionality reduction with the LFM information WB, the information entropy of the data after singular value decomposition and the joint entropy between the two. The generalized correlation function is calculated as the classification feature of teaching resource information, and the classification recognition of deception jamming signal is realized by SVM classifier.

The specific function operation steps are as follows:

The retrieval system receives teaching resource information and mutual information entropy parameters.

Wigner bispectrum analysis is carried out on the teaching resource information to obtain the three-dimensional WB retrieval data.

DSWB is calculated to obtain two-dimensional DSWB data of time retrieval frequency, and singular value decomposition is used to reduce the dimension of mutual information entropy.

The information entropy of the data after dimensionality reduction and singular value decomposition, as well as the joint entropy between them, is calculated by using the equidistance algorithm and the linear resource information WB.

The generalized correlation function is calculated as the classification feature of information entropy, and the SVM classifier is used to realize the classification and retrieval of English literature appreciation teaching resources.

The process of defining the generalized entropy function of English literature appreciation teaching resource information is shown in Fig. 1.

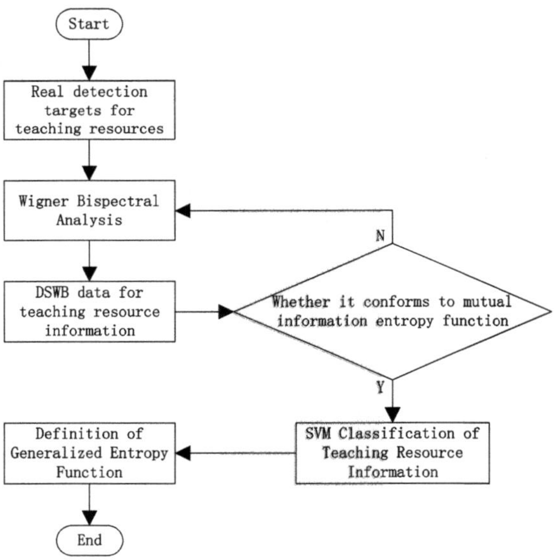


**Fig. 1.** Flow chart of definition of generalized entropy function of teaching resource information

The solution to the generalized entropy function of English literature appreciation teaching resources information satisfies the following expression:

$$U = \min_{\substack{e=1 \\ r=1}} |\dot{y}|^{(e-r)^2} + \partial_{\tilde{p}} \sum_{-\infty}^{+\infty} (u_{\max} - u_{\min})^2 \tag{3}$$

where, $e$、$r$ Represents two randomly selected entropy increasing vectors, and $e \neq r$ The inequality value condition of is always true, $\dot{y}$ It represents the real-time retrieval characteristics of English literature appreciation teaching resources, $u_{\max}$ Represents the maximum value result of the joint entropy parameter, $u_{\min}$ Represents the minimum value of the joint entropy parameter.

For a given number of teaching resource information, the larger the grid is divided, the more points will be in the grid, and the calculation of average probability will be more accurate, but the joint probability distribution obtained will change more smoothly, and the mutual information entropy will be lower; The smaller the lattice is, the greater the possibility that the joint probability distribution will change in a short distance, the more intense the change fluctuation, and the greater the mutual information entropy. Therefore, it is very important to select the appropriate lattice size for accurate estimation of mutual information entropy.

### 2.3 Processing of Teaching Resources

Since the query text input by the client on the query interface is natural language, the system must carry out a series of processing on the query text to automatically extract the key features of the query conditions and query objectives from the query English literature appreciation teaching resources. The process is as follows:

Query text → word segmentation → removing invalid words → extracting keywords → expanding synonyms.

Match the subject term after the extended synonym with the content description field in the database to find the records that meet the conditions.

For query text segmentation, the maximum positive matching algorithm is used.Relevant files used in word segmentation include: word segmentation dictionary (lastdictionary. Txt) and word segmentation function (fcresultl).

After the invalid words are removed, there are still some words in the string, which are meaningless to describe the characteristics of the query target. Therefore, it is necessary to extract words that can describe the characteristics of the query target from the remaining strings.

Using formula (3), the invalid words of English literature appreciation teaching resources information based on mutual information entropy can be expressed as:

$$\breve{W} = \sqrt{\dot{R}\frac{1}{\gamma}\left(\frac{E'^2 - E_0^2}{U}\right)^{-1}} \tag{4}$$

$\dot{R}$ Represent the descriptive characteristics of English literature appreciation teaching resources information, $\gamma$ Indicates the evaluation parameters of invalid words of resource information, $E'$ Represents the forward matching vector of resource information, $E_0$ Indicates the initial value of the teaching resource information matching parameter.

Because there are a large number of synonyms and synonyms in the information of teaching resources, it is difficult for users to list all the words expressing the same concept when querying, so it is easy to miss the inspection and the recall rate of the system is not high [5].

The result of solving the processing conditions of English literature appreciation teaching resources is as follows:

$$Q = (-\phi) \int_{\gamma=1}^{+\infty} \breve{W}\left(1 + \frac{s_1 + s_2 + \cdots + s_n}{q}\right)^2 \tag{5}$$

$\phi$ Indicates the calibration parameters of the transmission direction of English literature appreciation teaching resources information, $\gamma$ Represents the feature extraction coefficient of teaching resource information retrieval, $s_1$ 、 $s_2$ 、 $\cdots$ 、 $s_n$ express $n$ Unequal teaching resource information string definition vector, whose values belong to $(0, +\infty)$ Value range of, $q$ Represent resource information description parameters based on mutual information entropy.

The user's description of the query target in Chinese natural language on the query interface is presented in text form on the query interface. The retrieval system calls this descriptive text query text. The system should automatically extract the key features of the query conditions and query targets from the query text, and then find the records that meet the conditions in the database[6]. However, computers cannot directly understand natural language, which requires the processing of query text. Natural language word segmentation is a necessary part of query information processing.

## 3 Design Scheme of English Literature Appreciation Teaching Resources Retrieval System

On the basis of the principle of mutual information entropy, the design of the retrieval system for English literature appreciation teaching resources is completed by improving the connection form of the retrieval architecture and combining the necessary retrieval conditions.

### 3.1 Retrieval Architecture

The construction of retrieval architecture is based on metadata. The so-called metadata is a kind of structured data about the information or data of English literature appreciation teaching resources. It is a structured description of information resources, and it is machine understandable information for a specific application to describe resource attributes[7]. The structural characteristics of metadata can more accurately describe the semantics of resources, so that web data can be transformed from machine readable to machine understandable.

There are many metadata standards. RDF standard metadata can make the data compiled by web developers more consistent and effective in documents, and its main role is to describe and obtain metadata. RDF provides a basic dismissal for encoding, exchanging and reusing metadata on the web.

The commonly used RDF data model is the triple representation, and its basic object types are: Resource, Property, and Statement. Resources are identified by the unique resource identifier URI. Attributes are used to describe the common characteristics of resources. Declarations are composed of a resource, a property and the value of the property. Each declaration is a triple of "object, attribute and value", which is equivalent to the subject, verb and object in the sentence.

The complete teaching resource retrieval architecture is shown in Fig. 2.

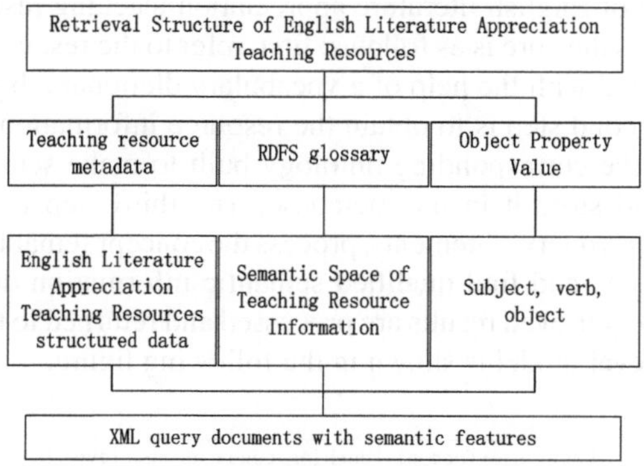


**Fig. 2.** Retrieval structure of English literature appreciation teaching resources

The RDF data model provides an abstract and conceptual framework for defining and using data. The data described according to the RDF specification is expressed in XML code to generate XML documents with semantic characteristics.

RDFS forms a complete semantic space. It provides the rules for using properties, defines a domain dictionary, organizes the dictionary with a type hierarchy, and provides a richer vocabulary to describe classes and class attributes.

Table 1 shows the composition of the RDFS vocabulary of the retrieval schema.

**Table 1.** RDFS vocabulary of teaching resource retrieval architecture

| Metalinguistic object | First level project object | Secondary project objects |
|---|---|---|
| Information category item | rdfs: Resource、rdfs:Class 、rdfs:Property | Rdfs、subClassof and rdfs:subPropertyof |
| Resource Properties | rdfs:domain、rdfs:range | RDFS、DAML + OIL and OWL |
| Constraint effect | Apollo、OILEd、OntoEdit、OntoSaurus | WebODE、Protege 、OKBC |

In order to achieve fast and accurate automatic word segmentation and part of speech tagging, it is necessary to consider the elimination of segmentation ambiguity, the recognition of unknown words and the elimination of multi category parts of speech in each link. In consideration of the above reasons, as well as the rapidity and practicality required by the system, the resource retrieval system has established a vocabulary dictionary based on mutual information entropy. The dictionary is saved in the dic folder under the system directory with the file name lastcitian.txt.

### 3.2 Resource Retrieval Method

The retrieval method of English literature appreciation teaching resources with mutual information entropy as the core is as follows: first, refer to the resource type of the target information source, and with the help of a vocabulary dictionary, build the ontology of related fields; The second step is to obtain the resource information in the information source, and refer to the corresponding ontology built to make semantic annotation of the obtained data and store it in the metabase; The third step is to extract relevant concepts from the user's query statements, process the concept semantics with the support of ontology technology, and find qualified semantic information documents from the metabase; Finally, the retrieved results are processed and returned to the user [8] (Fig. 3).

The general retrieval model is shown in the following figure.

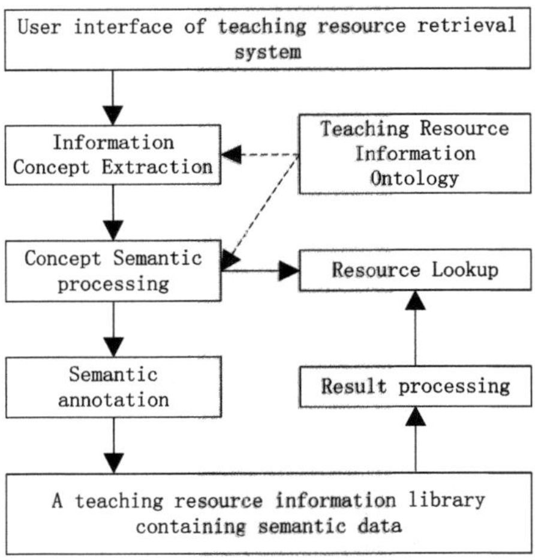


**Fig. 3.** Teaching resource retrieval model

Ontology is the key to realize the retrieval of teaching resources;The document library contains semantic information after semantic annotation; The feature items matched by the system are no longer keywords but domain concepts in the ontology; Conceptual semantic processing is the semantic expansion of user retrieval conditions under the guidance of ontology.

The following principles should be followed in the process of constructing the retrieval system of English literature appreciation teaching resources based on mutual information entropy:

(1) Analyze the discipline characteristics of resources, and construct the corresponding ontology of learning resources and knowledge.
(2) Create a metadata database containing semantic descriptions for learning resources.

(3) Word segmentation is required to convert the query statement entered by the user into a keyword set.
(4) Semantic expansion is needed to improve the recall and precision of retrieval.
(5) The retrieval result set should be processed to meet the needs of users.

Using formula (5), the resource retrieval expression followed by the system host is derived as follows:

$$A = \left. \frac{\prod_{a=1}^{+\infty} Q\left(\hat{d}\right)}{f \times |\Delta D|} \right|_{f \neq 0} \tag{6}$$

Among them, $a$ Represents the return coefficient of the teaching resource search results, $\hat{d}$ Metadata definition vector representing English literature appreciation teaching resources, $\Delta D$ Represents the unit cumulative amount of teaching resource information in the metabase, $f$ Represents the ontology retrieval coefficient.

Referring to the conceptual structure of knowledge point ontology, the corresponding semantic description of concepts is added with RDF (Resource Description Framework) language, and stored in the metadata base in the form of XML documents.Based on the concept structure of knowledge point ontology, the corresponding concept semantic information of teaching resources is expanded by using automatic semantic reasoning technology.

### 3.3 Key Technology Realization

The resource database building module in the English literature appreciation teaching resource retrieval system based on mutual information entropy allows users to upload learning resources to enrich the resource database, and simply describe and label resources according to the hierarchical relationship of knowledge points. In traditional retrieval systems, announcers usually use keywords to annotate resources. This standard method is simple and efficient, and is widely used; In the semantic web, such annotation information is no longer the keyword of natural language, but the concept, data attribute and value defined in the ontology.

regulations $\dot{g}$ It represents the semantic annotation features of English literature appreciation teaching resources, and the solution result is:

$$\dot{g} = \phi \times \sqrt{1 - \left| \frac{1}{A} \times \hat{h} \right|^2} \tag{7}$$

$\phi$ Indicates the description parameters of teaching resources, $\hat{h}$ Data attribute assignment vector representing teaching resource information.

There are two methods of semantic annotation: manual annotation and machine annotation. Among them, the manual annotation means that the standard direction is determined by the annotation personnel and the annotation items describing the resources are determined by themselves according to a certain process and under the guidance of the ontology. This method is strictly constrained by the ontology model, and the workload of annotation personnel is large, and the efficiency of annotation completion is low. Therefore, many researchers are committed to the automatic (or semi-automatic) technology of semantic annotation [9]. This semantic annotation process has both the simplicity and efficiency of traditional keyword based annotation and the structural normalization of ontology based annotation, which is an efficient way of semantic annotation.

The calculation formula for the result of the semantic standard of English literature appreciation teaching resources is:

$$K = \vec{j} \cdot \left(1 - \frac{\dot{g}}{\varphi}\right)^{\iota} \tag{8}$$

$\vec{j}$ Real time coding vector representing semantic information of teaching resources, $\varphi$ Represents automatic dimensioning parameters, $\iota$ The key value coefficient representing the information of English literature appreciation teaching resources.

Semantic reasoning has different meanings in natural language and machine language. The semantic reasoning in the teaching resource retrieval system is based on people's understanding of objective things, which is the deepening of understanding and the transfer of semantic expression; Semantic reasoning in machine language does not extend conceptual relationships as it does in natural language. It can only process formal symbolic expressions. It deals with logical relationships between symbolic objects [10]. In the semantic retrieval system, the symbolic object of machine language represents the concept of natural language, and the ontology structure defines the semantic relationship between concepts. The semantic reasoning of symbolic objects is completed using ontology technology. In a word, semantic reasoning is to enable computers to understand and understand the conceptual structure and metadata information of domain ontology, and complete the transformation from one concept to another with defined logical rules.

Using formula (8), the semantic derivation expression of English literature appreciation teaching resources is:

$$L = \frac{\prod_{-\infty}^{+\infty} \left|\lambda \cdot \tilde{H}\right|^2}{K - 1} \tag{9}$$

$\lambda$ Represent the logical authentication parameters of the retrieval system for English literature appreciation teaching resource information, $\tilde{H}$ The transfer behavior vector representing the teaching posture information under the condition of mutual information entropy.

In the retrieval system, semantic reasoning is expressed in the form that when the user enters a query statement, the system returns the reasoned result set to the user one by one, in order to meet the different needs of the user. The main function of online semantic reasoning is to expand the relevant semantics based on the query statements entered by the user. Its life cycle occurs in the session phase of interaction with the user. This online reasoning relationship is also called conditional extended semantic reasoning. The feature of this retrieval method is that it can expand the connotation and extension of the query conditions entered by users, which will inevitably reduce the workload of users in multiple retrieval. After the user submits the initial query statement, after the semantic expansion of the query statement, he or she will get a set of query statements with high relevance to the query statement. This set of query statements obtained through online semantic reasoning will greatly improve the recall and precision of information retrieval.

On the basis of formula (9), the execution conditions of key retrieval technologies can be expressed as:

$$X = \frac{1}{\dot{b}^2} \sum_{z=1}^{+\infty} v' \sqrt{\frac{L}{\psi \times \xi}} \tag{10}$$

Among them, $\dot{b}$ Represent the semantic reasoning features of teaching resource information based on mutual information entropy, $z$ Query parameters representing English literature appreciation teaching resource information, $\psi$ Represents the real-time query coefficient of the resource information to be retrieved, $\xi$ It represents the semantic expansion coefficient of English literature appreciation teaching resource information.

Under the support of mutual information entropy, the system host should also avoid repeating the value of semantic annotation parameters in the process of executing the retrieval instructions in order to achieve on-demand retrieval of English literature appreciation teaching resources.

## 4 Example Analysis

This paper takes the English literature appreciation teaching resource retrieval system based on mutual information entropy, the vertical retrieval system based on Lucene, the estimation retrieval system based on Grassberger, the literature [3] system and the literature [4] system as the experimental objects.According to the ratio of teaching resources information under the influence of different methods, the retrieval ability of host components to teaching information was analyzed.

### 4.1 Experimental Environment

Use the equipment components shown in Table 2 to build the operating environment of the teaching resource retrieval system.

In order to ensure the absolute fairness of the experimental results, in addition to the different experimental methods, the connection forms of other equipment components in the experimental group and the control group are always consistent.

### 4.2 Principle Description

For English literature appreciation teaching resources, in the process of implementing information retrieval, the balance of resource allocation affects the precise retrieval ability of host components to information parameters. Without considering other interference conditions, the higher the balance of resource allocation, the stronger the host components' ability to accurately retrieve information parameters; On the contrary, if the balance of resource allocation is relatively low, it means that the host components have relatively weak ability to accurately retrieve information parameters.

The specific implementation process of this experiment is as follows.

**Table 2.** Operation environment of retrieval system

| Project | Component Name | Equipment model |
|---|---|---|
| 1 | Resource information sharing chip | BASE version XC7K325T kit |
| 2 | Teaching Resource Master Microprocessor | S3C2416XH-40 main control CPU |
| 3 | Data information storage | BGA-676 SOC CORTEX-A9 |
| 4 | Resource sharing host | S3C2410AL-20 equipment |
| 5 | Information encryption component | Stc89c52RC programming motherboard |
| 6 | Information trigger | DS3231MZ + SOIC-8 clock chip |

- Connect the application equipment at all levels in Table 2 on demand to provide a stable transmission environment for English literature appreciation teaching resource information.
- Input the executive program of the English literature appreciation teaching resource retrieval system based on mutual information entropy into the application host, record the numerical changes of the resource allocation balance under the action of the system, and the results are experimental group variables.
- Input the executive program of Lucene based vertical retrieval system into the application host, record the numerical changes of resource allocation balance under the action of the system, and the results are the control (1) group variables.
- Input the executive program of the retrieval system based on the Grassberger estimation into the application host, record the numerical changes of the resource allocation balance under the action of the system, and the results are the control (2) group variables.
- The document [3] system executive program is input into the application host to record the numerical change of resource allocation balance under the action of the system, and the result is the control (3) group variable.
- The document [4] system executive program is input into the application host to record the numerical change of resource allocation balance under the action of the system, and the result is the control (4) group variable.
- Integrate the variable data obtained and summarize the experimental rules.

### 4.3 Discussion of Results

The following figure reflects the changes of experimental values of resource allocation balance in the experimental group, control (1) group, control (2) group control (3) group and control (4) group (Fig. 4).

Experimental group: With the extension of the experimental time, the balance of teaching resources in the experimental group kept increasing, and by the end of the 100min experiment, its maximum value reached 95.0%.

Control (1) group: The numerical change trend of the balance of teaching resources allocation in control (1) group is the same as that in the experimental group, but its average level is relatively low. By the end of the 100min experiment, its maximum value

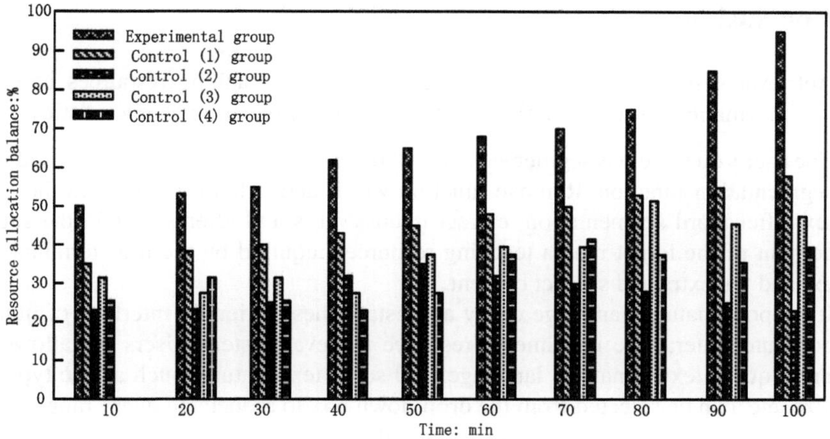


**Fig. 4.** Balance of resource allocation

can only reach 67.9%, which is 27.1% lower than the maximum value of the experimental group.

Control (2): Control (2) The balance of teaching resources allocation maintained the trend of increasing first and then decreasing. At the 50th minute, the maximum value was 35.0%, which was 32.9% lower than the maximum value of control (1) group, and 60.0% lower than the maximum value of the experimental group.

Control (3): The value of the system teaching resource allocation balance in literature [3] has a large trend of change, and the maximum value is 51%.

Control (4): The change trend of the value of the system teaching resource allocation balance in reference [4] is basically the same as that in control (3), and the maximum value is 43%.

To sum up, the conclusion of this experiment is:

- The application of the retrieval system based on Grassberger estimation can only keep the balance of teaching resources at a low numerical level, so the application of this system cannot solve the problem of unbalanced resource allocation.
- Although the application of Lucene based vertical retrieval system has properly improved the numerical level of the balance of teaching resources, it still does not meet the actual application needs.
- The application of the literature [3] system and the literature [4] system has appropriately improved the numerical level of teaching resource balance, but it still cannot meet the needs of practical application.
- Compared with the vertical retrieval system based on Lucene and the retrieval system based on Grassberger estimation, the application of the retrieval system of English literature appreciation teaching resources based on mutual information entropy has greatly improved the numerical level of the balance of teaching resources allocation, which can better solve the problem of unbalanced resource allocation, thus ensuring the accurate retrieval ability of the application host for teaching information.

## 5 Conclusion

The retrieval system of English literature appreciation teaching resources based on mutual information entropy mainly has the following application characteristics:

(1) The user's query text is segmented and part of speech tagged using the self used word segmentation function. Remove function words and default words from the query text after word segmentation, extract nouns, verbs and idioms, obtain the subject content of the target media teaching resources required by the user terminal, and expand the extracted subject content.
(2) It supports natural language query and establishes a friendly interface of human-computer interactive multimedia resource retrieval system. Users are allowed to input query text in natural language, and some text features such as file type, file size, etc. can be selected from the drop-down box to reduce the query range.
(3) The user terminal can intuitively observe the semantic characteristics of the search results and related teaching resources on the result output interface, and can enter the webpage where the media is located through the hyperlink on the interface.

In addition, since the system host searches English literature appreciation teaching resources indiscriminately, the actual value range of teaching resource information should be expanded as far as possible when defining the expression of mutual information entropy. The analysis of user query text should be further deepened. Conduct semantic analysis on user query statements, add weight to the obtained subject words, further determine the retrieval focus, and improve the retrieval accuracy. This is necessary for the further development of the system, but it is also the most difficult part to upgrade and realize. With the expansion of the database scale, when the query conditions are nested too much, the retrieval speed is relatively slow. The database retrieval algorithm should be further optimized to accelerate the speed and improve the practicability of the system.The system has some limitations in the semantic understanding and inference of user query, and can not accurately capture the user's intention and demand. In future studies, by introducing more advanced natural language processing technology, expanding data coverage, establishing user feedback mechanism and providing diversified search methods, the retrieval system of English literature appreciation teaching resources based on mutual information entropy can be further improved, and its retrieval accuracy, comprehensiveness and user experience can be improved.

## References

1. Aoyagi, S., Kamochi, K., Miisho, A., et al.: Interpretation of TOF-SIMS data based on information entropy of spectra. Surf. Interface Anal. **54**(4), 356–362 (2022)
2. Jiang, S., Ding, J., Zhang, L.: A personalized recommendation algorithm based on weighted information entropy and particle swarm optimization. Mob. Inf. Syst. **2021**(4), 1–9 (2021)
3. Yu, X., Zeng, F., Mwakapesa, D.S., et al.: DBWGIE-MR: A density-based clustering algorithm by using the weighted grid and information entropy based on MapReduce. J. Intell. Fuzzy Syst. **40**(6), 10781–10796 (2021)
4. Sinhababu, A., Chakravarty, R., Kaur, A.,et al.: Visual citation navigation of open education resources using Litmaps. Library Hi Tech News **39**(5), 7–11 (2022)

5. Gao, M.: Smart campus teaching system based on ZigBee wireless sensor network. Alex. Eng. J. **61**(4), 2625–2635 (2022)
6. Rublev, V.S, Kondakov, M.D.: Automated teaching system "sets" (research for organizing the 1st part of the project). Modeling Anal. Inform. Syst. **28**(1), 90–103 (2021)
7. Zhao, H., Guo, L.: Design of intelligent computer aided network teaching system based on web. Comput.-Aided Design Appli. **19**(S1), 12–23 (2021)
8. Kardoyo, E.: Development of e-learning management model for teaching system at the police academy. Turkish J. Comput. Mathem. Educ. (TURCOMAT) **12**(5), 188–196 (2021)
9. Yinping, Z., Gencheng, W.: Research on security structure retrieval simulation of sensitive information in mobile internet. Comput. Simulat. **39**(09), 451–455 (2022)
10. Liu, K.: On the construction of teachers' professional quality-oriented english practice teaching system—exemplified with the english major of sichuan university of arts and science. Theory Pract. Lang. Stud. **11**(4), 390–395 (2021)

# Design of Push Algorithm for Individualized Course Content of College Public Art Education Online Education

Fang Li[1(✉)] and Jie Li[2]

[1] Wuhan University of Technology, Wuhan 430070, China
fangdancing@163.com
[2] International Business School, Xi'an Fanyi University, Xi'an 710105, China

**Abstract.** In order to improve the adaptability of online education personalized course push resources and user demand resources, and reduce the push time, a new push method is designed for online education personalized course content of Public art education courses in colleges and universities. A collaborative filtering algorithm is introduced to determine the target content to be pushed. Through screening similar users, we can master the demand directions of different types of users for course content, and realize the calculation of user preferences. We introduce convolution neural networks to train the data information in the convolution layer of convolution neural networks, obtain the characteristic parameters of course content, and conduct directional extraction of course content of public art education. We introduce a weighted fuzzy calculation method to determine the recommendation levels of course content in combination with the spatial expression of course content, and realize the active recommendation of course content. Experimental results show that the proposed method can reduce the discrepancy between the content of push-forward course and user's demand, and ensure a higher adaptability between the content and user's demand.

**Keywords:** Convolution Neural Network · Fuzzy Weighting · Collaborative Filtering Algorithm · Resource Push · Teaching Resources · College Education · Public Art Education

## 1 Introduction

The public art education in colleges and universities refers to the public art courses set up in colleges and universities to improve students' artistic quality, aesthetic quality, cultural taste and understanding and understanding of art forms under different cultural backgrounds. Public art education in colleges and universities is different from professional art education in that it provides students with basic knowledge and skills of art literacy for all subjects. The development of public art education in colleges and universities can not only improve students' aesthetic ability and cultural quality, but also enhance their creativity and imagination. Public art education can make students more


G. Gui et al. (Eds.): eLEOT 2023, LNICST 543, pp. 172–184, 2024.
https://doi.org/10.1007/978-3-031-51465-4_12

open-minded and broadened horizons, but also can promote students' emotional experience and enhance students' mental health [1]. However, college public art education is facing some difficulties. Public art education is generally not the major of a student, and students may have limited time and energy to learn, so it is difficult to gain as much artistic culture and experience as possible in a short period of time. Online art education in colleges and universities refers to art-related learning activities through online platforms under the network environment. Online public art education in colleges and universities can learn independently according to individual needs and time without time and space constraints. Compared with the traditional public art education in colleges and universities, online public art education in colleges and universities is more convenient and flexible [2]. With the popularization and development of modern Internet technology, large-scale online open courses have become a new and popular trend in the field of education. With the characteristics of openness, free and accessibility, online teaching platform provides learners with diversified and high-quality online courses, which are not limited by time and place. Compared with the traditional teaching, the large-scale online open course provides a more flexible learning style for learners. Learners can learn according to their own schedule and requirements. In addition, the online teaching platform has no limit on the number of participants, and provides interactive, multimedia and other forms of online learning experience for learners through various teaching methods and forms, so as to enhance students' participation and learning enthusiasm, and enhance the quality and effect of courses. In a word, the large-scale online open course is an innovative form of education, which is loved by many learners with its flexibility and universality.

In today's globalization and informationization, online education has become the mainstream trend in the future. With the improvement of people's life quality, the demand for art is higher and higher. With college public art online education, students can learn art-related knowledge and skills to meet their needs and interests. The significance of online education of public art in colleges and universities lies in solving the limitation of time and space under the traditional education mode. College public art online education can improve people's learning enthusiasm and self-learning ability, and make learning more personalized and customized, attract more students to participate in art education. However, there are some difficulties in public art online education in colleges and universities. Because of the large amount of tedious steps and the complexity of information, the traditional scientific research elective system faces great challenges. Choosing courses not only needs time and energy, but also may bring stress and bad experience to students. The problem of information overload and difficult screening also makes it difficult for students to find valuable learning resources they need. These problems greatly hinder the improvement of students' academic performance and learning experience. Therefore, the accurate search and recommendation of online teaching resources has become a significant research topic.

Some scholars have proposed the use of cloud computing technology to build an e-learning resources recommendation system, featuring the use of Google cloud services to recommend learning resources based on students' needs and an incentive module to urge students to enhance learning [3]. Some scholars propose to use machine learning technology to provide a new Dirichlet framework for online teaching platform, which can provide users with curriculum suggestions according to their preferences and behaviors. Using Latent Allocation to mine text, using decision tree to generate decision rules, using Self Map to evaluate courses, and using rule-based fuzzy system to predict user preferences. In addition, the feature selection method is used to select important criteria for forecasting user preferences [4]. Another proposal is to design an enhanced e-learning hybrid recommendation system that adaptively matches learners' learning patterns and rules according to their behaviors and semantic relationships. Semantic extension methods including DBpedia and WordNet ontology are used to expand terms, and various mood analysis models are introduced to improve the accuracy and effectiveness of recommendation system. Text reviews in e-learning resources are classified into fine-grained emotional categories and applied to rating forecasts [5]. The methods mentioned above put forward different application techniques for searching and recommending learning resources, but when they are applied to public art education courses in colleges and universities, the problems such as frequent collapse of use, great time consumption and loose relevance of recommended contents are likely to occur due to the complexity of resource types and the large number of users concurrent [6], which brings great trouble to users. According to the market users' experience feedback, the existing recommendation systems have the characteristics of large deviation between recommendation resources and users' individual needs.

In order to solve the problem of poor application of traditional method in the process of individualized content push of college public art education courses, an algorithm is designed. Based on the calculation of user preferences based on Collaborative filtering algorithm, the Convolutional neural network method is used to achieve the directional extraction of Public art education curriculum content in colleges and universities. The personalized course content of online education was actively pushed through weighted fuzzy calculation, and the effectiveness of this study was verified through experiments. The main innovations of this approach are as follows:

(1) According to the personalized demands of college students, the user preferences are calculated based on the information such as the user's web browsing history and search history. The collaborative filtering algorithm is used in this process to preliminarily delineate the user's resource push resources and reduce the calculation amount.
(2) Using the convolution neural network algorithm to extract the resources within the user's preference range, through the cycle training related keywords, the course content resources with similar content are traversed and extracted, and a complete set of related resources is obtained.
(3) The weighted fuzzy algorithm is used to rank the weight of the course contents in the resource set, determine the relevance importance of the content resources, and give priority to the content resources with the highest relevance to users' interests and preferences, thus realizing the personalized recommendation of online education resources for public art education courses in colleges and universities.

This method can provide learners with more personalized art education curriculum resources, and also provide new ideas and methods for the research of adaptive recommendation algorithm.

## 2 User Preference Calculation Based on Collaborative Filtering Algorithm

In order to accurately push the individualized course content of public art education online in colleges and universities, this paper introduces collaborative filtering algorithm [7]. In this process, it is necessary to identify the target group of public art education curriculum content push, through the screening of similar users in the group, to master different types of users' demand for public art education curriculum content. Collect user's personal information, through the analysis of information, generate a user demand resource score matrix [3]. The matrix expression is as follows.

$$\mathbf{S} = \begin{bmatrix} s_{11} & s_{12} & \cdots & s_{1n} \\ s_{21} & s_{22} & \cdots & s_{2n} \\ \vdots & \vdots & \ddots & \vdots \\ s_{m1} & s_{m2} & \cdots & s_{mn} \end{bmatrix} \tag{1}$$

In formula (1): $\mathbf{S}$ means the matrix expression of the grading of the curriculum contents required by users; $s_{mn}$ means the scoring indicators of the curriculum contents required by users. By using the scoring matrix, the users who push the course content are screened, and the users with the same needs are classified into a same category. At the same time, the use of collaborative filtering algorithm to classify resources [8]. Randomly push the content of a public art education course for one user, and calculate the user's preference for the pushed content. According to the calculation results, master the user's demand for public art education curriculum content. The formula for calculating user preference is as follows.

$$B = \frac{L(X)^2}{J \times k} \tag{2}$$

In formula (2): $B$ represents user preference; $L$ represents course content category; $X$ represents collaborative filtering algorithm; $J$ represents automatic clustering parameters; and $k$ represents recommended capacity within courses. According to the above formula, the user preference based on collaborative filtering algorithm is calculated.

## 3 Orientation Extraction of Course Content Based on Convolution Neural Network

On the basis of the above design contents, convolution neural network [9] is introduced to conduct directional extraction of the contents of online teaching courses of public art education in colleges and universities. Considering the large amount of content resources of online teaching course of public art education in colleges and universities, the initial course content is input on the network interface. In the convolution layer of convolution neural network, the data information is trained to get the characteristic parameters of the course content. This process is illustrated by a formula.

$$w = \frac{r(c) - f(a)}{\|y\|^2} \tag{3}$$

In formula (3): $w$ represents the characteristic parameters of course contents; $r$ represents the convolution layer in convolution neural network; $c$ represents the training processing of data information; $f$ represents distributed fusion; $a$ represents reorganization model; and $y$ represents characteristic attributes. On the basis of the above contents, using the semantic representation tool in convolution neural network [10], the course contents are divided into several categories, and the course contents with the same characteristics are clustered in space, so as to make the transition from high-dimensional data to low-dimensional data and ensure the uniformity of data format in the terminal. This process is illustrated by a formula.

$$G = \frac{\overline{N}^j}{K\sqrt{HN}} \tag{4}$$

In formula (4): $G$ represents the unified processing of data format in the terminal; $\overline{N}$ represents high-dimensional data; $K$ represents semantic representation tools; $H$ represents the number of course contents with the same characteristics; $N$ represents low-dimensional data; and $j$ represents cluster centers. After finishing the treatment, we set up the content reorganization model of online teaching course of public art education in colleges and universities. At the same time, the design of directional extraction target function [11], so that users have the demand for curriculum content, the terminal can provide users with real-time curriculum content push services. The expression of the extraction objective function is as follows.

$$F = \vartheta_k \sqrt{\frac{\sum [v + c]^2}{M_k}} \tag{5}$$

In formula (5): $F$ represents the expression of the extraction objective function; $\vartheta_k$ represents the fusion of parameters; $M_k$ represents the directed set; and $v$ represents the hash table. According to the calculation formula, the content of the course is extracted from the nodes of convolution neural network to meet the real-time demand of college students for the content of public art education online course.

Based on the preference of college students, this paper constructs a model of course content extraction, and obtains the sample statistical regression analysis result as shown in Fig. 1.

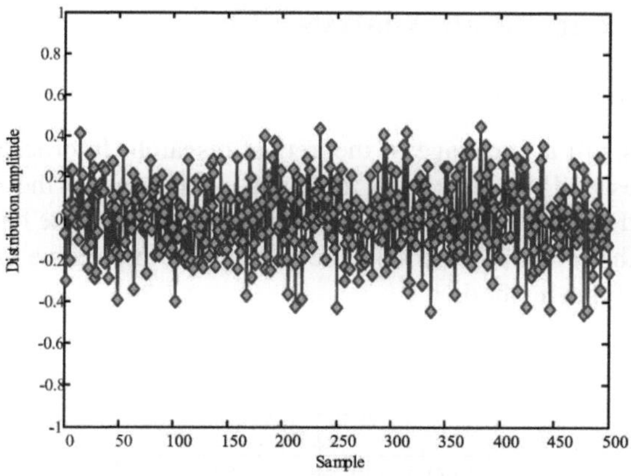


**Fig. 1.** Sample statistical regression analysis

# 4 Active Push of Course Content Based on Weighted Fuzzy Computation

After completing the above research, the weighted fuzzy calculation method [12–14] is introduced to calculate the recommended level of the course content. The formula is as follows.

$$\alpha = \left(AA^T + \partial D\right)^2 + \|\delta\|_{2,1}^z \tag{6}$$

In formula (6): $\alpha$ represents the recommended level of course content; $A$ represents the amount of access control; $\delta$ represents the position of nodes in space; $D$ represents the associated attributes of course content; and $z$ represents weighted fuzzy coefficients. On this basis, the proposed boundary data range of fitness matrix is designed to determine the corresponding data processing accuracy. According to the different categories of curriculum content and the attributes of corresponding curriculum content, the subordination degree is assigned, and then the feasibility of pushing curriculum content is analyzed through the adaptation of pushing curriculum content and user demand curriculum content. [15]. Through this way, improve the university public art education curriculum content of comprehensive push ability, realize the initiative to recommend the curriculum content. Design this process as shown in the following formula.

$$\mu = \sum_{q>1}^{q} \frac{1}{\gamma \times \omega} \tag{7}$$

In formula (7): $\mu$ means active recommendation of course content; $\gamma$ means fitness matrix; $\omega$ means suggested range of boundary data; $q$ means precision of data processing. In accordance with the above method, the active recommendation of curriculum content based on weighted fuzzy calculation is realized, and the individualized curriculum content push algorithm is designed.

# 5 Experiment and Result Analysis

## 5.1 Experimental Preparation

But this method is still at the stage of theoretical research. In order to popularize this method in colleges and universities or relevant institutions in the education market (Fig. 2), we should evaluate its comprehensive performance on the basis of the existing work. Therefore, the following will take the design of comparative experiments to test the effectiveness of this method.

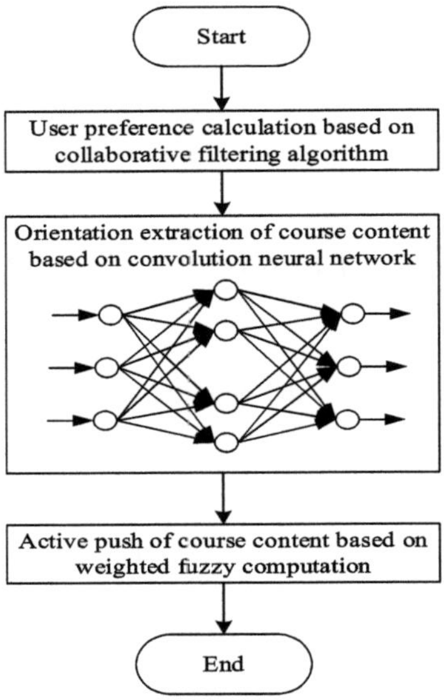


**Fig. 2.** Algorithm Flow

In order to ensure the authenticity of the test results and the objectivity of the data, the public art education majors in a key university in a certain area are selected as experimental sites to recommend online education courses. According to a university official, the school launched a comprehensive public art education program last year, and set up special subjects to give students special guidance on public art education 3–5 h a week. But public art is closely related to personal tastes and interests. The effect of ordinary education is not ideal. Students are not only weak in learning consciousness, but also poor in art identification. Therefore, after signing the relevant agreement with the person in charge of the college, it is decided to carry out the test of the application effect of the design method in the college. To test the application performance of the individualized content push algorithm of online art education courses designed in this paper.

Before carrying out the experiment, the public art education resources of the public art education course of the university in the past half a year shall be collected together with the online resources of the public art education course of the university obtained through the network to form a data set, and the data sources are various, including the development data of the relevant majors and market- related industries, the public art education course resources of the university, the art performance resources, etc. Statistical data samples are divided into two categories: value resources and general resources. The statistical data are collected and sorted as the test data in the comparative experiment. As shown in Table 1 below.

**Table 1.** Comparative Experimental Sample Data

| Data volume (piece) | Data Properties |
|---|---|
| 200000 | Total number of data |
| 140000 | Value resources |
| 600000 | General resources |
| 175000 | test data |
| 25000 | contrasting data |

The university's public art education curriculum resource data set includes more than a dozen art projects, each with 30 to 50 courses, with art appreciation, drama appreciation, drama and dance as an example. Some online teaching resources are shown in Fig. 3 below.

**Fig. 3.** Example diagram of online instructional resources

After the statistics of the experimental test samples is completed, the method designed in this paper is used to recommend the contents of public art education courses for students participating in the experiment. In the process of recommendation, collaborative filtering algorithm is introduced to extract users' history learning behavior and web browsing data, and user identity model is established to calculate user preference. On this basis, convolution neural networks are introduced to conduct directional extraction of university public art curriculum resources (existing resources). Through the weighted fuzzy calculation of the recommended resources, the active and accurate push service of public art resources is provided for users.

## 5.2 Push Performance Verification

Taking a college student user as an example, through the analysis of information such as history learning behavior and web browsing data, it is found that the user's main interest is oil painting, among which Richard Schmid is the most frequent keyword search. In this case, the push interface of this method is as follows:

**Fig. 4.** Push interface

Figure 4 shows that this method can effectively push the personalized content of public art education online teaching. The content pushed is closely related to the user's interests, and more push content can meet user needs.

## 5.3 Verification of Fitness

In the process of pushing the individualized course content of public art education courses online in colleges and universities, the probability distribution density of the content resources of public art education courses that college students click on or actively retrieve is calculated as follows:

$$Q = \sum_{i>1}^{\infty} e(t) + \frac{1}{\sqrt{c}\exp\left[R(t)^2\right]} \tag{8}$$

In the formula (8): $Q$ shall mean the probability distribution density of the recommended resources clicked or actively retrieved by the user; $e$ shall mean the number of times searched by the user; $t$ shall mean the valid range of probabilities; $R$ shall mean the number of iterations; $i$ shall mean the number of times of data mining. When the result is close to 1.0, the probability of students to click or retrieve the personalized course content resources is higher, and the adaptability of the proposed method is higher. Randomly select a college student user to participate in this experiment, according to the background record data, statistical experimental results, as shown in Fig. 5 below.

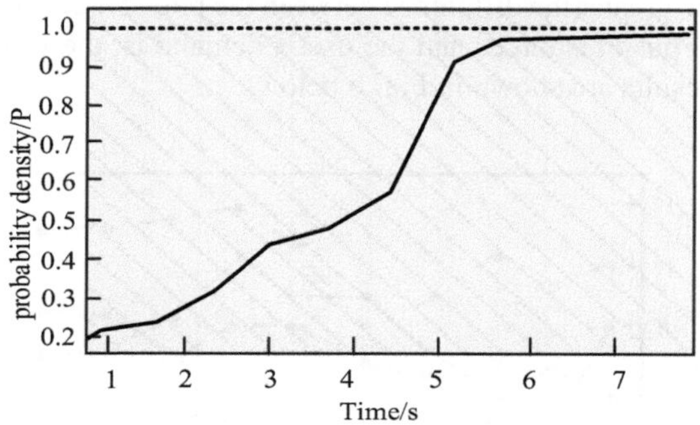


**Fig. 5.** Trend of probability distribution density for proactive retrieval of push resources

Based on the experimental results shown in Fig. 5 above, it can be seen that as the time of browsing the Web increases, the data of user behavior obtained by the terminal increases, and the probability distribution density of users clicking or actively retrieving the push resources of public art education personalized curriculum content increases. When the time of browsing the Web reaches 6 s, the probability distribution density of users clicking or actively retrieving the push resources tends to 1.0, that is, the fitness between the push resources of personalized curriculum content and the user demand resources tends to 100%. It can be proved that the algorithm designed in this paper is effective in practice, and can improve the adaptability between the public art education personalized course content and the user resources.

## 5.4 Difference Degree Contrast

On the basis of the above design contents, literature [3] method, literature [4] method and literature [5] method are introduced, and these methods are compared with the push algorithm designed in this paper. Using the method of this paper and the traditional method, we push the individualized course content of public art education to different users. The difference between push resource and user demand is used as evaluation index to calculate the evaluation index. The formula is as follows.

$$P = \frac{\sum_u |a_1 - a_2|}{n} \tag{9}$$

In formula (9): $P$ represents the difference between push resources and user needs; $a_1$ represents push resources; $a_2$ represents user needs resources; $n$ represents push times; and $u$ represents average errors. According to the above formula, the smaller the value of $P$ is, the smaller the difference between the public art education personalized curriculum content push resources and the user's demand is, the better the push effect is; the greater the value of $P$ is, the greater the difference between the public art education personalized curriculum content push resources and the user's demand is, the worse the push effect is. The statistical results are shown in Fig. 6 below.

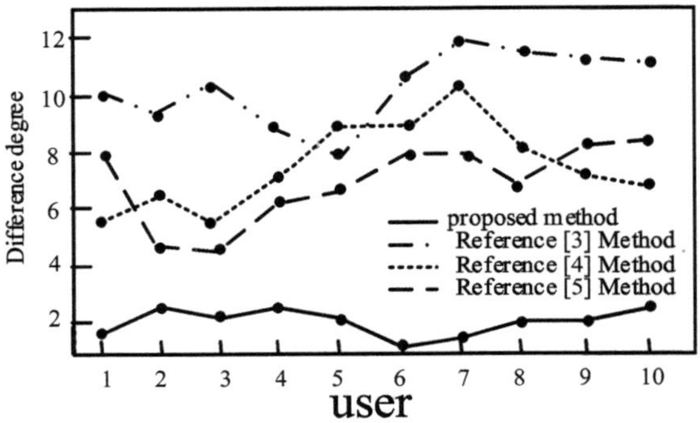


**Fig. 6.** Comparison of the difference between push resources and user requirements

Based on the experimental results shown in Fig. 6 above, it can be seen that the difference of the proposed method between the public art education personalized curriculum content push resources and users is small, with an average of 2.1. On the other hand, literature [3] method, literature [4] method and literature [5] method have significant differences in the average of 9.5, 7.8 and 6.1. It shows that the method can push the similar public art education personalized curriculum content, which makes the user experience of college students better, and is conducive to promoting the public art education curriculum.

### 5.5 Push Time Comparison

In order to further verify the application performance of the personalized course content push algorithm designed in this paper, five experiments were repeated to test the keywords of 10 different public art education courses by using the methods of document [3], document [4] and document [5] as the comparison methods. The results are shown in Table 2 below:

**Table 2.** Push Resource Time/ms

| group | The method of this paper | Reference [3] Methods | Reference [4] Methods | Reference [5] Methods |
|---|---|---|---|---|
| 1 | 146 | 501 | 387 | 586 |
| 2 | 251 | 533 | 339 | 688 |
| 3 | 188 | 496 | 376 | 641 |
| 4 | 267 | 467 | 540 | 689 |
| 5 | 207 | 528 | 486 | 643 |
| mean value | 211.8 | 505 | 425.6 | 649.4 |

From the Table 2, we can see that the speed of pushing the individualized curriculum content of public art education courses varies greatly among different methods. Under the application of this method, the pushing resource consumption is the shortest, averaging 211.8 ms, while the pushing resource consumption of document [3] method, document [4] method and document [5] method is high and fluctuating, averaging 505 ms, 425.6 ms and 649.4 ms respectively. The results show that this method can get the individualized course content of public art education with high response speed, and enhance the satisfaction of college students.

Compared with other methods, the proposed algorithm can reduce the difference between the push resource and the user's requirement, and ensure the higher adaptability between the push resource and the user's requirement.

## 6 Concluding Remarks

In this paper, we design an algorithm to push the individualized content of online art education courses in colleges and universities, and use convolution neural network to extract the content. After completing the design, the experiment proves that the method can reduce the difference between the personalized course content resources and the needs of college students, ensure the adaptability between the personalized course content resources and the needs of users, and reduce the overall push time. The purpose of this study is to provide some technical guidance for the rapid implementation of public art education in colleges and universities, and to enhance students' awareness of public art. In future research, multiple methods can also be considered for combination and integration to further improve the accuracy and effectiveness of personalized course content push algorithms. At the same time, attention should also be paid to issues such as privacy protection and data security to ensure that students' personal information is appropriately protected.

## References


1. Zagkotas, V., Fykaris, I.: Approaching the ‘Death of Socrates’ through art education. a teaching proposal and the introduction of a new typology for teaching with similar artworks. J. Classics Teach. **23**(45), 60–72 (2022)
2. Sabol, F.R.: Art education during the COVID-19 pandemic: the journey across a changing landscape. Arts Educ. Policy Rev. **123**(3), 127–134 (2022)
3. Rahhali, M., Oughdir, L., Jedidi, Y., Lahmadi, Y., Khattabi, M.Z.E.: E-learning recommendation system based on cloud computing. In: Bennani, S., Lakhrissi, Y., Khaissidi, G., Mansouri, A., Khamlichi, Y. (eds.) WITS 2020: Proceedings of the 6th International Conference on Wireless Technologies, Embedded, and Intelligent Systems, pp. 89–99. Springer, Singapore (2022). https://doi.org/10.1007/978-981-33-6893-4_9
4. Nilashi, M., Minaei-Bidgoli, B., Alghamdi, A., et al.: Knowledge discovery for course choice decision in massive open online courses using machine learning approaches. Expert Syst. Appl. **199**, 117092 (2022)
5. Ezaldeen, H., Misra, R., Bisoy, S.K., et al.: A hybrid E-learning recommendation integrating adaptive profiling and sentiment analysis. J. Web Seman. **72**, 100700 (2022)
6. Elpus, K.: Access to arts education in America: the availability of visual art, music, dance, and theater courses in US high schools. Arts Educ. Policy Rev. **123**(2), 50–69 (2022)
7. Papadakis, H., Papagrigoriou, A., Panagiotakis, C., et al.: Collaborative filtering recommender systems taxonomy. Knowl. Inf. Syst.. Inf. Syst. **64**(1), 35–74 (2022)
8. Aljunid, M.F., Huchaiah, M.D.: IntegrateCF: Integrating explicit and implicit feedback based on deep learning collaborative filtering algorithm. Expert Syst. Appl. **207**, 117933 (2022)
9. Ghimire, D., Kil, D., Kim, S.: A survey on efficient convolutional neural networks and hardware acceleration. Electronics **11**(6), 945 (2022)
10. Ali, R., Chuah, J.H., Talip, M.S.A., et al.: Structural crack detection using deep convolutional neural networks. Autom. Constr.. Constr. **133**, 103989 (2022)
11. Ghazal, T.M.: Convolutional neural network based intelligent handwritten document recognition. Comput. Mater. Continua **70**(3), 4563–4581 (2022)
12. Di Caprio, D., Ebrahimnejad, A., Alrezaamiri, H., et al.: A novel ant colony algorithm for solving shortest path problems with fuzzy arc weights. Alex. Eng. J. **61**(5), 3403–3415 (2022)
13. Pamucar, D., Deveci, M., Stević, Ž, et al.: Green strategies in mobility planning towards climate change adaption of urban areas using fuzzy 2D algorithm. Sustain. Cities Soc. **87**, 104159 (2022)
14. Jingjing, E., Yang, L., Feng, F.: Fuzzy clustering simulation study of big data based on improved sparse representation. Comput. Simul. **40**(01), 479–483 (2023)
15. Hesamian, G., Akbari, M.G.: Fuzzy time series model using weighted least square estimation. Iran. J. Fuzzy Syst. **19**(2), 63–81 (2022)

# Multi Agent Based High School Physics Network Course Automatic Generation System

Haiquan Chi[1(✉)], Zhonghua Zhao[1], and Xiaojun Jiang[2]

[1] Liao Ning Province Zhangwu Senior High School, Zhangwu 123200, China
18162766359@163.com

[2] School of Translation Studies, Xian Fanyi University, Xi'an 710105, China

**Abstract.** The construction of online courses is the key to the modernization of education. Due to the backwardness of the application means of the existing network course automatic generation system, the network course automatic generation takes a long time and the function of the network course is less perfect. In order to solve the problems such as long time and imperfect function of high school physical network course automatic generation, this paper puts forward the design and research of high school physical network course automatic generation system based on multi-agent. Take high school physics as the research subject, determine the principles that need to be followed in the automatic generation of online courses, build the automatic generation framework of online courses, design the database of online courses, construct and configure multi-agent according to the automatic generation requirements of online courses. The multi-agent value decomposition stage and the multi-agent communication mechanism design stage enable the multi-agent to have the corresponding function of automatically generating network courses, which can automatically generate the required high school physics network courses. The experimental data shows that after the application of the design system, the minimum time spent for automatic generation of online courses is 16 s, and the maximum value of functional perfection of online courses is 99%, which fully proves that the application performance of the design system is better.

**Keywords:** High school physics · Automatic generation · Online courses · Reinforcement learning · Multi-agent

## 1 Introduction

At the end of the last century, advanced information technologies such as network technology, Web Services, IPv6 and so on continued to emerge, and went deep into various industries. The development trend characterized by extensive application of information technology appeared in life, education, scientific research, national defense, urban construction and other fields. Education informatization was proposed under this background. Network education and network resource construction are the key to information education. Vigorously promoting the construction of network courses not only meets the


G. Gui et al. (Eds.): eLEOT 2023, LNICST 543, pp. 185–199, 2024.
https://doi.org/10.1007/978-3-031-51465-4_13

requirements of information technology, but also meets the needs of popular education and lifelong learning. ICT in education requires continuous reform of educational ideas, enrichment of educational means, innovation of teaching methods, and transformation of the interrelationship between the four elements (teachers, students, textbooks, and media) in the teaching structure, namely, the transformation of teacher centered teaching into student-centered teaching, and the transformation of collective face-to-face teaching of teachers into inquiry learning and collaborative learning guided by teachers. The teaching of fixed course content has changed to the extensive application of a variety of learning resources and learning environments [1]. The informatization of education in colleges and universities requires the addition of informatization equipment, the use of informatization means, the development of informatization classroom teaching and practical teaching in education related fields and departments, and the realization of informatization in the whole process and in all directions of education. The purpose is to spread new educational ideas, establish new teaching models, improve educational quality, improve educational environment, and cultivate innovative talents in the new century, realize the modernization of education.

"Curriculum informatization is the key content and way to realize education informatization". The carrier of curriculum informatization is the network, and the main component is network education. Network education has broken the traditional curriculum model. In addition to the training of students at school, it also meets the requirements of distance education, adult education, autonomous learning, exchange learning, personalized learning, and special education. The construction of educational informatization resources requires the transformation of traditional curriculum resources into network resources. The curriculum form, curriculum subject, teaching environment, learning environment and teaching media are different between them. Network education is the main method to solve the problem of unbalanced allocation of teaching resources in traditional education, and promote the realization of popular education, universal education and lifelong learning. With the development of information education, online education has also had a comprehensive and rapid reform and development. Various online courses have sprung up like mushrooms, and various course websites have emerged as the times require. More and more colleges and education related units have joined the ranks of developing and launching online course websites. Due to the high level of professional technology required for website development, most of the websites of online courses are currently developed by the course responsible units or teachers who contact professional companies or professional technicians for pre production and post maintenance. Therefore, the actual production, development, operation and maintenance process involves the difficulty and speed of communication between both parties. At present, the demand for online courses is large, the construction speed is slow, the teaching mode is outdated, the curriculum is difficult to modify, maintain, update, the development efficiency is low, and the operation and maintenance cost is high. Therefore, the majority of online course teachers urgently need an automatic generation system for online courses, which can automatically generate the required course website by defining the website structure and setting the plate columns by themselves. It is also able to update and maintain the generated course website in terms of data addition and deletion, online evaluation, message interaction, homework submission and correction [2].

The construction of online courses in foreign countries has developed earlier. At present, there are many mature teaching management software development platforms, such as EduCommons system, Sakai system and Moodle system. From the perspective of application, there are few automatic generation systems for online courses in China, and there are few software development platforms that integrate information based curriculum design mode and high-level website design. The automatic generation system of online courses has high application value and great demand, but few high-level products have been developed. At present, the online course automatic generation system based on fuzzy clustering and the online course automatic generation system based on FCM clustering are widely used in China. The quality of the generated online courses is poor, so the design of the high school physics online course automatic generation system based on multi-agent is proposed. According to the characteristics of online course website and the needs of users, B/S mode is adopted to realize the automatic generation of online course. Multi-agent can transform the problem of automatic generation of online courses into a Markov decision process of limited distributed observations, which simplifies the automatic generation of online courses to the maximum extent. Through multi-agent training stage, multi-agent value decomposition stage, multi-agent communication mechanism design stage, combined with the specific needs of users to automatically generate high school physics online course.

## 2 Design of Automatic Generation System for High School Physics Network Course

### 2.1 Automatic Generation Architecture Building Module of Online Courses

Take high school physics as the research subject, determine the principles that need to be followed in the automatic generation of online courses, build the automatic generation framework of online courses, and provide support for the subsequent module design.

To establish the principles of online curriculum design, we should refer to the principles of traditional teaching courses, and also combine educational theories, educational objectives under the new situation, and specific curriculum characteristics. Under the information education environment, the curriculum culture has undergone transformation, focusing on the construction of teaching research community and teaching community; Curriculum research insists on returning to the life world, integrating with humanism, and moving towards reflective practice; The quality evaluation system of curriculum construction is improved, from a single quality view to a diversified quality view, and from an academic quality view to an adaptive quality view, which will help to improve the overall quality of subject teaching and promote the sustainable development of the curriculum [3].

From the perspective of comprehensive quality assessment of system design, this paper proposes that the development of modern online courses should follow the following three principles, as shown in Table 1.

At present, there are mainly two operation modes of network application software: C/S mode and B/S mode. The former is more troublesome to upgrade and maintain, while the latter is easy to expand applications and upgrade and maintain. Therefore, it

**Table 1.** Principles for Automatic Generation of Online Courses

| ranking | principle | Content description |
|---|---|---|
| 1 | Principle of directionality | Online courses must achieve certain teaching and education goals. The automatic generation system must be able to design online courses that can construct learning tasks according to certain teaching goals, organize students to explore collaborative learning, guide learners to achieve dynamic learning activities, and achieve the expected learning results |
| 2 | Principle of universality | Online courses are open to public learning. Learners' knowledge level, learning ability and learning characteristics are different. The system design should take into account the universality of the audience. The way of knowledge organization and presentation should be flexible, and the establishment of knowledge modules should take into account the development |
| 3 | Human nature principle | Learners are the main body of cognition and active constructors of knowledge meaning. Website design and development should be integrated with humanism. The development concept should change from curriculum based to personality based. Each module should be arranged according to students' basic learning ability and actual needs. The content should be practical, consistent with learners' cognitive laws, and provide services for students |

has developed rapidly and been widely used in recent years. Based on the characteristics of online course website and user needs, the online course automatic generation system in this paper adopts B/S operation mode. Users can enter the website to browse and access the course content by sending a request to the web server through the browser on the client side. Based on the principles shown in Table 1, combined with B/S operation mode and multi-agent technology, an automatic generation framework of online courses is built, as shown in Fig. 1.

The system adopts a three-tier structure of user layer, business layer and data layer. Among them, the user layer provides a user interface for user operation, and users can fill in data, send requests, and view required information; The business layer is located between the user layer and the data layer, which acts as a bridge for data transmission. The BusinessFacade class is defined in this system to realize the specific business functions of this layer; The data access layer provides access to external systems such as databases, mainly involving ADO.NET database access technology. The DataAccess class is defined in this system for implementation [4].

The above process completed the construction of the automatic generation framework of online courses, laying a solid foundation for subsequent research.

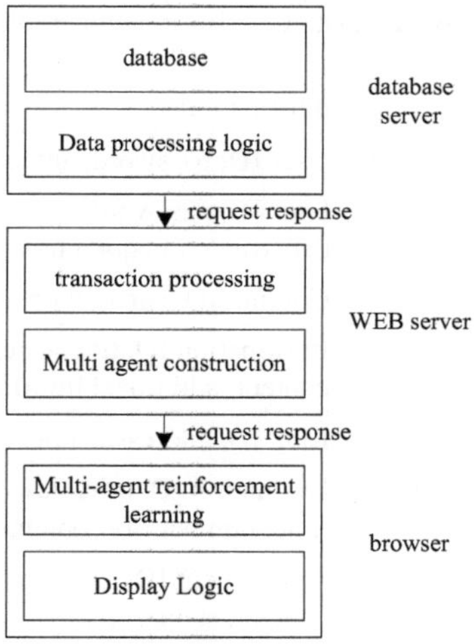


**Fig. 1.** Schematic diagram of automatic generation framework of online courses

## 2.2 Database Design Module

Through the analysis of the system function, the following data demand information is summarized according to the requirements of the automatic generation system of online courses in this paper:

One administrator can manage multiple students/columns/information /links/assessments/assignments/posts;

One student can be managed by multiple administrators;

One student can access multiple columns/information/links /assessments/assignments/posts;

One column/information/link/evaluation/assignment/post can be managed by multiple administrators;

One column/information/link/evaluation/assignment/post can be accessed by multiple students.

Through the analysis and demand summary of the above system functions, more than 10 data items have been designed, some of which are shown in Table 2.

The background database of the system should include administrator information, student information, column information, "information" information, link information, evaluation information, homework information, posting information and other relevant information, and ensure the safety, integrity and standardization of the data. The SQL Server background database designed in this system is JPKCMdf, which defines more than ten data tables, including ADMIN, STUDENT, BLOCK, INFO, LINK, TEST, HOMEWORK, and ARTICLE. Due to space constraints, it will not be detailed.

The above process completes the database design and provides support for the subsequent multi-agent construction.

**Table 2.** Data Item Information Table

| number | data item | information |
|---|---|---|
| 1 | Administrator Information | User ID, password, authority, email, phone, etc. |
| 2 | Student information | User ID, password, student number, name, grade, department, major, class, etc. |
| 3 | Column information | Column ID, name, type, display method, etc. |
| 4 | Information | Information ID, title, category, creator, creation time, content, additional information, etc. |
| 5 | Link Information | Link ID, address, name, etc. |
| 6 | Evaluation information | Evaluation ID, title, description, release time, end time, number of problems, etc. |
| 7 | Job information | Assignment ID, name, teacher, start time, end time, content, status, etc. |
| 8 | Post information | Post ID, title, content, publisher, publishing time, etc. |

## 2.3 Multi Agent Construction Module

Agent, as its name implies, is an entity with intelligence. Its English name is Agent.Based on the cloudAIAs the core, build a system of stereoscopic perception, global collaboration, accurate judgment, continuous evolution and openness. Multi agent can transform the problem of automatic generation of online courses into a Markov decision-making process with limited distributed observation, which can simplify the automatic generation of online courses to the greatest extent. Therefore, this section constructs and configures multi-agent [5].

There are many independent agents in the multi-agent system. Each agent can independently perceive and collect information about the environment. These agents share the same environment and often serve a common goal. The interaction process between multi-agent and environment is shown in Fig. 2.

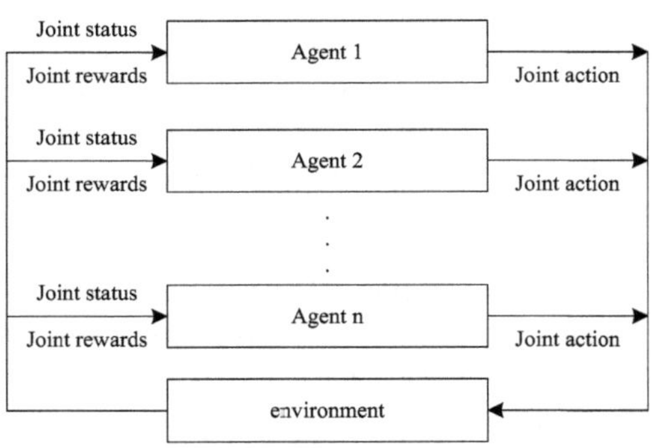


**Fig. 2.** Schematic diagram of interaction process between multi-agent and environment

From the perspective of one of the agents, the interaction process is not very different from that in the single agent system. However, because the environment is shared, each agent can execute actions into the environment, and the transfer of environment state is not only determined by one agent, but also determined by all agents. For example, agent in Fig. 2 $n$ status of $s_t^n$, possibly with agent 1 to $n$ all relevant. This mutual influence and coupling makes the analysis and optimization of multi-agent systems more complicated than that of single agent systems.

From the perspective of a single agent, the multi-agent system does not have the Markov property, but from the perspective of the combination of all agents, that is, if the multi-agent as a whole is regarded as a super agent, the Markov decision process of a single agent can be extended to the multi-agent system. Assume that the number of multi-agent in the system is $n$, then the joint state space can be expressed as $S = S^1 \times S^2 \times \cdots \times S^n$, where, $S^i$ represent agent $i$ state space; The joint action space can be expressed as $A = A^1 \times A^2 \times \cdots \times A^n$, where, $A^i$ represent agent $i$ space for action. At the moment $t$, federation status $s_t \in S$ in joint action $a_t \in A$ will be changed and transferred to $s_{t+1}$ the transfer probability is determined by the joint state probability transfer function of the environment, and the expression is

$$P = S \times A \times S \tag{1}$$

In Formula (1), $P$ it represents the transition probability.

At the same time, the environment will return a joint reward $r_t = \left\{r_t^1, r_t^2, \cdots, r_t^n\right\}$. In the cooperative multi-agent system, the multi-agent will optimize a common goal, so generally speaking, the environment will return the same reward for each agent, that is, the agent $i$ rewards for $r_t^i$ and Agents $j$ rewards for $r_t^j$ it is the same. The environment only considers the common impact of joint actions on the environment, but does not care about the merits of each agent's decision-making.

The multi-agent subsystem constructed above is used to transform the automatic generation problem of online courses into a distributed observation constrained Markov decision process, which can be defined as a seven tuple, expressed as

$$F = \langle S, A, P, R, Z, O, n \rangle \tag{2}$$

In Formula (2), $F$ it represents the result of problem transformation automatically generated by online courses; $R$ it means joint award; $Z$ it represents the mapping function inside the observation information simulation environment; $O$ it represents the observation information of agents.

All agents need to learn a cooperation strategy to maximize the cumulative discount reward. The calculation formula is

$$\alpha = E_{\pi_i}\left[\sum \beta^t r_t^i\right] \tag{3}$$

In Formula (3), $\alpha$ represents the cumulative discount reward calculation result; $E_{\pi_i}[\cdot]$ it represents the calculation function of multi-agent cumulative discount reward; $\beta^t$ indicates the auxiliary parameter for cumulative discount bonus calculation; $\pi_i$ it represents an agent $i$ policy.

Through the above process, the construction of multi-agent is completed, and the problem of automatic generation of online courses is transformed into a Markov decision-making process with limited distributed observation, which facilitates the realization of automatic generation of online courses.

## 2.4 Implementation Module of Automatic Generation of Online Courses

Through the application of multi-agent, the realization of automatic generation of online courses can be divided into three stages, namely, multi-agent training stage, multi-agent value decomposition stage and multi-agent communication mechanism design stage [6]. After passing the above stages, the multi-agent can automatically generate the corresponding functions of online courses, and automatically generate the required high school physics online courses according to user needs.

### 2.4.1 Multi Agent Training Phase

At present, the mainstream multi-agent reinforcement learning methods are mainly divided into two types. One is that agents communicate before making decisions, so as to master more comprehensive information and "negotiate" a cooperative strategy. This method requires agents to learn an efficient communication strategy. Therefore, the problem is mainly from when to communicate, what to communicate. How to carry out communication in these three aspects; The other method is to use centralized training and distributed execution. Each agent only uses its own observation information to make decisions during the execution process, but all agents are trained together during the training process, so that agents can easily obtain global information and learn cooperation strategies [7]. The multi-agent training program is shown in Fig. 3.

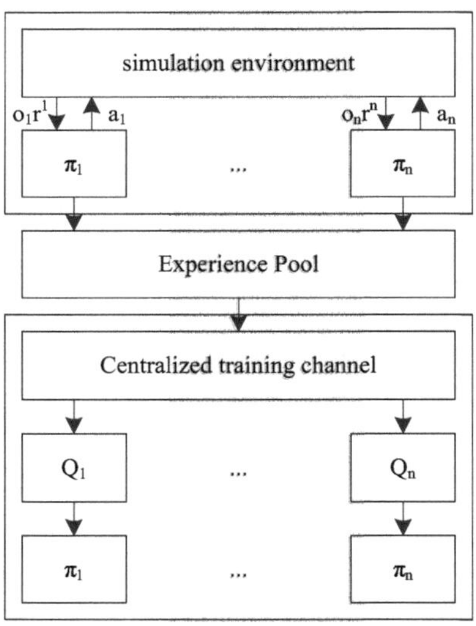


**Fig. 3.** Multi agent training program

Because the agent can only observe a part of the observation information in the multi-agent scene, and then make a decision based on the limited observation information, the decision is often a local optimal action rather than a global optimal action. In order to enable agents to learn a globally optimal strategy as far as possible, researchers have proposed a centralized training and distributed execution mechanism, which divides the training process and execution process of agents, making the two processes relatively independent. In the process of implementation, agents make decisions according to their local observation information, which meets the objective requirements; After the execution, all agents train together according to the global information during the training process. The advantage is that agents can not only obtain the global information for training, but also train together with other agents, making it easier for both parties to learn a cooperative strategy [8]at the same time. Figure 3 is the schematic diagram of centralized training and distributed execution mechanism. The lower part of the diagram represents centralized training, the upper part represents distributed execution, and the strategies of agents $\pi_i$, is responsible for making decisions in the execution phase to generate samples and storing the samples in the experience pool, and then its state action value function $Q_i$, responsible for using the global sample in the training phase $\pi_i$, update so that $\pi_i$ continuously update to the global optimal strategy.

Central-V is a basic centralized training and distributed execution algorithm. It uses Actor Critical as the infrastructure to directly train a centralized state value function $V(S)$ as a Critical, each agent maintains a policy network by itself $\pi_i(O_i)$ used for distributed decision making, and passed the $V(S)$ to calculate performance advantages $A(O_i, A_i)$ to update $\pi_i(O_i)$ the specific update gradient calculation formula is

$$\alpha = \pi \lg(A_i|O_i) \cdot A(O_i, A_i) \tag{4}$$

In Eq. (4), $\alpha$ it means $\pi_i(O_i)$ update gradient of; $\pi(A_i|O_i)$ it represents a state value function $V(S)$ time series difference error of, used to measure $O_i$ down execution action $A_i$ performance improvement.

Since Central-V is only a simple Actor Critical method, use $V(S)$ as the dominant function, the timing difference error of $V(S)$ is not enough [9]. Therefore, COMA first learns a global state action value function $Q(S, A)$ then, based on the counterfactual idea, a new dominance function is proposed, whose expression is

$$A_i(S, A) = Q(S, A) - \sum \pi_i(A_i|O_i)Q(S, (A_{-i}, A_i)) \tag{5}$$

In Formula (5), $A_i(S, A)$ it represents the dominance function.

Through the advantage function shown in Eq. (5), the agent can compare the actions that have been executed with other actions to optimize its own strategy $\pi_i$, preparing for the automatic generation of online courses.

### 2.4.2 Multi Agent Value Decomposition Stage

The multi-agent value decomposition method takes centralized training and distributed execution as the basic training architecture, and its core idea is to construct the individual value function of agents $Q_i(O_i, A_i)$ and global valued functions $Q_{total}(S, A)$ the expression is

$$Q_{total}(S,A) = \zeta\left[Q_1(O_1,A_1), Q_2(O_2,A_2), \cdots, Q_n(O_n,A_n)\right] \quad (6)$$

In Formula (6), $\zeta[\cdot]$ it represents the relationship between the individual value function and the global value function of the agent.

Through relationships $\zeta$ individual state action value function of agent can be used $Q_i(O_i, A_i)$ to approximate the global state action value function $Q_{total}(S, A)$ and then update it in the stage of centralized training $Q_{total}(S, A)$, via $Q_{total}(S, A)$ go through relationships $\zeta$ To update the individual value function of each agent $Q_i(O_i, A_i)$, each agent uses its own individual value function in the distributed execution phase $Q_i(O_i, A_i)$ make decisions. Therefore, most of the current value decomposition methods focus on constructing an accurate, stable and generalized functional relationship $\zeta$ to approximate a more accurate $Q_{total}(S, A)$ [10]. Centralized training stage $Q_{total}(S, A)$ use DQN to update, as shown below:

$$\Gamma(\varphi) = G\Big[Q_{total}(S,A,\varphi) - (R + \beta Q_{total}(S,A,\varphi))^2\Big] \quad (7)$$

In Eq. (7), $\Gamma(\varphi)$ it means $Q_{total}(S, A)$ update function; $\varphi$ represents the update parameter; $G[\cdot]$ it represents an auxiliary function expression; $\beta$ it means $Q_{total}(S, A)$ update step size.

In order to make the agent's strategy approach the global optimal strategy, $\zeta$ the structure of must meet the following conditions as far as possible:

$$\begin{aligned} \arg\max Q_{total}(S,A) =& [\arg\max Q_1(O_1,A_1), \\ & \arg\max Q_2(O_2,A_2), \cdots, \arg\max Q_n(O_n,A_n)] \end{aligned} \quad (8)$$

When the agent strategy reaches the global optimal strategy, the automatic generation performance of its online courses reaches the optimization.

### 2.4.3 Design Phase of Multi-agent Communication Mechanism

The core idea of the communication based method is to design a communication mechanism that allows the agent to communicate before the online course automatically generates the decision, implicitly allowing the agent to obtain the global information and the decision information of the teammates, so as to reach a cooperation strategy. Therefore, most communication based methods are committed to designing an efficient communication mechanism between agents. This mechanism needs to be designed from three aspects: when to communicate, what to communicate, and how to communicate. At present, mainstream methods directly provide a channel. When communicating, the optimal solution is to let the agent learn the communication protocol by itself, so as to intelligently determine the communication time and content.

The early CommNet is a multi-agent reinforcement learning network structure based on communication, which combines the policy networks of all agents into a large network, allowing agents to code their own network to obtain hidden states before making decisions $H_i$ send it out and accept the hidden state sent by other agents at the same time $H_{-i}$ and calculate the mean value $C_i$ so as to obtain sufficient information before making decisions $H_i$, and the average value of other agent information $C_i$, get a new hidden state $H_i$. At the same time, in order to prevent inconsistent communication results caused by a single communication, CommNet uses multiple communications to ensure consistent communication policies. Specifically, in the $j$ Step, agent $i$ the hidden state of is calculated as

$$H_i^{j+1} = \zeta_i\left(H_i^j, C_i^j\right) \tag{9}$$

In Eq. (9), $H_i^j$ it refers to the communication section $j$-one step agent $i$ hidden state of; $C_i^j$ it refers to the communication section $j$-average value of information of other agents in step 1.

CommNet allows agents to hide their own state every time $H_i$ in this way, the agent only learns the communication content, but has no time to learn communication. In many cases, communication is often unnecessary, because agents can make decisions based on their own observation information, and do not need the communication information of other agents. In addition, the information sent by some agents is likely to be redundant and noisy, which will interfere with the intelligence. So IC3Net designed a door $\xi$ communication action is obtained $g_i$, determine the agent $i$ whether communication is needed at present, and then in the communication phase $g_i$, for agents $i$ the specific processing method is

$$C_i^j = \frac{1}{n-1}\sum H_i^j \cdot g_i^j \tag{10}$$

In Eq. (10), due to $g_i$ It is a binary number. When it is 0, the agent $i$ wipe out the communication information of.

After the above three stages, multi-agent can automatically generate the corresponding functions of online courses, and can automatically generate the required high school physics online courses in combination with the specific needs of users.

## 3 Design System Application Performance Test

### 3.1 Multi Agent Task Target Adaptive Configuration

The design system takes multi-agent as the core, and realizes the automatic generation of high school physics network curriculum through the cooperation of multi-agent. In order to ensure the normal performance of the application of the design system, it is necessary to adaptively configure the task objectives of multi-agent to provide some convenience for subsequent experiments.

In order to guide different agents to explore to take advantage of different task target rewards, it is necessary to guide different agents to explore task targets belonging to different clusters. Because agents have a tendency to use all the targets they have explored, they need to build an adaptive task target allocation model $W_\psi(i, k)$ to the agent $i$ and mission objectives $k$ score the relationship between them, and conduct macro-control according to this score to judge whether to run the agent to discover this task target. This research design proposes an adaptive target allocation algorithm, which uses the self-monitoring learning theory to purposefully divide the task targets according to the historical running conditions of agents. The task target adaptive configuration of multi-agent is shown in Fig. 4.

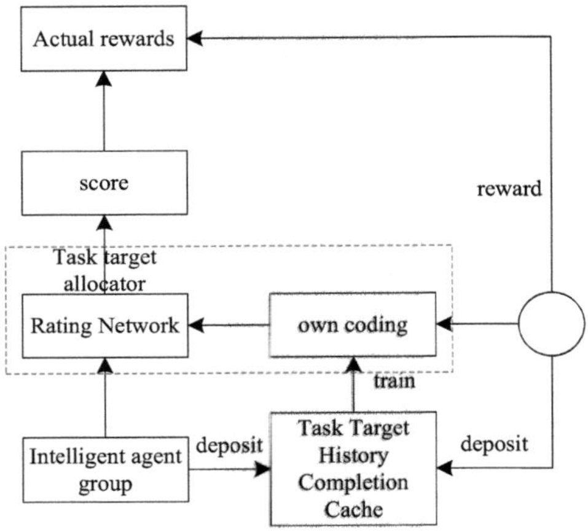


**Fig. 4.** Schematic diagram of multi-agent task target adaptive configuration

If the agent $i$ stay $t$ access to external task objectives in the environment at all times $k$, the task will be $k$ status information for $s_k$ input from encoder to get intermediate results $\chi_k$, and then calculate the task target status code through the scoring network $\chi_k$ and agent number $i$ the score of this combination, and calculate the actual reward that the agent should get, the expression is

$$r_{i,t} = W_{\psi}(i, k) * \delta * s_k * \chi_k \tag{11}$$

In Eq. (11), $r_{i,t}$ it represents an agent $i$ stay $t$ access task objectives at all times $k$ actual rewards obtained; $\delta$ represents a weight super parameter.

After completing a series of operations $\langle \chi_k, i \rangle$ update to the task target history completion cache. At the end of each episode, the central controller will call the task target history to complete the data training task target adaptive allocation network model in the buffer area.

### 3.2 Analysis of Experimental Results

On the basis of the above multi-agent task target adaptive configuration results, the comparison experiment of the automatic generation of high school physics online courses is carried out with the automatic generation system of online courses based on fuzzy clustering and the automatic generation system of online courses based on FCM clustering as comparison system 1 and comparison system 2. In order to intuitively display the application performance of the design system, the time consumption of automatic generation of online courses and the perfection of online courses' functions are selected as evaluation indicators. The specific analysis process of experimental results is as follows:

### 3.2.1 Time Consuming Analysis of Automatic Generation of Online Courses

The time consumption for automatic generation of online courses obtained through experiments is shown in Fig. 5.

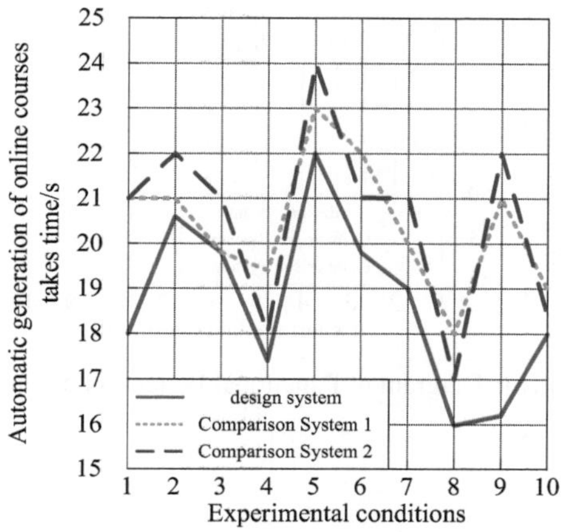


**Fig. 5.** Schematic diagram of time consuming for automatic generation of online courses

As shown in the data in Fig. 5, under different experimental conditions, the automatic generation time of online courses obtained by the design system is much lower than that of comparison system 1 and comparison system 2. Under the eighth experimental condition, the minimum automatic generation time of online courses obtained by comparison system 1 is 18 s, while the minimum automatic generation time of online courses obtained by comparison system 2 is 17 s. The minimum automatic generation time for online courses obtained under the eighth experimental condition was 16 s. The results show that under the specific experimental conditions, the designed system has achieved remarkable improvement and efficiency in the automatic generation of online courses.

### 3.2.2 Analysis on the Perfection of Online Course Functions

The degree of functional perfection of online courses obtained through experiments is shown in Fig. 6.

As shown in the data in Fig. 6, under different experimental conditions, the functional perfection of online courses obtained by the design system is much higher than that of comparison system 1 and comparison system 2. Under the background of the seventh experimental condition, the maximum functional perfection of online courses obtained by comparison system 1 is 85%; under the background of the seventh experimental condition, the maximum functional perfection of online courses obtained by comparison system 2 is 90%. Under the background of the seventh experimental condition, the maximum degree of functional perfection of online courses obtained by the design system is 99%. In this particular experimental condition, the designed system has made remarkable progress and improvement in the function of online course.

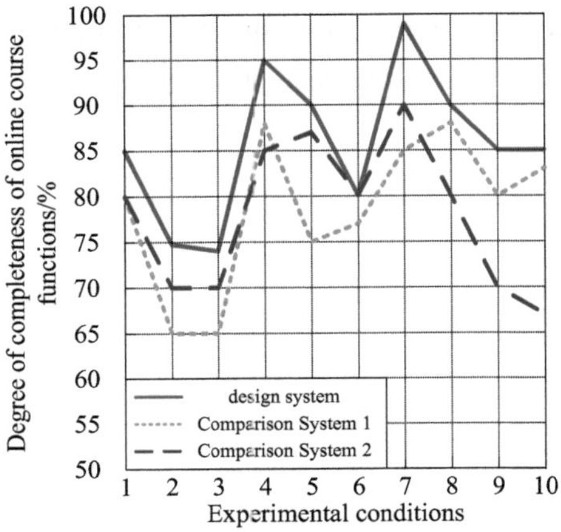


**Fig. 6.** Schematic Diagram of Functional Perfection of Online Courses

## 4 Conclusion

Online courses have the advantages of friendly interface, intuitive image, and multiple stimulation channels, which can help learners to play their initiative, and help to organize information and construct meaning. The need of network course construction is the requirement of information education. Network courses have the following advantages: First, flexible interaction. Traditional classroom interaction is poor. Except for a few questions and answers, it is difficult to accommodate in-depth communication in time and space. During online learning, real-time communication, discussion and interaction can be realized between teachers and students and between students through online question and answer system, BBS, FAQ and online collaborative learning system; The second is the asynchrony of teaching and learning. School education has its time limit and limitations, which cannot meet the internal requirements of education popularization and lifelong education. Network teaching has no time and space restrictions, knowledge space has unlimited extension, and learning time is completely free. Learners can design personalized curriculum and schedule; The third is the universality of learning information. In the process of online learning, the object of learning information service is students. Students can expand their learning according to the resources recommended by teachers, or choose learning resources in cyberspace individually, which not only enriches learning resources, but also helps students to cultivate their active learning ability. In order to meet the needs of high school physics teaching, this paper proposes the research on the design of the automatic generation system of high school physics network courses based on multi-agent, which shortens the time consumption of the automatic generation of network courses, improves the functional perfection of network courses, and provides effective system support for the generation of network courses.

## References

1. Ali, M.S., Agalya, R., Priya, B., et al.: Reliable controller for nonlinear multiagent system with additive time varying delay and nonlinear actuator faults. Math. Methods Appl. Sci. **45**(1), 561–574 (2022)
2. Liu, Q.: Pseudo-predictor feedback control for multiagent systems with both state and input delays. IEEE/CAA J. Automat. Sinica **8**(11), 1827–1836 (2022)
3. Luo, Y., Wang, X., Cao, J.: Guaranteed-cost finite-time consensus of multi-agent systems via intermittent control. Math. Methods Appl. Sci. **45**(2), 697–717 (2022)
4. Pang, K., Pang, K., Ma, L., et al.: Probability-guaranteed secure consensus control for time-varying stochastic multi-agent systems under mixed attacks. J. Franklin Inst. **359**(6), 2541–2563 (2022)
5. Weng, T., Xie, Y., Chen, G., et al.: Load frequency control under false data inject attacks based on multi-agent system method in multi-area power systems. Int. J. Distrib. Sens. Netw. **18**(4), 4610–4618 (2022)
6. Li, Z., Zhao, J.: Adaptive consensus of non-strict feedback switched multi-agent systems with input saturations. IEEE/CAA J. Automat. Sinica **8**(11), 1752–1761 (2022)
7. Sigmon, A.J., Bodek, M.J.: Use of an online social annotation platform to enhance a flipped organic chemistry course. J. Chem. Educ. **99**(2), 538–545 (2022)
8. Viennot, L.: Incomplete explanations in physics teaching: discussing the rainbow with student teachers. Eur. J. Phys. **42**(5), 055705 (2021)
9. O'Brien, D.J.: A guide for incorporating E-teaching of physics in a post-COVID world. Am. J. Phys. **89**(4), 403–412 (2021)
10. Sedova, N., Sedov, V., Bazhenov, R., et al.: Neural network classifier for automatic course-keeping based on fuzzy logic. J. Intell. Fuzzy Syst. **40**(2), 1–12 (2021)

# Multi Agent Based Network Collaborative Learning Support System for Mathematics Curriculum

Jufen Diao[1(✉)] and Songting Zhang[2]

[1] Changzhou College of Information Technology, Changzhou 213164, China
djf20233@163.com
[2] Fuyang Normal University, Fuyang 236041, China

**Abstract.** In the process of designing the learning support system, due to the low interaction flexibility between different modules, the running performance of the system is difficult to meet the application requirements under the condition of multi-user parallelism. Therefore, this paper proposes the design and research of multi-agent based mathematics curriculum network collaborative learning support system. The MYC-J335X-V2 core board equipped with TI AM335X processor and ARM Cortex-A8 core is used as the carrier of system development, ensuring that the running performance meets the application requirements under multi user parallel conditions. In the software design phase, based on multi-agent, a three-tier system architecture is constructed, and the resource allocation of each level is clarified. Each agent is refined from the perspective of structure and function, so that the information interaction between agents can be carried out independently, and its flexibility is improved. In the test, on the premise of 1400 concurrent requests, the corresponding CPU utilization and response time of the design system were 67.3% and 466.3 ms, respectively, which met the application requirements of the mathematics course network collaborative learning support system.

**Keywords:** Multi-Agent · Mathematics Curriculum Network · Support System · MYC-J335X-V2 Core Board · System Architecture · Information Interaction

## 1 Introduction

Compared with the traditional classroom, the information-based classroom has more resources, richer forms of interaction [1], and more wonderful forms of classroom expression, which can improve teachers' teaching and office efficiency, strengthen the interaction between teachers and students, and improve students' interest in learning [2]. Through the information classroom, students' data can be collected and analyzed, and students' learning behavior can be supervised. Students can use the information platform to use fragmented time for learning [3], and teachers can use the information platform to reduce workload and conduct personalized teaching for students. As the epidemic has made the information-based classroom a big step forward, various teaching systems have


G. Gui et al. (Eds.): eLEOT 2023, LNICST 543, pp. 200–216, 2024.
https://doi.org/10.1007/978-3-031-51465-4_14

sprung up like mushrooms [4]. Although this type of teaching system has various functions, its functionality is not highly targeted, and most teachers only use a small portion of these functions in actual teaching practice. As reference [6] analyzes the steady and long-term development of online teaching in the new era - taking the practical courses of music majors in universities as an example, reference [7] designs a new visual Q&A based online teaching effectiveness evaluation model. The above research shows that teachers are unable to customize the interface or the functions provided in the course according to the characteristics and different needs of their own courses, and the complex functional interface can actually lead to a decrease in user experience. Therefore, it is of great value and significance to design and implement a personalized teaching system that teachers can customize according to the characteristics of the mathematics curriculum.

For this reason, this paper proposes the research on multi-agent based mathematics mathematics curriculum network Collaborative learning support system, and the specific research process is as follows:

(1) The hardware design includes the design of a processor and a development board, ensuring that their performance meets the application requirements under multi user parallel conditions;
(2) In the software design, the multi-agent system architecture and the structure and function design of each agent are designed respectively to ensure the support effect of the network Collaborative learning of mathematics courses;
(3) The test experiment analyzed the server performance under different numbers of concurrent accesses, and verified the practical application effect of the designed system.

## 2 Hardware Design

In order to ensure that the designed mathematics course network collaborative learning support system can meet the operational requirements under the multi-objective application environment, realize the rapid parallel processing of multiple requests, and reasonably design the core board is very necessary [8]. For this reason, this paper takes MYC-J335X-V2 core board as the development carrier of the design system, which is equipped with TI AM335X processor, with strong compatibility and easy expansion attribute characteristics [9]. At the same time, the ARM Cortex-A8 core is also configured, and the corresponding operating frequency can be up to 1.0 GHz. With the characteristics of high performance and low power consumption, it can provide the highest DMIPS at the same cost; At the same time, it provides 3D graphics acceleration and key peripheral integration to meet various application needs [10]. The optional 3D graphics accelerator has a performance of up to 20 M/tri/s, supports LPDDR1/DDR2/DDR3 memory, and the independent PRU subsystem provides additional flexibility for product design. In terms of resource allocation, the MYC-J335X-V2 core board integrates gigabit Ethernet interface chips and PMU power management chips, which can meet the development and design requirements under different conditions.

The temperature of MYC-J335X-V2 core board's operating environment is required to be industrial grade, which can perfectly meet the external connection and expansion needs with the support of 200PIN golden finger interface.In terms of software resource configuration, the MYC-J335X-V2 core board perfectly supports the Linux 4.1.18 system. Combined with the above configuration analysis, it can be seen that MYC-J335X-V2 core board can meet the operation management requirements of the mathematics course network collaborative learning support system. In addition, the MYC-J335X-V2 core board also provides optional support for Ethercat and Profibus to further meet the needs of system design.

(1) Integrated configuration and extended signal settings

The specific structure of MYC-Y335X-V2 core board is analyzed. It is designed as a high-density high-speed circuit board, connected by stamp holes, with a size of 70 mm × The 50 mm board is integrated with TI AM3352/AM3358 processor, DDR3, NandFlash, PHY chip (gigabit) and other circuits. See Fig. 1 for details.

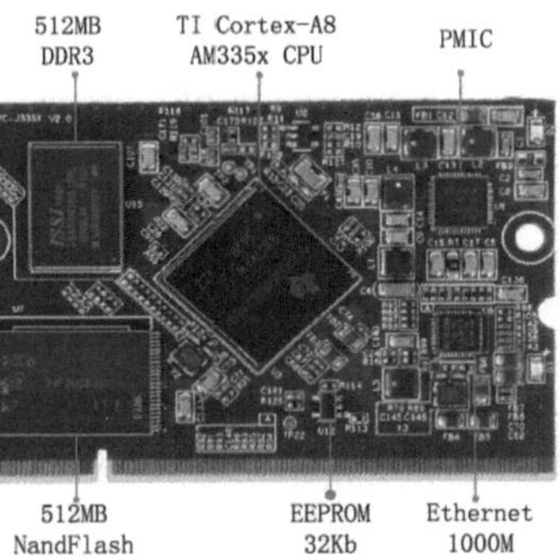


**Fig. 1.** MYC-Y335X-V2 Core Board Integration Configuration

In order to meet the integration requirements, MYC-Y335X-V2 core board adopts 8-layer PCBA design, gold deposition process, and independent and complete ground plane to ensure its quality reliability. On this basis, the extended signal setting of MYC-Y335X-V2 core board is analyzed, as shown in the table (Table 1).

It can be seen from the MYC-Y335X-V2 core board expansion signal settings shown in Fig. 1 that it has rich signal resources and can meet its application needs with strong scalability.

(2) Functional configuration

Figure 2 shows the function configuration of MYC-Y335X-V2 core board.

It can be seen from the information shown in Fig. 2 that the MYC-Y335X-V2 core board supports the implementation of multiple functions and can ensure the smooth operation of the network collaborative learning support system for designing mathematics courses in a multi-agent environment. Table 2 shows the parameter configuration of the MYC-Y335X-V2 core board backplane.

As can be seen from Table 2, the MYC-Y335X-V2 core board designed in this paper has multiple configuration parameters to choose from, which greatly ensures that it can meet the development needs of different levels.

**Table 1.** MYC-Y335X-V2 Core Board Extension Signal Settings

| S/N | project | parameter |
|---|---|---|
| 1 | Internet port | 2-way gigabit network interface |
| 2 | USB | Expandable 2-way independent USB OTG2.0 |
| 3 | Serial port | Expandable 6-channel serial port |
| 4 | I2C | Expandable 2-way I2C bus |
| 5 | CAN | Up to 2-way CAN bus can be expanded |
| 6 | SPI | Expandable 2-way SPI |
| 7 | ADC | 8-way ADC |
| 8 | PWM | 2-way PWM |
| 9 | SDIO | 3-channel SDIO (1 channel SDIO signal is shared with NAND FLASH signal) |

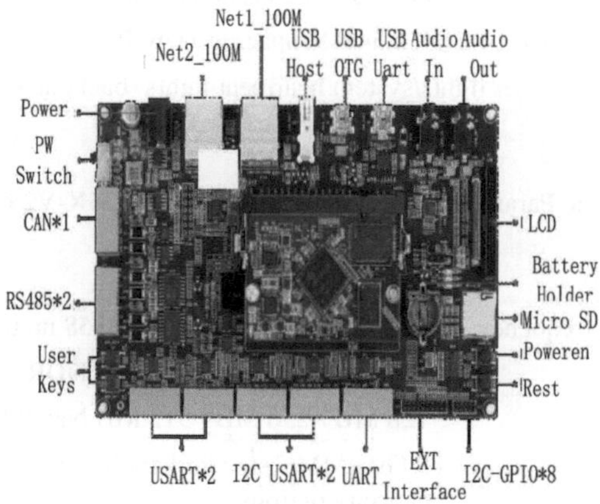


**Fig. 2.** Function Configuration of MYC-Y335X-V2 Core Board

(3) Parameter configuration

Table 3 shows the basic parameter configuration of MYC-Y335X-V2 core board.

Combined with the data information shown in Table 3, MYC-Y335X-V2 core board can realize the adaptive adjustment of its own running state in combination with the actual application of the mathematics course network collaborative learning support system to ensure that the system performance can meet the actual needs. In the actual operation stage, considering the differences of the objective environment, it is also extremely necessary to ensure that the performance configuration of the core board can adapt to the actual situation of different operation environments. Table 4 shows the basic operation parameter configuration of MYC-Y335X-V2 core board.

It can be seen from Table 4 that the adaptability of MYC-Y335X-V2 core board to the operating environment is of industrial grade, and it is characterized by low power

**Table 2.** Parameter Configuration of MYC-Y335X-V2 Core Board Bottom Plate

| S/N | project | parameter |
|---|---|---|
| 1 | audio frequency | One channel audio 3.5 mm output interface; One channel audio 3.5 mm input interface |
| 2 | display | 16 bit true color display interface, default 480 × 272 resolution (4.3 inch screen), support 7 inch screen (800 * 480) |
| 3 | USB | 1-way high-speed USB HOST interface |
| 4 | Serial port | 1-way mini USB HOST/Device interface |
| 5 | RS485 | 1-channel mini USB debugging interface |
| 6 | Micro SD | 5-way serial port, 1-way 3-wire, 4-way 5-wire |
| 7 | CAN | 2-way RS485 interface, shared by signal and serial port |
| 8 | Ethernet | 1-way Micro SD card interface |
| 9 | JTAG | 1 circuit (with electrical isolation) |
| 10 | User light | 2-way 10/100/1000 Mb/s Ethernet interface |
| 11 | RTC | One 14-PIN, 2.54MM spacing JTAGP |
| 12 | project | 2 user lights/system heartbeat lights (backplane: green) |

**Table 3.** Basic Parameter Configuration of MYC-Y335X-V2 Core Board

| S/N | name | main parameter |
|---|---|---|
| 1 | Core and main frequency | TI AM3352/AM3354/AM3358 up to 1 GHz |
| 2 | Memory | 128 MB / 256 MB / 512 MB DDR3 |
| 3 | Flash | 128 MB / 256 MB / 512 MB NandFlash |
| 4 | eMMC | 8 GB eMMC standard configuration, 16 GB and 32 GB capacity options |
| 5 | Ethernet | 1 channel gigabit network interface |
| 6 | Power management | External PMU power management chip |
| 7 | watchdog | External independent hardware watchdog |
| 8 | indicator light | One power indicator (red) and one user indicator (green) |

consumption. With this configuration, the impact of environmental factors on system operation status is minimized. In addition, MYC-J335X-V2 provides driver support for the Linux operating system, along with development kits and related materials. It provides stable design reference and perfect software development environment for developers, which can effectively help developers improve development efficiency, shorten development cycle, optimize design quality, and accelerate product development and time to market. The Boot Loader is set as Boot Loader, and the secondary boot program is responsible for system initialization and kernel boot.

**Table 4.** Operation Parameter Configuration of MYC-Y335X-V2 Core Board

| S/N | project | parameter |
|---|---|---|
| 1 | working temperature | −40~+85 °C industrial grade |
| 2 | ambient temperature | −50~100 °C |
| 3 | ambient humidity | 20%–90%, non condensing |
| 4 | Mechanical dimensions | 67.6 mm × 45 mm, 1.00 mm thick |
| 5 | PCB specification | 8 layers, produced by gold deposition process, independent grounding signal layer, lead-free |
| 6 | Power supply | DC 5 V |
| 7 | Core board interface type | 200PIN golden finger interface, spacing 0.6 mm |
| 8 | System power consumption | About 5 V/0.1 A |

It not only supports NAND Flash erasing, reading and writing, but also supports downloading images on the network, setting and saving environment variables, displaying, comparing and modifying memory contents, and adjusting system operation with bootcmd, bootargs and other settings.

(4) Driver settings and application configuration

Table 5 shows the drive configuration of MYC-J335X-V2 core board.

**Table 5.** MYC-J335X-V2 Core Board Drive Settings

| S/N | set up | Drive configuration |
|---|---|---|
| 1 | USB Host | Linux kernel specially designed for MYD-AM335X-J hardware |
| 2 | USB Device | USB Host drive, supporting OHC and EHCI transmission modes |
| 3 | Ethermet | USB Device Driver (Gadget) |
| 4 | MMC/SD | Ethernet drive |
| 5 | NAND Flash | MMC/SD card driver |
| 6 | I2C | NAND Flash/SmartMedia driver |
| 7 | PI | 12C drive |
| 8 | Audio | SPI drive |
| 9 | LCD | SGTL5000 audio driver |
| 10 | RTC | LCD screen drive, supporting 4.3 inch and 7 inch LCD screens |
| 11 | TouchScreen | Built in RTC clock drive |
| 12 | PWM | 4-wire resistance touch screen drive |

*(continued)*

**Table 5.** (*continued*)

| S/N | set up | Drive configuration |
|---|---|---|
| 13 | UART | PWM drive |
| 14 | CAN | Serial Drivers |
| 15 | PMU | CAN drive |
| 16 | LED | Power management drive |
| 17 | GPIO | LED drive. Including GPIO LED and PWM LED drive |
| 18 | 12c to UART/IO | GPIO drive |

On this basis, the file system is divided into rootfs and rootfs qt. Among them, rootfs is based on the file system driver customized by buildroot, and rootfs qt uses the Qt file system.

To drive, both are in binary form. For the corresponding application configuration, the specific settings of the MYC-J335X-V2 core board are shown in Table 6.

**Table 6.** MYC-J335X-V2 Core Board Application Configuration

| S/N | set up | to configure |
|---|---|---|
| 1 | Audio | Aduio test program |
| 2 | CAN | CAN test procedure |
| 3 | Key&LED | Key LED test procedure |
| 4 | NET | Network Test Procedure |
| 5 | RTC | RTC clock test experiment |
| 6 | NAND Flash | NAND Flash Clock Test Experiment |
| 7 | GPIO | GPIO Test Procedure |
| 8 | RS485 | RS485 Test Procedure |
| 9 | Qt | Qt environment and demo program |

Combined with the above comprehensive analysis of MYC-J335X-V2 core board, it can be seen that taking it as the development carrier of the web-based collaborative learning support system for the design of mathematics courses in this paper can effectively guarantee the smooth implementation of relevant functions and improve the reliability and smoothness of its operation.

## 3 Software Design

### 3.1 System Architecture Design Based on Multi-agent

The system studied in this paper adopts browser/agent/server server mode (and B/A/S mode). The browser is used to let users browse the page, and the server is used to store the database, mainly.

It is used to process applications and systems and interactively access the corresponding data in the database. This mode is called "thin user" mode. Users can surf the Internet through the browser, which can avoid installing different user programs for different clients, help to improve users' access speed, and is equivalent to providing a unified environment for users. In order to reduce the burden of the server, the client can also install some Java Applet plug-ins to improve the functions of the client, which not only increases the security, but also can perform corresponding operations on the user according to the permissions granted by the user. All agents are distributed in the intermediate agent layer, which is the communication bridge between the server and the client. Server communication requires protocols such as FTP and HTTP to assist. Various agents communicate on the intermediate agent layer through FIPA-ACL language.

The first layer of the system architecture is the presentation layer, which mainly provides the user with a Web browser, presents it to the user graphical interface, and is responsible for interacting with the user. The display logic of the system also includes the presentation layer. The main functions of this layer are to provide user information and behavior acquisition, realize the input and output of knowledge required for mathematics teaching, accept the tasks provided, and process the feedback results.

The intermediate agent layer is on the second layer of the system architecture. These agents are mainly divided into three types, which can be expressed as

$$S_a = \{a_y, a_g, a_r\} \tag{1}$$

Among them, $S_a$ Represents the agent of the intermediate agent layer, $a_y$ Represents the user agent, which can be subdivided into

$$a_y = \{a_{yt}, a_{ys}\} \tag{2}$$

Among them, $a_{yt}$ Represents teacher agent, $a_{ys}$ Represents a student agent. $a_g$ Represents the management agent, which can be subdivided into

$$a_g = \{a_{gj}, a_{gt}\} \tag{3}$$

Among them, $a_{gj}$ Stands for monitoring agent, $a_{gt}$ Represents the mathematics teaching management agent. $a_r$ Represents a task agent. The main workflow of agents in the middle agent layer is as follows:

(1) When logging into the system for the first time, you need to register through the monitoring agent, assign different permissions to users with different identities, generate teacher agents for teachers, and student agents for students;
(2) After the student agent logs in the system for the first time, it extracts the basic information of the user according to the user's identity, and uses this information as the user's system learning scheme;

(3) If the student is not logging in to the system for the first time, extract the learning record agent according to the student agent, and give the learning record saved by the student before, which can be used as the reference information for the student to continue learning;
(4) After students log on to the system, they can select their own course content according to the displayed learning interface. At the same time, the management agent also receives the information obtained by the student agent, and provides students with learning suggestions according to the student agent;
(5) After the teacher agent logs into the system, he can edit the syllabus and lesson plan, and assign homework, exam questions, correct homework, answer questions raised by students, etc. to the student agent of the course he has learned;
(6) The specific contents learned by students, exercises or assignments after class, solutions to problems encountered in learning, and examination questions after each chapter are provided by the mathematics teaching agent, homework agent, question answering agent, and examination agent respectively;
(7) Student Agent integrates the mathematics teaching agent, homework agent, question answering agent and exam required by students

    Agent is passed to students;

(8) In order to adjust the students' learning suggestions for the next step, the student agent collects the students' answer results, evaluates the returned exam results, and the management agent receives the evaluation results of the exam agent, and then adjusts the students' learning suggestions for the next step through this evaluation.

The data layer is the third layer, where various data resources are stored. The specific content can be expressed as

$$S_t = \{t(x), c(x), f(x), i(x), q(x)\} \quad (4)$$

$S_t$ Represents the composition of the data resource layer of the system, $t(x)$ Represents the mathematics teaching content library, $c(x)$ Indicates the question bank, $f(x)$ Represents the mathematics teaching strategy library, $i(x)$ Represents the student information base, $q(x)$ Question pool. It should be noted that the knowledge base is composed of specific mathematics curriculum knowledge taught by teachers. It plays the role of organizing materials needed for mathematics teaching, storing and managing all knowledge content required for courses in this mathematics teaching field. The test question database is composed of test questions. Its structure includes some basic attributes such as the body of the question, the specific answer to the question, the criteria for judging the question, the knowledge points involved in the question, the type of question, and the difficulty of the question. At the same time, the attributes of questions will serve as the basis of the examination agent, and according to the requirements of the examination, the questions with appropriate difficulty will be extracted from the question bank to form an examination paper. The difficulty of the questions also depends on the use.

The number of times varies, but the difficulty of the topic will decrease with the number of times it is used. The mathematics teaching strategy library mainly records various rules of software organization mathematics teaching and provides decision-making basis for the teacher agent. It records various rules such as the selection of learning environment, the amount of tasks for this learning, the difficulty of learning, and whether to enter the review stage, enter the test link, etc. In order to fully reflect the autonomy of students, different students should have different mathematics teaching strategies and rules. Students' personal information can be expressed as

$$i(x) = \{name, sex, years, number\} \tag{5}$$

Among them, *name* Indicates the student's name information, *sex* Gender information indicated, *years* Indicates the age information of the student, *number* Represent the student ID information of the student, and put it into the student information database. At the same time, the student's learning situation is also recorded in the student information database. The specific information includes

$$k(x) = \{t(i), s(i), T(i), q(t), w(t)\} \tag{6}$$

Among them, $k(x)$ It represents the learning information of students, $t(i)$ Represents the learning time information, $s(i)$ Represent learning content information, $T(i)$ Indicates the number of learning times, $q(t)$ Indicates the current level information of students, $w(t)$ Indicates learning ability information.

### 3.2 Structure and Function Design of Each Agent

For the monitoring agent, this paper designs it to provide users with functions such as registration, login, and cancellation exit. When a user logs in, the legitimacy of the user is detected according to the user's registration information. If the user is legitimate, the corresponding teacher agent or student agent is generated. If it is a newly registered user, student users should fill in their own learning ability evaluation form, improve the registration information in the user's basic information data table, so that the system can put forward learning suggestions according to the user's cognitive ability. If a student wants to quit the mathematics teaching system after learning, save the student's learning record in the learning record agent and cancel the corresponding agent. The specific structure of the monitoring agent is shown in Fig. 3.

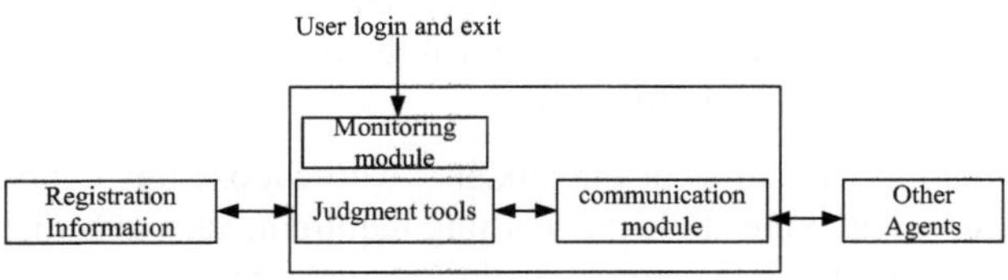


**Fig. 3.** Monitoring Agent Structure

Secondly, Student Agent Student Agent mainly communicates with other agents, among which communication with management agent is the most frequent. Its structure is shown in Fig. 4.

The functions of student agent include:

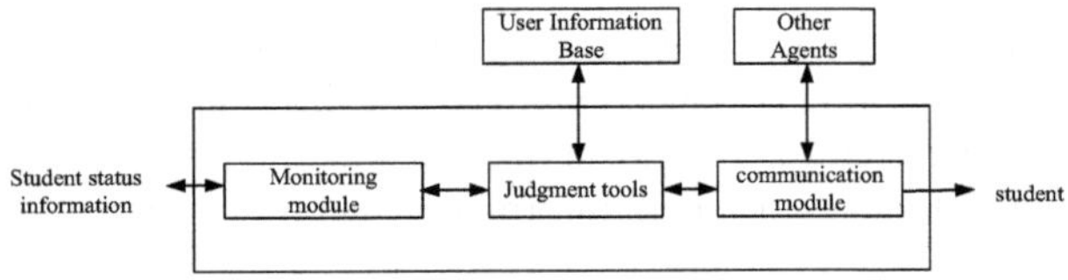


**Fig. 4.** Student Agent Structure

(1) Send the user's basic information and request to the management agent through the identification provided by the user, and the management agent feeds back the corresponding mathematics teaching strategy to the student agent;
(2) Assist students to interact with the system, effectively guide students' learning, master students' actual learning situation in the learning process according to the learning record agent, so as to better select the content learned;
(3) According to the student's choice, the homework generated by the student agent through the homework agent, or the exercises or exams generated by the exam agent, will be displayed to the student for viewing;
(4) Students submit the completed homework to the homework agent and obtain the evaluation results of the homework;
(5) The exercises or exam questions that students have completed within the specified time are returned to the exam agent, and the corresponding answers, knowledge points involved in the questions and the evaluation of the exam are obtained through review;
(6) But when encountering questions, you can establish a connection with the teacher agent, pass the questions to the teacher, and ask for answers;
(7) Collect the students' learning conditions (such as the length of learning time, the results of practice exams, etc.) and hand them over to the management agent, who will give suggestions for the students to continue learning through these information;
(8) When a student exits the system after learning, the student agent saves the student's learning record, and the corresponding student agent is also revoked.

The last is the design of teacher agent. When a teacher logs into the system, the teacher agent will be created by the monitoring agent. As the name implies, through the simulation of human teacher's wisdom, teacher agent should have rich knowledge level and mathematics teaching experience to control the mathematics teaching links in the system. It has the following main functions:

(1) Check the learning situation of the students who choose this course, put forward guidance according to the students' learning requirements and actual situation, and send the advice to the management agent for mathematics teaching guidance and management of students, which is conducive to personalized mathematics teaching of students;
(2) Assist teachers in editing, adding, deleting, modifying and updating mathematics teaching content, and help teachers formulate mathematics teaching strategies and rules;
(3) Check students' current learning psychology, learning attitude, learning progress, learning questions, learning achievements and students' comprehensive learning

ability, make statistics of these information, and then give students' learning evaluation, as well as reasoning to solve various problems encountered in the mathematics teaching process, reorganize the mathematics teaching content, adjust the mathematics teaching methods and steps, so as to give the best mathematics teaching scheme;

(4) Edit, modify, add, generate and publish assignments, exercises and test papers, and correct the assignments submitted by students, and update and maintain the exercise library and mathematics teaching content library in a timely manner;
(5) Enter the question answering system, view the question answering database, participate in the student's question answering, answer the questions that cannot be answered in the question answering agent, and update the answer results to the question answering database;
(6) Collect the information fed back by students and enrich the contents of student information database, knowledge database and mathematics teaching strategy database;
(7) Communicate with other agents.

The last is the design of management Agent. The main function of management agent is management and communication. It controls the cooperation and scheduling among multiple agents. The structure of the management agent is shown in Fig. 5

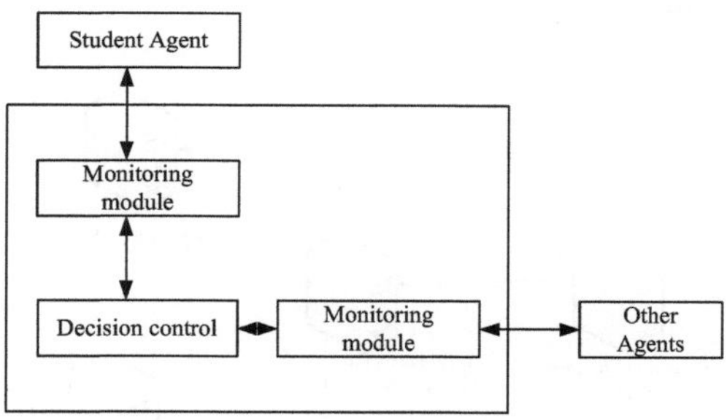


**Fig. 5.** Student Agent Structure

The main functions of the management agent are:

(1) According to student information (provided by student agent), communicate with learning record agent to obtain the history of student learning;
(2) According to the students' request, communicate with the mathematics teaching agent and provide the mathematics teaching content selected by the students to them;
(3) According to the student's request and historical information, give corresponding suggestions for the student's learning content;
(4) According to the student's request and the current learning situation of the student, communicate with the homework agent to provide students with difficult and appropriate homework; After students submit their homework, provide students with answers to the corresponding homework questions and the knowledge points involved;

(5) According to the student's request and referring to the student's historical learning situation, communicate with the examination agent, and provide exercises or examination questions with appropriate difficulty to the student; After the students finish answering the questions and submit the test questions, provide the answers to the corresponding questions and the knowledge points involved to the students;
(6) According to the student's request, communicate with the question answering agent and give answers to the student's questions;
(7) According to the evaluation results of the examination agent, provide students with further learning suggestions;
(8) According to the student learning information provided by the student agent, the corresponding learning suggestions are provided to students, so that students can learn more purposefully.

# 4 Test Experiment Analysis

## 4.1 Test Plan

According to the demand indicators of the web-based collaborative learning support system for mathematics courses, the system needs to meet the average concurrency of 1225 and the peak concurrency of 1326. To understand whether the concurrency performance of the server can meet the requirements, the test scheme developed in this paper is shown in Fig. 6.

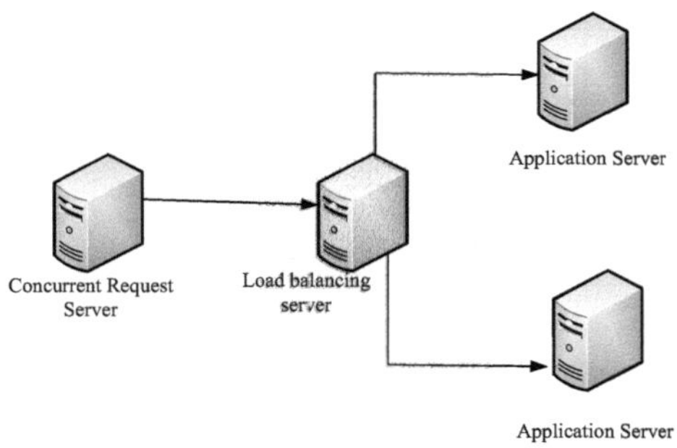


**Fig. 6.** Performance Test Scheme

First, run the load balancing server and business functions on different virtual machines, and then run a separate virtual machine as a concurrent request server to simulate user requests. Jmeter needs to be installed in the concurrent request server to simulate the concurrent request behavior of users. The configuration of each server is shown in Table 7.

In this test, the concurrent request server takes 100 users as the starting point, and adds 100 virtual users in turn.

The user records the CPU utilization response in the business function server through the built-in listener and plug-in of Jmeter Time and other parameters. Each concurrent request will be made many times. Finally, the average value measured many times will be recorded.

**Table 7.** Test Server Configuration

| Server name | Number of cores | Memory |
|---|---|---|
| Concurrent request server | 2 | 8.0 |
| Load balancing server | 2 | 8.0 |
| application server | 2 | 8.0 |
| application server | 2 | 8.0 |

## 4.2 Analysis of Test Results

Table 8 shows the server performance test results under different concurrent accesses. The average response time is a key indicator to measure the system response time.

**Table 8.** Server performance test results under different number of concurrent accesses

| Concurrent requests | 90% | 95% | 99% |
|---|---|---|---|
| 100 | 10 | 12 | 28 |
| 200 | 20 | 27 | 33 |
| 300 | 51 | 56 | 65 |
| 400 | 76 | 100 | 126 |
| 500 | 326 | 420 | 630 |
| 600 | 659 | 705 | 93 1 |
| 700 | 922 | 1001 | 1170 |
| 800 | 1360 | 1432 | 1604 |
| 900 | 1514 | 1 648 | 1885 |
| 1000 | 1624 | 1858 | 2225 |
| 1200 | 1834 | 2004 | 2259 |
| 1300 | 1835 | 2105 | 235 1 |
| 1400 | 2131 | 2309 | 2460 |

According to the test results shown in Table 8, with the increasing number of concurrent accesses, the performance test results of the designed system show a stable development trend, with the corresponding average performance rising steadily, but the overall stability is within 2500. On this basis, the CPU usage of the system is compared with the increase of concurrent requests; As the number of concurrent requests increases, the average response time of the system changes. The mathematics teaching support system based on big data and the mathematics teaching support system based on B/S are set as the control group for the test, and the specific operation conditions of different systems under the same test environment are counted respectively. The test results are shown in Fig. 7 and Fig. 8.

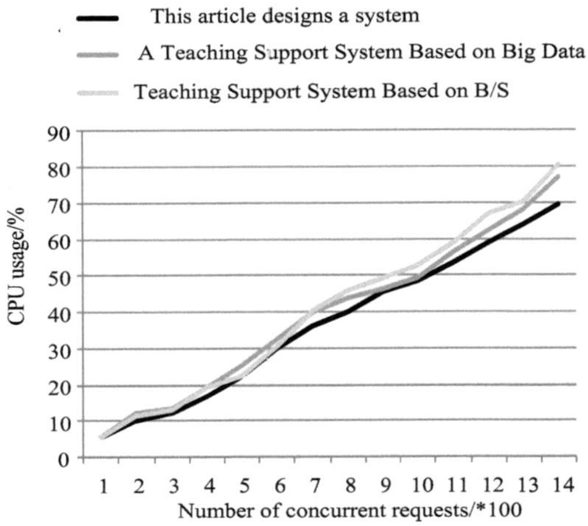


**Fig. 7.** Comparison Diagram of System CPU Usage

As can be seen from Fig. 7, as the number of concurrent requests of the system increases, the CPU utilization rate gradually increases. When the number of concurrent requests is 1400, the CPU utilization rate of the system designed in this paper is only 70.0%. At this time, the CPU utilization rate of the big data based mathematics teaching support system and the B/S based mathematics teaching support system reaches 82.01% and 76.44% respectively. In contrast, the running performance of the system designed in this paper is more stable. Not only that, but also from Table 9, the system did not reach the performance bottleneck when 1400 concurrent requests were made. When the number of concurrent users is 1300, the CPU utilization rate of the system designed in this paper is only 67.3%, and the probability of abnormal response requests is relatively low. Based on the above test results and analysis, it can be concluded that the system designed in this paper can support the concurrency of 1400 users and meet the requirements of 1226 Concurrency requirements during peak hours.

In Fig. 8, with the increase of the number of system users, the average response time of the three test systems gradually increases. When the number of users is 1400, the average response time of the system designed in this paper, the mathematics teaching support system based on big data and the mathematics teaching support system based on B/S are 466.3 ms, 512.40 ms and 535.20 ms respectively. The response rate of the system designed in this paper is significantly faster. Combined with the above test results and analysis, it can be concluded that the response time of the system in this paper can meet the response time index requirements in the actual application phase.

Analyze the changes in students' mathematical learning scores before and after the application of the system in this article. The analysis period is 3 months, and the changes in students' learning scores are shown in Table 9.

According to Table 9, after applying the system in this article, a total of 16 students' academic performance has been improved, while only 2 students' academic performance has decreased; Before the application of this system, only 5 students' academic performance improved, while 13 students' grades began to decline. The experiment

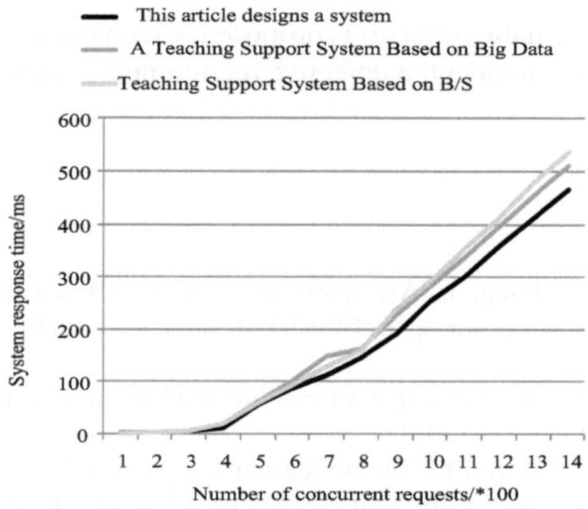


**Fig. 8.** Comparison Diagram of System Response Time

**Table 9.** Changes in student grades before and after the application of this system

| Group | Number of people | Increase/decrease situation | Total variation | Average change per person |
|---|---|---|---|---|
| Before applying the system in this article | 18 | 5 people increase by 11.4 points, | Reduce 28.4 points | Reduce 2.5 points |
| After applying the system in this article | 18 | 13 people reduced by 5.8 points | Increase by 40.3 points | Increase by 2.7 points |

proves that the application of this system can effectively improve students' math learning performance.

## 5 Conclusion

The rapid development of economy and society has changed people's production and living mode for a long time to a considerable extent. In education, the accelerating social rhythm makes the traditional face-to-face centralized mathematics teaching model unable to meet people's increasing learning needs. In recent years, with the rapid development of computer and multimedia technology, an information-based online mathematics teaching method relying on the Internet has gradually been accepted and recognized by people. At present, the popularity of the Internet in China is increasing day by day, and online mathematics teaching mode has gradually become a normal education mode that relies on and complements the traditional offline mathematics teaching mode with its advantages of fast transmission speed, wide coverage, and less impact from time and space. In this paper, the research on the multi-agent based network collaborative learning support system for mathematics courses is proposed, which ensures that the running performance of the system can meet the objective requirements in the practical application stage.

## References


1. Xiong, Y., Huang, R., Jiang, J., Asempapa, B., Fox, S.: Online teaching self-efficacy of group counseling instructors during the COVID-19 pandemic. Int. J. Group Psychother. **72**(3), 228–256 (2022)
2. Dolighan, T., Owen, M.: Teacher efficacy for online teaching during the COVID-19 pandemic. Brock Educ. J. **30**(1), 95–116 (2021)
3. Siegel, V., Moore, G., Siegel, L.: Improving nursing students' knowledge and assessment skills regarding skin cancer using online teaching resources. J. Dermatol. Nurses Assoc. **13**(6), 305–308 (2021)
4. Wang, J., Chia, I.: Engaging students via Nearpod? In synchronous online teaching. Manag. Teach. Rev. **7**(3), 245–253 (2022)
5. Jesus, L.C.D., Cabral, L.M.: Synthetic biology as a tool to online teaching undergraduate level molecular biology. Biochem. Mol. Biology Educ. **50**(1), 122–123 (2021)
6. Nihui, Z.: A brief analysis of how online teaching can develop steadily and be far-reaching in the new era-a case study of practical course for college music programs. Psychol. Res. **12**(7), 525–529 (2022)
7. Cui, Y., Han, G., Zhu, H.: A novel online teaching effect evaluation model based on visual question answering. J. Internet Technol. **23**(1), 91–98 (2022)
8. Dahabiyeh, L., Najjar, M.S., Wang, G.: Online teaching during COVID-19 crisis: the role of technostress and emotional dissonance on online teaching exhaustion and teaching staff productivity. Int. J. Inform. Learn. Technol. **39**(2), 97–121 (2022)
9. Wang, H.J., Wang, Z.F.: Design of simulation teaching system based on modular production and processing. Comput. Simul. **39**(4), 205–209 (2022)
10. Liao, J., Hou, B., Zhang, J.,et al.: Practical exploration of online teaching of animal product processing. Asian Agric. Res. **14**(12), 54–56,59 (2022)

# Research on English Online Video Teaching System Based on Streaming Media Technology

Yanli Ge[1] and Ying Gao[2](✉)

[1] Office of Foreign Language, Basic Teaching Department, Changchun University of Architecture and Civil Engineering, Changchun 130607, China

[2] Academic Affairs Office of Sanda University, Shanghai 201209, China

ygao@sandau.edu.cn

**Abstract.** With the rapid development of Internet and digital technology, education methods and learning modes are also changing. Online education has become a trend, so the research of online video teaching system is helpful to the quality of English learning. The existing English online video teaching system mainly uses the spring MVC (model - view - controller) architecture to generate the video teaching interface, which is affected by the code maintenance relationship, resulting in some functions unable to operate normally. Therefore, it is necessary to design a new English online video teaching system based on Streaming Media Technology. The hardware part designs the ARM S3C2440 processor and LCD display, the software part designs the video teaching transmission protocol based on the streaming media technology, develops the core streaming media online teaching program, and designs the English online video teaching function module, thus realizing the English online video teaching.The system test results show that each functional module of the designed online English video teaching system based on streaming media technology can operate normally, which proves that the designed online video teaching system has good performance, reliability, and certain application value, and has made certain contributions to improving the quality of online English teaching.

**Keywords:** Streaming Media Technology · English · Online Video · Teaching · System Study

## 1 Introduction

Under the trend of globalization, English as the main language of international communication has become more and more important [1]. However, there are some limitations in traditional English teaching methods. The rapid development of Internet and digital technology provides new opportunities for online education [2]. Therefore, it is of great significance to study the background of English online video teaching system. The system can provide flexible learning methods. Regardless of geographical location and time constraints, learners can learn anytime and anywhere [3]. At the same time, personalized learning and teaching are also possible. The system can provide personalized


G. Gui et al. (Eds.): eLEOT 2023, LNICST 543, pp. 217–232, 2024.
https://doi.org/10.1007/978-3-031-51465-4_15

learning content and teaching methods according to learners' level, interest and learning style [4]. In addition, the system can integrate rich and diverse learning resources and expand learning opportunities and resources. Through multimedia, interaction and practice, English online video teaching system can improve the learning effect and results [5, 6]. To sum up, the background and significance of studying English online video teaching system is to explore and develop a flexible, personalized and efficient English learning method, promote the development of English education, improve the English level of learners, and promote the fairness and popularization of education.

Reference [7] proposes an English online video teaching system based on cloud platform. Firstly, the framework of the English online practice system of cloud computing platform is designed. The infrastructure layer is used to provide users with all facility services, and the platform service layer is used to provide users with application development, testing and custody functions. The software service layer evaluates users' English learning status according to the scores of users' knowledge points and question types. Reference [8] proposes an English online video teaching system based on mybatis framework. Combined with statistical information analysis and big data regression analysis, it carries out big data mining, and combines with relevant information feature matching to carry out the sharing and scheduling design of multi terminal interoperability online teaching resources. Build a multi terminal interoperability online teaching resource scheduling model and resource sharing design, and carry out the software development and human-computer interaction design of the multi terminal interoperability online teaching platform under the mybatis framework. Although the above two systems can realize the online teaching function, there are still some deficiencies in improving learning performance.

In order to solve the problems existing in the existing teaching system, a new English online video teaching system based on streaming media technology is proposed. From the two aspects of hardware and software, the hardware is designed to meet the online video teaching function of the system and improve the stability of system operation. The software part improves the security and reliability of system resource transmission through the design of transmission protocol, and designs the online teaching program to complete the online video teaching function of English.

## 2 Hardware Design

It is necessary to design an English online video teaching system from both hardware and software aspects. From a hardware perspective, reasonable selection and configuration of hardware devices can ensure the operational requirements and user experience of the system, such as servers, network devices, cameras, etc. At the same time, the performance of hardware devices and network bandwidth directly affect the implementation of video quality and interactive functions. From a software perspective, designing a simple, intuitive, and easy to operate user interface can provide a good user experience. At the same time, it is necessary to provide rich and diverse teaching content and resources, and achieve personalized teaching support through learning analysis and data mining technologies. In summary, designing an English online video teaching system from both hardware and software aspects can ensure the improvement of system functionality, performance, and user experience, providing a good video experience, interactive functions, and personalized teaching support to meet the needs of learners.

### 2.1 ARM S3C2440 Processor

For an embedded system application, the selection of CPU is very important.Embedded microprocessors generally need to have the following characteristics:

(1) High reliability and integration.The chip integrates as many interfaces or controllers as possible to meet user needs, and expands off chip resources as little as possible.
(2) The overall cost of the product is low, and processors and peripherals that are cheaper, more widely used, and have a long life cycle are selected.
(3) Low development cost, short development cycle, using operating system, driver and other software to support perfect processors can effectively reduce the risks and uncertainties in development.At present, there are more than 1000 kinds of processors with embedded features in the world [9]. The popular architecture includes more than 30 series such as MCU and MPU, with faster speed, stronger performance and lower price.Compared with industrial control computers, embedded microprocessors have the advantages of small size, light weight, low cost and high reliability. At present, such embedded processors include ARM, MIPS, Am186/88, 386EX, PowerPC, 68000, etc. The performance comparison table is shown in Table 1 below.

**Table 1.** Processor Performance Comparison Table

| Processor Type | Processor price | Main performance and application |
|---|---|---|
| ARM | low | Low power consumption, suitable for personal portable devices |
| Dragon Ball | low | Low speed, mainly used in PDA |
| Power PC | high | Communication, network and other equipment;High unit added value and small market;Especially for It is applied to high-end embedded systems when there are high performance requirements |

It can be seen from Table 1 that, considering the application field, cost, development difficulty and other factors, the embedded processor selected in this paper is ARM, which is widely used in 16/32 bit embedded RISC solutions, has become the standard processor on mobile phones, PDAs and other portable devices, and is the most representative architecture of embedded processors.At the beginning of 2007, ARM's 32-bit RISC processor market share exceeded 95%.The kernels provided include the following series: ARM7, ARM9, ARM9E, ARM10, SecurCore, StrongARM, InterXScale, etc.The time of each series of products should follow the principle of high performance and low power consumption to meet the increasingly complex application needs of users[10]. ARM microprocessor with RISC architecture generally has the following characteristics:

(1) Small size, low power consumption, low cost and high performance;
(2) It supports Thumb (16 bit)/ARM (32 bit) dual instruction set, and can be well compatible with 8-bit/16 bit devices;
(3) Using a large number of registers, the instruction execution speed is faster;
(4) Most data operations are completed in registers;
(5) The addressing mode is flexible and simple, and the execution efficiency is high;
(6) The command length is fixed.

According to the system requirements, this paper selects the S3C2440 processor based on ARM9 core produced by SAMSUNG Company.

S3C2440 is a 32-bit RISC processor based on ARM920T core produced by Samsung, and a CMOS standard macro cell and memory unit with 0.18 um process. It provides a solution of low-cost, low-power, high-performance small microcontroller for handheld devices and general type applications. The highest frequency reaches 533 MHz, and it is cheaper than other manufacturers' products of the same type,Therefore, S3C2440 is used as the embedded processor in the implementation of this system, and its main structure is shown in Fig. 1 below.

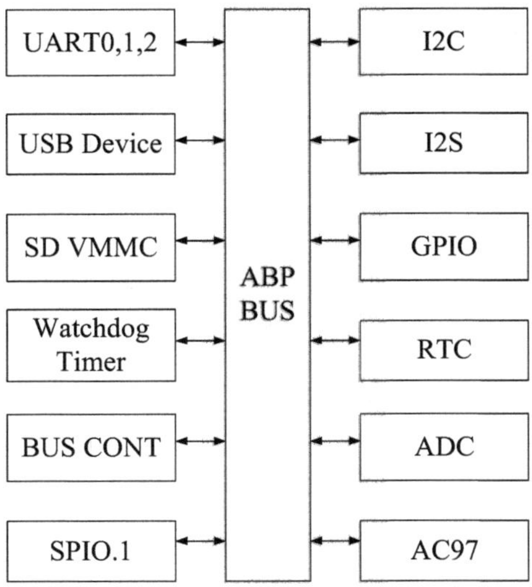


**Fig. 1.** Main Structure of S3C2440 Processor

It can be seen from Fig. 1 that the S3C2440 processor contains a 16/32-bit RISC architecture and a powerful instruction set of the ARM920T core. It contains MMUs, can use virtual storage systems, and can support WINCE, EPOC 32, and LINUX operating systems.Instruction high-speed storage buffer, data high-speed buffer, write buffer and physical address TAG RAM reduce the impact of main memory bandwidth and responsiveness, and reduce the loss caused by cache loss;Support ARM debugging architecture;Internal Advanced Micro Control Bus (AMBA) architecture;Support large/small end mode;1G addressing space in total;Support 8/16/32 bit data bus bandwidth;From bank0 to bank6, fixed bank start addressing is adopted;Bank7 has a programmable bank start address and size.

The S3C2440 processor has: independent 16 KB instruction cache and 16 KB data cache, MMU, TFT capable LCD controller, NAND flash memory controller, 3-channel UART, 4-channel DMA, 4-channel Timer with PWM, I/0 interface, RTC, 8-channel 10 bit ADC, Touch Screen interface, IIC-BUS interface, IIS-BUS interface, 2 USB hosts, 1 USB device, SD host and MMC interface, and 2-channel SPI.Up to 533 MHz.

S3C2440 is the internal 32-bit address, the external 27 bit address, and the data bus width is 32 bits.400 M main frequency, 100 – 133 MHz bus speed.If the peripheral chip with 8-bit or 16 bit data width is connected to the CPU, the data bus width of the core board is configurable, which can be configured as 32-bit, 16 bit or 8-bit modes respectively.The setting is implemented in BW bit of BWCON.When assigning a slice selection to a peripheral, set the two bits in its BWCON, and change the data width when accessing its address.For 16 bit data width, the lowest 16 bit data line is valid;In 8-bit mode, the lowest 8-bit data line is valid. The interface connected to the processor is shown in Fig. 2 below.

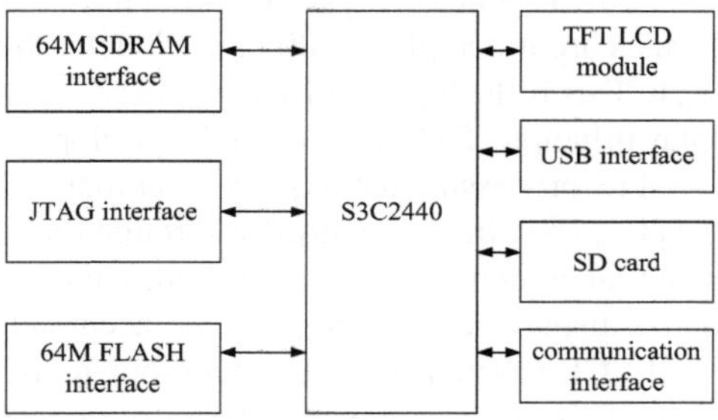


**Fig. 2.** S3C2440 Processor Connection Interface

It can be seen from Fig. 2 that the S3C2440 provides 8-way chip selection. Each chip selection has a fixed address, and each chip selection has a fixed interval of 128M bytes.This is invalid for CSO during startup, because CSO is a memory chip for storing startup code, which is generally FLASH. When the CPU is just powered on, the data width cannot be set with BWCON, and it is only implemented by hardware.The width of data is determined by the hardware configuration after reset. The default value for reset is 0x000000000.

### 2.2 LCD Display

At present, the display equipment of portable multimedia player mainly adopts LCD (Liquid Crystal 1 Display) display, which is a kind of display that uses T liquid crystal to control the transmittance technology to achieve color.Compared with CRT display, LCD has obvious advantages.The light and dark are controlled by controlling whether the light is transmitted. When the color is unchanged, the liquid crystal also remains unchanged, so the refresh rate need not be considered.For LCD with stable picture and no flicker, the refresh rate is not high but the image is also stable.The LCD display also uses the technical principle of liquid crystal to control the light transmittance to make the bottom plate glow as a whole, so it is truly completely flat and has no radiation. Even if you watch the LCD display for a long time, the screen will not cause great harm to your eyes.In addition, its power consumption is relatively small, so it is very common in portable devices at present.

At present, LCD used in media player mainly includes TFT and STN.TFT liquid crystal display technology adopts the "active matrix" mode to drive. The method is to use the transistor electrode made of thin film technology, and use the scanning method to "actively" control the opening and closing of any display point.When the light source irradiates, it first passes through the lower polarizing plate and transmits light with the help of liquid crystal molecules.When the electrode passes through, the liquid crystal molecules will change like the arrangement state of STN liquid crystal. The purpose of display is achieved through refraction and light transmission. It seems that this is similar to the principle of STN.But the difference is that since TFT transistor has capacitive effect and can maintain the potential state, the liquid crystal molecules that have been exposed to light will remain in this state until the TFT electrode is powered up again next time to change its arrangement, while STN liquid crystal does not have this characteristic. Once the liquid crystal molecules are not applied with electric field, they will return to their original state immediately,This is the biggest difference between TFT liquid crystal and STN liquid crystal display principle.TFT liquid crystal is equipped with a semiconductor switch for each pixel, and its processing technology is similar to large-scale integrated circuit.Because each pixel can be directly controlled through the dot pulse, each node is relatively independent and can be continuously controlled. This design not only improves the response speed of the display screen, but also can accurately control the display grayscale. Therefore, TFT LCD has more realistic, smoother, more delicate, and stronger sense of hierarchy. TFT LCD is more expensive in terms of price.Since TFT screen will be the mainstream of future application, 5.7 inch TFT digital LCD CLAA057VA01 produced by Shydar Company is selected in this paper. Its basic parameters are shown in Table 2.

**Table 2.** LCD Display Parameters

| parameter | Specifications | Company |
|---|---|---|
| Screen size | 5.7 | Inch |
| Display Format | 640*(R,G,B)*480 | Dot |
| Display Color | 262, 144 | \ |
| Effective area | 140(H)*100(V) | mm |
| Pixel spacing | 0.1815(H)*0.1815(V) | mm |
| Outer frame size | 127(W)*100(H)*7(D) | mm |
| weight | TBD | g |
| response time | 30 | ms |

Table 2 shows that the LCD controller of S3C2440A chip is used to transmit image data located in the video buffer in the system memory to the LCD driver and generate necessary LCD control signals (VFRAME, VLINE, VCLK and VM).The LCD controller uses the time jitter algorithm and frame rate control method to support monochrome, 4-level grayscale (each dot occupies 2 bits), 16 level grayscale (each dot occupies 4 bits) display on a gray white LCD, and also supports up to 256 colors (each dot occupies 8 bits) display on a color LCD.The LCD controller can support LCD with different horizontal and vertical points (1024 * 768, 640 * 480, 320 * 240, etc.), different data line widths, different interface timing and refresh rates through programming, support 4-bit dual scan, 4-bit single scan, 8-bit single scan LCD displays, and support horizontal/vertical scrolling to support larger screen displays (such as 1280 * 1280),Some internal connection structures of the display are shown in Fig. 3 below.

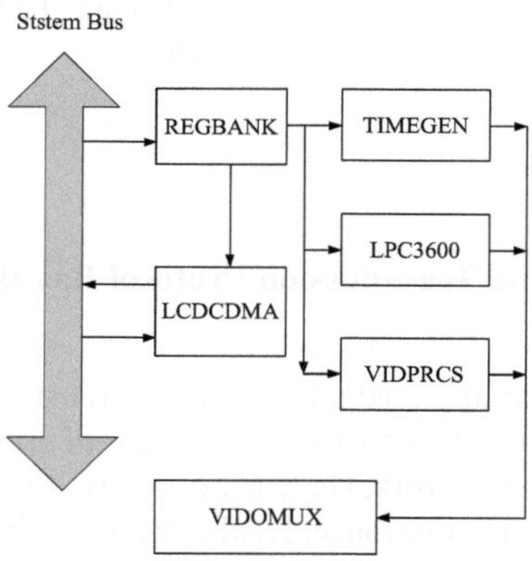


**Fig. 3.** Internal Structure of LCD Display

It can be seen from Fig. 3 that the flow of LCD controller transmitting image data is as follows: when the FIFO memory area in the LCDCDMA (LCD dedicated DMA, which is used to automatically transmit the video data in the video buffer to the LCD driver without the participation of the CPU) is empty or partially empty, LCDCDMA requests to prefetch data from the video buffer (using burst transmission mode, prefetching 4 words at a time, and bus control transfer is not allowed during transmission). Its interface is shown in Table 3 below.

It can be seen from Table 3 that when the request is accepted by the bus arbitration in the memory controller, the data of four consecutive words will be sent from the video buffer to the FIFO storage area of the LCDCDMA.The total size of the FIFO storage area is 24 words (12 words belong to FIFOL and 12 words belong to FIFOH, which are used to support double scanning. In the single scanning mode, only one FIFO is available).The S3C2440A supports TFT/STN type LCDs, but cannot be directly connected to LCDs. It needs an interface board to drive LCDs.

**Table 3.** LCD Display Connection Interface

| Symbol | explain | function |
|---|---|---|
| VCLK | Refresh clock | Provide clock signal for data transmission |
| VLINE | Horizontal synchronizing pulse | Provide line signal, i.e. line frequency |
| WFRAME | Frame synchronization signal | The frame displays the effective control signal, after the complete frame is displayed |
| VM | AC control voltage | Change of polarity controls the display of liquid crystal molecules |
| VD[3:0] | data line | Data input, high 4-bit data input in double scan |
| VD[7:4] | data line | Data input, high 4-bit data input in double scan |

# 3 Software Design

## 3.1 Design Video Teaching Transmission Protocol Based on Streaming Media Technology

The key technology of streaming media is streaming transmission.Streaming is widely defined, and now it mainly refers to the technology of transmitting media (such as video and audio) through the network.There are two ways to realize streaming transmission: sequential streaming transmission and real-time streaming transmission.Sequential streaming is a sequential download. Users can watch online media while downloading files. At a given time, users can only watch the downloaded part, not the first part that has not been downloaded.The sequential streaming mode is suitable for high-quality short fragments, which are placed on standard HTTP or FTP servers, easy to manage, basically independent of firewalls, and does not need other special transmission protocols. It is often called HTTP streaming.Sequential streaming is useful for publishing short clips through modems, allowing video clips to be created at higher data rates than modems.Despite the delay, it is possible to release high-quality video clips.However, it is not suitable for videos, lectures, speeches and demonstrations with long clips and random access requirements, nor does it support live broadcasting.

Real time streaming transmission is always real-time transmission, especially suitable for on-site events. It also supports random access. Users can fast forward or backward to view the content in front or behind.It ensures that the bandwidth of the media signal matches the network connection so that the media can be viewed in real time.Theoretically, the real-time stream will never stop once played, but in fact, periodic pause may occur.Real time streaming must match the connection bandwidth, which means poor image quality when connecting at modem speed.Moreover, because the information lost due to errors is ignored, the video quality will be poor when the network is congested or there are problems.To ensure video quality, sequential streaming may be better.In addition, real-time streaming transmission requires specific servers, such as

QuickTime Streaming Server. For the advantages of streaming media technology, this paper designs an effective streaming media transmission protocol. The implementation diagram of this protocol is shown in Fig. 4 below.

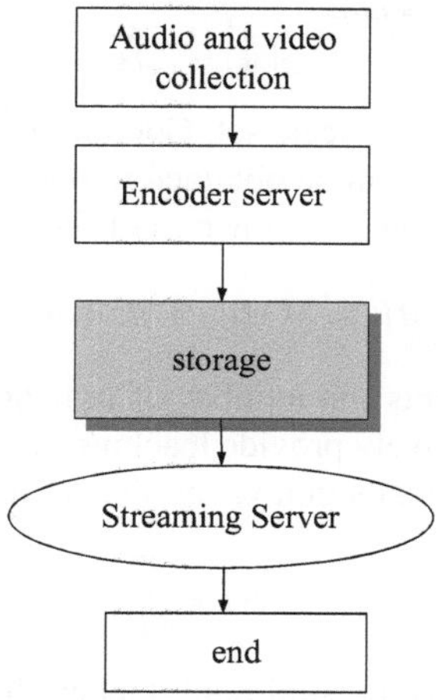


**Fig. 4.** Schematic Diagram of Streaming Media Video Transmission Protocol Implementation

It can be seen from Fig. 4 that after encoding and compression, the original audio/video stream is stored as a media file or directly transmitted to the streaming media server, which transmits the live media stream (or media file) to the streaming media player at the user's request.In the middle of media transmission, proxy servers can also be used to distribute or forward media content.The remote client can see the video data as long as it logs in to the server using the streaming media player.

Real time Transport Protocol (RTP) is defined as a transport protocol for transmitting real-time data such as audio, video and analog data.Originally designed for multicast of data transmission, it is also used for unicast.Compared with the traditional transport layer protocol that focuses on high reliability data transmission, it focuses more on the real-time nature of data transmission.The services provided by this protocol include time load identification, data sequence, time stamp, transmission control, etc.RTP usually uses UDP to transmit data, but RTP can also work on other protocols such as TCP or ATM.When the application starts -- RTP sessions, two ports will be used, one for RTP and one for RTCP. RTP itself cannot provide a reliable transmission mechanism for sequentially transmitting data packets, nor does it provide flow control or congestion control. It relies on RTCP to provide these services, which can generate video teaching resource combination $u_i$, as shown in (1) below.

$$u_i = p_b - p_{ij} \tag{1}$$

In formula (1), $p_b$ represents the matching degree of video resources, and $p_{ij}$ represents the resource combination coefficient. Based on the above video teaching resources, the operating occupancy rate $u_s$ can be estimated, as shown in (2) below.

$$u_s = u_i \bullet otherwise - p_j^s \tag{2}$$

In formula (2), *otherwise* represents the occupancy rate of video resources after the transaction ends, and $p_j^s$ represents the total occupancy rate of video resources. At this point, the transmission utility $u_0$ of the video transmission protocol is shown in (3).

$$u_0 = \sum_{b \in w} p_j^s - \sum_{b \in w} p \tag{3}$$

In formula (3), $p$ represents the scale set. Combining the transmission utility calculated above, the scale difference can be obtained to obtain the user node weight $MR$ for obtaining video teaching resources, as shown in (4) below.

$$MR = M \backslash (u_0 + u_s + u_i) \tag{4}$$

In formula (4), $M$ represents the number of user nodes, and different users have different preferences. To effectively provide teaching services to them, it is necessary to calculate the comprehensive satisfaction $v$, , as shown in (5) below.

$$v = w_k \bullet \frac{1}{MR} \tag{5}$$

In formula (5), $w_k$ represents the minimum standard for video resource transmission, and resource synthesis can only be carried out after meeting the above satisfaction standards. At this time, the resource synthesis scale $bs$ is shown in (6).

$$bs = \sum_{k=1}^{c} r_k w_k \tag{6}$$

In formula (6), $r_k$ represents the transmission basis coefficient, and combined with the resource comprehensive scale mentioned above, an effective transmission decision variable $Q$ can be generated, as shown in (7) below.

$$Q = \max bsS_i \tag{7}$$

In formula (7), $S_i$ represents the matching coefficient. According to the above decision variables, the streaming Media Transfer Protocol operation model $LD$ can be generated, as shown in (8) below.

$$LD = \frac{Q}{bs} w_k \bullet v \backslash u_0 + u_s + u_i \tag{8}$$

Combined with the above transport protocol operation model, traffic control and congestion control can be carried out.Send some RTCP packets periodically between RTP sessions to transmit monitoring quality of service and exchange session user information and other functions.The RTCP packet contains statistics such as the number of sent packets and the number of lost packets.Therefore, the server can use this information to dynamically change the transmission rate, or even change the payload type.The combination of RTP and RTCP can optimize the transmission efficiency with effective feedback and minimal overhead, so it is particularly suitable for transmitting real-time data on the network.

### 3.2 Develop Core Streaming Media Online Teaching Program

The system is developed by Dreamweaver MX2004, combined with ASP technology to generate dynamic web pages, to achieve remote management of the system and learners' remote video learning.Dreamweaver MX2004 is a "what you see is what you get" web page editing tool produced by Macromedia, which can be used to design, code and develop web sites, web pages and web applications. ASP is the abbreviation of Active Server Page, which is launched by Microsoft.ASP is not a pure technology, more accurately, it is a server script environment in which users can realize dynamic interactive WEB page design.ASP script can be written together with HTML, VBScript, JavaScript and other script languages, which greatly enriches and expands the functions of ASP applications.ASP has the following four important features that make it very versatile.ASP can include server-side script;ASP provides some Built in objects, which can be used to receive and send information from the browser; ASP can be extended with other elements. ASP itself is derived from a considerable number of standard server ActiveX elements. These components allow pages to display different contents according to browser capabilities, etc.;ASP can easily connect with the database. By using some special object set ADO (Active Data Object), you can use SQL language in ASP. The execution process of this program is shown in Fig. 5 below.

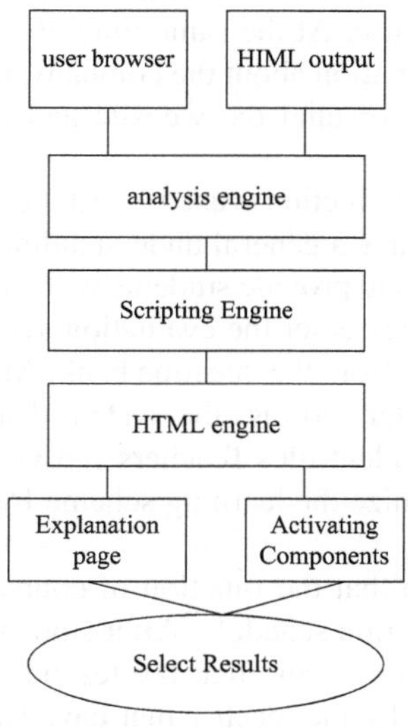


**Fig. 5.** ASP Program Execution Process

It can be seen from Fig. 5 that ASP provides five built-in objects: Application object: an application level object, which is used to share information among all users and can maintain data persistently during the running of the Web application.Request object: The Web page (. htm file) used to connect the client and the server can obtain client data or exchange data between them.Response object: used to send data from the server to the client. It can be displayed in the client browser, redirected to browse the page, and created cookies on the client.This function is the opposite of that of the Request object.Serve: Object: It is used to complete many advanced functions: it can create instances of various Server objects, and provide methods and properties to access the Web Server.Session object: it provides an identifier for each visitor. Session can be used to store some preferences of visitors and track their habits.

Each page of the system is generated dynamically, and the displayed content of the page is extracted from the database in real time.The system adopts ADO mode for database connection and access.ADO (ActiveX Data Objects) is a database access technology, which is actually a connection mechanism providing access to various data types.ADO is designed as a very simple format, which is connected to the database interface through ODBC.Users can use any ODBC data source, which is not only suitable for database applications such as SQL Server 2000 and Oracle Access, but also suitable for Excel tables, graphic files and unformatted data files.

### 3.3 Design English Online Video Teaching Function Module

The student module mainly introduces the seven function points of English proficiency test, course appointment, course cancellation, course viewing, student class, card purchase and recharge, and account management.The homepage of the website includes various functions such as registration, login, online customer service, novice guide and proficiency test for tourists to use. At the same time, the website will also post corresponding announcement information about the company, news plate and other dynamic information for tourists to understand the website and the services provided by the company.

The English proficiency test function is used to test the level of students' English proficiency, so that teachers can have a general understanding of students' current English learning, and facilitate teachers to provide students with corresponding curriculum programs.After students log in, they enter the evaluation system. At this time, the system randomly selects test questions from the question bank. After students finish answering, they submit their answers. After scoring, the system displays the results to students, and saves the test results in student files.Teachers can view the test results of students through the system and customize the learning scheme for students. The business flow chart is shown in Fig. 6 below.

It can be seen from Fig. 6 that the function of course reservation depends on the function of viewing the reservation schedule. After students view the teachers who can be reserved in a certain day, they can click the teacher's name to enter the detailed schedule that can be reserved by the teacher that day. The space displaying the word "reservation" in the schedule is the time when students can book courses, and students can click to enter the reservation details,At the top of the timetable, there is a specific introduction about the teacher for students to refer to.After logging in, students can view the teachers who can make an appointment within their expected time, and then make an appointment for courses.If the balance in the student account is insufficient, the system will prompt the student, on the contrary, it will prompt that the appointment is successful, and save the information in the student and teacher files.

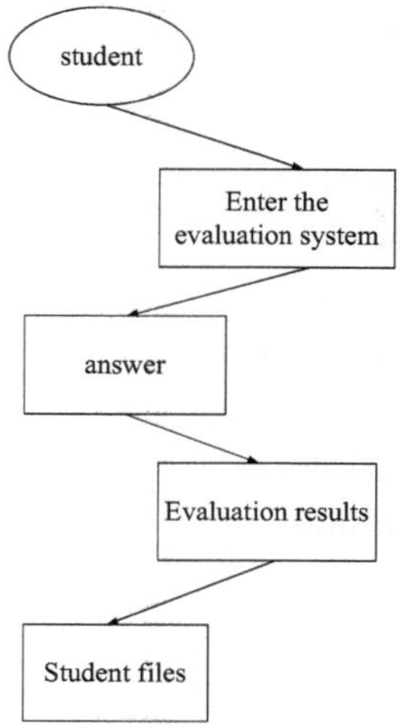


**Fig. 6.** Business Flow Chart

# 4 System Test

In order to verify the running performance of the designed English online video teaching system based on streaming media technology, this paper builds a test platform, runs the design system, and conducts system testing, as follows.

## 4.1 Test Preparation

From the perspective of application systems, testing generally includes functional testing and performance testing.Function test is to test the functions required by the developed application system one by one; The testing of web applications has its own characteristics. In addition to the different contents of performance testing and function testing, it also needs to test from the aspects of UI and security.General web application testing includes user interface, function, interface, compatibility, strength and security testing.

User interface test: referred to as UI test, it tests whether the style of the user interface meets customer requirements, whether the text is correct, whether the page is beautiful, whether the combination of text and pictures is perfect, and whether the operation is friendly.Function test: to test whether the function of the software system is correct, which is based on the requirements documents, such as the Requirements Specification.Since correctness is the most important quality factor of software, functional testing is indispensable.Database test: in web application technology, database plays an important role. Database provides space for the management, operation, query of web application system and the realization of user's request for data storage.In a web application system that uses a database, two types of errors may occur in general, namely data consistency errors and output errors.Data consistency errors are mainly caused by incorrect form information submitted by users, while output errors are mainly caused by network speed or program design problems. For these two cases, tests can be conducted separately. The test environment built at this time is shown in Table 4 below.

**Table 4.** Test Environment

| equipment | main parameter | explain |
|---|---|---|
| application server | processor | IntelP87002, 53 GHz |
| | Hard disk | 2TB |
| | Memory | 8GB |
| | network card | 100\1000 M |
| | operating system | Windows Server |
| | processor | Intel P87002, 53 GHz |
| | Hard disk | 2 TB |
| database server | Memory | 8 GB |
| | network card | 100\1000 M |
| | data base | SQL Server 2012 |
| | operating system | Windows Server2012 |
| | processor | Intel P87002.53 GHz |
| Client computer | Hard disk | 1 TB |
| | Memory | 4 GB |
| | network card | 100\1000 M |
| | operating system | Windows 10 |

It can be seen from Table 4 that subsequent system performance tests can be carried out under the above preset test environment.

### 4.2 Test Results and Discussion

Under the above test environment, the system test can be carried out, that is, run the English online video teaching system based on streaming media technology designed in this paper, and record the operation effect of each functional module. The test results are shown in Table 5 below.

Table 5 shows that all functional modules of the online English teaching system based on streaming media technology designed in this paper have passed the test, proving that the designed system has good performance, reliability and certain application value.

In order to further validate the teaching performance of the system in this paper, the average final English score of 50 students in a class was used as an indicator to compare and verify the system with the reference [7] system and the reference [8] system. The average final grades of students under the three systems are shown in Table 6.

From the comparison results of average grades shown in Table 6, it can be seen that the system in this article can improve students' English learning performance, and students' average English scores are higher than the two comparison systems. Therefore, it indicates that this system has high practical application value.

**Table 5.** Test Results

| process | Expected test results | test result |
|---|---|---|
| Log in to the network video teaching system | Successful login | Test passed |
| Upload teaching video | Display upload success | Test passed |
| Select the video file to learn | Prompt that the video is uploaded successfully | Test passed |
| Update resource description information | Update succeeded | Test passed |
| Submit video resource modification | Modified successfully | Test passed |
| Select the client server and log in | Login succeeded | Test passed |
| Watch teaching resources | Successfully opened the viewing interface | Test passed |

**Table 6.** Student average score

| Systems | Score |
|---|---|
| This paper system | 86.85 |
| Reference [7] system | 70.49 |
| Reference [8] system | 75.63 |

## 5 Conclusion

The so-called online learning refers to a series of learning processes in which students watch the teacher's online teaching live broadcast in real-time through a computer network, or access the course related knowledge data previously released by the teacher. The course related knowledge data mentioned in this learning process can be divided into teaching videos, teaching plans, teaching documents, teaching test questions, etc. Online course teaching in the network environment can improve the pertinence of teaching and the sharing of teaching resources. Therefore, this article designs a new English online video teaching system based on streaming media technology and conducts system testing. The results show that the designed system has good performance, reliability, and certain application value, making a certain contribution to improving the effectiveness of English teaching. However, the issue of maximum user concurrency in the system was not considered in this study. When there are too many students, further verification is needed in future research to ensure the system can continue to operate stably.

## References

1. Wang, H., Wang, Z.: Design of simulation teaching system based on virtual reality. Comput. Simul. **39**(4), 205–209 (2022)

2. Zhang, C., Guo, Y.: Mountain rainfall estimation and online English teaching evaluation based on RBF neural network. Arab. J. Geosci. **14**(22), 178–183 (2021)
3. Ma, X.: Study on college English online teaching model in mixed context based on genetic algorithm and neural network algorithm. Discret. Dyn. Nat. Soc. **41**(11), 201–205 (2021)
4. Wu, X.: Research on the reform of ideological and political teaching evaluation method of college English course based on "online and offline" teaching. J. High. Educ. Res. **3**(1), 87–90 (2022)
5. Chen, S.: Design of internet of things online oral English teaching platform based on long-term and short-term memory network. Int. J. Contin. Eng. Educ. Life-Long Learn. **31**(1), 104–109 (2021)
6. Chen, J., Huang, R.: Providing in-service online language training for primary teachers of English as a foreign language: a brief report. Lang. Teach. Young Learn. **4**(1), 171–183 (2022)
7. Wang, J., Zhao, C.: English online practice system based on cloud computing platform. Inf. Technol. (07), 26–30+35 (2022)
8. Zhuang Fang, T., Zhen.: Design and implementation of multi-terminal interoperability online teaching platform based on MyBatis framework. Tech. Autom. Appl. **41**(01), 182–185 (2022)
9. Yu, Y.: Online teaching of college English during COVID-19 --- taking Shandong vocational college of industry as an example **23**(5), 961-965 (2021). Francis Academic Press
10. Mohideen, S.: The perspectives of online English language teaching and learning during the pandemic. Hum. Resour. Manage. Acad. Res. Soc. (HRMARS) **15**(10), 56–59 (2021)

# Online Educational Video Scoring System for Physical Education

Wei Li[1(✉)] and Meiling Hou[2]

[1] Guangzhou Huali College, Guangzhou 511325, China
liwei0010012023@163.com
[2] Private Hualian College, Guangzhou 510653, China

**Abstract.** In order to meet the needs of online education score calculation for sports subjects, an online education video scoring system for sports subjects has been designed and developed. The system uses an 80C51 microprocessor as the core device, which uses not many data units and the system program occupies not much space, which can save system space. Developing database programming with Visual Basic 6.0 eliminates the need for users to master tedious operating skills, which is beneficial for improving the simplicity of system operation. On the basis of hardware design, optimize the software functional structure and complete the design of online education video scoring system. The experimental results confirm that the online educational video scoring system for sports disciplines can better quickly and accurately score sports videos, and has certain reference value.

**Keywords:** Sports Discipline · Online Education · Educational Video · Scoring System

## 1 Introduction

In the process of sports practice at this stage, the timely, accurate and effective conversion of sports scores measured in the process of sports testing into percent has certain guiding significance for students' performance evaluation, teaching and training. At this stage, in the process of physical education teaching, manual scoring is basically adopted, and a scoring table is used to find the original score of each item of physical education. There is a certain deviation in this statistical process, which takes a long time and has a large workload. Therefore, it is particularly important to study the application and implementation of effective sports score video scoring system [1]. In the calculation process of sports scores, teachers should change the manual calculation method in the traditional calculation process, fully recognize the efficiency, accuracy and timeliness characteristics of the sports education video scoring system, give a positive attitude to try and accept the application of the sports education video scoring system in sports score statistics. In addition, physical education teachers should also constantly improve their ability to use computer related knowledge and skills while accepting the sports education


G. Gui et al. (Eds.): eLEOT 2023, LNICST 543, pp. 233–248, 2024.
https://doi.org/10.1007/978-3-031-51465-4_16

video scoring system, overcome computer related knowledge and training difficulties, and constantly learn the relevant knowledge and skills of the corresponding scoring system, so as to improve the effectiveness of using the sports education video scoring system to achieve high efficiency accurate and timely scoring. With the development of times and technology, computers have gradually penetrated into the teaching process of various disciplines at this stage. To some extent, online sports education video scoring guides students to learn independently, helps students build an overall knowledge system, changes the traditional teaching mode, integrates new teaching methods, and makes teaching more mature and efficient. Physical education achievement is mainly an important indicator to evaluate students' physical education learning level. It is necessary to publish the examination results timely, effectively and accurately after the examination. The traditional manual calculation method takes a long time, lacks timeliness, and errors often occur in the calculation process [2]. In the process of building the sports education video scoring system, it can improve the timeliness, effectiveness and scientificity of sports performance evaluation to a certain extent. It will carry out statistical analysis on the needs of theory and skills, directly export the corresponding analysis table, so that viewers can see clearly.

## 2 Optimization of System Hardware Configuration

The system uses 80C51 microprocessor as the core device.80C51 on-chip data memory (RAM) space is 256B, address O0H-0FFH: on-chip program memory (ROM) space is 4KB, address 000H0FFH.The microcomputer score input system uses only a few data units, and the space occupied by the system program is not large, so the RAM and ROM in 80C51 chip are enough, and external data memory and program memory are not needed. The hardware composition of the microcomputer fraction input device is as follows: chip address latch 74LS373 pieces of digital tube segment display driver chip ULN2003AN, six Darlington tubes drive digital tube 6-bit display. 3-bit 3-inch high brightness nixie tube and a small nixie tube display. Chip 825 programmable parallel I/0 expansion interface [3]. (The microcomputer scoring input device has the functions of input and display, and 8255 is used as the interface between keyboard and display). The MAX232 chip can realize level conversion and drive. In order to make the system reliable and prevent power interference and crash, a power filter watchdog reset circuit is added in the hardware design. The camera equipment selected in the camera module includes the sports teaching video decoding security PTZ. The decoding of sports teaching video is shown in Table 1.

YA9045 PTZ is a built-in, all-weather environment PTZ, which can be hoisted or wall mounted, with a double-layer cover design, prefabrication function and built-in digital decoder. The video capture module mainly collects multi-channel video signals in real time through the video capture card. The selected video capture card is AVZE1000X, which can output, store, digitize and perform other operations including zooming, editing, etc. on the captured and captured pictures. The module diagram of the video capture card is shown in Fig. 1.

In the interim, the embedded processor is selected as the processor module of the system, and the selected model is Samsung SC23440A. The embedded processor has

**Table 1.** Technical Parameters of Sports Teaching Video Decoding

| number | project | date |
|---|---|---|
| 1 | model | VC-7XXS |
| 2 | image sensor | HAD Super 1/3 CCD |
| 3 | Photosensitive area (mm) | 6.3 × 3.7 |
| 4 | Effective pixels | PAL: Horizontal * Vertical: 562 * 542<br>NTSC: Horizontal * Vertical: 678 * 498 |
| 5 | Installation method of lens | CS /A format |
| 6 | signal system | NTSC/PAL |
| 7 | Auto iris lens | DC/ VIDEO Servo type |
| 8 | White balance method | White balance automatic tracking |
| 9 | minimum illumination | 1.5 lx |
| 10 | Signal-to-voice ratio | > 10db |
| 11 | power supply | AC 22V |
| 12 | Power consumption | < 4.8W |
| 13 | Size (mm) | 58*50*115 |

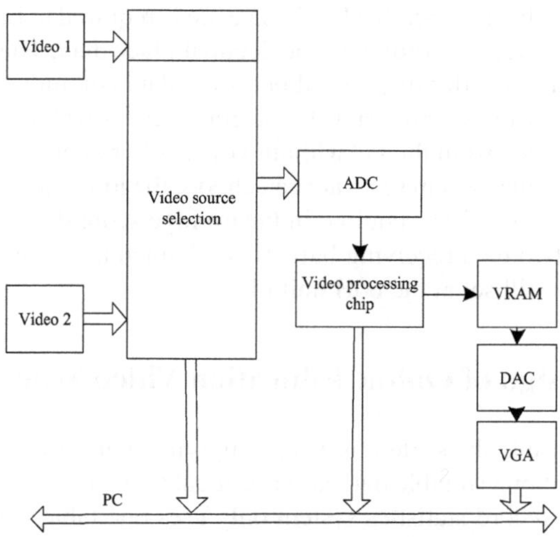


**Fig. 1.** Structure of Motion Video Capture Device

the characteristics of full static design, low power consumption, low cost, etc., which is very suitable for application in the system. The specific technical data of the embedded processor is shown in Table 2.

The design method of the average score display is basically the same as that of the score input device. The system displays data sent from PC through communication with

**Table 2.** Specific Technical Data of the Embedded Processor

| Number | project | date |
|---|---|---|
| 1 | model | SC33665A |
| 2 | structure | CACHE |
| 3 | Peripheral Addressing Space Bytes | 1.2 G |
| 4 | Data and instruction capacity (KB) | 32 |
| 5 | dominant frequency (MHZ) | 200 |
| 6 | AMBABus interface bits | 64 |
| 7 | ARMInstruction Set Bits | 46 |
| 8 | equipped | Universal I/O interface (140) |
| | | clock generator (PLL) |
| | | External interrupt (24 channels) |
| | | Camera Interface |

MCU. In this system, the display data is the data of one, ten, hundred and decimal places. However, during system communication, the data of one and ten places are combined into one byte data, and the data of one hundred places and decimal places are combined into one byte unit data. To display specifically, BCD code is required to be separated, and the actual display is rearranged according to the decimal place data. Therefore, the average score display program includes display subprogram, data communication subprogram, and display data processing subprogram. The average score display is used to display the average score transmitted from the PC without keyboard or operator control. Therefore, the design structure of the system software can choose the job sequence scheduling type. There are not many data buffers required in the average score display system, but three display buffers and two data receiving buffers are defined at the high end of the RAM address. The stack is still set at the 60H unit [4].

## 3 Database Design of Online Education Video Scoring System

The design of database in the system is a very important part of the application system, and the establishment of a suitable database is critical to the maintenance and use of the system. The scoring record statistics system only uses one table, so it adopts the form of free table, which is conducive to the synthesis and statistics of scores. The data table is named pingdata. The database structure is shown in Table 3:

It can be seen from the table structure of the database that most fields are of character type. The reason for this definition is that it is convenient to query and operate the database using SQL statements [5]. The serial port of the computer is used for communication between the decoder and the application program to realize the control of the lens and the PTZ. The communication protocol of the video scoring monitoring control module is as follows:

**Table 3.** Database Result Table

| Field Number | Field Name | Field type | weight | illustrate |
|---|---|---|---|---|
| 1 | Csh | character | 8 | Number |
| 2 | Xm | character | 10 | Name |
| 3 | Fz | character | 6 | Sports Zub |
| 4 | Cj2 | character | 6 | Teacher grading |
| 5 | Sex | character | 8 | Action rating |
| 6 | Address | character | 12 | average |
| 7 | school | character | 12 | Comprehensive score |

(1) The baud rate is 9.7BPS/22.085 crystal oscillator.
(2) A frame uses 10 bits together, and the number of start bits is 1; The number of data bits is 8;The number of stop bits is 1, and there is no check bit.
(3) The interface standard is RS845.
(4) The format that the computer sends the serial port instruction is control code+address code, in which the control code has a total of 16 bits and 2 bytes, which are represented by hexadecimal binary data; The address code has a total of 32 bits and 4 bytes, which are also represented by hexadecimal binary data. The instructions sent by the computer to the serial port instructions are shown in Table 4, and the returned information is represented by the status code+address code.

**Table 4.** Commands sent by the system to serial port commands

| Code | describe | Code | describe |
|---|---|---|---|
| 0149 | Control the magnification of the camera lens | 0140 | Stop pan tilt scanning |
| 014A | Control the reduction of camera lens magnification | 0141 | Upward pan tilt action |
| 014B | Patrol through PTZ | 0142 | Downward pan tilt action |
| 013A | Control query does not exist | 0143 | Increasing focal length |
| 013B | Stop camera action and pan tilt action | 0144 | Defocus |

The score uses character data for data security. If the score is defined as numerical type, the initial value of the score is 0.00. In order to ensure the security of the data, the system stipulates that if there is already data in the position to be modified in the database, the original data must be deleted by authorization before it can be re entered by the single-chip score input device. The standard for deleting data is that the original data is empty characters. Therefore, the types of these score data are also set to character type. When performing arithmetic operations on the score data, the conversion functions

Strtofloat() and FloatTostr() in Delphi can be used. The scoring system defines sub elements and scoring criteria for each element. It is divided into two sub elements: one is the proportion of 13.333% of the score in the level of action technology, and the other is the proportion of 13.333% of the score in the level of diversity of action elements. Make progress in interpreting its various elements, so as to calculate the single factor variance value. Assume that the characteristic index of the original data is $\alpha$, the commonness of information is $\beta$, and the difference of information is $\chi$. Combine the weighted TOPSIS method to calculate the single factor variance of teaching information. The specific algorithm is as follows:

$$\Delta F = \frac{\alpha}{\chi - \sqrt{\beta}} - 1 \tag{1}$$

Combining the above algorithm, further analyze the characteristics of the original information category, and statistically calculate the difference value $d$ in the quality indicators of different categories of teaching information. Furthermore, use factor analysis and cluster analysis principles to iteratively process the average $R$ of information management evaluation indicators, and record the teaching management indicators as $A$, $B$, $C$, $D$, $E$ five levels. Based on this, Standardize the evaluation parameters of teaching management at different levels, with specific algorithms as follows:

$$level(A \rightarrow E) = d \times \frac{(A \rightarrow B \rightarrow C \rightarrow D \rightarrow E)}{\Delta F + R} \tag{2}$$

Based on the above algorithm, the weights of evaluation indicators for online sports education videos in China are set uniformly, and different registered indicators are standardized, so that the quality of online sports education videos can be accurately evaluated later. From the scoring elements of physical fitness, it can be seen that the competition has very high requirements for the physical fitness of participants: strength, speed, endurance, coordination, flexibility Sensitivity and other qualities are very important. It is particularly critical for competitors to effectively use their physiological advantages, upgrade their physiological advantages to a higher level of ability, and turn their disadvantages into advantages [6]. The scoring system makes the evaluation results of sports events a relatively objective evaluation. It is a scoring system that allows the referee to judge the contestants with a more rational attitude. Although there are many indicators in the scoring system, it is not a one size fits all evaluation, but a more comprehensive and objective evaluation of the contestants, providing new ideas for sports teaching and promoting the development of sports teaching [7].

## 4 Software Function Design of Online Education Video Scoring System

The system runs under the Windows operating system. With VVisBasic6.0 as the programming tool, it is an information analysis and processing tool that integrates multiple functions such as data tables and databases. The sports education video scoring system includes student data entry, information entry and competition performance management. The system can not only query and print the results through the computer, but also timely release the results of the game through automatic voice play, LED large screen display, Web publishing and other forms. See Fig. 2 for system function module.

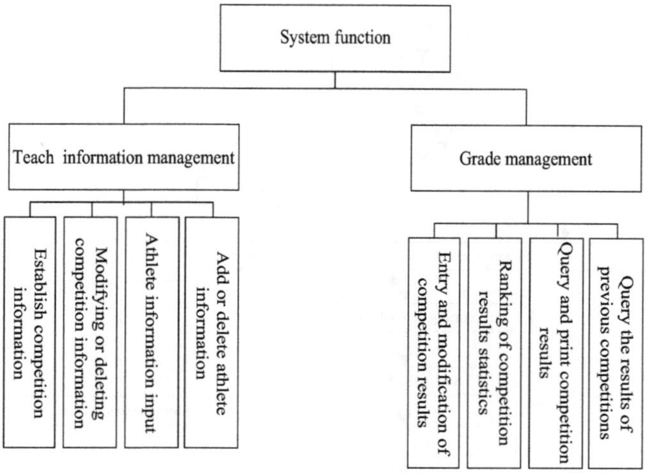


**Fig. 2.** Structure optimization of system function module

The system is programmed with Visual basic 6.0 and runs on the Windows operating system. It is a graphical user interface application software supported by the fully object-oriented programming concept. It is also the first set of application software used to calculate the results of figure skating competitions in China. To some extent, it reflects the level of competition performance statistics. The system adopts the object-oriented programming method and has the typical style of Windows application program [8]. Users do not need to memorize any code and master tedious operation skills. As long as they are familiar with Windows, they can carry out actual operation after a few minutes. The system can closely monitor the operation and operation. According to the operation status and the competition process, error proofing programs are set in good time. Once the operation is wrong, the system will immediately "sound" and display error prompt information. The system can also automatically save the data in the current operating environment, and even in the event of power failure and other unexpected circumstances, it can recover to the state before the accident after restarting. Based on the above collection mode, the collected common characteristic data and difference characteristic data are described and explained, and the original data is compared and tested. To ensure the accuracy of the evaluation results, the information management characteristic parameters are collected, and the specific collection steps are as follows (Fig. 3):

The scoring results will be further recorded and analyzed. In order to ensure the accuracy of the analysis, different feature categories will be recorded as $f(i), f(j), f(x)$, $f(y), f(n), f(z)$ and $f(m)$ for subsequent calculation and analysis. Based on the above content, further optimize the evaluation method of educational informatization management quality. In order to ensure the effectiveness and reliability of the evaluation of higher education informatization management quality, it is necessary to further define teaching information, student information, campus information, etc. in order to evaluate information accurately. Due to the huge amount of information, online sports education

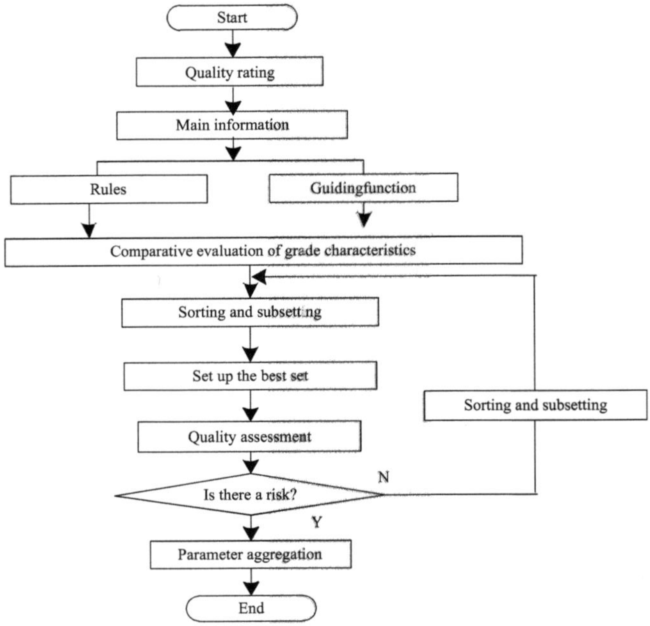


**Fig. 3.** Video scoring feature information acquisition steps

evaluation is relatively complex, which needs to be defined from different perspectives. Based on this, it is necessary to further improve and adhere to the principles of sports education video evaluation: complex, connotative, personalized, academic, democratic and innovative. This further carries out a comprehensive analysis on the standard indicators of teaching informatization management quality judgment, and carries out a consistency test on the structural and independent characteristics of physical education video scoring indicators [9]. Combined with the analytic hierarchy process, professional, objective and overall calculation and evaluation are carried out, and the relative importance values of teaching evaluation indicators are given, and the characteristic values are analyzed consistently. The numerical matrix of the relative importance of students' evaluation indicators is:

$$R_1 = \begin{Bmatrix} level(A), \frac{1}{2}, \frac{1}{3}, 1, 2, 0, 0, 1 \\ level(B), 2, \frac{1}{2}, 1, 0, 1, 9, \frac{1}{3} \\ level(C), 1, 3, \frac{1}{2}, \frac{1}{3}, 2, 1, 1 \\ level(D), 0, 3, \frac{1}{2}, 0, \frac{1}{3}, 0, 1 \\ level(E), 1, 2, \frac{1}{3}, 2, \frac{1}{2}, 2, 1 \end{Bmatrix} \tag{3}$$

The maximum characteristic value can be calculated through the above algorithm, which is recorded as: $\lambda_{\min}$=3.154, the average value is:

$$CI = \Delta F \prod (\lambda_{\min} - R_1)/K - 1 \tag{4}$$

Among them, $K$ is a consistency index, its randomness ratio algorithm is:

$$CR = CI_1 - \lambda_{\min}/RI \tag{5}$$

If in the calculation process, the weight value of students' teaching evaluation is: $s = (0.1219,\ 0.183\,5,\ 0.4862,\ 0.2084)$

Then further standardize the student evaluation matrix, as follows:

$$r = \begin{Bmatrix} A: 1, 0, 1, 0, 0, 0, 1, 0, 1 \\ B: 0, 1, 2, 1, 2, 0, 1, 2, 1 \\ C: 1, 2, 0, 1, 2, 1, 0, 2, 1 \\ D: 0, 2, 1, 2, 0, 2, 0, 1, 1 \\ E: 1, 2, 0, 0, 1, 2, 1, 0, 2 \end{Bmatrix} \tag{6}$$

If the teacher's teaching attitude can be recorded as $U_n$, with a consistency ratio of 1:0.328, then the weight of the teaching attitude can be recorded as $m = (0.124, 0.232, 0.187)$. Further select the average weighted value $M$ and combine it with fuzzy algorithm to calculate the first level evaluation model. The specific algorithm is:

$$\begin{cases} W = U_n \sum CI - R_1 * s \\ N = 0.328 \sum CR - rm \end{cases} \tag{7}$$

Further standardize the secondary evaluation model, as follows:

$$C = \sum \lambda_{\min}(W - N)/2 \tag{8}$$

Assuming that during the teaching process, the difference in teaching effectiveness before and after is 0; But in reality, there are certain cross differences before and after the teaching ends. On the basis of this hypothesis, hypothesis testing is conducted on the teaching difference parameters, and a calculation method is set based on data mining and Analytic Hierarchy Process principles. $p$ is set as the influence parameter of sports education video scoring. If $|p|>\varphi$ is set, it indicates that the teaching effectiveness evaluation is poor; On the contrary, if $|p|<\varphi$, it indicates that the teaching evaluation effect is good. Then, starting from the zero hypothesis, we use the Proof by contradiction method for reasoning. If the difference before and after teaching is $\varphi \geq 1$, it will be recorded as $x$, indicating that it is a factor with high influence value. If $\varphi < 1$, it will be recorded as $1-x$, indicating that it is a factor with low influence value. On this basis, we conduct a unified evaluation and analysis of the learning effect of the training objects, and we can get the following algorithm for the influence parameter of physical education video scoring:

$$V = \frac{\lambda_{\min}}{m\sqrt{\frac{(p-\varphi)s_1^2+(p_1+\varphi)s_1^2}{1-x}}\sqrt{\frac{1}{W}+\frac{1}{N}}} - \frac{\overline{z}}{s_z/\sqrt{Cn}} \tag{9}$$

where, $z$ represents the average difference of teaching effect test samples before and after evaluation, $s_z$ is the standard parameter value of the teaching scoring effect of physical education, $m$ is the maximum influence degree, $n$ is the minimum influence degree. Through the above algorithm, we can calculate the influencing parameters of different influencing factors on the teaching scoring effect of physical education, and evaluate the influencing factors of teaching effect according to the influencing parameters. In order to better evaluate the influencing factors of the effect, the scoring effect statistics is carried out in combination with the network platform. Mining and integrating the marketing value and influence degree of teaching content under the condition of big data, and conducting online evaluation on sports education video scores according to the integration results, so as to timely and effectively collect the characteristics of students' learning behavior, and retain the collected data: learning duration, online number of people, learning progress, examination results, etc. And input the obtained data into the knowledge inventory storage system, and set set evaluation rules to evaluate the influencing factors of teaching effect [10]. Set up $L = (Q, R, T)$ is the evaluation value of an information, $\xi = \{a_1, a_2, \cdots, a_m\}$ is the reference coefficient in the evaluation rules, then:

$$Ea \leq \widehat{V} \frac{C, \{level(A \to E)\}}{H(E) - H_a(E)} - L\xi \tag{10}$$

Among them, $H(E)$ is the associated influence value, $H_a(E)$ it is a reference parameter for data evaluation.Then the impact assessment parameters between a and E are:

$$RH_E(a) = Ea - \sum \widehat{V} \frac{H_a(E)}{H(E)} - C \tag{11}$$

If $RH_E(a)$ is less than or equal to zero, the hypothesis is not tenable, which indicates that the evaluation results of the factors affecting teaching effectiveness are effective, otherwise, it indicates that the evaluation results are uncertain and need further optimization. In the sports education video scoring system, the operation page is simple, highly operable and intuitive. The page mainly includes the corresponding list import link, score input link, score query link and score statistics link. In the list import link, students' names, learning, classes, teachers, sports class hours and other information are counted in the form of EXCEI. Have certain comprehensiveness and accuracy; In the score input link, statistics are mainly made for each sports item in the process of physical education teaching, such as standing long jump, special event, theory, process score and usual score. Among them, standing long jump accounts for 10%, theoretical knowledge mastery accounts for 20%, special event accounts for 40%, and process score accounts for 10%. The peacetime percentage is 10%, and each item shall be statistically calculated based on 100 points. The score inquiry link is mainly based on the input of student number and name to accurately obtain students' individual exam scores, which is fast and accurate. The last part is the link of score statistics, which is mainly aimed at the statistics of students' peacetime scores, final scores, overall evaluation scores, technical achievement statistics, theoretical scores, etc., and the number of test scores, the lowest score, the highest score, the number of people, the average score and other ratios in the process of students' examination, so as to facilitate teachers to better statistics of sports and physical education video scores and teaching levels. The application of video scoring system of physical education can reduce the workload of physical education teachers to a certain extent, improve the accuracy of statistical scores of physical education teachers, and has a certain advantage of timeliness.

On the basis of the above software and hardware design, the overall design of an online education video scoring system for sports subjects has been completed. The following is a schematic diagram of the login interface of the system.

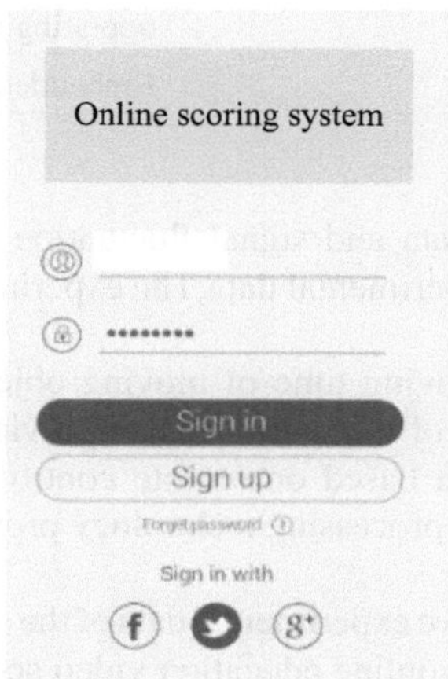


**Fig. 4.** System Login Interface

As shown in Fig. 4, users only need to have an account and password to log in, and the system has good privacy.

## 5 System Test

Build an experimental environment to test the online education video scoring system for sports disciplines. The simulation tool used in the experiment is matlab 7.0. Use the moving target detection digital video capture equipment to conduct a digital video scoring experiment on a place with moving targets, and compare the traditional scoring system based on remote control technology and the scoring system based on image coding processing technology in the same experimental environment. The specific experimental environment is shown in Table 5.

Based on the above environment, the digital video sampling frame rate data and signal fluctuation data of moving objects are obtained as experimental data. In order to enhance the contrast of the experimental results, the traditional scoring system based on remote control technology and the scoring system based on image coding processing technology are used as the comparison system in the experiment. The two digital video dynamic scoring systems are also used to conduct digital video scoring in the experimental place,

**Table 5.** Built Experimental Environment

| Number | Experimental environment configuration | project | date |
|---|---|---|---|
| 1 | hardware configuration | CPU | intel core i8 9800 |
| | | Memory | 32GB |
| | | Hard disk | wdf-069T |
| | | Graphics card | GV-N0903GAMING |
| | | Number of hosts | 6 |
| 2 | software configuration | operating system | Win7 |
| | | Embedded system | LINUX |

and the sampled frame rate data and signal fluctuation data of the two systems are obtained as the comparison experimental data,The experimental data were recorded and compared.

In the case of different moving time of moving objects, the sampling frame rate comparison experimental data of the online education video scoring system for sports disciplines, the scoring system based on remote control technology and the scoring system based on image coding processing technology proposed in this paper are shown in Table 6.

According to the comparative experimental data of the sampling frame rate in Table 6, the sampling frame rate of the online education video scoring system for sports disciplines proposed in this paper is higher than the sampling frame rate of the system based on remote control technology scoring and the scoring system based on image coding processing technology, when the moving time of the moving target is different. The great improvement in the video sampling frame rate helps to make more clear and accurate scoring decisions. The higher the sampling frame rate, the closer the scoring will be to the standard.

The experimental data of signal fluctuation comparison between the online education video scoring system oriented to physical education, the scoring system based on remote control technology and the scoring system based on image coding processing technology is shown in Fig. 5.

In the figure, A is the online education video scoring system for sports discipline proposed in this paper, B is the scoring system based on remote control technology, and C is the scoring system based on image coding processing technology. The lighter the color in the figure, the smaller the impact of interference on the system score. According to the signal fluctuation comparison experimental data, as shown in Fig. 6, under the interference environment, the online education video scoring system for sports discipline proposed in this paper, B is a system based on remote control technology scoring. The digital video dynamic monitoring system based on motion target detection has a lower signal fluctuation frequency and is more stable. Finally, the accuracy of the system scoring is compared. The scoring accuracy of the three systems is compared based on the on-site scoring of 10 expert teachers. The specific results are shown in the following table (Table 7):

**Table 6.** Experimental data of sampling frame rate comparison

| Target Movement Time (s) | Sampling frame rate (frames/s) | | |
|---|---|---|---|
| | This article system | A Scoring System Based on Image Coding Processing Technology | A scoring system based on remote control technology |
| 0 | 86 | 42 | 38 |
| 5 | 88 | 43 | 38 |
| 10 | 89 | 44 | 37 |
| 15 | 91 | 48 | 36 |
| 20 | 89 | 41 | 36 |
| 25 | 97 | 40 | 36 |
| 30 | 92 | 39 | 35 |
| 35 | 91 | 42 | 38 |
| 40 | 91 | 40 | 32 |
| 45 | 93 | 38 | 37 |
| 50 | 88 | 37 | 30 |
| 55 | 88 | 40 | 29 |
| 60 | 87 | 40 | 35 |

**Table 7.** Comparison and Analysis of Video Scoring Results of Three Systems

| Video frequency (min) | Expert scoring (average score) | This article system | A Scoring System Based on Image Coding Processing Technology | A scoring system based on remote control technology |
|---|---|---|---|---|
| 15 | 88.45 | 88.33 | 85.46 | 82.46 |
| 30 | 91.26 | 91.45 | 89.33 | 86.39 |
| 45 | 73.58 | 73.89 | 80.12 | 70.56 |
| 60 | 90.44 | 90.89 | 86.44 | 87.23 |
| 75 | 96.34 | 96.34 | 88.12 | 86.43 |
| 90 | 87.23 | 87.65 | 80.56 | 82.12 |

Based on the above comparison results, it can be seen that the highest scoring value of the designed system in this article reaches 96.34, which is significantly higher than the scoring system based on remote control technology and image encoding processing technology. The online education video scoring system proposed in this article for the

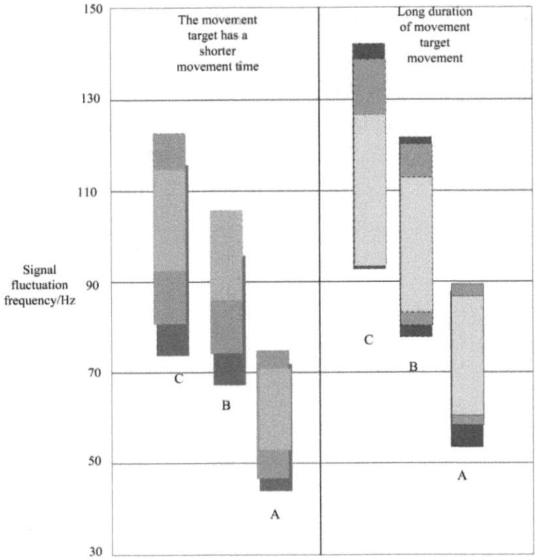


**Fig. 5.** Signal fluctuation comparison experimental data

discipline of physical education has high stability and accuracy in practical application, and repeatedly meets the design requirements.

In order to further verify the performance of the system designed in this article, the system response time was used as a testing indicator to compare the application effects of the three systems mentioned above. The results are shown in Table 8.

**Table 8.** System Response Time Test Results/s

| Number of experiments/time | This article system | A Scoring System Based on Image Coding Processing Technology | A scoring system based on remote control technology |
|---|---|---|---|
| 10 | 1.23 | 2.30 | 1.97 |
| 20 | 2.05 | 2.97 | 2.48 |
| 30 | 2.41 | 3.56 | 3.07 |
| 40 | 2.59 | 4.02 | 3.99 |
| 50 | 2.87 | 4.28 | 4.52 |

From the data in Table 8, it can be seen that the minimum response time of the designed system in this article is 1.23 s, while the response time of the other two systems is higher than that of the designed system, indicating that the application effect of the system in this article is better.

# 6 Conclusion

This article has optimized the design of an online education video scoring system for the physical education discipline. According to the experimental results, the lowest response time of the system designed in this article is only 1.23s, and the highest scoring value reaches 96.34. This indicates that the application effect of the system is good and good results have been achieved. This is because the system uses an 80C51 microprocessor as the core device and uses Visual Basic 6.0 to develop database programming. This not only saves system space, but also helps to improve the simplicity of system operation. However, in the application of sports score statistics for physical education video scoring system, teachers should also enhance the security, reliability and stability of data by setting worksheet protection password and cell protection password. In the process of statistics of online education video scoring system for physical education disciplines, teachers should also realize the statistics of list import link, score input link, score query link and score statistics link by implementing the transformation of traditional calculation methods and calculation concepts of physical education scores and the application process of physical education scores in the sports education video scoring system, improve the effectiveness, timeliness and accuracy of sports score statistics.

**Aknowledgement.** One of the research results of the 2022 private university education research project initiated by Guangdong Provincial Private Education Association: "Research on practical teaching of integrating outward bound training into public physical education in private universities" (project number: GMG2022048).

# References

1. Ajloni, M., Psych, E.D., O'Toole, M.: Adopting TPACK to video technology in the context of the Jordanian education system. Turk. Online J. Educ. Technol. **20**(2), 13 (2021)
2. Malick, H., et al.: Moving postgraduate ophthalmology education online—experiences of a nationalised live video-linked series. Nat. Publ. Group **9**, 2633–2635 (2021)
3. Liu, S., et al.: Human inertial thinking strategy: a novel Fuzzy reasoning mechanism for IoT-assisted visual monitoring. IEEE Internet Things J. (2022). https://doi.org/10.1109/JIOT.2022.3142115
4. Wang, J.: Intelligent system for interactive online education based on cloud big data analytics. J. Intell. Fuzzy Syst.: Appl. Eng. Technol. **40**(2), 2839–2849 (2021)
5. Noetel, M., Griffith, S., Delaney, O., et al.: Video improves learning in higher education: a systematic review. Rev. Educ. Res. **91**(2), 003465432199071 (2021)
6. Lee, K.: Teaching entrepreneurship education (EE) online during COVID-19 pandemic: lessons learned from a participatory action research (PAR) in a Malaysian public university. SAGE Open **12**(1), 730–767 (2022)
7. Tudini, D.V., Dooly, D.M.: Complaining for rapport building: troubles talk in a preservice language teacher online video exchange. Linguist. Educ. **64**(2), 100941 (2021)
8. Qiang, C., Cun, Z.: Adaptive compression method of embedded online video inter frame signal. Comput. Simul. **38**(03), 87–91 (2021)

9. Espasa, A., et al.: Does the type of feedback channel used in online learning environments matter? Students' perceptions and impact on learning. Act. Learn. High. Educ. **23**(1), 49–63 (2022)
10. Zhou, M., et al.: Consumer behavior in the online classroom: using video analytics and machine learning to understand the consumption of video courseware. J. Mark. Res. **6**, 58 (2021)

# Design of Online Network Multi Module Teaching System for ERP Sand Table Simulation Course

Biling Lu(✉) and Caili Wang

Hunan Traffic Engineering College, Hengyang 421001, China
xingjuunmn@163.com

**Abstract.** In order to provide auxiliary tools for ERP sandbox simulation course teaching, an online network multi-module teaching system was designed and developed. The system database is constructed from conceptual models, logical structures, physical structures, and other aspects to provide storage space for the operational data of the teaching system. In terms of system software, user role division and authorization modules are used to determine the permissions of users in the system. By determining the course arrangement of the ERP sand table simulation course, simulating the role of enterprise operation participation, simulating the ERP sand table business process, and enterprise evaluation, the online teaching module of the ERP sand table simulation course has been designed. By designing and connecting the online network interaction module, network resource query module, and teaching evaluation module, the system software functionality has been completed. Through system testing experiments, it has been concluded that compared to traditional teaching systems, the module teaching cases of the optimized design system have a higher success rate in operation and a 29 s reduction in operation delay, proving that the optimized design system has obvious advantages in functional operation, performance operation, and application performance.

**Keywords:** ERP Sand Table Simulation Course · Online Network · Multi Module Teaching System

## 1 Introduction

ERP, Enterprise Resources Plan, is MRP II Next generation manufacturing system and resource planning software. ERP, in addition to production resource planning, manufacturing, finance, sales, procurement and other functions, also includes Quality Assurance, laboratory management, operation flow Administration, product data management, inventory, distribution and transportation management, Human Resources Management and periodic report System. The meaning of ERP in China has been expanded. All kinds of software used in enterprises have been included in the category of ERP [1]. It breaks away from tradition Enterprise boundary, optimize from the scope of supply chain. Enterprise resources is based on internet economy, the new generation of information system of the era. It is mainly used to improve enterprise business processes


G. Gui et al. (Eds.): eLEOT 2023, LNICST 543, pp. 249–266, 2024.
https://doi.org/10.1007/978-3-031-51465-4_17

to improve Enterprise core competitiveness. Enterprise resources Planning is a management platform based on information technology and systematic management ideas, which provides decision-making and operation means for enterprise decision makers and employees. ERP System support discrete, process type and other mixed manufacturing environments, scope of application. The ERP sandbox simulation course focuses on cultivating students' ability to apply ERP systems in real scenarios. The online network multi module teaching system can provide a virtual practice environment, allowing students to learn and practice real ERP system applications in simulated enterprise operations, thereby better mastering relevant knowledge and skills. It can enhance interactivity and collaboration, provide personalized learning support, monitor and evaluate students' learning situation in real-time, and provide flexible learning methods. These characteristics make the teaching system important and necessary in cultivating students' practical operational abilities, promoting student interaction and cooperation, and providing personalized learning support. From manufacturing to retail, service banking, telecommunication industry, government agencies, schools and other public institutions, through integration database technology, graphical user interface, the fourth generation query language, client server structure, computer-aided development tool, portable open system, so as to effectively integrate enterprise resources. ERP sand table simulation course is set up for the professional ability, collaboration ability, hands-on ability and innovation and entrepreneurship ability of students majoring in economics and management. ERP sand table simulation course is a professional course of economics and management in higher vocational colleges, a comprehensive course integrating theory and practice, and an important teaching method in innovation and entrepreneurship education.

This course is mainly based on manufacturing enterprises. Students can simulate a set of systematic processes of enterprise operation by playing the roles of general manager, financial director, production director, procurement director, sales director, etc. Through the study of this course, students can learn about enterprises in an all-round way, and carry out business innovation, technological innovation, concept innovation, strategic innovation, etc. in the process of active participation and interaction. In order to improve the teaching effect of ERP sand table simulation course and break the limitations of course teaching in time and space, an online network multi module teaching system for ERP sand table simulation course was designed and developed.

Under the guidance of certain teaching theories and ideas, online network teaching has many applications media and network technique. It is a kind of teaching mode to achieve teaching goals through multi-lateral and multi-directional interaction among teachers, students, media and the collection, transmission, processing and sharing of teaching information in multiple media. The online network multi module teaching system refers to teachers and students. Joint participation aimed at achieving Teaching objectives, Activities for system. From the current research situation of the teaching system, the more mature teaching systems include: the teaching system based on the project teaching method, the teaching system based on the auxiliary teaching mode, and the teaching system based on the hierarchical teaching theory. However, the above teaching systems are mainly targeted at computer professional courses, and are applied to the teaching of ERP sand table simulation courses. There are obvious problems such as poor teaching quality and poor system performance.

In order to address the issues of poor teaching quality and system performance in the aforementioned transmission teaching system, the ERP sandbox simulation course was taken as the research object and a multi-module teaching approach was adopted to optimize the online network teaching system. This system has designed and developed an online network multi module teaching system, providing auxiliary tools for ERP sandbox simulation course teaching. The system achieves the storage of teaching system data, user permission management, and online teaching functions by constructing a database, determining user permissions, and designing online teaching modules. Compared with traditional teaching systems, the optimized design system has achieved significant improvements in operation success rate, operation delay, and student performance. This innovation makes the ERP sandbox simulation course teaching more convenient and efficient, and improves students' learning experience and performance.

## 2 Database Design of Online Network Multi Module Teaching System

Database is a warehouse that organizes, stores and manages data according to data structure computer. A collection of large amounts of internal, organized, shareable, and uniformly managed data. In the optimized design of ERP sand table simulation course online network multi module teaching system, the database can provide storage space for ERP sand table simulation course resources, and can also store real-time data generated during the operation of the teaching system. In order to ensure the normal operation of the database, the redesign of the database should follow the principles of practicality, advancement, scalability and security, of which the security principle mainly refers to that when designing the database, the confidential data should be the center, and the authority of each user should be taken into account, and the level should be limited at the same time; The database shall be maintained during infrequent use, and management tools shall be provided to back up the data in the system on a regular basis, so as to prevent the data from being lost. The database shall be able to recover automatically after being damaged [2]. This ERP sand table simulation course online network multi module teaching system database is carried out from the conceptual model, logical structure, physical structure and other aspects. Based on the analysis of the system's needs, the database is designed for conceptual structure, needs are synthesized, summarized and abstracted, and an E-R diagram is designed. The design result of the E-R diagram of the teaching system is shown in Fig. 1.

According to the E-R diagram, the logical structure of the database is designed, and several database tables are constructed according to the characteristics of the system operation. The system database table can be roughly divided into three aspects: basic information table, core business table, and system parameter table. The ERP sand table in the core business table is used to simulate the construction results of the course information database table, as shown in Table 1.

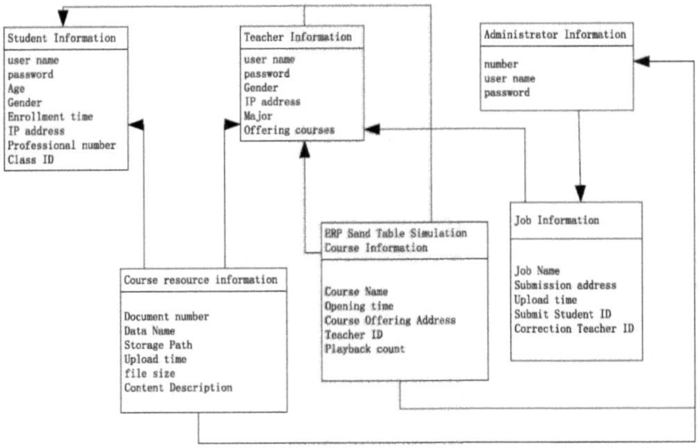


**Fig. 1.** E-R Diagram of Multi module Teaching System Database

**Table 1.** ERP sand table simulation course information database

| Field Name | Field Description | data type | Storage length | Is it empty |
|---|---|---|---|---|
| Curriculum_id | Course No | Int | 10 | no |
| Curriculum_Name | Course name | Varchar | 50 | no |
| Curriculum_OpeningTime | Opening time | Varchar | 20 | no |
| Curriculum_url | Course running address | Varchar | 100 | yes |
| Curriculum_imageUrl | Course cover address | Varchar | 100 | no |
| Curriculum_teacherId | Teacher No | Varchar | 100 | no |
| Curriculum_Description | Content introduction | Varchar | 250 | yes |

The construction results of other database tables in the system database can be obtained according to the above methods. In order to ensure the security of the database, effective control needs to be carried out through the database role. When the server is successfully accessed by the user, the user name [3] required is generally queried through the corresponding database role on the server. If the user information is found in the corresponding database role, the user can access the corresponding database name and related dataset list. However, this user can only view related data tables that have been assigned database roles. If the required user name cannot be found in the database role, the user cannot access or query any object on the server. In the process of system operation, real-time data will be generated, so the data in the database needs to be updated according to the operation of the system to facilitate the storage and reading of all data resources in the database.

# 3 Software Function Design of Online Network Multi Module Teaching System

With the support of the system database, the software functions of the system are optimized by using the multi module teaching method.Through user role division, ERP sand table simulation course implementation, teaching resource sharing and retrieval, teaching process synchronization and other modules, the teaching function of the system is realized.

## 3.1 User Role Division and Authorization Module

Users in the system can be divided into three types: administrator, teacher and student. Set an administrator account in the system. This role is set manually. Only the system administrator can access the system background, and other users are prohibited from accessing. During system initialization, the system administrator can create a new user for the experimental instructor, modify the instructor's user password, and delete the user. The new user created has all permissions except the system management module. The teacher role has the authority of student information management, course opening, question reply, etc., while the student user has the authority of personal information management, resource retrieval, resource download, ERP enterprise role simulation, etc. In order to prevent illegal access to the system, the default user of the system must be a registered student. Before starting the teaching of ERP sand table simulation course, the student must, according to his/her student ID. The system can only be used after the name and other information are registered as official users of the system, which also provides guarantee for the safe operation of the system [4]. To facilitate the system's management of users, user information is recorded in the form of Formula 1.

$$u = \{b, \chi, \omega\} \tag{1}$$

Variables in Formula 1 $b$, $\chi$ and $\omega$ They correspond to the user name, user type, and user permission. Quantify all users in the system according to formula 1 and input them into the system database.Teachers can make preparations for courses on the system, such as making courseware, writing teaching plans, building relevant curriculum resources and test question database, and uploading reviewed multimedia video, audio, pictures, text and other material resources; Teachers can also prepare lessons for traditional teaching, assign and wholesale homework, and provide synchronous or asynchronous tutoring to students through the network through this platform. Students can understand, preview, study and review courses under the system, complete online homework provided by teachers, complete online tests of units and courses, use the network to help online, and communicate with teachers or classmates online. The administrator can manage users and resources on this platform, understand teachers' teaching and guidance as well as students' comprehensive learning situation, and master students' learning effects through online examinations, online feedback and other forms.

## 3.2 Online Teaching Module of ERP Sand Table Simulation Course

The course teaching function is the core part of network teaching, which serves as a bridge between teachers, students and system administrators. Teachers design teaching courses according to teaching objectives, develop corresponding courseware, create corresponding courses and determine teaching plans by analyzing students' learning characteristics. After the course is created, you can properly select some related resources to add to the course. This teaching resource is not optional, but should be closely related to the curriculum, and it is necessary to explain, introduce and supplement the specific curriculum content. The curriculum teaching management in the design system mainly includes curriculum management, teaching management, teaching materials, homework and examination, teacher-student interaction and other related functions. Students can solve their own problems by inquiring about the course introduction, selecting the teaching course suitable for them, improving their learning ability, and meeting course problems directly through the interactive program between teachers and students, and sending an email to the teaching mailbox [5]. The teacher is the organizer and implementer of the online teaching process. The whole process of online teaching starts with the establishment of a course for a certain teaching, and has supplemented and explained the relevant materials and data, making the course more rich and interesting, and then providing it to students for learning and downloading, students actively study and explore according to the online teaching of teachers. In addition, the course created by the teacher is also the basis of all the follow-up links of online teaching. It should be classified according to the relevant information of the course to provide greater convenience for students to download and search.

### 3.2.1 Determine the ERP Sand Table Simulation Course Schedule

ERP sand table simulation course consists of five parts: sand table teaching aids, course design, teaching subject, ERP sand table simulation course software and ERP sand table simulation learning guide. ERP sand table teaching takes a set of sand table teaching aids as the carrier. The sand table teaching aids mainly include sand table surface, various logos and other parts. The sand table surface is divided into functional centers according to the functional departments of manufacturing enterprises, including marketing and planning center, production center, logistics center and financial center. Each functional center covers all the key links of enterprise operation: strategic planning, marketing, production organization, procurement management, inventory management, financial management, etc. It is the epitome of a manufacturing enterprise [6]. Figure 2 shows the construction result of the sand table surface.

The ERP sand table simulation course is divided into six stages: organization preparation, basic situation description, market rules and enterprise operation rules, initial state setting, enterprise operation competition simulation, and on-site case analysis. Among them, organizational preparation is the first step of the ERP sand table simulation course. The first step is to group students into groups. Each group is usually 5–6 people, including CEO, Marketing Director, Business Director, Purchasing Director, Financial Director, etc.; From this, 6 to 8 competitive simulation enterprises are formed. On this basis, it is necessary to explain the basic situation of the enterprises with the same conditions

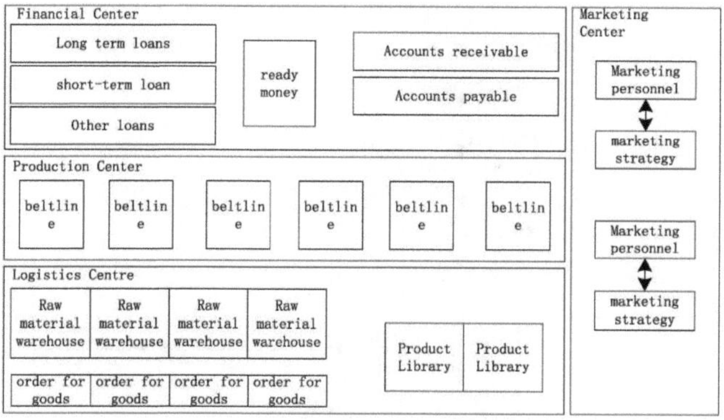


**Fig. 2.** ERP Sand Table Construction Results

that each simulation enterprise is ready to take over, including shareholders' expectations, the current financial situation of the enterprise, market share, products, production facilities, profitability, etc. In addition, enterprise operation competition simulation is the main part of ERP sand table simulation course, which is carried out according to the enterprise operation year. At the beginning of each year, according to the market forecast data, make a forecast on the overall demand, unit price and development trend of each product in the relevant market, and determine the enterprise strategy and business strategy. The forecast formula of demand and unit price is as follows:

$$\begin{cases} W = W_0 + \eta_W \Delta t \\ p = p_0 + \eta_p \Delta t \end{cases} \tag{2}$$

In the above formula $W_0$ and $p_0$ They are the demand quantity and unit price of the current enterprise's products, $\Delta t$ Is the forecast time, $\eta_W$ and $\eta_p$ It corresponds to the change rate of demand quantity and unit price.Under the leadership of the CEO, we carried out business activities throughout the year in accordance with market rules and business operation rules [7]. Field case analysis is an important part of the sand table simulation course. According to the annual business results, enterprise managers should analyze the success and failure of their own enterprises, investigate the situation of competitors, and make necessary adjustments to the enterprise strategy. The teacher combines the overall situation of the classroom, finds out the problems that everyone is confused about, and analyzes the typical cases that appear on the scene. With the support of the ERP sandbox simulation course software and the ERP sandbox simulation learning guide, determine the implementation process of the ERP sandbox simulation course, as shown in Fig. 3.

Thus, the implementation process of ERP sand table simulation course is arranged.

### 3.2.2 Role Simulation of Enterprise Operation Participation

When students form a group to operate an enterprise, they need to serve as CEO of the general manager of the enterprise, CMO of the marketing director, COO of the

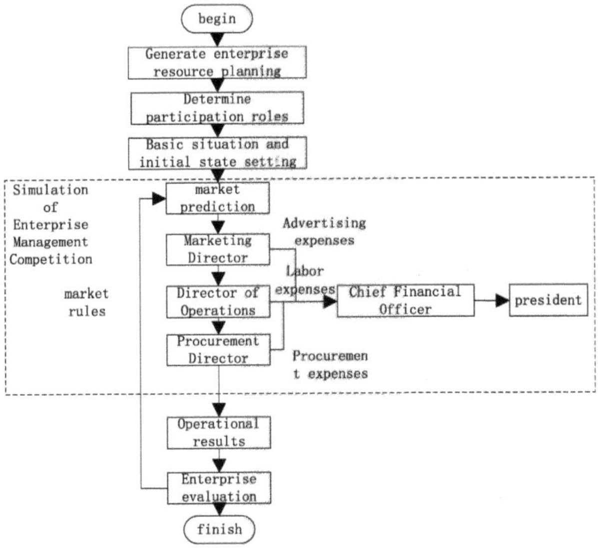


**Fig. 3.** ERP Sand Table Simulation Course Implementation Flow Chart

production director, CFO of the financial director, CLO of the logistics director, CIO of the information director, HR of human resources management and other positions, register users according to different identities, and operate different enterprise function modules.Table 2 shows the setting of enterprise operation participation roles.

**Table 2.** Roles of Enterprise Operation Participation

| Enterprise management participates in teaching | Operation Center | Operation permission content |
|---|---|---|
| general manager | CEO cockpit | Decision making |
| Chief Financial Officer | Enterprise Decision Query | Loan, A/R and A/P management, report query |
| Marketing Director | Business Settlement Center | Product quotation, bidding, delivery |
| Logistics Director | Marketing Center | Purchase and transfer of raw materials |
| Production Director | Purchase and Production Center | Raw material procurement and product production |
| Product Director | Purchase and Production Center | Product design and R&D |
| HR Director | Product R&D Center | Human Resources Management |

The general manager can preside over the annual work plan and summary meeting; Assist the Chief Financial Officer to make financing decisions according to the company's needs and the information provided by the Chief Information Officer; According to the annual task list, guide the heads of functional departments to complete the work in the year on time; According to the results of financial analysis, point out the problems existing in the company's operation and propose improvement measures; Be responsible for the implementation of job rotation. The chief financial officer's main responsibilities include: preparing the detailed statement of comprehensive expenses; Annual financial statements, including preparation of balance sheet and annual profit statement; Formulate the dividend distribution plan for shareholders. Similarly, we can get the simulation results of the role of enterprise management participation.

### 3.2.3 ERP Sandbox Business Process Simulation

Take the role of CFO in ERP sandbox as an example to simulate the ERP sandbox business process [8]. The financial part of ERP sand table business is divided into two parts: accounting and financial management. Accounting mainly records, calculates, reflects and analyzes the capital in the enterprise economic activity. The simulation result of enterprise economic general ledger is:

$$M_{\text{ledger}} = M_{\text{income}} - M_{\text{pay}} + M_{\text{x}} + M_{\text{fixed assets}} \tag{3}$$

Variables in Formula 3 $M_{\text{income}}, M_{\text{pay}}, M_{\text{x}}$ and $M_{\text{fixed assets}}$ They respectively represent the income amount, expenditure amount, cash and fixed assets of the enterprise. Where variable $M_{\text{income}}$ and $M_{\text{pay}}$. The calculation formula of is as follows:

$$\begin{cases} M_{\text{income}} = M_{\text{bill}} + M_{\text{bills due}} + M_{\text{order}} \\ M_{\text{pay}} = M_{\text{material}} + M_{\text{check}} + M_{\text{other}} \end{cases} \tag{4}$$

among $M_{\text{bill}}, M_{\text{bills due}}$ and $M_{\text{order}}$ Invoices, arrears and order payments, $M_{\text{material}}, M_{\text{check}}$ and $M_{\text{other}}$ The corresponding costs are production material costs, operation and management costs and other costs. Substitute the calculation result of Formula 4 into Formula 3 to get the general ledger calculation result of accounting. The business process simulation results of other roles in the ERP sandbox can be obtained according to the above methods.

### 3.2.4 Enterprise Evaluation

Evaluate the operation status of the ERP sand table simulation target enterprise from multiple dimensions such as finance, customer, and internal operation capability. The financial dimension indicators can provide a certain guarantee for the realization of other related dimension goals. It is necessary to invest in raw materials and plants reasonably, and manage effectively. On this basis, it can win the market through reliable products, improve their comprehensive competitiveness, actively attract customers to obtain funds, and then use the information system and improve their capabilities, improve the coordination of the organization, and reasonably improve the skills of employees to meet the relevant management requirements [9]. The goal of the customer dimension is to improve customers' recognition of products and promote the further development of the enterprise. The performance of the enterprise's customer dimension is investigated from two aspects: customer satisfaction and brand market value. The specific measurement indicators of customer satisfaction are: on-time delivery rate, product qualification rate, etc. The calculation formula of the on-time delivery rate is:

$$\mu_{\text{delivery}} = \frac{N_{\text{delivery}}}{N_{\text{order}}} \times 100\% \tag{5}$$

In the above formula $N_{\text{delivery}}$ and $N_{\text{order}}$ They are the quantity of orders completed on time and the total quantity of orders within the enterprise. In addition, the solution result of product qualification rate index is:

$$\mu_{\text{qualified}} = \frac{N_{\text{qualified}}}{N_{\text{product}}} \times 100\% \tag{6}$$

among $N_{\text{qualified}}$ and $N_{\text{product}}$ They correspond to the quantity of qualified products and the total quantity of produced products. From the perspective of brand market value, specific measurement indicators include market share, service quality, sales ratio, etc. After determining the financial dimension and customer dimension, the enterprise needs to focus on the corresponding internal process dimension. In the process of management, enterprises can provide support for the realization of financial objectives on the basis of optimizing and improving the corresponding internal business processes. The internal process dimension indicators include marketing capability, production volume, etc. The calculation formula of marketing capability is:

$$\psi = \gamma \cdot z \cdot (\psi(i) + M_{\text{advertisement}}) \tag{7}$$

among $\gamma$ and $z$ It indicates that the enterprise has relevant market certification and access qualification coefficient, $\psi(i)$ For employees in the enterprise $i$ Marketing capabilities, $M_{\text{advertisement}}$ It is the sum of advertising expenses invested by enterprises in the market. The production measurement structure is:

$$Q = \sum_{j=1}^{n_{\text{farm}}} q_j \tag{8}$$

where $q_j$ For workshop $j$ Production, $n_{\text{farm}}$ Indicates the number of workshops included in the enterprise. Based on the above indicators, the evaluation results of the enterprise are as follows:

$$f = \varpi_1 \mu_{\text{delivery}} + \varpi_2 \mu_{\text{qualified}} + \varpi_3 \psi + \varpi_4 Q \tag{9}$$

In the above formula $\varpi_1$, $\varpi_2$, $\varpi_3$ and $\varpi_4$ Corresponds to the weight value of the above evaluation indicators. The enterprise evaluation output results can be obtained by substituting the calculation results of each indicator into Formula 9. Through the above process, complete the implementation of the system ERP sand table simulation course module.

### 3.3 Course Online Network Interaction Module

When the logged in user clicks the online question answering hyperlink on the home page of the course learning system, the learning exchange platform interface will be launched. The learning and exchange platform interface should provide links for users to further view the details of messages, post messages, return to the home page, modify user information and user passwords and other functions. The main task of the online question answering interface is to establish a link to the database, retrieve all article records from the database in chronological order, and display several records in the front according to the page size, and generate pagination links for the rest. After the student user uploads the interactive information, it will be received by the teacher through the communication network. The online network interaction process can be quantified as:

$$x_{\text{receive}} = x_{send} \times \kappa_{m-d} \times \varsigma \tag{10}$$

In Formula 10 $\kappa_{m-d}$ and $\varsigma$ They are modulation and demodulation coefficient and communication channel parameter respectively. After receiving the interactive information, the teacher end can enter the page for posting messages, which should provide a complete interface for writing message titles, message content, uploading pictures, picture descriptions and publishing time; In order to ensure the integrity of the record, the system needs to verify the legitimacy of the content entered by the user; Provide the submit message button and insert it into the BBS article table, and give the user the corresponding prompt according to whether the insertion is successful or not; If the user does not want to leave a message at this time, the "Back to the previous page" option is also provided, allowing the user to return to the online question answering interface at this time.

### 3.4 ERP Sand Table Simulation Course Network Resource Query Module

When setting up ERP sand table simulation course, teachers upload relevant resources of the course to the system database and extract the characteristics of the course resources $\tau_{\text{resources}}(i)$ As a tag item for a resource. When students enter the system, input keywords according to the resource query content, and extract the query keyword features using Formula 11.

$$\tau_{\text{keyword}} = \sqrt{\frac{1}{N_{\text{keyword}}} \sum_{i=1}^{N_{\text{keyword}}} (x_i)^2} \tag{11}$$

among $N_{\text{keyword}}$ Is the number of keywords, $x_i$ It represents the input keyword content. The specific feature matching process can be expressed as follows:

$$s = \frac{\tau_{\text{keyword}} \cdot \tau_{\text{resources}}(i)}{\left\| \tau_{\text{keyword}} \right\| \cdot \left\| \tau_{\text{resources}}(i) \right\|} \tag{12}$$

If calculated $s$ The value of is above the threshold $s_0$, describe the current keywords and teaching resources $i$ Consistency, i.e. teaching resources $i$ It is the query result of online network resources of the current course. If the calculation result of Formula 12 is lower than the threshold value $s_0$, you need to match the next teaching resource, and finally output all the matching results that meet the conditions in a certain order to complete the resource query task of the system.

### 3.5 Online Online Teaching Assessment Module of Sand Table Simulation Course

In order to ensure the online network teaching effect of the system, in addition to the basic teaching module, it is also necessary to set up a teaching assessment module, which outputs the final assessment results of online network teaching of ERP sand table simulation courses from three aspects of students' daily learning behavior, written examination results and practical assessment results. The output results can be expressed as:

$$H = H_{\text{daily}} + H_{\text{written}} + H_{\text{practice}} \tag{13}$$

among $H_{\text{daily}}$, $H_{\text{written}}$ and $H_{\text{practice}}$ Respectively corresponding to the scores of daily learning behavior, written examination results and practice assessment results[10]. Finally, the teaching assessment results of all students in the system will be output visually and displayed in the system interface.

### 3.6 System Background Load Balancing Control

In order to avoid uneven load distribution, service request blocking, computing resource waste and other situations in the case of multi concurrent operation of the system, it is necessary to further improve the design of system load balancing. In the process of system load balancing control, first calculate the congestion probability of the server, and the calculation result is:

$$P = \frac{N_b}{\sum G} \tag{14}$$

among $N_b$ Is the number of concurrent users in the system, $G$ The total number of resources contained for the system. It is calculated that the higher the congestion probability is, the greater the load of the current system server is, and the request submitted by the user needs to be dynamically allocated to other servers for processing. This completes the load balance control of the system background, and ensures the running performance of the online network multi module teaching system of ERP sand table simulation course.

In summary, the design process of the online network multi module teaching system for ERP sandbox simulation course is shown in Fig. 4.

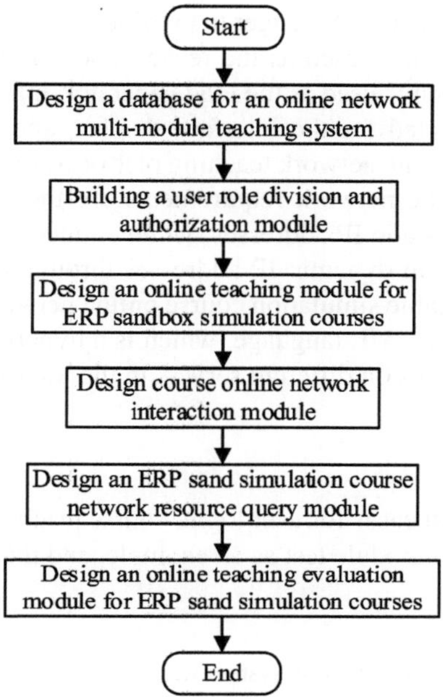


**Fig. 4.** Design flowchart of online network multi module teaching system for ERP sandbox simulation course

## 4 System Test

After completing the previous software code design and interface design, the next unit must be the necessary system test. System test is not only to test software code, but also to test various aspects such as data verification. Like software code development, system testing is also a highly demanding and technical content, without many principles and skills. System testing is the main component of developing application software quality assurance. The system test experiment is divided into two parts: function test and performance test. The function test is mainly to test whether the program module has achieved the functions required in the software design. The performance test is to judge whether the optimized design system can achieve the expected functions under different operating conditions.

### 4.1 Preparation for System Test Experiment

Before the experiment begins, the experiment is prepared from two aspects: system operation and test environment, as well as test cases.

### 4.2 System Test Environment

In order to ensure the efficiency and reliability of the system operation, the system server should generally have a high software and hardware configuration. The operating system uses Ubuntu 12.04 and Apache + Pssenger to provide application services. MySQL 5.0 is used as the database, Solr is used as the retrieval server, Memcache is used as the cache server, Apache Bench is used as the load generator, mainstream Firefox, Chrome and IE browsers are selected for the interface display, and multiple versions of the above browsers are tested. The network teaching platform software system is developed based on B/S mode, so the network requirements are the most basic configuration. Generally, all servers use static IP addresses, while clients can use either manually set static IP addresses or obtain dynamic IP addresses through dedicated DHCP servers. The optimized ERP sand table simulation course online network multi module teaching system is developed with HTML language, which is a hypertext markup language that can connect information files on different servers in the Internet.

### 4.3 System Test Cases

Generate multi module test cases for user login, course teaching, resource retrieval, etc. Take the resource retrieval module test as an example, and the specific case preparation is shown in Table 3.

**Table 3.** Test Cases of System Resource Retrieval Module

| Case number | Search keywords | Expected retrieval quantity/piece |
|---|---|---|
| J01 | financial analysis | 102 |
| J02 | Marketing Center | 95 |
| J03 | Production Center | 87 |
| J04 | Logistics services | 113 |
| J05 | Material procurement | 98 |

Similarly, test cases of other modules of the system can be obtained. In order to ensure the credibility of the experimental results, the number of test cases prepared for each teaching module is 200.

On this basis, evaluate whether the system has the necessary functions, including course management, learning material sharing, learning progress tracking, homework submission and evaluation, to ensure that the system can meet teaching needs. Evaluate the stability and reliability of the system, including its response speed, operation delay, etc.

### 4.4 System Test and Experiment Process

In the configured system test environment, complete the development of the online network multi module teaching system for the optimized design of ERP sand table simulation course. This system test adopts the test method of combining black box and white box. The black box test is mainly used to test the performance of the system, while the white box test is used to test the function of the teaching module of the system.Input the prepared system test cases into the corresponding running program of the developed online network multi module teaching system, and obtain the test output results of module functions. Figure 5 shows the test run interface of the ERP sandbox business process simulation module.

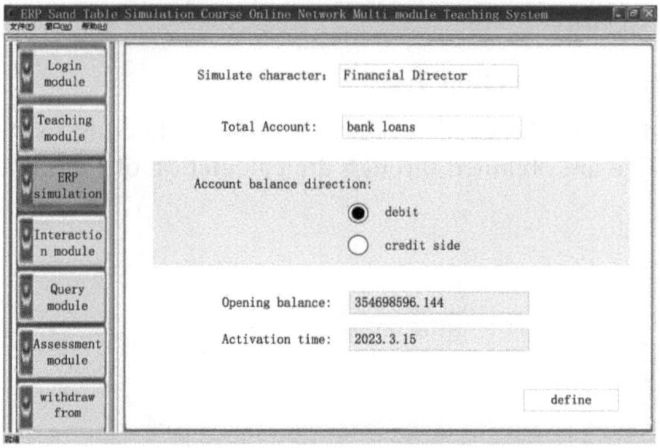


**Fig. 5.** Operation interface of ERP sandbox business process simulation module

Similarly, the operation test results of other module functions of the system can be obtained. The quantitative test index of system functions is set as the success rate of module teaching case operation $\eta_{suc}$ The numerical results of this indicator are as follows:

$$\eta_{suc} = \frac{n_{suc}}{n_{\text{Use case}}} \times 100\% \tag{15}$$

In the above formula $n_{suc}$ and $n_{\text{Use case}}$. It respectively represents the number of successful use cases of module functions and the total number of use cases set in the experiment. In addition, the system performance test is mainly divided into two parts: running performance test and application performance test. The main principle of running performance test is to adjust the concurrent number of system running tasks, and observe the change of system response speed under different concurrent conditions. The quantitative test results of running performance in system performance are as follows:

$$\Delta\tau = t_{in} - t_{out} \tag{16}$$

among $t_{in}$ and $t_{out}$ They are the start time and output time of the system task. The application performance test is to judge the change of students' scores after the application of the ERP sand table simulation course online network multi module teaching system. The test results of system application performance can be directly obtained through the statistics of students' scores. Final calculation $\eta_{suc}$ The higher the value of, the better the function of the corresponding system teaching module, $\Delta\tau$ The larger the value is, the higher the student's score is, which means the better the operation performance of the corresponding system is. In order to reflect the advantages of the optimized design system in terms of function and performance, the traditional project-based teaching system and the teaching system based on the auxiliary teaching mode are set as the two comparison systems of the experiment. The development of the comparison system is realized under the same experimental environment, and the corresponding operating results are obtained.

## 4.5 System Test Results

### 4.5.1 System Teaching Function Test

Through the statistics of relevant data, the test results reflecting the teaching function of the system module are obtained through the calculation of Formula 15, as shown in Fig. 6.

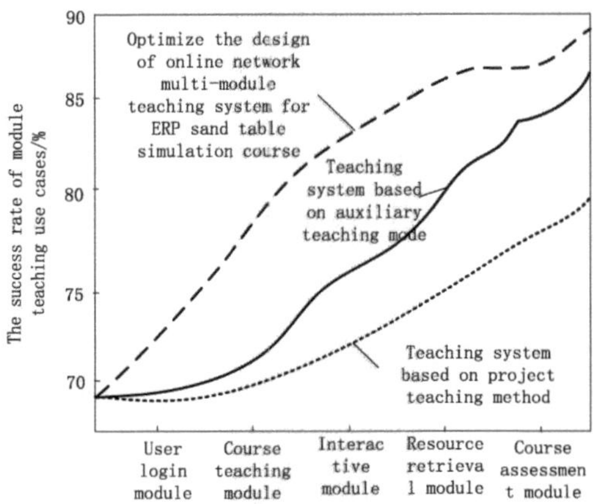


**Fig. 6.** Comparison curve of teaching function test of system module

It can be seen intuitively from Fig. 6 that, compared with the two comparative teaching systems, the module teaching use cases of the optimized design ERP sand table simulation course online network multi module teaching system have a higher success rate, that is, the teaching function of the optimized design system is better.

### 4.5.2 System Operation Performance Test

Under different concurrent conditions, the running time of each teaching task is counted, and the test results reflecting the running performance of the system are obtained through the calculation of Formula 16, as shown in Fig. 7.

It can be seen from Fig. 7 that under different concurrency conditions, the average response delay of the optimized design system is 10.4 s, while the average response delay of the comparison system is 42.3 s and 36.5 s respectively, which proves that the optimized design system has higher operation performance.

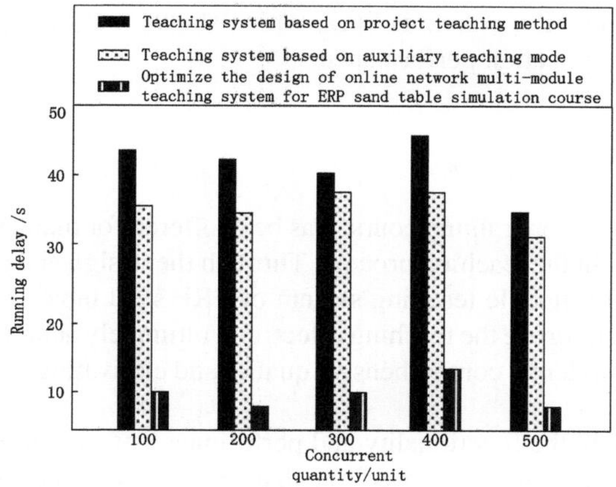


**Fig. 7.** System Operation Performance Test Results

### 4.5.3 System Application Performance Test

The two contrast teaching systems and the optimization design system are respectively applied to the actual teaching work of ERP sand table simulation course, and the test results of system application performance are obtained through the statistics of scores of multiple students, as shown in Table 4.

**Table 4.** Data Sheet of System Application Performance Test

| Student ID | Student assessment scores/points of the teaching system based on project-based teaching method | Students' assessment scores/scores by applying the teaching system based on the auxiliary teaching mode | Student assessment score/score of applying optimized design of multi module teaching system |
|---|---|---|---|
| 1 | 86.6 | 90.2 | 97.5 |
| 2 | 89.2 | 91.4 | 98.6 |
| 3 | 78.5 | 85.7 | 94.4 |
| 4 | 73.4 | 84.2 | 92.9 |
| 5 | 80.9 | 86.5 | 93.5 |
| 6 | 85.5 | 88.1 | 96.2 |
| 7 | 84.3 | 87.6 | 97.4 |
| 8 | 89.8 | 92.1 | 98.8 |

Through the calculation of the average value, it can be concluded that the average value of the students' assessment scores of the two comparison teaching systems is 83.5 and 88.2 respectively, while the average value of the students' assessment scores of the online network multi module teaching system of the application optimization design

ERP sand table simulation course is 96.2, which shows that the optimization design system has higher application performance.

## 5 Conclusion

ERP sand table simulation training course has been offered for many years, but there are still many problems in the teaching process. Through the design and development of the online network multi module teaching system of ERP sand table simulation course, it will be beneficial to improve the teaching effect, and ultimately achieve the teaching purpose of improving students' comprehensive quality and cultivating students' application ability.

In future research, the functionality and performance of each module in the system will be further optimized and improved to enhance user experience and teaching effectiveness. For example, improving the realism and interactivity of the sandbox simulation module, and increasing the functionality and operability of the ERP system module.

**Aknowledgement.** 2022 Key Project of Teaching Reform Research in Hunan Province's General Colleges and Universities;Project name: Research on the Mixed Teaching Reform of ERP Sand Table Simulation Course oriented to the Cultivation of Digital Intelligence Talents; Project number: HNJG-2022–0386.

## References

1. Liu, X., et al.: Self-attention negative feedback network for real-time image super-resolution. J. King Saud Univ. – Comput. Inf. Sci. **34**(8B), 6179–6186 (2022)
2. Liu, S., Li, Y., Fu, W.: Human-centered attention-aware networks for action recognition. Int. J. Intell. Syst. **37**(12), 10968–10987 (2022)
3. Huang, Y., Mai, Q.: Research on the construction of O2O teaching system of cross-cultural knowledge in college English based on MOOC. J. Intell. Fuzzy Syst. **5**, 1–10 (2021)
4. Luo, J., et al.: Research on construction of innovative teaching system of transportation engineering and talent evaluation based on CDIO. Int. J. Electr. Eng. Educ., 002072092098355 (2021)
5. Long, C., Wang, S.: Music classroom assistant teaching system based on intelligent speech recognition. J. Intell. Fuzzy Syst. **14**, 1–10 (2021)
6. Chen, H., Huang, J.: Research and application of the interactive English online teaching system based on the internet of things. Sci. Program. **2021**(S1), 1–10 (2021)
7. Pang, X., Ning, Y.: Fuzzy control based on genetic algorithm in intelligent psychology teaching system. J. Intell. Fuzzy Syst. **5**, 1–9 (2021)
8. Wang, P.: Modeling of badminton intelligent teaching system based on neural network. Wirel. Commun. Mob. Comput. **2021**(8), 1–10 (2021)
9. Pakinee, A., Puritat, K.: Designing a gammed e-learning environment for teaching undergraduate ERP course based on big five personality traits. Educ. Inf. Technol. **4**, 26 (2021)
10. Wang, W., Hu, J.: Extraction of PE online teaching resources with positive psychology based on advanced intelligence algorithm. Front. Psychol. **13**, 948721 (2022)

# Japanese Online+Offline Hybrid Educational Resources Sharing System Based on Data Classification

Yi Wei(✉)

School of Foreign Languages and International Education, Chengdu Technological University, Chengdu 611730, China
weiyiry0855@163.com

**Abstract.** In the process of online+offline mixed educational resources sharing, due to the lack of effective data classification, the response rate of student terminal education server is slow, and it is difficult to share Japanese teaching resources quickly. Therefore, a Japanese online+offline mixed educational resources sharing system based on data classification is studied. Improve the hardware design of the sharing system from three aspects: resource management module, resource retrieval module, and user management module. On this basis, the principle of support vector machine is combined to define the sample data set, and relevant parameter indicators are combined to solve the expression of data classification model. Then, by analyzing the specific functional requirements of each application unit, the processing of mixed educational resources is realized. Combined with the relevant hardware application structure, the design of Japanese online+offline mixed educational resources sharing system based on data classification is completed. The experimental results show that under the effect of the data classification model, the average response rate of the student terminal education server has significantly improved, which is in line with the original intention of the system design to quickly share Japanese teaching resources.

**Keywords:** Data classification · Japanese teaching · Online education · Offline education · Mixed educational resources · Resource sharing · Support vector machine · Functional requirements

## 1 Introduction

Data classification is to combine data with certain common attributes or characteristics, and distinguish data by their attributes or characteristics. In order to realize data sharing and improve processing efficiency, we must follow the agreed classification principles and methods, and divide all information in the system into different sets according to a certain structural system according to the connotation, nature and management requirements of information, so that each information has a corresponding position in the corresponding classification system. In other words, the information with the same


G. Gui et al. (Eds.): eLEOT 2023, LNICST 543, pp. 267–282, 2024.
https://doi.org/10.1007/978-3-031-51465-4_18

content, the same nature, and the information that requires unified management are gathered together, and the different information and the information that needs to be managed separately are distinguished, and then the relationship between each set is determined to form an organized classification system. According to the purpose of classification, the most stable essential characteristics of the classification object are selected as the basis and basis of classification to ensure the most stable classification results. Therefore, in the process of classification, we should first clearly define the most stable and essential feature [1] of the classification object. Systematically arrange the features (or characteristics) of the selected classification objects according to their internal laws to form a classification system with clear logical hierarchy, reasonable structure and clear category. In the setting of categories or the division of levels, there is appropriate room to ensure that the established classification system will not be disturbed when the number of classification objects increases. Starting from the actual needs, the specific classification principles are determined by integrating various factors, so that the resulting classification results are optimal, meet the needs, comprehensive and practical, and easy to operate. If there are relevant national standards, the national standards shall be implemented; if there are no relevant national standards, the relevant industrial standards shall be implemented; If neither exists, relevant international standards shall be referred to. In this way, the coordination and conversion between different classification systems can be ensured as far as possible.

With the development of the Internet and the improvement of the level of science and technology, modern education has developed from the traditional face-to-face teaching of teachers and students in the classroom to the coexistence of multiple teaching methods, in which the education mode of online education has become the key goal of modern education services. The traditional face-to-face education mode is limited by time, space, manpower and material resources, which is difficult to meet the requirements of today's information construction and education reform. In contrast, online education transcends space and time constraints and provides people with a more convenient and flexible way of learning. Through the network, schools can be extended to families, companies and even any corner of society. People can flexibly allocate their learning time to integrate work, learning and life [2].Whether students, workers unable to study off the job or other social figures, regardless of social level or age level, there are conditions and opportunities to accept education at all levels. The promotion and development of online education has improved the information literacy of teachers and students, accelerated the updating of knowledge resources, changed the way people access resources and read, and provided more learning opportunities and better learning environment for learners. One of the advantages of online education is to realize the sharing of educational resources. The so-called educational resources refer to all objectively existing entities such as people, media, strategies, methods and environment that can improve and promote teaching. Network education needs to digitize educational resources, and the resources after digital processing can run in the multimedia computer and network environment. In order to further realize the new educational ideas, we will introduce a hybrid educational mode of online and offline learning in all fields of learning to improve the efficiency of educational learning.

In the process of online+offline mixed educational resources sharing, due to the lack of effective data classification, the response rate of student terminal education server is slow, and it is difficult to share Japanese teaching resources quickly. Therefore, a Japanese online+offline mixed educational resources sharing system based on data classification is studied. Through reasonable data classification and storage strategies, common and popular educational resources can be placed on online servers closer to students, so as to respond to students' requests quickly. The less commonly used and unpopular educational resources can be stored on the offline server, reducing the load on the online server and improving the performance of the whole system. In this paper, the principle of joint support vector machine is adopted to define the sample data set, and the expression of data classification model is solved by combining relevant parameter indexes. Then, by analyzing the specific functional requirements of each application unit, the processing of mixed educational resources is realized. Finally, combined with the related hardware application structure, the design of Japanese online+offline mixed educational resource sharing system based on data classification is completed. The experimental results show that the average response rate of the server is greatly improved under the effect of the data classification model, which provides strong help for the rapid sharing of Japanese teaching resources.

## 2 Shared System Design Scheme

The improvement of the hardware design scheme of Japanese online+offline hybrid education resource sharing system should be carried out simultaneously from three aspects: resource management module, resource retrieval module and user management module. This chapter will study its specific design methods.

### 2.1 Resource Management Module

In the Japanese online+offline hybrid educational resource sharing system, the resource management module processes the shared information parameters by improving the storage behavior of teaching resources. Educational resources often have multiple forms of existence, such as documents, pictures, videos, and so on. Most of these massive digital resources exist in an unstructured form, which cannot be effectively stored using a unified data structure, thus making resource sharing difficult to achieve. In view of the characteristics of massive educational resources such as diversity, heterogeneity and low degree of sharing, the first problem to be solved in realizing the goal of massive educational resources sharing is the description of educational resources, that is, a standardized and feasible way should be defined to uniformly describe and package educational resources, so as to realize the unified storage and retrieval of resources. This is the basis for effective resource sharing [3].Therefore, the system should first carry out unified and standardized representation of resources.

Defining a consistent data resource description framework through data classification standards is an effective means to solve this problem. Metadata is the description of the data structure and content characteristics of the original data resources. Users browse metadata to access the original data resources, that is, the education resources themselves.

The so-called metadata standard is the collection of all rules when describing the specific objects of educational resources.

In addition, the hybrid education resource sharing system also provides 9 optional data elements, which are: publisher - the person responsible for making the resource available and available, usually identified by the name of the publisher; Other authors - other authors who have contributed to the creation of resource content; Related resource - another related resource identifier, but there is a relationship between the current resource and this resource, and the "relationship description" element describes this relationship; Relationship description - the relationship between the current resources and the resources represented by "related resources"; Coverage, the extension and coverage of resource content, including spatial location description, time period description or permission description; Permission - information about the permission owned or granted by the resource itself, including the permission statement for the resource, or a reference to the service that provides this information; Evaluation - comments or identification of resources from a third party who is not the author or publisher; Evaluators - individuals, organizations or institutions associated with evaluation; Version - the version of the learning object.

On the system page, users can view the metadata information of Japanese teaching resources and the content information of the resources themselves (displayed on the page in preview mode). When they need to obtain resources, they can obtain the corresponding resources in HDFS through the storage location field of the resources in the database table. Table 1 shows the design principles of the resource management module description information table ResourceInfo.

**Table 1.** ResourceInfo data description of resource management module

| Field name | Field type | Explain |
|---|---|---|
| Title | Varchar(50) | Title of Japanese teaching resources |
| TypeId | Integer | Types of Japanese teaching resources |
| ResourceId | Integer | Japanese teaching resource ID |
| UserId | Integer | Owner of Japanese teaching resources |
| FormatId | Integer | Japanese teaching resource file format |
| Value | Integer | The value of Japanese teaching resources |
| Identify | Varchar(255) | Identification of Japanese teaching resources |

The specification allows users to expand metadata elements according to the needs of the system, but it must conform to the format and technical specifications defined by the specification elements. With reference to this specification, the system designs the storage mode of resources as follows:

(1) The educational resources themselves and the resource description information are named with the same file name and stored in the designated folder of the HDFS distributed file system through Hadoop. The resource description information is

generated by the resource name and the resource content introduction in a fixed format for generating index files during resource retrieval.

(2) The metadata information of Japanese education resources is stored as a record in the MysQL database table, and the storage location of the resources in HDFS is recorded, which is the way to download and obtain resources. Metadata information is used for users to view various attributes of resources when resources are displayed.

### 2.2 Resource Retrieval Module

The resource retrieval module provides users with a simple retrieval method to quickly and accurately retrieve the desired resources. In this system, users search resources by keyword. Due to the huge amount of educational resources involved in the system, it is difficult to achieve fast and accurate retrieval results only through traditional relational database queries. In order to improve the speed and accuracy of retrieval, the retrieval process is implemented on multiple DataNodes in the background through the MapReduce program in Hadoop.

The retrieval of online+offline hybrid educational resources mainly includes the establishment of inverted index files and the realization of parallel search. MapReduce programming model is used to establish inverted documents or realize parallel search. Every MapReduce program is a combination of map and reduce. The search content implemented by this system is based on resource description information, which consists of resource name and resource content introduction [4]. In the design of parallel retrieval, the user sends a query command to retrieve in real time, and the efficiency of user query is determined by the efficiency of parallel search. The operation of creating inverted documents is issued regularly, and the inverted index has been established before receiving the user's query command, so the efficiency of creating inverted index does not affect the efficiency of query. The implementation process design of the entire resource retrieval module is shown in Fig. 1.

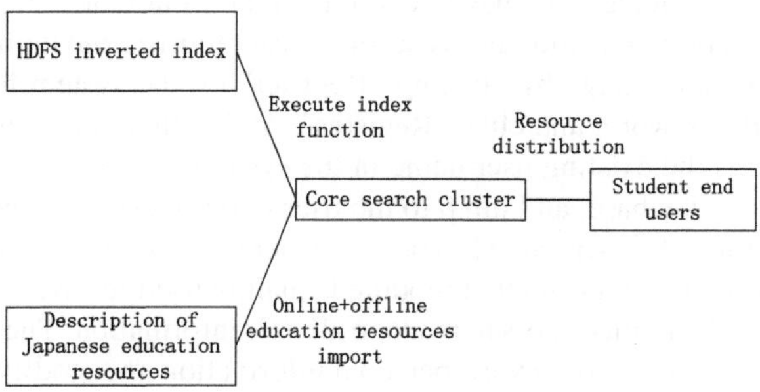


**Fig. 1.** Implementation process of resource retrieval module

The establishment of inverted index is the first stage of parallel retrieval, that is, to establish inverted index documents for resource description information imported into HDFS to provide input data for subsequent searches. It adopts Hadoop's Map/Reduce parallel programming mode. During the index establishment process, JobTracker coordinates the distributed processing of each DataNode node in the system. After the index processing of each DataNode node, the generated index fragments are reduced and merged into an index whole, and finally saved to HDFS. The design process of the entire distributed index is described as follows:

(1) Read the file description information from the specified location of HDFS as input, segment the input file through FileSplit, and process the input data with the key value in the form of < name, content > to the map function allocated to different DataNodes.
(2) Each map parses the input key values of < name, content >, name, value, content, extracts keywords, assigns the word frequency of each keyword to 1, and outputs them to the combiner in the format.
(3) Combine: complete the statistics and sorting of the word frequency corresponding to the same keyword. (Note: The word frequency statistics of map and combiner are different. A keyword is extracted in the map operation, and the word frequency assigned to it is 1, while the word frequency of combine is the accumulation of the same key value in the same DataNode, that is, the word frequency value corresponding to the keyword.). Then each combiner outputs its own statistical results, that is, the inverted sort index. At this time, the index is not perfect and needs to be merged by reducer.
(4) The reducer receives the output of the combiner, traverses all nodes to obtain the required intermediate data set, and then performs post processing such as de duplication, filtering, accumulation, and sorting to obtain the results.
(5) Finally, the OutputFormat class outputs the inverted index document as a file and stores it on HDFS.

## 2.3 User Management Module

The user management module of the Japanese online+offline hybrid educational resource sharing system consists of four parts: user registration and login unit, user information management unit, user integral management unit, and user authority management unit.

The user registration login module is used to register tourists and login users. Tourists can enter the registration page by clicking "Register" on the system homepage, enter the user name and password, and click "Register". At this time, judge whether the user name is the same as the existing user name in the system. If not, add a new user name and password to the database, and jump to the user login interface. Otherwise, the user will be prompted that "the user name has been registered", and the user needs to rename.

The user information management module is mainly used for users to manage their own information and administrators to manage all user information. The function design is as follows: all system users can view personal information and modify personal information. Ordinary users can apply for upgrading to authenticated users. Administrators can find users, view user information, add, delete, and modify user information according to conditions [5]. At the same time, the administrator needs to review the upgrade application submitted by the user, and agree or reject the user's upgrade.

User credit management module provides users and administrators with the function of managing user credit. In the system, you can view your own point use details list at any time, including point change details, change time, change product score, and current remaining product score. Where the details of points change include downloaded resources, the name of downloaded resources, download time and the number of points deducted will be displayed; If the comment gets points, the comment resource name, comment time and added points will be displayed. Users can obtain points by uploading resources for others to download and commenting on resources. The administrator can view the change details of the points of the specified user and manage the user points.

User permission management refers to that according to the permission rules set by the system, users can only perform their own authorized operations and access their own authorized resources. A good privilege management system should assign different system operation privileges to each class or user, and should be extensible. In this system, different user roles have different operation permissions. The administrator manages the permissions of all roles through the permission management module. The realization of this unit structure function involves three subjects, one is the user who owns the permission, the second is the user role set by the system, and the third is the executable permission operation for the system [6]. By assigning different operation permissions to different roles and then assigning the roles with permissions to a user, that is, there is no direct relationship between users and permissions. Users are associated with permissions through roles, so that users can implement the corresponding rights. The E-R model of the user rights management unit is shown in Fig. 2.

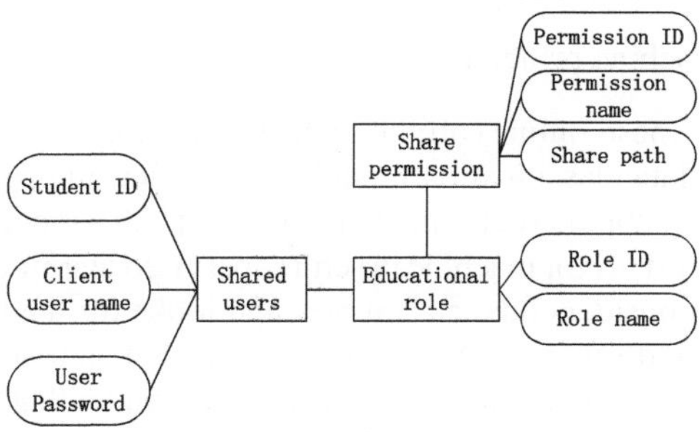


**Fig. 2.** E-R Model of User Rights Management Unit

In order to simplify the relationship in the Japanese online+offline hybrid education resource sharing system, each user only corresponds to one role. The administrator can directly view the role of the user and the operation permissions of the role through the browser, and can directly modify the user role and role permissions on the page according to the system function needs. After modification, when the user logs in to the system again, the operation interface will directly display the modified operation permissions. In this way, users and permissions are associated through roles, which not only conforms to the logic in real life, but also has simpler program design, clearer thinking, and simpler and more convenient access management for administrators. After a user logs into the system, the application program performs the following operations to obtain the user's operation permissions:

The program obtains the user ID from the session. If not, the page will locate the error prompt information page.

Query the role ID from the user role relationship table according to the obtained user ID.

Query the role permission relationship table through the user role to obtain all operation permission IDs of the role.

Query the operation authority table according to the authority ID, obtain the operation authority name corresponding to the ID and the operation page link corresponding to the authority, and display them in the user operation interface in order. Click the operation name to jump to the corresponding operation interface. If the user role does not have the corresponding operation permission, the corresponding prompt will be given on the user operation page.

# 3 Mixed Educational Resources Processing

On the basis of application modules at all levels of the system, in order to realize the sharing and processing of Japanese online+offline hybrid educational resources, the functional requirements of component structures at all levels should also be analyzed according to the data classification model.

## 3.1 Data Classification Model

(1) Support vector machine principle

The design of Japanese online+offline hybrid educational resource sharing system needs to refer to the data classification model, and the design of model structure must follow the principle of support vector machine. Direct push support vector machine is a generalization of support vector machine in semi supervised learning. Traditional support vector machine only considers labeled samples and looks for the maximum separating hyperplane from labeled samples. After taking unlabeled samples into consideration, direct push support vector machine looks for the hyperplane that can separate labeled samples and pass through areas with low data density.

As the key point of the whole educational resource sharing platform, the relevant educational resource system integration module realizes the reorganization of the existing system, uses the principle of support vector machine to SOA the existing system and reorganize the services, and then rearranges it. At the same time, it integrates the existing educational resources in the relevant system, In order to truly realize the integration of all systems related to educational resources in the whole school, and truly realize the sharing platform of educational resources.

The relevant education resource system integration module mainly integrates other existing teaching management systems through SOA, web service, EBS and other technologies. For various existing education resource systems in schools, SOA technology is used to realize service arrangement and reorganization, and then re open to the outside world, so as to make use of existing resources and combine existing services, Quickly integrate to form new business services, realize resource sharing faster, and reduce costs [7].

Due to the uniqueness of Japanese online+offline hybrid educational resources, the educational resources running on the system are more valuable, and it is not easy to retrieve them after they are lost. Therefore, the reliability requirements for the system are high, especially for the reliability of hardware devices such as file storage servers and database servers. The servers should have high reliability. In addition, the server should also have better redundancy, backup and recovery and other disaster recovery schemes, so that the relevant data stored on it can be easily and safely recovered in case of system hardware failure, thus ensuring the security and reliability of relevant Japanese education sharing education resources from the software level.

Given tagged sample set $P_n = \{(p_1, i_1), (p_2, i_2), \cdots, (p_n, i_n)\}$, where, $p_1, p_2, \cdots, p_n$ respectively $n$ different online education resource marking parameters, $i_1, i_2, \cdots, i_n$ respectively $n$ different offline education resource marking parameters are shared $\chi$ the value always belongs to $[1, +\infty)$ the support vector machine expression can be defined as:

$$Y = \beta \times \frac{\min \frac{1}{\chi} |p_1^2 + p_2^2 + \cdots + p_n^2|}{\sum_{\alpha=1}^{+\infty} i_1^2 + i_2^2 + \cdots + i_n^2} \tag{1}$$

Among them, $\alpha$ represents the redundancy coefficient of educational resources, $\beta$ represents the educational resource information identification parameters selected based on the data classification model.

Direct push support vector machine successfully uses a small amount of labeled data and a large number of unlabeled data to train a more ideal support vector machine model. Compared with the traditional support vector machine, the direct push support vector machine effectively uses the information implied in the unlabeled data, and successfully improves the classification accuracy of the support vector machine by combining the distribution information of the unlabeled data. But the direct push support vector machine needs to traverse all unlabeled data during the training process. When the problem size is small, it can be solved directly, but when the data size is large, the algorithm takes too long, or even the problem is unsolvable.

(2) Sample data set

In the process of implementing the data classification of Japanese online and offline mixed educational resources, the expression of sample data set can be used to describe the application ability of support vector machine principle. The definition of sample data set refers to the transformation of data samples in the real world into mathematical representations for training and classification of support vector machines. Specifically, the sample data set includes a set of labeled data samples, and each sample has multiple characteristics or attributes. These features can be text, images, audio and other different types of data. The abstract definition of sample data set represents each sample as a vector and associates it with the corresponding label.

Assume that there is a training set in a linear nonseparable space $W$, where exist respectively $\delta_1$ and $\delta_2$ two types of samples, sample points $e_1$ for this category $\delta_1$. A sample in the training set that has been mapped $\tilde{q}$ obtain $\tilde{q}(e_1)$, the same category $\delta_2$ sample points in $e_2$ mapped $\tilde{q}$ obtain $\tilde{q}(e_2)$. After mapping, the sample points become linearly separable, and the simultaneous formula (1) can $\tilde{q}(e_1)$, $\tilde{q}(e_2)$ shared distance between $D_{e_1 \leftrightarrow e_2}$ expressed as:

$$D_{e_1 \leftrightarrow e_2} = \frac{\sqrt{\sum_{a=1}^{+\infty} |\tilde{q}(e_2) - \tilde{q}(e_1)|^2}}{w_1 \times w_2} \tag{2}$$

where, $a$ linear coefficient representing Japanese education resource information, $w_1$ Representation and $\delta_1$ sample related education resource description vector, $w_2$ representation and $\delta_2$ the description vector of educational resources related to the sample, and $w_1$, $w_2$ there are always value conditions shown in Formula (3).

$$w_1, w_2 \in W \tag{3}$$

It is used to realize real-time query of course resource list and course resource information according to the data classification model. You can query the list of all course resources corresponding to the query criteria through such query criteria as subject name, course resource owner (teacher name), course resource name, upload time, and school. According to different user permissions,Each time, a different number of course resource lists and brief descriptions that meet the query criteria are returned in the form of pagination.The detailed information of the course resource can be queried through the conditions such as the course resource number, course resource name, etc., including the metadata such as the course resource name, owner, upload time, file size, modification times, and download times. At the same time, the storage address of the course resource can be returned, so as to facilitate the whole process of viewing and downloading the course resource.After the metadata of relevant course resources is passed in, the relevant information is recorded in the database after uploading the course resources to the file server, so as to realize the operation of uploading course resources[8].Pass in the course resource ID, return the storage address of the course resources corresponding to the resource ID, and then download the specified course resources through the address, so as to realize the download function of course resources.Through the course resource ID, modify the description of the course resource, the course resource file and other information or data corresponding to the resource ID, so as to realize the dynamic maintenance function of the existing course resources.

If the classification conditions are met, set $\phi$ represents the classification coefficient of Japanese online+offline mixed educational resources in the sharing system, $f$ represents the educational resource import parameters in the shared system, $\overline{h}$ represents the unit cumulative amount of online+offline mixed educational resources, $\dot{k}$ indicates the directional transmission characteristics of resource information. With the support of the above physical quantities, formula (2) can define the sample dataset expression based on the data classification model as:

$$G = \frac{1}{\phi}\left(\sum_{-\infty}^{+\infty} f \cdot D_{e_1 \leftrightarrow e_2}\right) \cdot \sqrt{\frac{|\overline{h}|}{\dot{k}^2 - 1}} \tag{4}$$

Active learning is carried out for unbalanced data with few labels. If the initial training set is constructed by random sampling, it cannot guarantee that the initial training set has a high amount of information. Using these unreliable samples to train the initial classifier will lead to a large deviation from the correct position of the initial classifier, increasing the calculation cost of subsequent active learning iterative learning. And the initial training set selected randomly is largely unbalanced, which cannot improve the generalization accuracy for a few classes. Therefore, it is necessary to study the initial training set selection strategy of active learning.

When the resource sharing system adds educational resources according to the data classification model, first fill in the relevant information of the newly added educational resources, then select the file of educational resources to upload, then enter the relevant details, and finally select the operation of adding resources. The system verifies the file format, size, input information and other relevant information. After the verification is passed, the system uploads the fileThen write to the database, refresh the page, and add educational resources.

### 3.2 Functional Requirement Analysis and Realization of Shared Services

According to the business demand analysis of the Japanese online+offline hybrid education resource sharing system and the current demand of related systems, the whole system is divided into several modules, including user management, education resource management and related education resource system integration modules. The detailed functional requirements of each module are shown below.

The user management module includes two functional modules: user login and user information management. The user information management includes user information modification, adding new users and deleting users, which is used to maintain the user system of the whole system [9]. The user management module mainly includes user login and user information management related modules. The user information management module includes administrators adding new users. Administrators can add new users by importing the obtained new user list into the system. At the same time, all users have the right to modify their personal information. User information management includes user information modification, adding new users, deleting users and other functions to maintain the user system of the whole system.

Curriculum resource management is used to manage curriculum related resources, including the function of managing curriculum related resources such as curriculum documents and reference materials. You can add curriculum resources, view curriculum resources, and download selected curriculum resources through the system. At the same time, teacher users or administrators can maintain the information of curriculum resources,Delete or modify relevant course resources [10].

The solution result of the function requirement analysis expression of the resource sharing system is as follows:

$$L = \frac{\prod_{c=1}^{+\infty} \lambda \cdot \dot{j} \cdot |\Delta X|}{G} \tag{5}$$

Among them, $c$ represents the education resource information transmission parameters in the system host, $\lambda$ represents the resource information storage coefficient, $\dot{j}$ it represents the recognition characteristics of the shared host for Japanese online+offline hybrid educational resources, $\Delta X$ represents the unit cumulative amount of education resource information. In order to realize real-time sharing of Japanese online+offline mixed educational resources, the inequality conditions shown in Formula (6) and Formula (7) must be established at the same time.

$$\Delta X > 0 \tag{6}$$

$$\begin{cases} \lambda > 0 \\ \dot{j} \geq 1 \end{cases} \tag{7}$$

The integration of educational resources should quickly and conveniently complete the integration of other existing educational resources and existing systems, so as to achieve the great integration of the whole school's educational resource system. In the implementation process, the following technical problems need to be solved. (1) Processing of existing redundant data: at this stage, various independent applications have produced a lot of teaching resource data in the process of system operation, and there is a lot of redundancy between these data, resulting in poor data consistency. How to better handle the existing redundant dataProviding highly consistent educational resource data for educational resource sharing platform is the first problem that should be dealt with in the integration of educational resources. (2) Processing of existing redundant functions: there are many existing educational administration systems and teaching resource systems in the school, among which there is a large part of functional redundancy. Many systems have similar functions, operate and process similar data, and after integration, these similar data will be integrated into one,At this time, these similar functions operate on the same data from different levels, making the maintenance of system data consistency more difficult. How to integrate these redundant functions is also helpful to shorten the development cycle of the system.

On the basis of formula (5), the calculation formula of hybrid education resource sharing service can be expressed as:

$$M = \frac{\xi L}{\sqrt{\dot{B}(\omega + 1)}} \tag{8}$$

where, $\xi$ represents the real-time sharing coefficient of mixed educational resources, $\dot{B}$ represents the response parameters of education resource sharing service based on data classification, $\omega$ represents the shared service execution vector. So far, it has realized the calculation and processing of sharing behavior parameters, combined with hardware application structures at all levels, and completed the design of Japanese online+offline hybrid educational resource sharing system based on data classification. The system design flow chart is shown below (Fig. 3).

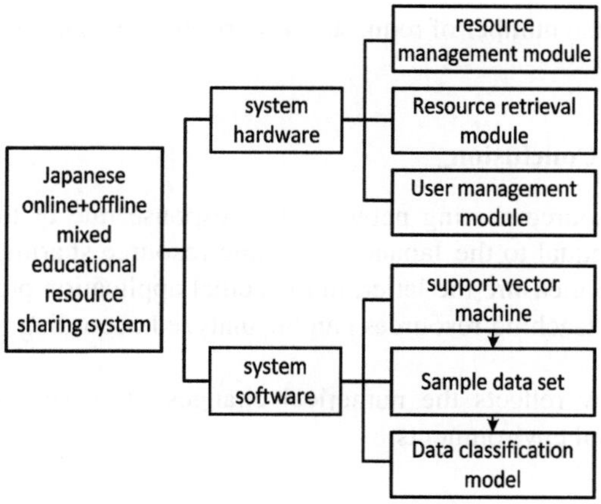


**Fig. 3.** System design flow chart

# 4 Example Analysis

## 4.1 Experimental Process

In order to verify the practical value of Japanese online+offline hybrid education resource sharing system based on data classification, sharing system based on neural artificial network, and sharing system based on SOA propagation model, the following comparative experiments are designed.

Step 1: Use Windows host cluster as the network terminal server, Mainframes host cluster as the client server, and use IPC channel organization to establish the data information transmission relationship between host and server.

Step 2: Input the running program of the Japanese online+offline hybrid education resource sharing system based on data classification in the client server, record the data change of the server response rate under the effect of the system, and the results are experimental group variables.

Step 3: Input the running program of the sharing system based on the neural artificial network in the client server, record the data change of the server response rate under the action of the system, and the result is a control group of variables.

Step 4: Input the running program of the shared system based on the SOA propagation model in the client server, record the data changes of the server response rate under the action of the system, and the results are compared with two groups of variables.

Step 5: Collect the variable data and summarize the specific experimental rules.

## 4.2 Experimental Index

Throughput: indicates the number of requests that the server can handle in a unit time, which can effectively reflect the response rate of the server. Its expression is:

$$v = \frac{N \cdot G}{T} \tag{9}$$

where $N$ represents the number of requests, $G$ represents the data size, and $T$ represents the total time.

### 4.3 Principle and Conclusion

In the education resource sharing network, the response rate of the student terminal education server is equal to the Japanese teaching resource sharing rate. Because it is relatively difficult to measure the latter, in the actual application process, the real-time sharing of Japanese teaching resources can be analyzed according to the response rate level of the server.

The figure below reflects the numerical changes of server response rate under different experimental environments.

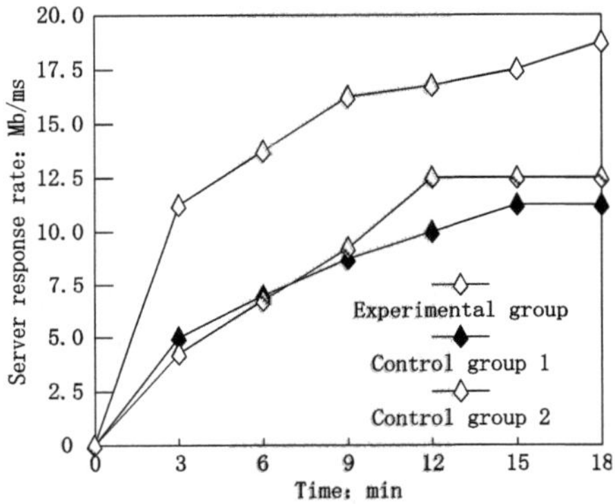


**Fig. 4.** Server Response Rate (Network System Busy)

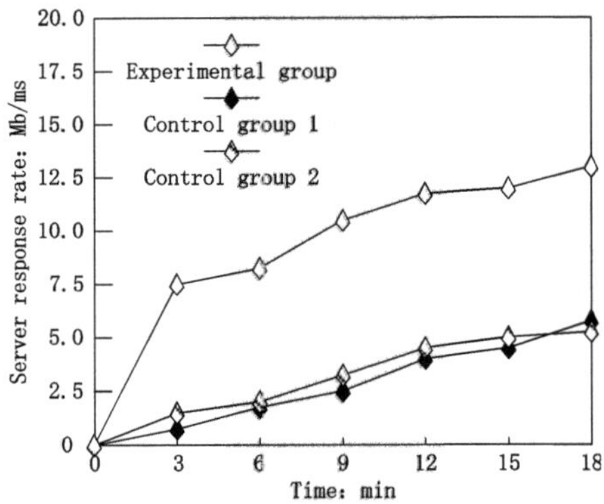


**Fig. 5.** Server Response Rate (Network System Idle)

In Fig. 4 and Fig. 5, respectively, take the maximum value of the server response rate of the experimental group and the control group, and calculate the average response rate. The specific calculation results are shown in formula (10).

$$\begin{cases} \overline{v}_1 = 15.76 \\ \overline{v}_2 = 8.51 \\ \overline{v}_3 = 8.84 \quad (\text{Unit}: \ \text{Mb/ms}) \end{cases} \tag{10}$$

Among them, $\overline{v}_1, \overline{v}_2, \overline{v}_3$ represent the average server response rate of the experimental group, control group 1 and control group 2 respectively.

According to the calculation result of formula (10), the average speed of the experimental group is the highest, with a mean difference of 7.25 Mb/ms from the control group 1 and 6.92 Mb/ms from the control group 2.

To sum up, the conclusion of this experiment is:

(1) The sharing system based on neural artificial network does not meet the application demand of improving the average response rate of the server, so its application ability in solving the problem of slow response rate of student terminal education server is relatively weak.
(2) Compared with the sharing system based on neural artificial network, the application of the sharing system based on the SOA propagation model can appropriately improve the average response rate of the server, but it still cannot meet the actual demand standard.
(3) The application of Japanese online+offline hybrid education resource sharing system based on data classification has significantly improved the average response rate of the server. Compared with the sharing system based on neural artificial network and the sharing system based on neural artificial network, this new system can better solve the problem of slow response rate of the student terminal education server,So as to realize the rapid sharing of Japanese teaching resources, which is consistent with the original design intention of the sharing system.

## 5 Conclusion

Among educational resource sharing technologies, Hadoop is a popular framework for distributed storage and parallel computing at this stage.In the process of designing and implementing the education resource sharing system, Hadoop storage model HDFS is used to store massive Japanese mixed education resources, and Hadoop parallel processing framework MapReduce is used to retrieve massive digital education resources. The use of distributed file system HDFS storage resources has the characteristics of low hardware requirements, low storage costs, simple backup mechanism, and easy capacity expansion. The sharing system uses the characteristics of HDFS tree structure directory and the method of classified storage of resources to store different kinds of resources in different directories of HDFS to optimize the storage results and facilitate resource management. In terms of data retrieval, the popular full-text retrieval is adopted at this stage, and the inverted index is established and the parallel search is realized by using MapReduce programming model on the Hadoop platform. In the technology of sharing educational resources, remarkable achievements have been made by using Hadoop storage model HDFS and parallel processing framework MapReduce. However, in the process of online+offline mixed educational resources sharing, the sharing time did not achieve the expected effect due to the complex algorithm. In the following research, we will dig deep into the information and patterns in educational resources to further promote the development of educational resources sharing technology, aiming at shortening the computing time and providing more efficient and intelligent resource management and services for the education field.

**Aknowledgement.** The first batch of "Research and Development and Application of Intelligent Proofreading Corpus for Japanese Courses in Colleges and Universities Based on Blockchain Technology" by the Production and Learning Coordination Center of the Department of Higher Education of the Ministry of Education in 2022 Project No.: 20220603242103215.

## References

1. Barakaz, F.E., Boutkhoum, O., Moutaouakkil, A.E.: A hybrid nave Bayes based on similarity measure to optimize the mixed-data classification. TELKOMNIKA (Telecommun. Comput. Electron. Control) **19**(1), 155–162 (2021)
2. Brahmane, A.V., Krishna, C.B.: Rider chaotic biography optimization-driven deep stacked auto-encoder for big data classification using spark architecture: rider chaotic biography optimization. Int. J. Web Serv. Res. **18**(3), 42–62 (2021)
3. Hza, B., Jing, B.A., Yw, A., et al.: Few-shot electromagnetic signal classification: a data union augmentation method. Chin. J. Aeronaut. **35**(9), 49–57 (2022)
4. Ferraiolo, D.F., Defranco, J.F., Kuhn, D.R., et al.: A new approach to data sharing and distributed ledger technology: a clinical trial use case. IEEE Netw. **35**(1), 4–5 (2021)
5. Chigozie, M.P., Ogbo, A.I., Okoh, A., et al.: The effect of education, research and development on women entrepreneurial proclivity. Solid State Technol. **65**(5), 881–888 (2021)
6. Shi, Y., Zhao, Z.: Computer-aided software development and application in physical education in colleges and universities. Comput.-Aided Des. Appl. **19**(S1), 59–69 (2021)
7. Narwaria, M.: The transition from white box to black box: challenges and opportunities in signal processing education. IEEE Signal Process. Mag. **38**(3), 163–173 (2021)
8. Akpolat, A.N., Yang, Y., Blaabjerg, F., et al.: Design implementation and operation of an education laboratory-scale microgrid. IEEE Access **9**(99), 57949–57966 (2021)
9. Schor, D., Teng, J.L., Kinsner, W.: The future of engineering education. IEEE Pot. **40**(2), 4–6 (2021)
10. Tien, N.H.: Formative assessment in business and entrepreneurship education in Poland. Xinan Jiaotong Daxue Xuebao/J. Southwest Jiaotong Univ. **56**(1), 176–187 (2021)

# Research on Resource Classification Method of Mobile Education Platform for Physics Theory Teaching

Han Xu and Qiong Chen(✉)

Department of Basic Courses, Wuhan Donghu University, Wuhan 430212, China
MiuMiu1993@163.com

**Abstract.** There are various types of resources on mobile education platforms, but these resources often appear fragmented and lack systematicity and integration. Therefore, the classification research of physics theory teaching resources can help students better find and utilize resources that are suitable for their learning needs. A mobile education platform resource classification method for physics theory teaching is proposed to solve the problems of low accuracy and recall rate, as well as long resource classification time in traditional mobile education platform resource classification methods. Build a data collection architecture for physics theory teaching resources on the mobile education platform by using web page parsing module, text processing module, search strategy module, and supplementary mechanism module. Extract relevant resource features based on the collected data of physics theory teaching resources. Utilizing cost sensitive learning to improve Ada Boost ensemble learning algorithm, and combining resource feature extraction results to achieve resource classification on mobile education platforms. The experimental results show that the average accuracy of this method is 96.9%, the average recall rate is 96.8%, and the minimum time required for resource classification on mobile education platforms is 2.1 s. The classification results are reliable.

**Keywords:** Teaching physics theory · Mobile education platform · Resource classification · Cost sensitive learning · Ada Boost ensemble learning algorithm

## 1 Introduction

With the popularity of mobile Internet and the wide application of smart terminals such as smart phones, mobile education platform has become one of the hot spots in the current education field, which is particularly important for physics theory teaching [1]. Compared with traditional education, mobile education platform is not limited by time and space, has the advantages of flexibility and interaction, provides students with more learning possibilities, and can realize personalized teaching and the sharing of high-quality teaching resources. Mobile education platform resource classification refers to the classification of various learning resources on the mobile education platform in


G. Gui et al. (Eds.): eLEOT 2023, LNICST 543, pp. 283–299, 2024.
https://doi.org/10.1007/978-3-031-51465-4_19

accordance with a certain way, so that students can quickly find the required learning resources on the platform. These classification methods can be divided according to different dimensions, such as subject classification, knowledge point classification, difficulty level classification, non-curriculum resources classification, etc.The significance of studying the classification of mobile education platform resources is that through classification and organization, it can better improve students' learning efficiency and quality. The number of learning resources on mobile education platforms is huge [2]. If not classified and organized, students may feel confused and anxious during the process of searching and selecting learning resources, which affects learning efficiency and quality. Meanwhile, studying the classification of mobile education platform resources can also help improve the user experience of the platform, enhance students' learning experience, and enhance the brand value of the education platform. However, due to the numerous and complex knowledge points of physics theory, as well as the wide variety of educational resources, educators need to classify and manage resources to meet students' learning needs and achieve the best teaching results.

Aiming at the problem of resource classification on mobile education platform, literature [3] combined with a novel data enhancement method and calculated its attention matrix through attention mechanism according to the contribution of word vector to classification results, aiming at the characteristics of teaching material resource data set, such as rich text information, not obvious feature presentation and uneven sample distribution. Then the word vector matrix is combined with input into the model, so as to propose a text classification model Io META combined with attention mechanism, and use Io META to carry out deep learning of textbook resources, so as to realize resource classification. Reference [4] proposes an information resource classification method based on association rules to address the issue of current methods being unable to accurately analyze information feature relationships, resulting in low accuracy of information resource classification results. Utilize information gain to extract features of the information to be classified, and establish an evaluation function based on the difference in information gain. Using the distance from the feature to the corresponding category center as an association rule, deep mining of the internal relationship between information is achieved. By determining the itemset and using training, the classification of information resources is completed.

However, problems such as low accuracy of classification results, low recall rate and long classification time are found in the application of these two methods, leading to poor classification effect of mobile education platform resources. To solve this problem, this paper proposes a resource classification method for mobile education platform oriented to physics theory teaching. Through reasonable classification and integration of resources, it provides educators with effective educational resource management schemes, which aims to ensure effective management and utilization of educational resources and bring more and better learning resources to students. At the same time, the method will also consider students' academic needs and interests, in order to better meet the learning needs of different students. The structure of this article is as follows:

1) Build a data collection architecture for physics theory teaching resources on the mobile education platform using web page parsing module, text processing module, search strategy module, and supplementary mechanism module, and obtain relevant data collection results.
2) Extract relevant resource features based on the collected data of physics theory teaching resources. Cost sensitive learning is used to improve Ada Boost Ensemble learning algorithm, and resource feature extraction results are combined to achieve resource classification of mobile education platform.
3) The accuracy and recall rate of resource classification on mobile education platforms, as well as the time spent on resource classification, were used as indicators to comprehensively test the effectiveness of this method.
4) Summarize the entire article and draw a conclusion.

The main contributions of resource classification research on mobile education platforms for physics theory teaching are as follows:

1) Personalized resource recommendation: This study can achieve personalized recommendation of physics theory teaching resources by analyzing students' learning behavior, interest preferences, and learning needs. By associating student portraits with resource classification, students' personalized learning needs can be better met, and learning effectiveness and motivation can be improved.
2) Resource integration and organization: In response to the diversity and fragmentation of physics theory teaching resources, this study can integrate and organize different forms of resources to build a more complete and coherent learning resource chain. By categorizing and organizing resources such as videos, PPTs, PDFs, and codes, we aim to provide students with a more diverse learning experience and support.
3) Resource quality assessment and assurance: This study can establish standards and indicator systems for resource evaluation, evaluate and screen resources through automated or semi-automatic methods, and improve learners' trust and effectiveness in resource utilization. By evaluating and ensuring the quality of resources, high-quality physics theory teaching resources can be provided to improve learning outcomes.
4) Teaching strategy optimization: By analyzing the behavior data of learners on mobile education platforms, it is possible to understand the usage and effectiveness of different resources by students. Based on these data, teaching strategies can be optimized, resource classification and recommendation strategies can be adjusted, and teaching effectiveness and student satisfaction can be improved.
5) Cross platform sharing and interoperability: This study can explore the establishment of unified resource classification standards and norms, achieving resource sharing and interoperability among different mobile education platforms. This helps to promote the cross platform circulation and sharing of resources, improve their accessibility and sustainability.

# 2 Design of Resource Classification Method for Mobile Education Platform

## 2.1 Data Collection Architecture of Physics Theory Teaching Resources on Mobile Education Platform

The data collection architecture for physics theory teaching resources on the mobile education platform designed in this article adopts a B/S architecture as a whole. The MySQL database stores crawling data, the Redis cache database serves as a middleware database, the Neo4j graph database stores Fin Graph knowledge graphs, and the front-end page developed based on the Vue.js framework is used to complete user interaction. The back-end server provides logical processing, and the database stores the collected webpage information, The functions are mainly divided into web page parsing module, text processing module, search strategy module, and supplementary mechanism module. The data collection architecture is shown in Fig. 1.

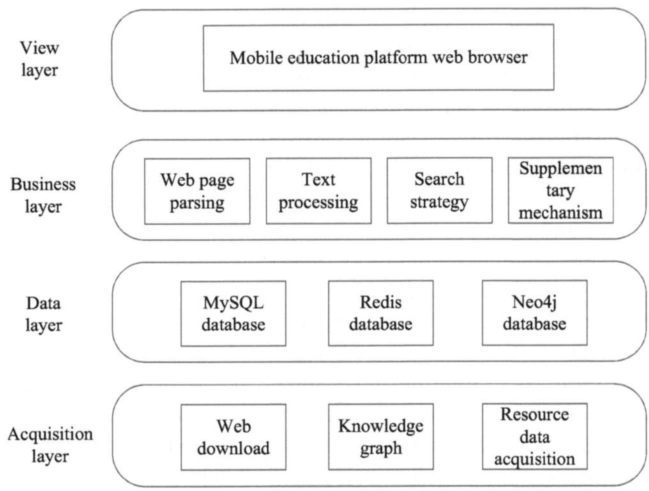


**Fig. 1.** Data collection architecture of physics theory teaching resources on mobile education platform

The user interacts with the view through the web browser. The browser is responsible for the front page display, and the back end is responsible for responding to the corresponding operations of the front end. The business layer includes webpage parsing module, text processing module, search strategy module and supplementary mechanism module. The data layer includes My SQL database, Redis database and Neo4j database. My SQL and Neo4j are mainly used to store subject-related webpage text data and Fin Graph knowledge graph, while Redis database is used for url reprocessing.The collection layer includes data collection function, which downloads webpage content based on URLs. Fin Graph assists in extracting key phrases from webpage text for topic semantic similarity calculation. According to the supplementary mechanism of the business layer, high correlation webpage crawls are extracted from triples to update Fin Graph, thereby building relevant knowledge graphs and achieving data collection of physics theory teaching resources on mobile education platforms.

(1) Design of web page parsing module

The webpage parsing module is responsible for extracting text, page title and link information from the obtained HTML source code [5], and removing redundant data and label structure of physical theory teaching resources on mobile education platform. This paper uses Xpath selector for preliminary screening. Xpath selector uses path expressions to select nodes or node sets in webpage documents, and extracts field data to webpage documents of mobile education platform by locating target nodes. Compared to CSS selectors, Xpath selectors' expressions are more concise, flexible, and efficient in finding complex elements. After the preliminary screening, regular expressions are used to extract the specific requirements.

(2) Text processing module

The text processing module is responsible for processing the extracted text of mobile education platform web pages. As the extracted text may contain residual web page tags, irrelevant punctuation mark and characters, and stop words, the text of the web page text should be cleaned to get clean physical theory teaching resource data of mobile education platform by removing miscellaneous content. Afterwards, the APKGram algorithm and Fin Graph knowledge graph were combined to extract key phrases from the cleaned web page text. Finally, word vector training is conducted based on relevant corpora to extract key phrase segmentation from the webpage body and map the segmentation to the training results to obtain the word vector for each word. If there are missing values, a word vector representation with the same dimension is randomly initialized. The word vectors of each key phrase are the average of the constituent word vectors, and the set of word vectors of these key phrases serves as the text feature vectors of the entire mobile education platform webpage.

(3) Search strategy module design

The search strategy module has the function of judging strategy based on the mixed content and link structure of mobile education platform. New links found by theme web crawler in the process of crawling web pages can be divided into two categories. One is directory page link, which is usually seen as the next page link. The other is the web content link, that is, the link that needs to parse the extracted fields of the web page, pointing to the actual mobile education platform physical theory teaching resource data information page. Theme web crawler [6, 7] extracts multiple content page links and web contents from each directory page link, selects the required links according to the set link structure rule expression and adds them to the cache database Redis to be downloaded, and removes the interference of irrelevant pages. And by calculating the semantic similarity between the content of the web page and the topic to decide whether to store the text of the web page in My SQL database.

This article uses the Redis database to store the URL queue. The Redis database is a high-performance non relational database that can support multiple data structures and can support persistence logs based on memory. The key of the crawler from

Redis is next_ When the link extracts its value value, the initial link starts running. The downloader returns a response to obtain the webpage content text. During the parsing of the webpage content, the following judgment process is performed:

1) Determine whether the webpage content has a link to the next page, and if so, store it in the Redis download queue;
2) Judge whether the webpage content matches the detail content page. If so, consider the page link and text content. For the link, use the set regular expression to extract the page link that meets the requirements and store it in the Redis download queue; For the text content, the topic similarity calculation based on the mobile education platform physics theory teaching resources text content is used to determine whether it is stored in the database. By comparing the semantic similarity between the text feature vector obtained from the text processing module and the topic feature vector, the semantic matching degree between the text content and the topic is calculated. The cosine similarity is used to calculate the topic similarity of the webpage text. If the calculated topic similarity is greater than or equal to the set threshold, the text content of the web page and its related information will be stored in My SQL database, otherwise it will not be recorded. After completing the above steps, if the next_link list is not empty, the crawler continues to fetch urls from the Redis queue for the above judgment steps until the waiting queue is empty. If the next_link list is empty, the process ends.

(4) Supplementary mechanism module

The supplementary mechanism module further supplements the Fin Graph knowledge graph based on a certain amount of physical theory teaching resource text data collected by crawlers, making the knowledge graph more complete. This article sets up to crawl 1000 physics theory teaching web pages, extract entity and relationship triplets through a joint extraction learning model of constructing a knowledge graph, and then perform entity disambiguation and co referential resolution to complete knowledge fusion. The fused "entity relationship entity" triplets are obtained and stored in the Neo4j graph database. Its significance lies in improving the accuracy of extracting key phrases from webpage text based on the supplemented Fin Graph knowledge graph, thereby affecting the crawler's ability to crawl webpage content that is more in line with the theme. The two complement each other [8].

(5) My SQL database is mainly used to store the webpage information of mobile education platform collected by crawler, including webpage URL, title, text, publication time, source and storage time.

The main detailed process of themed web crawler for data collection of physics theory teaching resources on mobile education platform is described as follows:

1) The crawler reads the initial URL in the URL queue and sends the request to the server. After obtaining the response returned by the server, the webpage is downloaded and the HTML source code is obtained [9];
2) The webpage parsing module analyzes the obtained HTML source code, removes irrelevant content and structure, and retains the webpage text;
3) The text processing module processes the text of the web page to some extent, and extracts key phrases in the text with the help of Fin Graph to get the feature vector of the text of the web page;

4) The search strategy module is used to determine a strategy based on a mixture of web page content and link structure. It calculates the semantic similarity between the web page text feature vector and the input topic vector. If the set threshold is met, the relevant information of the text is stored in the database, and the page links that meet the requirements are extracted and stored in the URL queue according to the rules.
5) Finally, determine whether the stop condition has been met. If the URL queue is empty, the program ends. If the URL queue is not empty, the next URL is passed to the webpage download section and the program continues to run.
6) The supplementary mechanism module stores a certain amount of physical theory teaching resource text data on a mobile education platform in a database, and then inputs these text data into a joint extraction learning model to obtain triplets, in order to supplement the Fin Graph knowledge graph and achieve data collection of physical theory teaching resources on mobile education platforms.

## 2.2 Resource Preprocessing of Mobile Education Platform

Based on the collected data, extract the characteristics of physical theory teaching resources on mobile education platforms to ensure subsequent classification accuracy.

The TF-IDF algorithm was proposed by Professor Salton in 1973 [10]. It is a statistical method used to evaluate the importance of a word or phrase to a document or category in a corpus. The main idea is that if a word or phrase appears frequently in one category and rarely in other categories, it is considered to have good category differentiation ability and is suitable for resource feature extraction.

*TF* represents the total frequency of a feature item $t$ appearing in document $d$. In the early stages of artificial intelligence, the *TF* algorithm is usually chosen for text processing of physical theory teaching resources on mobile education platforms. The formula is as follows:

$$TF(t,d) = \frac{f(t,d)}{\sum_{k=1}^{n} f(w_k,d)} \tag{1}$$

where, $f(t,d)$ represents the total number of occurrences of feature item $t$ in document $d$, and $f(w_k,d)$ represents the total number of occurrences of feature item $d$.

IDF is used to see if a feature item $t$ is ubiquitous in the document. The main idea is: if the fewer documents contain the feature item $t$, the larger the IDF value, indicating that the feature has good distinguishing ability. The formula is as follows:

$$IDF(w) = \log\left(\frac{N}{1+df_t}\right) \tag{2}$$

Among them, $N$ represents the total number of documents in the corpus, and $df_t$ represents the number of documents containing feature item $t$.

TF-IDF evaluates feature terms from two aspects during calculation. The weight of feature item $t$ increases proportionally with its frequency in the corpus, but at the same time decreases inversely with its frequency in the corpus. The complete formula is as follows:

$$IF - IDF = IF(t, d) \times IDF(t) \tag{3}$$

It can be seen from the definition of IDF formula that IDF mainly considers the category differentiation of feature item $t$ from the perspective of the whole corpus set, and lacks consideration of the distribution of feature item $t$ among classes, thus affecting the classification accuracy.

Since the traditional IDF calculation method does not consider the distribution between classes, an improved IDF calculation method is proposed here. The logarithmic molecule of the IDF formula is changed from the number of the whole document set to the number of all documents under a certain category, and then the IDF value under each category is calculated separately, and then the IDF value of all categories is used for variance calculation $D(t)$, the specific formula is as follows:

$$D(t) = \frac{\sum_{i=1}^{m} (IDF(t, c_i) - IDF(t))^2}{m} \tag{4}$$

Among them, $D(t)$ represents the distribution of the concentration degree of feature item $t$ in different categories of text sets. It can be seen that the value of $D(t)$ is inversely proportional to the distribution of feature item $t$ in different categories. The less concentrated the feature item is, the better the degree of differentiation, and the more representative it is of a class. The improved formula is as follows:

$$IF - IDF = IF(t, d) \times IDF(t) \tag{5}$$

The whole mobile education platform physics theory teaching resource data set is trained by the word vector model, so as to obtain the word vector of each feature item $t$. The word vectors of feature item $t$ appearing in text $w_i$ are summed respectively to obtain the sentence vector $R(w_i)$ of text $w_i$. Where, $word2vec(t)$ indicates the word vector of the feature item $t$.

$$R(w_i) = \sum_t word2vec(t), t \in w_i \tag{6}$$

Then, the improved TF IDF 'formula is used to weight the word vector and obtain $weight\_R(w_i)$.

$$weight\_R(w_i) = word2vec(t) \times weight_t, weight_t = TF - IDF \tag{7}$$

The feature extraction process of physics theory teaching resources on mobile education platform is as follows.

Input: mobile education platform physics theory teaching resource data set $c$, document set $D_j$ of each category, and each text $d_i$, optimal feature item set $T$.

Output: Resource feature extraction results.

1) The sentences in the data set of physics theory teaching resources on the mobile education platform are processed by word segmentation, words that do not belong to the optimal feature set $T$ are filtered out, only words belonging to the optimal feature set $T$ are reserved, and the results are saved in the Word2Vec training model;
2) Train the Word2Vec model on the model and set the size length to 50;
3) Calculate the IDF values of each feature item in the optimal feature set in different categories of documents;
4) Perform variance calculation on the IDF value of each feature item $t$, and then multiply it by its corresponding TF value to form the improved TF-IDF';
5) The word vectors trained using the Word2Vec model represent each text, and TF-IDF' is used to weight each feature item that appears in the text;
6) Return the text vector representation matrix and use it to extract the characteristics of physics theory teaching resources on mobile education platforms.

### 2.3 Resource Classification of Mobile Education Platform Based on Improved Integrated Learning

Ada Boost ensemble learning algorithm adopts Boosting ensemble idea, which links up multiple classifiers in series. With two weights, namely sample weight and base classifier weight, Ada Boost ensemble learning algorithm can achieve key learning of the misclassified samples, so as to improve the classification effect of resources on the mobile education platform. The specific process is as follows.

(1) Initialize the sample weights of the training set of resource data of the mobile education platform, so that all samples have the same weights

$$D_1 = \left(W_{1,1}, W_{1,i}, ..., W_{1,m}\right), W_{1,i} = \frac{1}{m}, i = 1, 2, ..., m \tag{8}$$

(2) Train the base classifier using a training set of mobile education platform resource data samples with a weight of $D_t$ to obtain the $t$ weak classifier $D_t(x)$.

(3) Calculate the classification error rate of $D_t(x)$ in the mobile education platform resource data training set:

$$e_t = P(G_t(x_t) \neq y_i) = \sum_{i=1}^{m} W_{ti} I(G_t(x_t)) \neq y_i \tag{9}$$

The weight of weak classifier $D_t(x)$ in strong classifier is calculated according to the classification accuracy of weak classifier

$$\alpha_t = \frac{1}{2} \ln \frac{1 - e_t}{e_t} \tag{10}$$

(4) Update the weights of the samples in the training dataset based on the results of the previous iteration

$$D_{t+1} = \left(W_{t+1,1}, ..., W_{t+1,i}, ..., W_{t+1,m}\right) \tag{11}$$

$$W_{t+1,i} = \frac{w_{t,i}}{Z_t}\exp(-\alpha_t y_i G_t(x_i)) \tag{12}$$

where, $Z_t$ represents the gauge factor.

(5) Construct the linear combination of weak classifiers for resource classification of mobile education platform, specifically as follows:

$$f(x) = \sum_{i=1}^{T} \alpha_t G_t(x) \tag{13}$$

(6) The final strong classifier for resource classification on mobile education platforms is as follows:

$$G(x) = sign(f(x)) = sign\left(\sum_{i=1}^{T} \alpha_t G_t(x)\right) \tag{14}$$

It can be seen from the above process that the key of Ada Boost integrated learning algorithm is adaptive dynamic updating of sample weights, and samples of resource classification results on different mobile education platforms have different weight updates.

When the sample prediction is correct:

$$W_{t+1,i} = \frac{w_{t,i}}{Z_t}\exp(-\alpha_t) \tag{15}$$

When the sample prediction is incorrect:

$$W_{t+1,i} = \frac{w_{t,i}}{Z_t}\exp(\alpha_t) \tag{16}$$

where $\alpha_t \geq 0.5$, when the classification of resource data samples on the mobile education platform is correct, the weight of the samples will be reduced; when the classification of resource data samples on the mobile education platform is wrong, the weight will also increase, so as to realize the focus of learning on the wrong samples. However, in the unbalanced data classification problem, due to the small number of minority samples, the standard machine learning algorithm which takes the overall optimization as the optimization strategy is easy to classify the minority samples incorrectly. Therefore, through multiple learning, better identification results of minority samples will be obtained compared with other ensemble learning models.

The traditional machine learning classification algorithm takes the improvement of the overall classification accuracy as the optimization goal, and treats the misclassification cost of each type of sample equally in the loss function, but in the unbalanced classification problem, this is not very appropriate. Moreover, in imbalanced data, the error cost of misclassifying minority samples into majority samples is much higher than that of misclassifying majority samples into minority samples. For imbalanced classification problems, different types of misclassification costs should be treated differently based on the consideration of misclassification costs, in order to achieve the minimum comprehensive misclassification cost. Therefore, in the imbalanced data classification problem, the difference in misclassification costs of samples from different categories is fully considered, and cost sensitive learning is introduced to transform the learning objective of the classification algorithm from reducing overall error to reducing classification costs. Cost sensitive learning can be divided into input stage introducing cost sensitive learning, algorithm stage introducing cost sensitive learning, and output node introducing cost sensitive learning based on the timing considered.

The cost sensitive learning is introduced into the algorithm, the algorithm is improved, the loss function is modified, and the change of the optimization objective of the loss function is used to realize the effective identification of a few types of samples while ensuring the overall accuracy, and FP and FN in the confusion matrix are treated differently. That is:

$$R_L = R(i,j) * L(FP) + R(j,i) * L(FN) \tag{17}$$

Among them, $R(i,j)$ represents the loss cost when Class $j$ is misclassified as Class $i$, $R(j,i)$ represents the loss cost when Class $i$ is misclassified as Class $j$, and $R(i,j) \neq R(i,j)$. $x$ represents an instance. If $j = i$, it indicates that the model classifies mobile

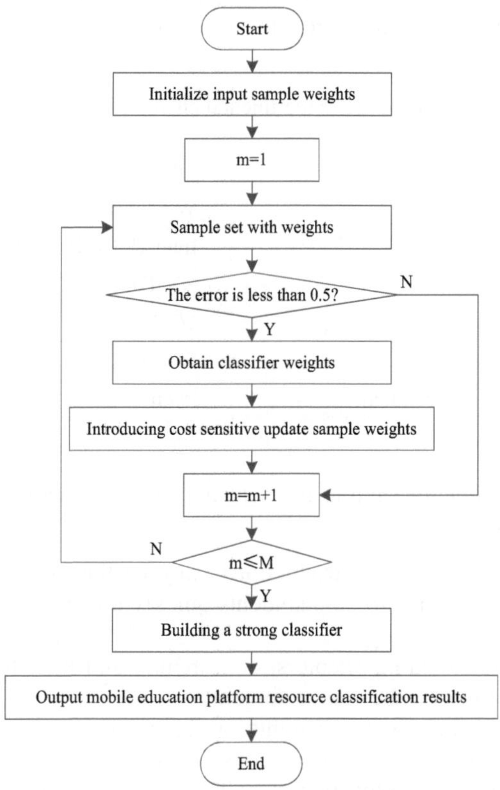


**Fig. 2.** Resource Classification Process for Mobile Education Platform

education platform resource samples correctly. The cost sensitive classification loss function involved in this concept no longer takes the overall mobile education platform resource classification accuracy as the optimal goal, but the expected cost of classification is the smallest, namely:

$$\arg\min E(x, y)\ :\ C\left[t_{yR(x)}\right] \tag{18}$$

where, $E$ represents the expected cost of classification, $C$ represents the unbalanced data distribution, $R(x)$ represents the structural risk value of $x$, and $t_{yR(x)}$ represents the misclassification cost of a certain category. In order to achieve the iteration process to achieve the specified class of samples in the loss function to increase the discourse power, to achieve the focus of the iteration process. The resource classification process of mobile education platform is shown in Fig. 2.

## 3 Experimental Design

The configuration of the experimental platform in this article is diverse, mainly conducting simulation experiments on computers. The specific operating system is Windows 10, and Pandas is used as a tool for reading and preprocessing file data. The specific experimental environment is shown in Table 1.

**Table 1.** Experimental environment

| Environment name | Environment configuration |
|---|---|
| Operating system | Windows 10 |
| CPU | Inter CoRE i5-5200U |
| GPU | NVIDIA GTX 1650 |
| Memory | 16 GB |
| Programming language | Python 3.8 |
| Integrated development environment | Pych |

The types of experimental sample data selected during this experiment are as follows:
Type 1: Text Data

1) Image data: Course name and introduction of physics theory: Describe the name and main content of the course to help students quickly understand the overview of the course.
2) Textbook content: including chapters, class hours, and knowledge points, to help students learn and master the course content.
3) Study notes: This includes notes, insights, and summaries of students' physics theory courses, which helps them review and consolidate course knowledge.
4) Teacher's handouts and lesson plans: including teacher's handouts and classroom lesson plans to assist teachers in lesson preparation and teaching.

5) Evaluation and feedback: This includes students' evaluation and feedback on physics theory courses, which helps to provide feedback, improve and improve course quality.

Type 2: Audio data

1) Course audio: including the recording and explanation of the physics theory course, students can listen to the class anytime and anywhere through mobile devices.
2) Teaching audio: including teachers' lectures and answers, to help students better understand and master the content of physics theory course in learning.
3) Evaluation and feedback: including students' evaluation and feedback on the physics theory course, which is helpful to provide feedback and improve and perfect the quality of the course.
4) Voice interaction: including voice assistant and voice recognition, to help students to carry out interactive learning, improve the interest and effect of learning.

Type 3: Video Data

1) Course video: including videos recorded for physics theory teaching, which can be watched anytime and anywhere through mobile devices.
2) Teaching video: including teacher's explanations, demonstrations, problem-solving, etc., to help students better understand and master the content of physics theory courses during learning.
3) Evaluation and feedback: This includes students' evaluation and feedback on physics theory courses, which helps to provide feedback, improve and improve course quality.
4) Virtual simulation videos: including virtual simulation experiments, virtual demonstrations, etc., can provide more vivid and vivid learning methods.

Type 4: Evaluation data

1) Evaluation data of mobile education platform refers to students' evaluation data on courses and teaching, which mainly includes the following contents:
2) Course evaluation: including the evaluation of the difficulty, learning content, curriculum setting and other aspects of the physics theory course.
3) Teaching evaluation: including the evaluation of teachers' explanation, solution, guidance, interaction and other aspects.
4) Teaching environment evaluation: including the evaluation of physical theory teaching classroom environment, learning equipment, learning atmosphere and other aspects.
5) Evaluation of learning experience: including evaluation of learning style, learning effect, learning resources, sense of experience and other aspects.

Type 5: Behavioral Data

The behavior data of mobile education platforms refers to the learning and operational behavior data of students on the platform, mainly including the following content:

1) Learning records: including students' learning duration, visit frequency, learning content, learning progress, etc.
2) Learning interaction: including interaction between students and teachers, interaction between students, etc., such as questioning, discussion, etc.

3) Learning outcomes: including homework, exam, experimental data, and other outcome data during the student learning process, reflecting the student's learning outcomes in a timely manner.
4) Operational behavior: including students' click behavior, search behavior, collection behavior, evaluation behavior, etc., reflecting students' interest and inclination towards learning resources.

Each experimental sample data category contains 10,000 records, with 80% randomly designated as the training set and 20% as the test set respectively. After training the simulation software, the data of the test set is input into the simulation software to obtain the relevant experimental results. The method of literature [3], literature [4] and the method in this paper are used as experimental comparison methods, and the accuracy rate, recall rate and classification time of different methods are compared to verify the effectiveness of this method.

Classification accuracy rate refers to the proportion of all samples classified as a certain category, which really belongs to that category. It is one of the important indicators to evaluate the performance. The higher the classification accuracy rate is, the higher the proportion of the samples of this category is correctly classified by the classification method, and the higher the classification accuracy is. The comparison results of the accuracy rates of the methods in literature [3], literature [4] and the methods in this paper are shown in Table 2.

**Table 2.** Precision Comparison Results (Unit:%)

| Number of experiments | Reference [3] Method | Reference [4] Method | Proposed method |
|---|---|---|---|
| 1 | 75.6 | 81.3 | 96.8 |
| 21 | 76.3 | 80.6 | 97.2 |
| 41 | 74.9 | 84.7 | 98.7 |
| 61 | 72.5 | 81.3 | 95.6 |
| 81 | 73.4 | 81.4 | 96.1 |
| Mean Value | 74.5 | 81.9 | 96.9 |

By analyzing the results in Table 2, we can see that with the increase of experiment times, the accuracy rates of the three methods all show a fluctuating trend. Among them, the average accuracy rate of the method in literature [3] is 74.5%, the average accuracy rate of the method in literature [4] is 81.9%, and the average accuracy rate of the method in this paper is 96.9%, which is much higher than that of the experimental comparison method, indicating that the method has a high accuracy for the classification of resources on mobile education platform and good practical application effect. The reason is that this method uses cost sensitive learning to improve Ada Boost Ensemble learning algorithm to achieve resource classification of mobile education platform by extracting relevant resource characteristics. Therefore, the classification accuracy of this method is high.

Classification recall rate refers to the percentage of all samples that actually belong to a class that are classified into that class. It is another important index to evaluate the performance of the classification method. The higher the classification recall rate is, the better the classification method can capture the samples of this category, and the better the classification effect is. The comparison results of the recall rate of the method in literature [3], literature [4] and the method in this paper are shown in Table 3.

**Table 3.** Comparison results of recall rate (unit: %)

| Number of experiments | Reference [3] Method | Reference [4] Method | Proposed method |
|---|---|---|---|
| 1 | 86.3 | 79.6 | 98.7 |
| 21 | 85.4 | 86.3 | 95.6 |
| 41 | 85.6 | 85.2 | 94.7 |
| 61 | 84.8 | 81.3 | 97.6 |
| 81 | 81.7 | 80.7 | 97.5 |
| Mean Value | 84.8 | 82.6 | 96.8 |

By analyzing the results in Table 3, we can see that with the increase of experiment times, the recall rates of the three methods all show a fluctuating trend. Among them, the average recall rate of the method in literature [3] is 84.8%, that of the method in literature [4] is 82.6%, and that of the method in this paper is 96.8%, which is much higher than the experimental comparison method, indicating that the method has a higher recall rate and better classification quality for the mobile education platform resources. The reason is that this method uses cost sensitive learning to improve Ada Boost Ensemble learning algorithm, and combines the resource feature extraction results to achieve resource classification of mobile education platform. The improved Ada Boost Ensemble learning algorithm has the advantages of improving classification accuracy, handling unbalanced data sets, enhancing robustness, maintaining interpretability and adjustability, and using parallel computing capabilities in resource classification. These advantages make the improved Ada Boost algorithm an effective and feasible method for resource classification tasks, resulting in a higher recall rate of classification results.

Classification time index refers to the time index required to classify resources of mobile education platform in the process of data processing. In order to improve the efficiency and accuracy of classification, these indexes should be evaluated and optimized during resource classification of mobile education platform. The comparison results of resource classification time of mobile education platform based on literature [3], literature [4] and this paper are shown in Fig. 3.

The analysis of experimental results in Fig. 3 shows that with the increase of experiment times, the resource classification time of the three methods of mobile education platform also changes to some extent. Among them, the minimum time of resource classification of mobile education platform in literature [3] is 5.3 s, the minimum time of resource classification of mobile education platform in literature [4] is 4.5 s, and the

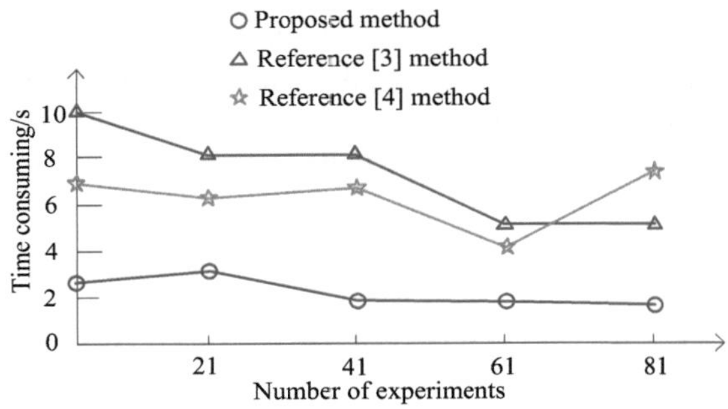


**Fig. 3.** Comparison results of classification time consumption

minimum time of resource classification of mobile education platform in this paper is 2.1 s, indicating that the resource classification of mobile education platform in this paper is shorter and more efficient. The main reason is the introduction of the improved Ada Boost Ensemble learning algorithm, which can realize parallel computing in resource classification, so the classification time of this method is always kept at a low level.

## 4 Conclusion

With the popularization of mobile internet and intelligent terminals, more and more educators are beginning to realize the importance of mobile education platforms in education and teaching. Especially in the field of physics theory teaching, the advantages of mobile education platforms are particularly evident. Through mobile education platforms, students can learn at any time, anywhere, and according to their own learning progress and interests. The research on resource classification methods for mobile education platforms for physics theory teaching has become one of the hotspots in the current education field. Therefore, this article proposes a mobile education platform resource classification method for physics theory teaching. The experimental results show that the accuracy and recall of this method are high, and the classification time is short. It can achieve accurate and fast classification of mobile education platform resources, promoting further improvement of physics theory teaching level. However, the resource classification methods studied for mobile education platforms still face some challenges and shortcomings, such as a lack of consistency and standardization, improvement in classification accuracy, and difficulty in resource evaluation and quality assurance. Future research can focus on addressing these issues, improving the accuracy, personalization, and quality of resource classification, in order to provide a better learning experience and support.

**Acknowledgement.** 1. 2022 Hubei Provincial Department of Education Science and Technology Research Program Project B2022315.

2. 2021 Wuhan Donghu University Youth Fund Project Approval (Natural Science) 2021 dhzk0077.

## References


1. Lin, H.: The construction of mobile education in cloud computing. Procedia Comput. Sci. **183**(8), 14–17 (2021)
2. Wu, Y., Chen, J.: Realization of mobile education resource sharing method based on wireless broadband connection. Sci Program. **7**(1), 1–10 (2021)
3. Guo, S.W., Chen, J.H.: Textbook classification method of index of moral education based on deep learning. Comput. Moder. **9**, 106–112 (2021)
4. Zhou, M.: A Classification method for personnel archive information resources based on association rules. Jiangxi Commun. Sci. Technol. **3**, 28–30 (2021)
5. Liu, D.L., Lv, M.: User information extraction based on web crawler and associated big data. Comput. Simul. **38**(8), 482–486 (2021)
6. Yu, L., Li, Y., Zeng, Q.: Design of topic Web crawler based on improved PageRank algorithm. J. Phys: Conf. Ser. **1754**(1), 012210–012217 (2021)
7. Kuze, D.: Classification of diversified web crawler accesses inspired by biological adaptation. Int. J. Bio-Insp. Comput. **17**(3), 1–12 (2021)
8. Luo, M., Lin, J.: Research on the impact of credit, brand and service recovery on online sales based on web crawler technology and regression analysis methods. J. Phys: Conf. Ser. **1955**(1), 012083–012095 (2021)
9. Han, D.H., Lee, Y.K.: Design of action-based web crawler structural configuration for multi-website management. KIISE Trans. Comput. Pract. **27**(2), 98–103 (2021)
10. Yu, H., Ji, Y., Li, Q.: Student sentiment classification model based on GRU neural network and TF-IDF algorithm. J. Intell. Fuzzy Syst. **40**(2), 2301–2311 (2021)

# Ceramic Art Teaching Resource Sharing Platform Based on Classroom Behavior Analysis

Zhiyan Zhang[1], Yongshun Xu[2], Yu Xia[3], and Senyang Lu[4(✉)]

[1] Fine Arts of Nanjing Xiaozhuang University, Nanjing 211171, China
[2] School of Communication, Jiangsu Second Normal University, Nanjing 211171, China
[3] Aviation Services and Music School, Nanchang Hangkong University, Nanchang 330063, China
[4] Yunnan Normal University, Kunming 650500, Yunnan, China
zzy135851@163.com

**Abstract.** Aiming at the problem of poor sharing effect of modern pottery teaching resources, this research proposes and designs a pottery teaching resource sharing platform based on classroom behavior analysis. In terms of hardware, the API sharing interface is designed, the information transmission master station is connected to the collection device through GPRS public network communication channel, and the structure of XML parser is designed to realize cross-regional resource sharing. In terms of software, the Grobeis criterion is used to pre-process the teacher-student interaction graph data and determine the resource center. The sharing center determined according to the classroom behavior of the interactive map and the ranking method of the remote sharing mode of resource library resources are established to realize the integration of teaching resources. The experimental results show that the maximum shared resource of the platform is 4500bit, which proves that the proposed method has a good resource sharing effect.

**Keywords:** Classroom Behavior Analysis · Ceramic Art · Teaching Resources · Sharing Platform

## 1 Introduction

The rapid development of Internet technology has provided new teaching means for traditional education. Teaching resource sharing technology has been widely used in various fields. Its application in ceramic teaching has effectively improved the limitations of traditional ceramic art teaching resource sharing. In the context of mobile Internet + education, a variety of learning based teaching resource platforms are in full bloom, including MOOC, micro classes, online open courses, etc. These platforms provide learners with a good autonomous learning environment.But educators often ignore the construction of another type of teaching resource platform, which is the data based teaching resource platform.


G. Gui et al. (Eds.): eLEOT 2023, LNICST 543, pp. 300–315, 2024.
https://doi.org/10.1007/978-3-031-51465-4_20

Year after year, day after day, data based teaching resources are increasing, and their storage, classification, sharing, and use are all topics that need special consideration at present: first, although all majors or teachers now save these teaching achievements every year in the form of burning CDs or computer storage, this traditional data storage method has virus threats, hardware damage. The storage device is unstable, the space is limited and cannot be shared. Once the course is over, over time, these precious teaching resources will sink into the sea and no one will care about them. Second, the traditional way of storing data on hard disk or optical disk is basically privatized. Except that all teachers can obtain the teaching results of their subjects, other professional teachers and students cannot directly or timely obtain effective resources or information, resulting in the problem of asymmetric information resources in education, which leads to repeated waste of resources. Third, in terms of the transformation of teaching achievements, the evaluation, exhibition, competition and other forms each semester can not let more enterprises understand the works designed by the school, but at best it is only a small exhibition within the school. This situation directly leads to the fact that students' teaching resources are hard to see and unknown to outsiders, resulting in a huge waste of design resources, which is not conducive to the effective connection between teaching and the market. Therefore, building a shared platform for data based teaching resources is also a necessary means to further deepen teaching reform and speed up education informatization. Through sorting, summarizing and surfing the Internet of various teaching resources, a new open and shared network sharing platform can be formed.

At present, the heterogeneous data fusion algorithm based on BP neural network is proposed in literature [1]. This algorithm takes variable factors as input factors, obtains relevant data by screening factor variables, and combines neural network data fusion technology to fuse heterogeneous network information on this basis. The heterogeneous data sharing algorithm based on the twin neural network proposed in literature [2] uses the relationship based heterogeneous network information sharing model, uses the multitask twin neural network, approximates the similarity of the same and different nodes to low dimensions, and uses the multitask twin neural network to realize the deep sharing of multiple nodes. Literature [3] proposed a fusion method based on privacy protection. This method uses BGN encryption system to share the key, and shares the encrypted data to the perception platform through differential privacy awareness data. However, the current three methods are vulnerable to cross platform operations between different formats of information when exchanging different information, and the amount of computation is large, which tends to shorten the network life and lead to poor information exchange results. Therefore, a ceramic art teaching resource sharing platform based on classroom behavior analysis is designed.

## 2 Platform Structure Design

The ceramic art teaching resource sharing platform based on classroom behavior analysis provides users with better resource sharing services, integrates rich ceramic art teaching resources, improves the utilization rate of teaching resource sharing, and solves the problems in teaching resource storage. There are two design functions of the ceramic art teaching cloud sharing plaorm, one is to meet the needs of users for resource utilization, the other is to provide users with personalized cloud sharing service experience to meet the needs of communication between users [4]. The basic functions of the platform design include resource browsing, resource query, resource download and other functions. Users can search the required resources in the platform according to the keywords of information. In order to meet the needs of user communication, the platform has added instant chat, personal space and other functions in the function design to meet the requirements of personalized learning of users. The function of community learning module is added to the functional design of the platform, and websites such as QQ space are introduced for teachers and students to use, which promotes students' enthusiasm for learning and strengthens the exchange of learning between teachers and students [5, 6]. Through cloud services, teachers and students can achieve two-way real-time interaction, and students and teachers can experience the fun of learning anywhere. The structural design of ceramic art teaching resource sharing platform based on classroom behavior analysis is shown in Fig. 1.

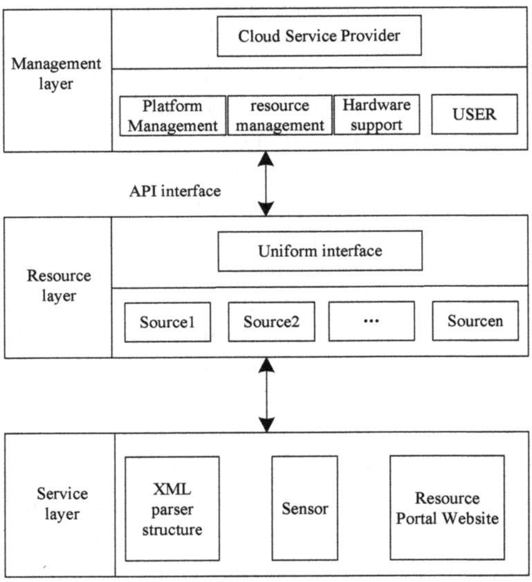


**Fig. 1.** Structure of ceramic art teaching resources sharing platform

The system platform is a service layer for users, which provides users with a resource sharing interface. Users can access, browse and download ceramic art teaching resources cloud sharing platform anytime and anywhere through mobile terminal devices such as computers and mobile phones. Users can download ceramic art teaching resources they need at any time and any place. The use of cloud platform in ceramic art teaching resources allows users of mobile terminals to access resources and improve users' experience. Cloud sharing services promote the sharing services of ceramic art teaching resources [7]. Users can query and visit ceramic art teaching resources through the website through the keyword search function, which is fast and accurate. The sharing service of the cloud platform can not only provide users with the function of resource access, but also provide users with personalized services. Compared with traditional resource sharing platforms, the cloud sharing platform not only meets users' needs for resource access and download, but also provides the function of communication between users. It attaches more importance to the application of user interaction.

## 2.1 Sharing Management

The management layer manages the cloud sharing platform of ceramic art teaching resources. The cloud service provider provides the management layer with the architecture based on the Pass platform. The cloud service provider also provides the management layer with hardware equipment, storage and other services, and the cloud service provider is responsible for management. The managers of ceramic art teaching resources can easily manage platform resources, services and accounts through API management. The management of accounts is mainly to allocate legal and authorized authentication IDs, and users can access the resource pool by applying for IDs [8]. An API interface is designed in the sharing management layer, as shown in Fig. 2.

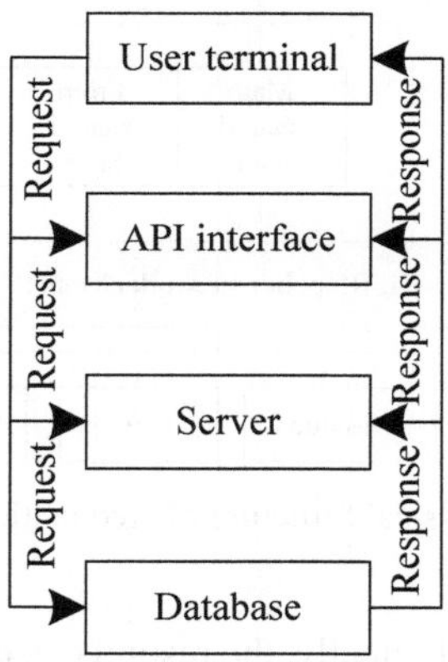


**Fig. 2.** Schematic diagram of API interface of management layer

In the resource management layer, applications and resources are decoupled through API interfaces, ensuring the stability of the front-end application system, so that it will not be disturbed by the back-end heterogeneous resource environment, nor affected by changes in the implementation technology. In this way, resource management and applications can be separated, while ensuring the stability of the management interface.

## 2.2 Shared Resource Layer

The resource layer is the key layer for the integration and summary of ceramic art teaching resources. The design advantage of the platform system is to improve the utilization efficiency of resource sharing, facilitate users' access to ceramic art teaching resources, make the storage of ceramic art teaching resources more secure, and save manpower and material resources [9]. The resource layer provides resource services for the cloud sharing platform. It collects ceramic art teaching resources and stores them in the cloud resource pool in a virtual way. The teaching resources in the resource pool are shared by various institutions. Users submit their own resources to the resource pool for sharing with other users after being approved by the cloud platform.

The physical structure of the acquisition system used by the shared resource layer is shown in Fig. 3.

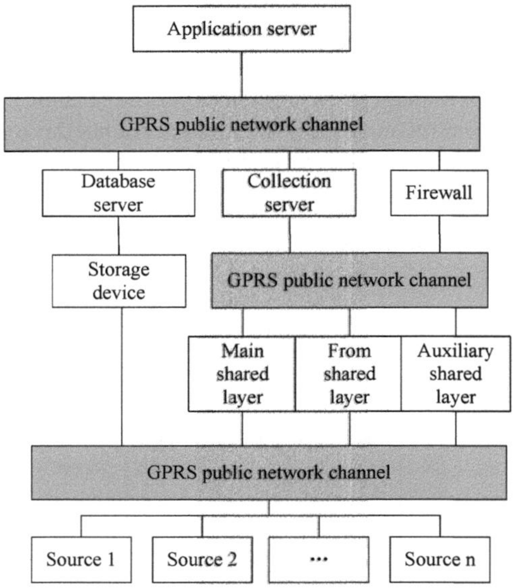


**Fig. 3.** Physical Structure of Acquisition System

As can be seen from Fig. 3, logically, the resource acquisition system is divided into the main sharing layer, the secondary sharing layer and the auxiliary sharing layer. The platform is connected to other application systems through interfaces. The acquisition master sharing layer mainly uses the GPRS public network communication channel, which supports the information interaction between the master sharing layer and the slave sharing layer, and is the connection between the information transmission master station and the acquisition equipment. GPRS public network communication is a 32-bit wireless module, which uses an embedded operating structure to provide an RS232 interface for the system, facilitate direct connection with serial devices, and realize rapid transmission of resources [10]. The auxiliary sharing layer has metering and statistics functions. It is divided into N terminal layers to be responsible for resource collection and realize resource interaction between different users.

### 2.3 Shared Service Layer

In order to facilitate the rational use of resources, a set of template mapping between resource database patterns is designed. XML analysis software is used to read, write, count and report XML resources, which solves the problems of heterogeneous conflict and cross platform resource exchange in the process of resource exchange and resource processing, and realizes resource transmission at any time and anywhere.

XML parser structure, as shown in Fig. 4.

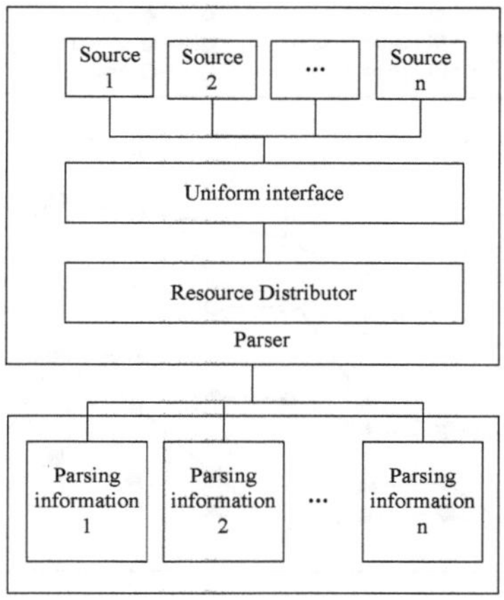


**Fig. 4.** XML parser structure

As shown in Fig. 4, in an XML document, the parser will scan the internal or external subset of the declaration to establish a syntax tree. The syntax tree stores the attributes in the XML validator and stores the syntax tree information in the array.

Redundant arrays are resources stored in different locations of multiple disks. These resources overlap evenly to improve the system performance. The system fault tolerance performance is improved by increasing the average time between disk failures. Use dual storage disk cabinets to store resources on local disks, and use the replication function of dual storage arrays to back up the stored resources to other storage arrays to ensure that resources will not be lost.

# 3 Platform Function Realization

## 3.1 Determination of Sharing Center Based on Interaction Map Classroom Behavior

In order to more intuitively see the comparison of teacher talk, student talk, technology application and silence behavior time share in ceramic art class, it is necessary to analyze the teacher-student interaction map. First, use the Grobeis criterion to preprocess the atlas data. The formula is:

$$g = \frac{\sum_{l=1}^{\beta} g_n}{\beta} \tag{1}$$

In formula (1), $\beta$ indicates the quantity of data; $l$ indicates the number of calculations. Using the i-FIAS analysis program matched with the i-FIAS interaction analysis system, the original code table is imported into the analysis program, and the corresponding teacher-student interaction map is obtained, as shown in Fig. 5.

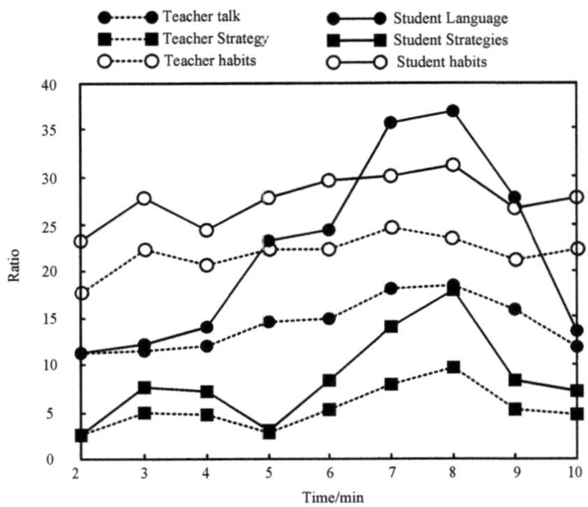


**Fig. 5.** Interaction map between teachers and students

In the teacher-student interaction map in Fig. 5, the ratio of teacher's language five minutes before class is significantly higher than that of other behaviors, which indicates that teacher's language is mainly used during this period. From the 5th minute to the 15th minute, the ratio of teachers, students and technology accounted for a certain proportion, indicating that teachers interacted with students through the use of technology during this period. From the 15th minute to the 23rd minute, the teacher's language ratio is significantly higher than other ratios, which indicates that most of the time in this ten minute period is dominated by teachers' teaching. From the 23rd minute to the 33rd minute, the teacher's language, student's language and technology ratio intersect in turn, indicating that the teacher-student interaction is very active during this period, and technology application also accounts for a certain proportion. From the 33th minute to the 36th minute, the ratio of silence beneficial to teaching is significantly higher than the ratio of teachers' and students' language and technical behavior, which indicates that students are mainly silent and self-study practice during this period. Between 36–40, the teacher's language ratio, silence ratio and student's language ratio intersect one by one, indicating that teachers and students are interacting during this period of time, while in the last period of time, the teacher's language ratio is far greater than the student's language ratio, indicating that teachers are summarizing the classroom at the last period of time.

Based on the results of classroom analysis, the ceramic art teaching resources sharing center was determined. First of all, the Resource Sharing Center integrates a variety of resource management technologies, adheres to the principle of resource centric in technology selection, and does not blindly pursue the basic principles of advanced, fast, and clear order. For many fields of circular economy, especially in market regulation, the requirement for resource consistency is not high, and the key is integration. It pays attention to the high availability of resources and the scalability of the structure. Technical factors such as resource sharing in the large resource supply chain. Data visualization is also an important part of resource data processing. Its main purpose is to present the data integration in an easy to understand form on the circular economy integration platform, which is the specific expression of the integrated data. Then, the integrated resource can be processed on various resource receiving devices.

Based on this, the Content Center is determined as follows:

$$O = \frac{1}{\log(1 + \frac{m}{n})} \cdot \frac{1}{\sqrt{\sum_{m=1}^{N} m}} \tag{2}$$

In formula (2), $m$ is the number of attribute values in the local ontology; $n$ is the total number of all local noumenons; $N$ is the total number of attribute values in all local ontologies. Through this formula, the sharing center of classroom behavior based on interaction map can be determined.

### 3.2 Integration of Teaching Resources

According to the determined sharing center based on the interaction map classroom behavior, the teaching resource integration mechanism is established by establishing the sequencing method of the remote sharing mode of resource library resources. The specific process is as follows:

Set the threshold and iterative adjustment parameters, and construct a complementary judgment matrix when the time is 0:

$$E(t) = \left(E(t)_{ij}\right)_{m \times n} \tag{3}$$

In formula (3), $E(t)_{ij}$ represents the judgment matrix $j$ at point $i$.

Obtain the minimum non negative deviations $a_{\mathrm{ij}}^{(t)-}$ and $a_{\mathrm{ij}}^{(t)+}$. Calculate the consistency index and optimal weight vector of the complementary judgment matrix according to the following formula:

$$\gamma(E) = \frac{\sum\limits_{\mathrm{i<j}} \left| e_{\mathrm{ij}}^{(t)-} - e_{\mathrm{ij}}^{(t)+} \right|}{n} \tag{4}$$

In formula (4), $e_{\mathrm{ij}}^{(t)-}$, $e_{\mathrm{ij}}^{(t)+}$ represent the minimum non negative and non positive deviation respectively. Output the complementary judgment matrix and consistency index, and sort the data to be integrated according to the value.

When two sorting arrays have the same dimension, the size difference between them is only a constant, which is compatible array. Only compatible arrays can perform resource fusion. When merging qualified resources, the calculation result of resource fusion degree between heterogeneous networks is taken as the basis, and the formula is:

$$\iota_{ij} = \int_{M_j}^{M_i} \frac{1}{\sqrt{2\pi\phi}} \exp\left\{-\frac{1}{2}\left[\frac{M_i - M_j}{\sigma_j}\right]^2\right\} dM \tag{5}$$

In formula (5), $M$ represents teaching resources; $M_i, M_j$ represents the teaching resources $j$ listed in $i$; $\phi$ is a Normal distribution function.When the calculation result of the formula is close to 0, it indicates that the coincidence degree of these two resources is large, and the integration effect of these two resources is good.

### 3.3 Sharing of Teaching Resources

On the basis of bionics principles, with ant colony as the optimization goal, and according to the distribution law of ant colony, the distribution of ant colony is constantly adjusted to achieve the goal of searching. Therefore, a platform sharing technology based on ant colony algorithm is proposed. The detailed process is as follows:

Step 1: Initialize the parameters, train the ceramic art teaching resource sharing process, and construct the ant colony adaptive function. In the shared platform, the input terminal contains only one neuron, which is responsible for the overall output of the neural network. The adaptive function input obtained from this can be expressed as:

$$a_{k+1}(t) = \sum_{k=1}^{t} w_k a_k(t) \tag{6}$$

In formula (6), $w_k$ represents the weight of $k$; $a_k(t)$ represents the input result at sampling time $t$. The corresponding output layer is:

$$b_{k+1}(t) = \begin{cases} 1 & a_{k+1}(t) > 1 \\ a_{k+1}(t) & -1 \le a_{k+1}(t) \le 1 \\ 1 & a_{k+1}(t) < -1 \end{cases} \tag{7}$$

The result obtained by formula (7) is equivalent to the overall output of the entire sharing platform. Through intelligent control of the sharing platform, the difference between the real input and the expected input of the platform is maximized, that is, the maximum stable state. With the entity resource type and resource data supply chain in this state as the only identification, a comprehensive and unique circular supply mode sharing data cloud is established.

Step 2: In a secure resource data cloud system, resource sharing is necessary. The processing method for shared resources is mainly to use resource data re encryption, which combines attribute based encryption sharing with resource re encryption, and makes full use of encryption algorithms to ensure the security of resource sharing. Therefore, a secure encryption resource sharing method is designed. In order to ensure the confidentiality of resources, resources are stored in the cloud after the client is encrypted by the user using the symmetric encryption method, as shown in Formula (8).

$$DP = (A_p, A_q, B_p, B_q) \tag{8}$$

In formula (8), $A_p, A_q$ are finite non empty sets with encrypted identity and non encrypted identity respectively; $B_p, B_q$ are finite time sets with encrypted identity and non encrypted identity respectively. In this way, unencrypted resources to be shared will not be exposed during data sharing.

Step 3: In the ant colony algorithm, set guidance parameters and adjust its convergence. When the guidance parameter value is greater than 1, the ant colony will expand the range and launch a global search; When the guidance parameter value is less than 1, the ant colony will shrink and concentrate on hunting. The guidance parameters are determined by the convergence factor, so the convergence factor can have a great impact on the improvement results of the ant colony algorithm. Based on this situation, a nonlinear convergence factor is proposed, and the expression formula is:

$$\lambda = \lambda_0 \cdot e^{\left(\frac{1}{\max d}\right)} \tag{9}$$

In formula (9), $\lambda_0$ represents the initial convergence factor; $\max d$ represents the maximum number of iterations; $e$ is the derivative. At the initial stage of the algorithm, with the increase of the number of iterations, the convergence factor presents a nonlinear trend of slow first and fast later. At this time, the convergence factor decreases slowly, which also indicates that the proportion of iteration $a > 1$ is large, and then the Ant colony optimization algorithms also has a strong global optimization capability, which can obtain an efficient resource matching effect.

Step 4: In order to achieve uniform sharing, it is necessary to introduce different sharing radii in the shared nodes to reduce the number of "hot zone" problems.The formula for calculating the shared radius is:

$$r = 1 - \frac{W_0 - W'}{W_0} \cdot \frac{S_{\max} - S'}{S_{\max} - S_{\min}} \rho \tag{10}$$

In formula (10), $W', W_0$ represent the initial and current energy of the node respectively; $S'$ represents the distance between any two nodes; $S_{\min}, S_{\max}$ represent the nearest and farthest distance of any two nodes in all nodes respectively; $\rho$ indicates node density. The shared node uses the existing data to construct a new node, and takes it as the initial shared leader node. After the initial leader node is determined, broadcast the leader node message. The unselected leader node will no longer be in sleep state, and select the leader node with the lowest communication cost to complete the creation of the shared radius.

Step 5: Visually operate the resource database, extract the data of each resource to the general data center interface according to the data resource association database and the objectified circular sharing of ceramic art professors, visually load the circular integration data resource platform, combine the multi resource data into a tree like circular structure, and at the same time establish index mapping for each resource, establish resource sharing index for the platform, and complete resource sharing.

# 4 Experiment

## 4.1 Experimental Environment Setting

The simulation experiment is carried out with Cooja network simulator, which is carried out under Contiki operating system, uses the message authentication code generated by HMAC MDS algorithm, and authenticates the data source by combining tinyDTLS library. The topology used in the experiment is shown in Fig. 6.

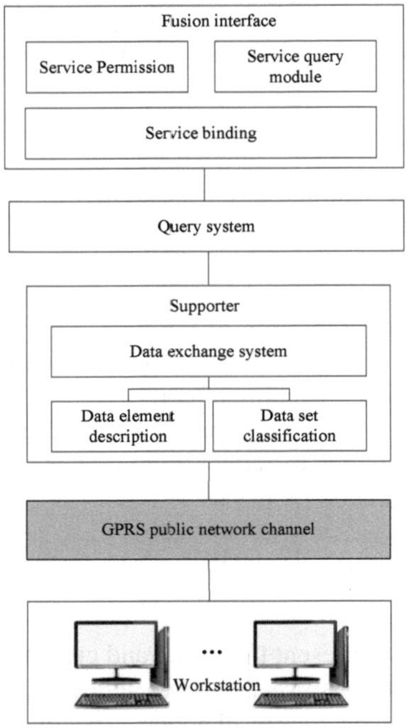


**Fig. 6.** Experimental Topology

During the experiment, the information delay is not taken into account. The previous trust value has the same importance as the newly generated trust value in the current trust value, so the weight factor is set to 0.5. In order to comprehensively evaluate the overall trust value of the node, without the wrong judgment caused by the high proportion of direct experience value, the decline of the overall trust value of the normal node caused by the misinformation of messages can be ignored during the simulation.

### 4.2 Source of Experimental Data

The application function in ceramic modeling design teaching is realized under the support of various software, mainly including 3ds max, Unity, After Effect and other software, which plays an important role in the setting of virtual scenes in ceramic modeling design teaching. 3ds max software is used in advertising production, film and television production, industrial design and other fields. It is based on 3D software, applied to ceramic modeling design, and made ceramic models with the use of modeling tools. You can also set simulated real lights to render decorative graphics for 3D ceramic modeling. Unity software can create 3D video games, realize 3D animation and other multiple interactive functions. Teachers can use this software to release ceramic teaching courseware to various platforms, which is convenient for students to learn. After Effect software is an important tool for making dynamic images. Teachers can produce post synthesis effects when they apply it to ceramic modeling design teaching. The use of ZBrush software can increase the depth, material, lighting and other special effects of ceramic modeling design pixels. To sum up, in 2D and 3D, we can see the functions of digital media software, which fully meets the teaching requirements of teachers in the production of digital interactive ceramic modeling design courses, realizes the simplification of courses, and solves the difficulties of traditional digital interactive ceramic modeling design. It improves the effect of teaching and learning.

Resources are divided into three categories, as shown in Fig. 7.

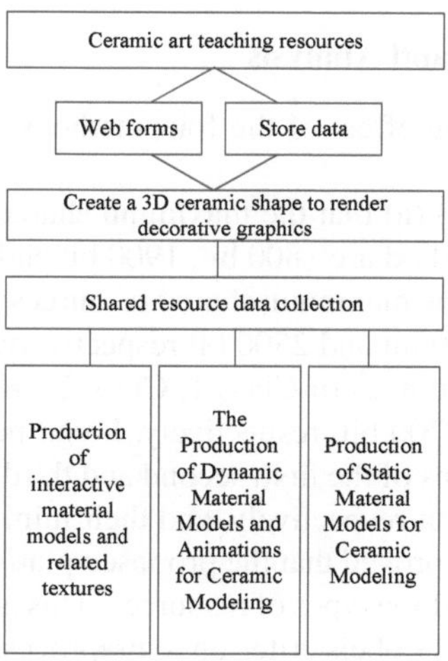


**Fig. 7.** Experimental Resources

The experimental resources are divided into the following three categories:

Class I: production of interactive material models and related maps. The application of digital interactive technology in ceramic modeling design requires that ceramic models can be observed from multiple angles. To meet the demand of multi angle observation, the real-time rendering model is mainly made by 3dmax, and maps of relevant models are made with the help of photoshop. In the 3dmax software, the model is made according to the porcelain picture that needs to be made.In the demonstration process of ceramic modeling design under digital interaction technology, only one 3D model can be displayed and interacted at the same time, and the number of faces of the model is limited to about 10000. After that, the ceramic modeling map is designed according to the digital interaction technology.

Class II: the production of ceramic modeling dynamic material model and its animation. The production of ceramic modeling dynamic material model aims to enhance the atmosphere of the page. Most of the time, this dynamic material is located at the bottom of the page, so you only need to make simple model maps.

Class III: Production of static material model of ceramic modeling. Ceramic modeling static materials mainly refer to various pictures. In order to save memory, these pictures need to be sorted into a large picture. When a picture is needed, read out the required part from the large picture. Through text information retrieval in the engine, unnecessary consumption caused by heavy reading can be avoided.

In this study, these three types of resources were extracted as data samples, and their memory size was 80 GB, which was carried out in the experimental environment designed in 4.1. Heterogeneous data fusion algorithm based on BP neural network, heterogeneous data sharing algorithm based on double neural network and fusion method based on privacy protection were selected as comparison methods to carry out comparative experiments, and the practicability of the proposed methods was verified by comparing the sharing effects.

### 4.3 Experimental Results and Analysis

Compare the resource sharing effect of the four methods. The comparison results are shown in Fig. 8.

It can be seen from Fig. 8 (a) that the maximum shared resources of Class I, Class II and Class III using this method are 1800 bit, 1900 bit and 1700 bit respectively; from Fig. 8 (a), it can be seen that the maximum shared resources of Class I, Class II and Class III using this method are 3100 bit and 2500 bit respectively. As can be seen from Fig. 8 (c), the maximum shared resources of Class 1, Class 2, and Class 3 using this method are 3500 bit, 3500 bit, and 3700 bit, respectively. It can be seen from Table 8 (d) that the maximum shared resources of the first, second and third levels using this method are 4500 bit, 4500 bit and 4500 bit respectively, and their minimum values are also greater than 4000 bit. Thus, it can be proved that the proposed platform for resource sharing has the best sharing effect for the three types of resources. This is mainly because on the basis of hardware design, it adopts Grobeis criterion to preprocess teacher-student interaction data to determine resource center and sharing center, so as to achieve a high degree of integration of teaching resources and thus improve the effect of resource sharing.

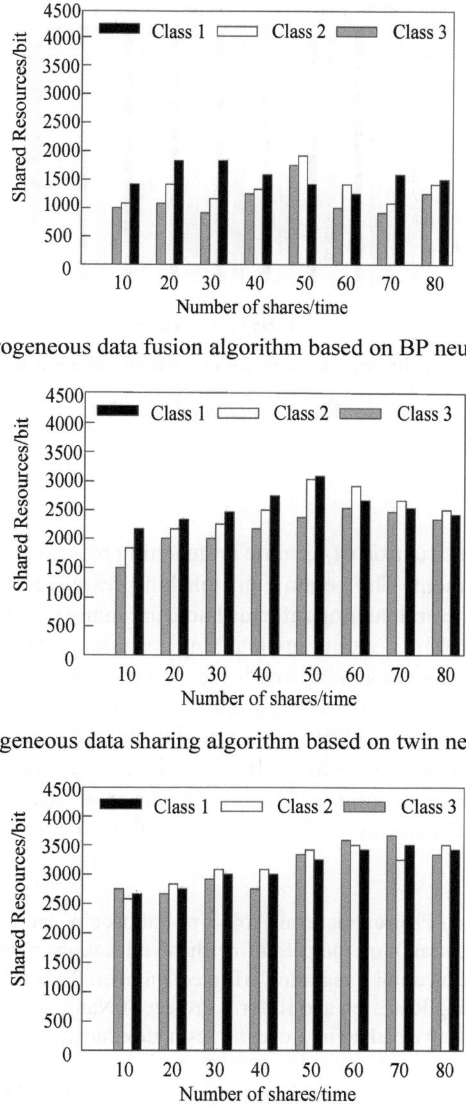


(a) Heterogeneous data fusion algorithm based on BP neural network



(b) Heterogeneous data sharing algorithm based on twin neural network



(c) Fusion method of privacy protection

**Fig. 8.** Comparison Results of Shared Resources by Different Methods

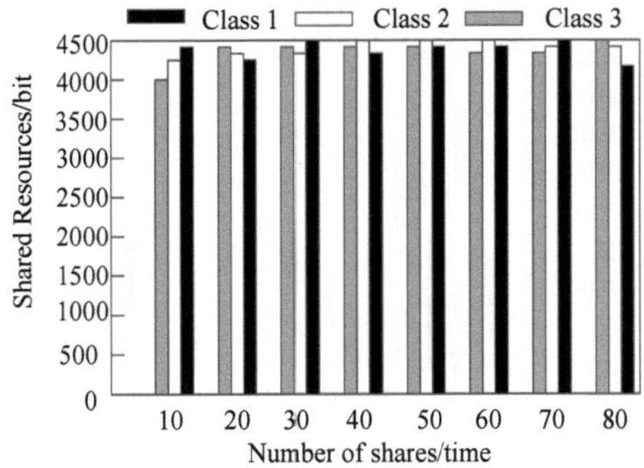


(d) Resource sharing platform for classroom behavior analysis

**Fig. 8.** (*continued*)

## 5 Conclusion

The informatization construction of ceramic art teaching resources is an inevitable trend of ceramic art development. The ceramic art teaching resource sharing platform is an important part of ceramic art teaching reform. There are many problems in the traditional resource sharing mode. The ceramic art teaching resource sharing platform designed based on classroom behavior analysis provides technical support. The experiment proves that this research platform can effectively improve the sharing efficiency.

The applied ceramic art teaching resource sharing platform based on classroom behavior analysis has produced positive effects in the application of ceramic modeling design, provided a new development direction for ceramic design teaching, improved the technical content of ceramic design, and strengthened the application of various high-tech.

**Acknowledgements.** Fund Project: General Project of Philosophy and Social Science Research in universities in 2023: Research on the path of aesthetic education in normal universities from the perspective of "Five Education Integration" (Project number: 2023SJYB0573);

Education and Teaching Research and Reform Project of Nanjing Xiaozhuang University in 2023: Research on the effective path to improve the aesthetic education quality of college students in the new era;

Nanjing Xiaozhuang University 2023 Ideological and Political Work thematic research project: Research on the Teaching Reform of Ideological and Political Education in Aesthetic Education Course, (Project number: 2023SZKT14).

## References

1. Zhiwei, W., Li, W., Guanwen, H., et al.: Research on multi-source heterogeneous data fusion algorithm of landslide monitoring based on BP neural network. J. Geomech. **26**(04), 575–582 (2020)

2. Xiong, L., Xinze, H., Chaoliang, W., et al.: A deep heterogeneous network embedding algorithm based on twin neural network. Telecommun. Eng. **60**(11), 1271–1277 (2020)
3. Long, H., Zhang, S.K., Zhang, L.: Data fusion method based on privacy preserving in crowd sensing network. Comput. Eng. Des. **41**(12), 3346–3352 (2020)
4. Shibayama, S., Lawson, C.: The use of rewards in the sharing of research resources. Res. Policy **50**(7), 19 (2021)
5. Tucker, B.V., Kelley, M.C., Redmon, C.: A place to share teaching resources: speech and language resource bank. J. Acoust. Soc. Am.Acoust. Soc. Am. **149**(4), A147–A147 (2021)
6. Xiang, J.: Evaluation of the college English flipped classroom teaching model based on data mining algorithms. Mob. Inf. Syst., 1–10 (2021)
7. Li, G., Liu, F., Wang, Y., et al.: A convolutional neural network (CNN) based approach for the recognition and evaluation of classroom teaching behavior. Sci. Programm. **2021**(pt.9), 1–8 (2021)
8. Lu, Y., Lizhi, W.: Construction of multimedia assisted legal classroom teaching model based on data mining algorithm. Sci. Programm. **2021** (Pt.14), 1–11 (2021)
9. Tedre, M., Toivonen, T., Vartiainen, H., et al.: Teaching machine learning in K–12 classroom: pedagogical and technological trajectories for artificial intelligence education. IEEE Access **9**, 110558–110572 (2021)
10. Li, X., Zhou, Y., He, Y., et al.: The fusion of eye movement and piezoelectric sensing technology assists ceramic art process optimization and mechanical characterization. J. Sens. **2021**(Pt.11), 1–11 (2021)

# Research on Online Education System for College English Majors Based on Cloud Computing

Meizhi Wu(✉)

School of Foreign Languages, Sichuan University Jinjiang College, Meishan 620010, China
wzm202303@163.com

**Abstract.** A new cloud computing based online education system for English major teaching in universities is proposed to address the issues of poor system usage and resource storage efficiency in online education systems. The system is based on cloud computing to construct the overall architecture of the system. The functions of each layer of the online education system are designed based on the overall structure. A low redundancy data storage algorithm based on data dependency is introduced to store system resource data. Combined with the CP-ABE encryption algorithm, the system is designed to share and improve the security performance of system resources, achieving research on online education systems for English majors in universities. The experimental results show that the system has a very satisfactory usage effect with a proportion of over 65.0%. The proportion of abnormal data stored in system resources is only 0.3%, and the probability of abnormal modification of resource data is less than 0.4% under all three conditions. This verifies that the system has higher system usage efficiency, resource storage efficiency, and resource data encryption effect. The CPU ratio of the system is studied to reduce the ratio and improve the operation effect of the system in the follow-up research work to further improve the performance of the system.

**Keywords:** Teaching English Majors in Universities · Online Education System · Cloud Computing · CP-ABE Encryption Algorithm

## 1 Introduction

The learning mode carried out under the information technology environment is constantly changing with the rapid development of computer technology and network technology. Every new technology can bring new learning methods and learning experience to the field of education. From computer-aided instruction to distance education, and then to computer network education are all the same [1, 2]. Cloud computing [3, 4] in this process, a concept proposed by Google for commercial use, it is another new computing mode after parallel computing, distributed computing and grid computing. The virtualization technology provided by cloud computing can solve the shortage of online learning resources and integrate the most abundant educational resources for


G. Gui et al. (Eds.): eLEOT 2023, LNICST 543, pp. 316–334, 2024.
https://doi.org/10.1007/978-3-031-51465-4_21

online learning. Online teaching and learning under various "cloud education services" provided by cloud computing can greatly reduce the configuration requirements for mobile terminal devices. Therefore, with the development of cloud computing, online education can break through the bottleneck, usher in new development space, and form a new online education model - based on cloud computing online education model. This education model is mainly based on the education system of cloud computing. However, there are certain limitations in this education system at the present stage. For example, abnormal data in the resource data stored in the system accounts for a high proportion, leading to the unavailability of some resource data and the high probability of abnormal modification of resource data, which indicates that the encryption effect of resource data is not good and the system has security problems.

Relevant scholars have devoted themselves to in-depth research on this issue. Reference [5] studied a continuous water cycle ecological impact and remote English education system based on sequence matching. The system analyzed generation rules, designed an interface that can provide a free form, and had dynamic feedback function. Using the cognitive counseling creation tool developed by Carnegie Mellon University, an online tutoring system based on production rules was designed, Implement the design of the education system, but the system has poor performance in the actual use process. Reference [6] studied a constant water cycle ecological impact and remote English education system based on sequence matching. The system introduced JavaBean components and designed the system's software architecture. This paper analyzed the nonlinear model of water cycle ecology, combined it with English, and designed a remote English teaching system. The system shortened the development cycle and simplified system maintenance measures, but its resource storage effect was poor, Mainly due to the high proportion of abnormal data stored in system resources. Reference [7] studied a virtual reality action interactive teaching artificial intelligence education system. This study utilized VR technology to develop a human-machine interactive teaching process design for learning scenarios, introducing 3D modeling technology, model building, image and text panel production, video material production, and virtual guided 3D scene establishment. The principle is to use 3DMAX and Unity 3D engines to build 3D vision, construct 3D views for educational needs, and design high-quality images and video animations. Then, we introduced the use of VR glasses, smartphones, and Bluetooth wireless controllers to build a simple interactive teaching platform. The virtual reality action interaction effect of this system is good, but its resource data has a high probability of abnormal modification, which poses a threat to system security.

Aiming at the problems of the above methods, this paper studies a new online education system for college English major teaching based on cloud computing. Cloud computing is introduced into the system. The overall system architecture is built and the system functions are designed based on cloud computing technology. The system logic algorithm is designed to realize the functions of the online education system for college English major teaching according to the system architecture of cloud computing.

## 2 Online Education System Based on Cloud Computing Technology

### 2.1 Overall System Architecture Based on Cloud Computing Technology

The construction of online education system for college English major teaching based on cloud computing is to make up for the shortcomings of the current online learning mode, maximize the integration of rich learning resources, maximize the utilization of resources, and eliminate the information silo phenomenon as far as possible to improve the learning efficiency of learners. Therefore, the design of an online education model based on cloud computing is shown in Fig. 1.

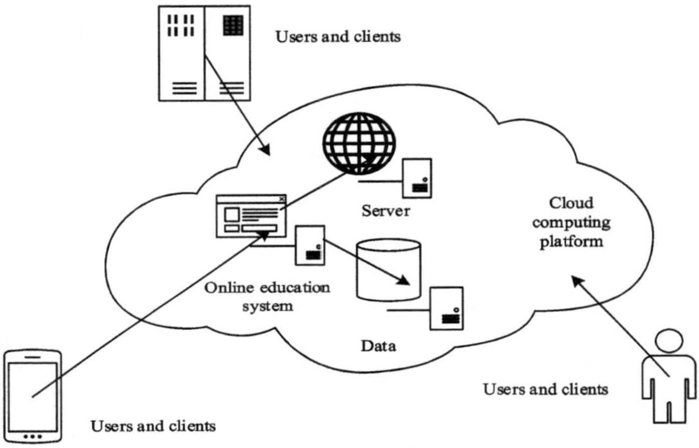


**Fig. 1.** Online Education Mode Based on Cloud Computing

According to Fig. 1, the realization of the online education department of English major teaching in colleges is based on the cloud platform of cloud computing [8]. In the online education mode based on cloud computing, education units no longer independently develop education systems, but enter the cloud service platform through interconnection. They can realize uninterrupted access at any time and place by using the cloud computing services provided by the cloud service platform, and share bandwidth and education resources with other users in the cloud platform. Cloud computing mainly provides infrastructure services, including storage, servers, and network devices. It can manage infrastructure in a unified manner and provide powerful computing power, data storage space, and network communication resources. End users through a unified user interface for online education in the cloud computing teaching system. At the same time, the online education resources of college English major teaching are stored in the cloud, and the cloud computing platform provider is responsible for the security of the resources. College education no longer needs to feel anxious about the inaccessible resources caused by the server failure. Based on this, with the functional needs of students and teachers as the core, the overall architecture of online education system for college English major teaching based on cloud computing technology is designed, as shown in Fig. 2.

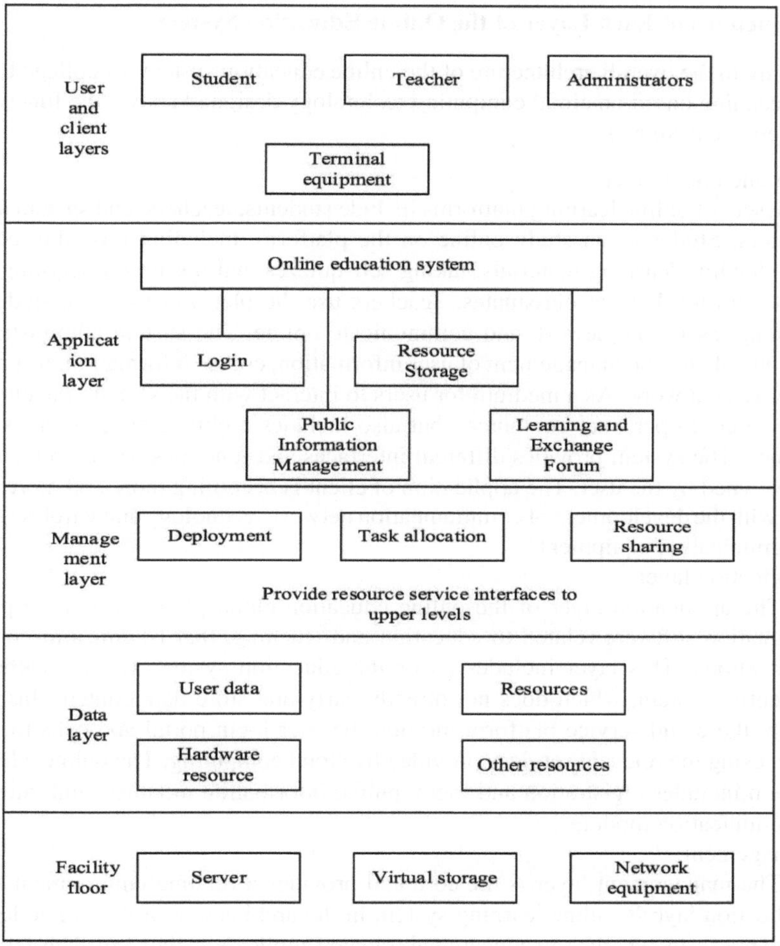


**Fig. 2.** Overall architecture of online education system for English major teaching in universities based on cloud computing technology

The overall architecture of the online education system for English major teaching in universities based on cloud computing technology is divided into five layers according to Fig. 2, namely user and client layers, application layers, management layers, data layers, and facility layers. The user and client layers are the consumers in the cloud computing system, while the application layer, management layer, data layer, and facility layer are the supporters and providers of cloud computing. The specific functions of each layer are as follows.

## 2.2 Functions of Each Layer of the Online Education System

According to the overall architecture of the online education system for college English major teaching based on cloud computing technology designed above, the functions of five layers are designed.

1) User and client layer

   Users of online learning platforms include students, teachers, and system administrators. Students can study online on the platform, including browsing courses, downloading learning materials, taking self-quizzes and discussing learning problems with teachers or classmates. Teachers use the platform to guide students in learning, assign homework and communicate online. The system administrator is responsible for the management of user information, course information, forums and other related work. As a medium for users to interact with the system, the client not only refers to personal computers, but also includes mobile devices such as smart phones. The system provides different interfaces and functions based on the device type owned by the user. The application of client is becoming more and more extensive with the development of communication network technology and wireless mobile communication equipment.

2) Application layer

   The application layer of the online education cloud platform aims to provide application software related to education and teaching, that is, education oriented applications. This layer includes an online education system as the backbone of the entire system, which does not directly carry and store data content. Instead, it enters the cloud service platform through the user login portal and calls the interface, using the relevant services provided by cloud computing. The online education system includes registration and login, public information modules, and interactive communication modules.

3) Management

   The management layer is the core and provides a running environment for the application layer's online learning system in the architecture of the online learning cloud platform, which is an educational oriented application platform. This layer represents the platform or service layer of cloud computing, using third-party application platforms launched by the system and deployed on a unified infrastructure. Users do not need to worry about the reliability, performance, and security of the platform, as its operation is monitored and maintained by service providers. The platform implements a load balancing mechanism internally in addition, which can automatically distribute a large number of request tasks to idle application servers for processing. This layer provides various services, data persistence storage mechanism and necessary management control functions for user applications, which are mainly realized by providing programming interfaces. The user, resource, and other data in the online education system are managed, shared, and interacted with by the components of this layer through interfaces.

4) Data layer

   It as the core of the architecture, the data layer is responsible for storing all types of data, both structured and unstructured. The core and foundation of online education system is the construction of educational resources. However, educational resources cannot be fully utilized under the condition that each online education platform operates independently. Unified resource pool for users to share to solve this problem, data storage services in cloud computing consolidate resources into a common. The data storage service of cloud computing is provided by a cluster of one million servers. The storage space can be dynamically expanded as required without worrying about the capacity. The data layer stores two types of data: structured data and unstructured data.

5) Facility layer

It as the foundation layer of the entire architecture, the infrastructure layer corresponds to the infrastructure as a service in the cloud computing service layer, which determines the service scope and service capabilities of online education systems. The infrastructure layer provides users with hardware resources such as servers, storage space, and network devices, which are virtualized through virtualization technology, namely server virtualization, storage virtualization, and network virtualization. This method can generate multiple virtual machines on a physical server and achieve comprehensive isolation between multiple virtual machines, virtualizing storage resources into a "storage pool", consolidating many scattered storage resources, and improving overall utilization. Computer cluster technology virtualizes a unified cloud computing service platform through unified scheduling management. Its powerful computing power and massive storage space just meet the growing number of online learning users, the growing demand for educational resources and the purpose of hardware resource sharing. By using the infrastructure provided by cloud computing, educational institutions do not need to consider issues such as servers and storage space, and it can focus on the development and services of online learning platforms.

Wireless communication network is used to complete the communication in the online education system architecture based on cloud computing. The mobile learning system is used by learners to communicate through WIFI or 4G/5G network [9], which can be the private network of some specialized organizations or the 4G/5G service provided by network operators.

## 3 System Logic Algorithms Based on Cloud Computing Technology

After completing the architecture design of the online education system for English major teaching in universities based on cloud computing, the system logic algorithm of cloud computing technology is designed to achieve the system's functions based on the system of cloud computing technology. The low redundancy data storage algorithm based on data dependency and CP-ABE encryption algorithm [10] are introduced in this part. The online education system can store and share educational resources through the combination of algorithms and the complete system logic algorithm design, so that the system has application performance.

Firstly, the system designed in this article stores online education digital resource data for English major teaching in universities, making it easy for teachers, students, and management personnel to use teaching digital resources during the teaching process. A low redundancy data storage algorithm based on data dependency was introduced in the process of data storage design, and the structure of the algorithm is shown in Fig. 3.

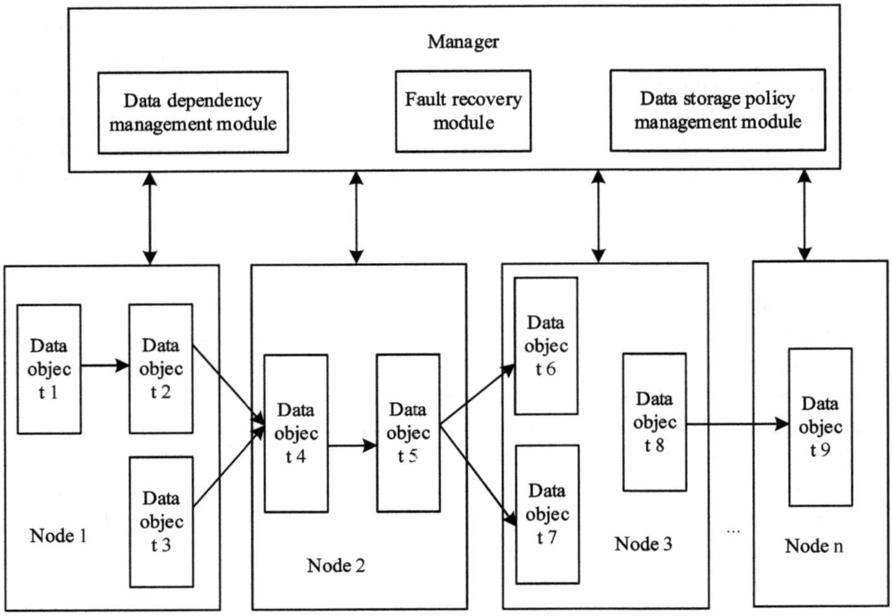


**Fig. 3.** Low redundancy data storage algorithm structure based on data dependency relationships

The low redundancy data storage algorithm based on data dependency mainly consists of three modules according to Fig. 3, which are data dependency management module, fault recovery module and data storage policy management module. Among them, the data dependency management module records the dependency relationship between resource data in the school education system. According to Fig. 3, $x_1, x_2, \cdots, x_n$ data object of educational digital resources is constructed in this module. The data object is set as A and the dependency relationship of the data object is designed.

$$x_k = \overline{x_i x_j}, k > j > i \tag{1}$$

where, $x_i, x_j$ represents the data object, belonging to $x_1, x_2, \cdots, x_n$ mentioned above, $\overline{x_i x_j}$ represents the directed edge, and $x_k$ represents the generated data. According to formula (1), only when the data object $x_i, x_j$ points to $x_k$ and $x_i, x_j$ is ready can $x_k$ be generated.

After determining the dependency relationship of digital resource data in the online education system for English major teaching in universities, abnormal data is recovered through a fault recovery module to avoid unavailability when teachers or students use resource data. Build the data generated through dependency relationships into a dataset, with the formula:

$$X = \{x_1, x_2, \cdots, x_i, x_j, x_k, \cdots, x_n\} \tag{2}$$

After determining the abnormality of digital resource data, the required data objects are found in the educational resource data set, and the resource data is re-generated by combining the generation operator. The formula is as follows:

$$x_k' = \alpha_k x_k, x_k \in X \tag{3}$$

where, $\alpha_k$ represents the generation operator. Reply to abnormal resource data through formula (3) to provide the system with usable data.

After the complete system resource data is recovered, the resource data storage policy is designed in the data storage policy management module, and the formula is:

$$x_k'' = \begin{cases} b_k(x_k, x_k'), 0 \le b_k \le 3 \\ 4, \text{Use the (10,14) erasure code store policy} \end{cases} \tag{4}$$

where, $b_k$ represents the number of copies of the data object.

Considering the resource data storage overhead of online education system for college English major teaching, the overall storage overhead of online education system is first determined in order to reduce the storage overhead and optimize the overall overhead of resource data storage, and the formula is as follows:

$$d(t) = \sum_{k=1}^{n} \{d_i(t) + (1 - \beta_i(x_k'')e_k d_k(x_k''))\} \tag{5}$$

where, $d_i(t)$ represents the storage cost of recovering faulty resource data, $\beta_i(x_k'')$ represents the availability coefficient of resource data, $e_k$ represents the storage cost factor of system resource data, and $d_k(x_k'')$ represents the storage cost of system resource data $x_k''$. The overall system storage cost for optimizing formula (5) is as follows:

$$F(t) = \min \sum_{k=1}^{n} d(x_k'', t) \tag{6}$$

Formula (4) and formula (6) are combined to obtain the final storage strategy. The formula is:

$$\begin{aligned} & x_k'' = \begin{cases} b_k(x_k, x_k'), 0 \le b_k \le 3 \\ 4, \text{Use the (10,14) erasure code store policy} \end{cases} \\ & s.t\ F(t) = \min \sum_{k=1}^{n} d(x_k'', t) \end{aligned} \tag{7}$$

where, the (10, 14) erasure code store policy is by storing redundant blocks together with the original data blocks, which can be recovered in case of data loss, and 4 means that there are 4 additional redundant blocks for fault tolerance, $d(x_k'', t)$ Indicates the storage cost of system resource data $x_k''$ at time $t$.

After completing the storage of digital resource data in the online education system for English major teaching in universities based on cloud computing, design a sharing algorithm for storing resource data, link the storage and sharing of system resource data, and achieve system functions. The system sharing considers the security of educational resource data and adopts CP-ABE encryption algorithm to achieve resource data sharing.

First, select a bilinear group $G$, the generator is $g$, the order of the group is a prime number $L$, and randomly select $\chi, \delta$, both of which belong to the addition group $G'$, and then generate the public key and master key of the online education system for English majors in colleges and universities. The formula is:

$$\begin{aligned} M &= G, g, o, p, q \\ M' &= (\delta, g^{\chi}) \end{aligned} \tag{8}$$

Among them,

$$\begin{aligned} o &= g^{\delta} \\ p &= g^{\frac{1}{\delta}} \\ q &= (g, g)^{\chi} \end{aligned} \tag{9}$$

where, $M$ represents the public key of the education system, and $M'$ represents the master key of the education system.

After the public key and master key of the system are designed, the shared access control tree is designed, and the threshold of the node of the shared access control tree is set as $J_k$, then the access control is:

$$H = J(x_k''), J(x_k'') = J_k = 1 \tag{10}$$

Among them,

$$0 \le J_k \le n \tag{11}$$

where, $J(x_k'')$ represents the node polynomial of data $x_k''$ on the access control tree.

Connect formula (8) and formula (10) to generate ciphertext for online education system, with the formula:

$$M'' = (H, \widetilde{R}, R, R') \tag{12}$$

Among them,

$$\begin{aligned} \widetilde{R} &= Sq \\ R &= H(0) \\ R' &= H(att(x_k'')) \end{aligned} \tag{13}$$

where, $S$ represents the ciphertext of the education system.

To calculate the attribute private key of an online education system user, the formula is:

$$T = g^{\frac{\chi+\varepsilon}{\delta}} + g^{\varepsilon} H \tag{14}$$

where, $\varepsilon$ represents an element in the additive group $G'$.

After determining the user's attribute private key, recursively calculate the system resource data using the formula:

$$Derypt(M'', M, T, k) = e(g, g)^{\varepsilon H(0)} \tag{15}$$

where, $e(\cdot)$ represents a recursive function.

Through recursive calculation, the final ciphertext $S$ is obtained, and the formula is as follows:

$$S = \frac{\widetilde{R} \cdot Derypt(M'', M, T, k)}{e(R, M')} \tag{16}$$

Resource access under system resource data sharing can be achieved by using the ciphertext obtained above, achieving the purpose of system interaction. So far, the logical algorithm design of the online education system for English major teaching in universities based on cloud computing has been completed, and the system functions have been implemented.

# 4 Experimental Analysis

## 4.1 Experimental Scheme

The application performance of the system in actual online teaching is analyzed in order to verify the effectiveness of the cloud-based online teaching system for college English majors designed in this paper. Therefore, the comparative analysis experiment is designed. The specific scheme is as follows:

1. Before starting the experimental analysis, it is necessary to prepare the experimental environment to lay a foundation for verifying the method designed in this paper. The experimental preparation provides the online course information, system interface, and experimental equipment configuration.
2. Before analyzing the system performance, it is necessary to test the basic performance of the system designed in this paper to ensure the normal operation of the system and avoid affecting the experimental results due to the abnormal operation of the system.
3. After completing the system test, set the experimental parameters to ensure that the parameter settings are reasonable and scientific.
4. Set experimental conditions. In this step, considering that the number of concurrent online users may affect the system performance, set three experimental conditions about the number of concurrent online users. The experimental analysis was carried out under this condition.
5. Result analysis: After the preliminary preparation, the reference [6] method and the reference [7] method are used as comparison methods, compared with the method in this paper, and the effectiveness of system use, resource storage and resource data encryption are taken as evaluation indicators.

## 4.2 Experimental Environment

It is necessary to prepare for the experiment before the experiment starts. The object of the experiment is the online English major teaching course of a university. The system resource information for the course is shown in Table 1.

The online education system for college English majors designed according to the method in this paper is shown in Fig. 4.

The experimental configuration is shown in Table 2.

Prepare the experiment according to the above content.

**Table 1.** Online Course Information

| Serial Number | Name | Content |
|---|---|---|
| 1 | System course resource data volume | 50G |
| 2 | Resource data type | Electronic documents, videos, images, audio files |
| 3 | Number of course chapters | Chapter 12 |
| 4 | Course arrangement | Two classes per week in the afternoon |

### 4.3 Experimental System Testing

It is also necessary to ensure the normal operation of the designed online education system for college English major teaching based on cloud computing to avoid inaccurate experimental analysis results due to system problems before starting the experimental analysis. Therefore, targeted tests are conducted on the online education system, and the test results are shown in Table 3.

It can be seen that all functions of the system designed in this paper can be used independently and run normally according to the test results of the online education system in Table 3, and the system can run normally when multitasking is concurrent. Therefore, the system meets the basic application conditions, has the application performance and can be verified and analyzed.

### 4.4 Experimental Parameter Settings

Set experimental parameters to avoid different numerical values that may affect the experimental results. The specific settings of experimental parameters are shown in Table 4.

Set the experimental parameters according to the values in Table 4, complete the preliminary work of the experiment, and start the experimental analysis.

### 4.5 Experimental Conditions

Considering the different effects of the number of concurrent online users on the performance of the cloud-based online education system for college English major teaching, three experimental conditions were set and the experimental analysis was carried out under the three experimental conditions. The specific experimental conditions are shown as follows:

Condition 1: The number of concurrent online users of the online education system is 200;

Condition 2: The number of concurrent online users of the online education system is 400;

Condition 3: The number of concurrent online users of the online education system is 600.

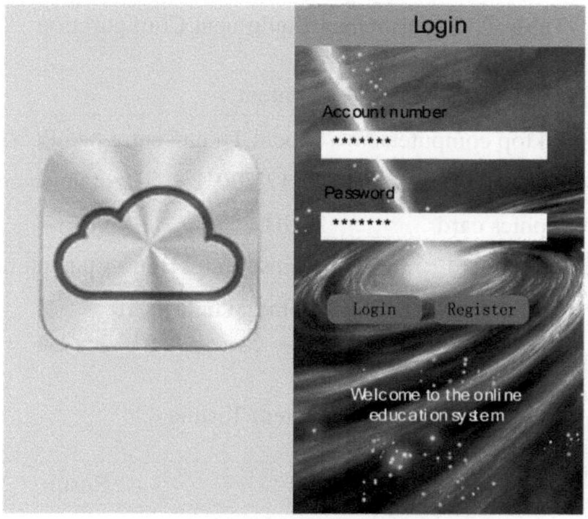


(a) System login interface

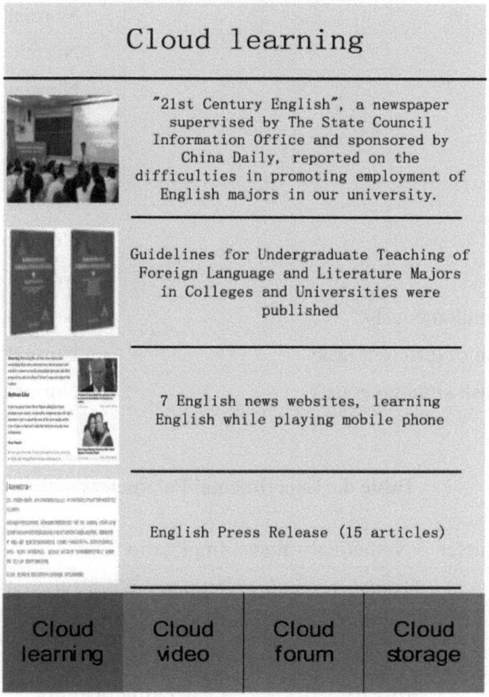


(b) Internal interface of online education system

**Fig. 4.** System Interface

Based on the above three experimental conditions, the system in this paper, the reference [6] method and the reference [7] method are compared to analyze the effect of system use, resource storage and resource data encryption.

**Table 2.** Experimental Equipment Configuration

| Serial Number | Name | Content |
|---|---|---|
| 1 | Desktop computer | Model ThinkCentre neo P600 |
| 2 | CPU | I7-12,700, 2.1 GHz, twelve core |
| 3 | Graphics card | 6 GB |
| 4 | Motherboard | Chipset Intel B660, standalone graphics card |
| 5 | Operating system | 64 bit, Windows 10 |

**Table 3.** System Testing

| Function | Result |
|---|---|
| Register | Normal |
| Land | Normal |
| Cloud learning | Normal |
| Cloud Video | Normal |
| Cloud Forum | Normal |
| Cloud storage | Normal |
| Cloud sharing | Normal |
| Cloud access | Normal |
| Single-user access | Normal |
| 500 users accessing simultaneously | Normal |
| Simultaneous execution of different tasks | Normal |
| Performing the same task simultaneously | Normal |

**Table 4.** Experimental Parameters

| Serial Number | Parameter | Numerical value | Implication |
|---|---|---|---|
| 1 | $n$ | 1000 | Number of educational digital resource data objects |
| 2 | $k$ | $\leq$1000 | The $k$-TH of the generated data |
| 3 | $\alpha_k$ | (0,1.0) | Generating operator |
| 4 | $e_k$ | [0,0.874] | System resource data store cost factor |
| 5 | $L$ | 11 | The order of the group, which is a prime number |

### 4.6 Result Analysis

#### 4.6.1 Analysis of System Usage Effectiveness

Firstly, analyze the effectiveness of the online education system for English major teaching in universities based on cloud computing, which includes resource data storage, resource data sharing, interaction, cloud learning, cloud video, cloud forum, and cloud access. Due to the differences in the functions of different literature systems and the lack of comparability, the analysis of this system ensures a certain degree of reliability in the experimental analysis by increasing the number of users participating in the use of the system. The number of users participating in the system usage is 500, and the experimental results of the system usage effect are shown in Fig. 5.

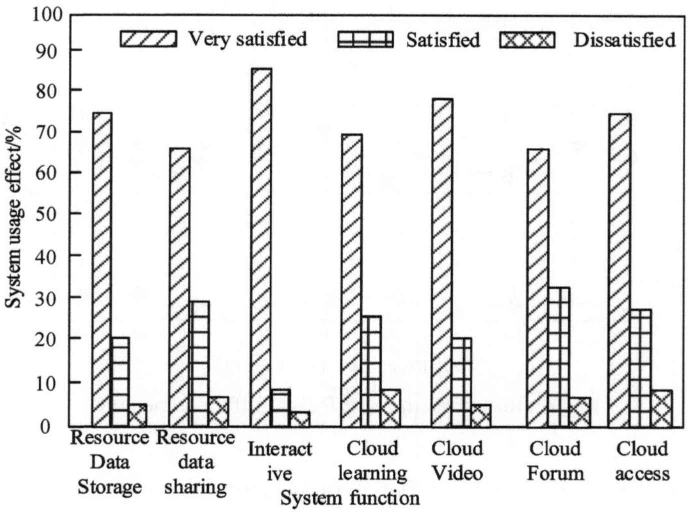


**Fig. 5.** System Usage Effect

The system usage effect in Fig. 5 is the percentage of very satisfied, satisfied, and dissatisfied users. An analysis of the system use effect data in Fig. 5 shows that the users of the cloud-based online education system for college English major teaching designed in this paper give a very satisfied proportion of over 65.0% for different functions of the system, and the users who are satisfied with the system use effect are less than 10.0% for the interactive function in addition to 3. While the functions of other systems are above 20.0%, and the proportion of interactive functions is low, because the users of this system are very satisfied with 86.2% of the interactive functions. By analyzing the dissatisfaction of system users, it can be seen that the proportion is only 8.3% at the highest level and 3.7% at the lowest level, indicating that most users after the system designed in this paper, The use effect of the homosensory system is good, which verifies that the use effect of the system in this paper has been recognized and has a certain feasibility and effectiveness.

### 4.6.2 Analysis of Resource Storage Effectiveness

The performance of the system in the storage of educational resource data is further analyzed on the basis of the above experiments. The effect of resource storage is reflected by the proportion of abnormal data in resource storage. The lower the proportion of abnormal data, the better the effect of resource storage is. Process of experimental analysis The system of this paper is compared with the method of literature [6] and the method of literature [7], and the experimental results are shown in Fig. 6.

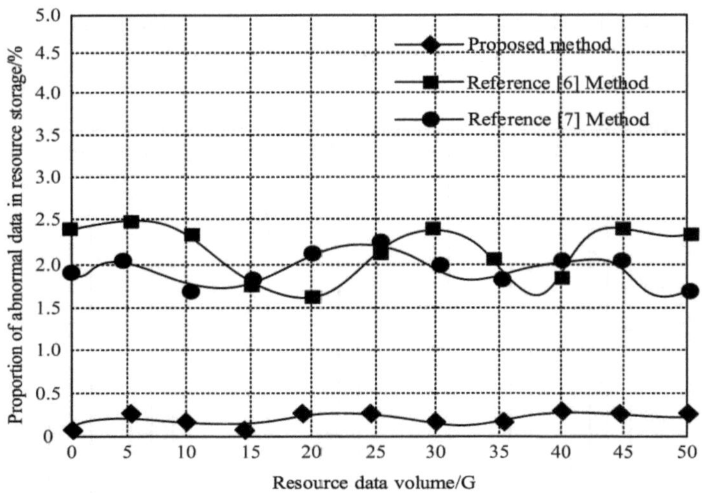


**Fig. 6.** Resource storage effects of different methods

Abnormal data accounts for less than 3.0% of storage resources in the three systems according to the effects of different storage methods in Fig. 6, meeting application requirements. However, among the three kinds of online education systems, the system designed in this paper has the lowest proportion of abnormal data in resource storage, and the highest value is only 0.3%. However, among the comparison systems, the abnormal data in literature [6] system and literature [7] system both account for about 2.0%, and the lowest proportion of abnormal data in the two systems is only 1.6% and 1.7%. In this paper, the proportion of abnormal data in resource storage is reduced by more than 1.3%. Therefore, it can be seen that the proportion of abnormal data in resource storage in this system is the lowest. The experimental results verify that the system in this paper has better resource storage effect.

### 4.6.3 Analysis of Resource Data Encryption Effect

The probability of resource data being abnormally modified is used to reflect the effect of resource data encryption in order to further analyze the performance of the system and the effect of resource data encryption in this paper. The lower the probability of resource data being abnormally modified, the better the effect of system resource data encryption is. The expected target is that the probability of resource data being abnormally modified is less than 1.0%. The effect of resource data encryption of the three methods under three experimental conditions is analyzed, and the experimental results are shown in Fig. 7.

According to the data in Fig. 7, different systems have different effects of resource encryption under the three conditions, and with the increase in the number of concurrent online users, the probability of resource data being abnormally modified in the literature system has increased, while the probability of resource data being abnormally modified in the system in this paper has not increased, and the numerical curve has been lower than 0.4%. However, the probability of resource data being abnormally modified in the literature [6] system and the literature [7] system is above 0.7%, and the maximum probability of resource data being abnormally modified in the two systems is over 1.0%. Therefore, the resource encryption effect of the literature system can meet the application requirements when the number of concurrent online users is small. However, when there is a large number of online users at the same time, the literature system does not meet the requirements, while the paper system does.

### 4.6.4 Effect Analysis of Resource Sharing

After analyzing the resource encryption effect of different systems, the resource sharing effect of the system designed in this paper is analyzed, and the resource sharing effect is reflected by the resource sharing rate. The higher the resource sharing rate, the better the resource sharing effect of the system is shown in Table 5.

According to the data in Table 5, the resource sharing effect of the three methods is above 95.0%. However, detailed analysis shows that when the resource sharing data reaches 50G, the resource sharing effect of this method is the highest, reaching 99.6%, while the resource sharing rate of reference [6] method is only 97.6%. The resource sharing rate of reference [7] method is 95.1%, and the resource sharing rate of the proposed method is all above 99.0%. Therefore, the comparison shows that the resource sharing rate of the proposed method is increased by more than 2.0%, and the experimental results fully demonstrate that the proposed method effectively improves the resource sharing effect.

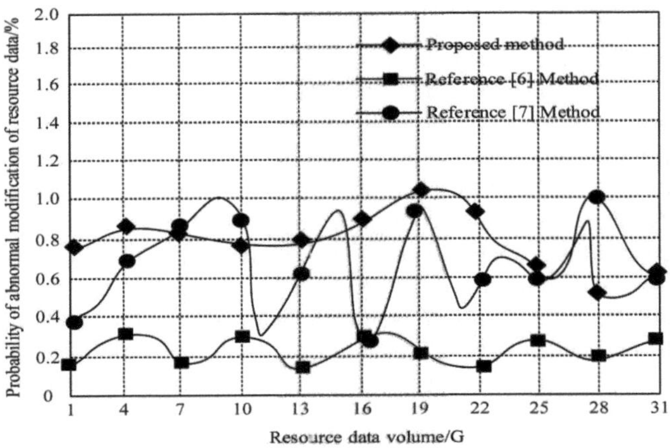


(a) Condition 1

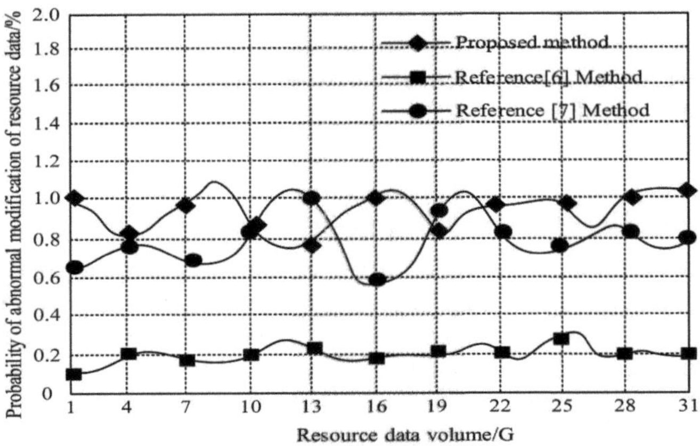


(b) Condition 2

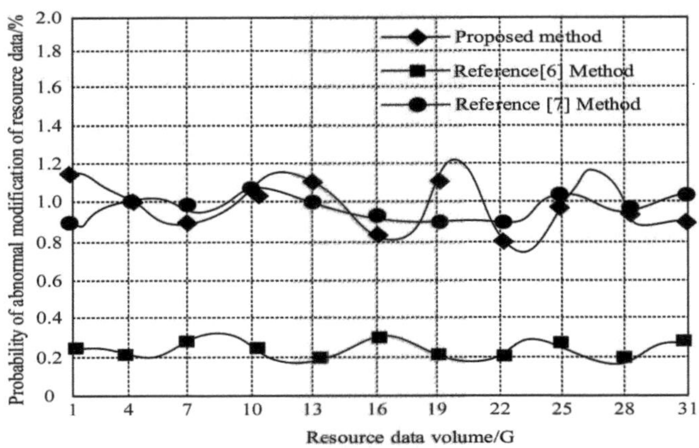


(c) Condition 3

**Fig. 7.** Resource encryption effects of different systems

**Table 5.** Resource Sharing Effect (%)

| Amount of resource data/G | Proposed method | Reference [6] method | Reference [7] method |
|---|---|---|---|
| 5 | 99.7 | 97.2 | 95.3 |
| 10 | 99.5 | 97.3 | 96.5 |
| 15 | 99.2 | 97.0 | 94.7 |
| 20 | 99.6 | 97.1 | 95.3 |
| 25 | 99.3 | 96.5 | 97.1 |
| 30 | 99.1 | 97.2 | 96.8 |
| 35 | 99.5 | 97.2 | 95.8 |
| 40 | 99.7 | 97.4 | 94.3 |
| 45 | 99.8 | 97.0 | 94.0 |
| 50 | 99.6 | 97.6 | 95.1 |

## 5 Conclusion

A new cloud computing based online education system for English major teaching in universities has been designed in order to improve the effectiveness of online education systems for English major teaching in universities and address issues such as poor storage of system resource data. The system introduces cloud computing. Based on cloud computing, the overall architecture of the system is designed, and the system functions are designed. Based on this, the low redundancy data storage algorithm based on data dependency and CP-ABE encryption algorithm are introduced. Through the combination of algorithms, the complete system logic algorithm design realizes the storage and sharing of educational resources in the online education system, so that the system has application performance. Finally, the performance of the designed system was verified through experiments. The experimental results showed that the system performed well, with a very satisfactory rate of over 65.0% and a satisfactory rate of over 20%. Additionally, the proportion of abnormal data stored in resources was reduced by over 1.3%, and the probability of abnormal modification of resource data was lower than 0.4%, which was 0.3% lower than other systems. Therefore, it can be concluded that the system has higher application performance. An in-depth study will be conducted on the CPU ratio of the online education system for English major teaching in colleges and universities in the follow-up work. The CPU ratio is an important indicator to measure the practical application effect. The lower the CPU ratio, the better the system performance will be.

## References


1. Haoran, Z., An, H.: Shanxi merchant economic history education system based on fuzzy control and quantum evolution algorithm. J. Intell. Fuzzy Syst. **9**(1), 1–10 (2021)
2. Busquets, P., Segalas, J., Gomera, A., et al.: Sustainability education in the Spanish higher education system: faculty practice, concerns and needs. Sustainability **13**(15), 1–14 (2021)

3. Fang, Q., Yan, S.: MCX Cloud—a modern, scalable, high-performance and in-browser Monte Carlo simulation platform with cloud computing. J. Biomed. Opt. **27**(8), 1083–1095 (2022)
4. Ayeh, M., Behrang, B., Mehdi, A.: LATOC: an enhanced load balancing algorithm based on hybrid AHP-TOPSIS and OPSO algorithms in cloud computing. J. Supercomput. **78**(4), 4882–4910 (2022)
5. King, E.C., Benson, M., Raysor, S., et al.: The open-response chemistry cognitive assistance tutor system: development and implementation. J. Chem. Educ. **99**(2), 546–552 (2022)
6. Zhang, X.: Constant water circulating ecological influence and remote English education system development based on sequence matching. Arab. J. Geosci. **14**(16), 1–11 (2021)
7. Jiang, L.: Virtual reality action interactive teaching artificial intelligence education system. Complexity **2021**(14), 1–11 (2021)
8. Eshratifar, A.E., Abrishami, M.S., Pedram, M.: JointDNN: an efficient training and inference engine for intelligent mobile cloud computing services. IEEE Trans. Mobile Comput. **20**(2), 565–576 (2021)
9. Li, G., Deng, J., Xin, S., et al.: A radio over fiber system compatible with 3G/4G/5G for full spectrum access and handover with multi-scenarios. J. Lightwave Technol. **39**(24), 7885–7893 (2021)
10. Sowjanya, K., Dasgupta, M., Ray, S.: A lightweight key management scheme for key-escrow-free ECC-based CP-ABE for IoT healthcare systems. J. Syst. Archit. **117**(2), 1383–1392 (2021)

# Construction of Music Intelligent Interactive Teaching System Based on J2EE Platform

Yu Xia[1](✉) and Zhiyan Zhang[2]

[1] School of Aviation Services and Music, Nanchang Hangkong University, Nanchang 330063, China
xylxm2022@njust.edu.cn

[2] Fine Arts of Nanjing Xiaozhuang University, Nanjing 211171, China

**Abstract.** In response to the problems of low data interaction efficiency, long system response time, and poor quality of music teaching in traditional teaching systems, this article proposes a study on building a music intelligent interactive teaching system based on the J2EE platform. Choose J2EE as the system development platform, analyze and explore its main service functions, allocate short addresses of each device reasonably, and complete the system network communication design. The use of ASP and ADO technology to achieve intelligent interaction of teaching data provides a foundation for achieving intelligent interactive teaching of music. Using genetic algorithm to intelligently generate test papers, complete the design of the music teaching exam module, and thus achieve the operation of the music intelligent interactive teaching system. The experimental data shows that after applying the designed system, the maximum interaction efficiency of teaching data reaches 188MB/s, the minimum response time of the system is 0.45 s, and the highest score for music teaching is 98 points, fully verifying the better application performance of the designed system.

**Keywords:** Music Teaching · Intelligent Teaching · Teaching System · Student Exercises · j2ee Platform · Interactive Teaching

## 1 Introduction

As a very important carrier of culture and art, music plays an increasingly important role in people's life and learning. With the progress of education and teaching system reform, cultivating students' overall quality has become the latest goal of teaching, which has gradually improved the status of music teaching in the teaching system. As an important part of cultivating students' quality education, music education in primary and secondary schools has attracted the attention of the educational community and the whole society. At the same time, teachers are required not only to impart basic knowledge and skills of music to improve students' cultural skills and knowledge, but also to guide and cultivate students. In the process of teaching according to the teaching plan, teachers should effectively use teaching means to give full play to students' independent learning and


G. Gui et al. (Eds.): eLEOT 2023, LNICST 543, pp. 335–349, 2024.
https://doi.org/10.1007/978-3-031-51465-4_22

exploration ability, become the main body of teaching activities, and cultivate students' good learning interest, create a positive learning atmosphere, let students actively learn and receive knowledge under the correct guidance of teachers, and through absorption and reengineering, systemize and organize knowledge, build their own learning system, cultivate students' core literacy, and achieve students' all-round development[1].

In recent years, the development of computer software technology has changed people's work and life patterns. In terms of teaching, people's way of acquiring knowledge is also changing significantly. The situation of a single mode of receiving traditional education in the classroom is changing. Especially in recent years, the breakthrough development of Internet technology has enriched and diversified the original online education model. People gradually accept the mode of completing various learning tasks through the network. With the continuous development and application of information technology, the field of education has gradually integrated the trend of intelligence and interactivity. As an important art discipline, music education also needs to keep up with the times and improve teaching effectiveness and learning experience through advanced technological means. The traditional music teaching method has problems such as limited teaching resources, insufficient interactivity, and high difficulty in personalized teaching, which cannot meet the diverse learning needs of students.

Reference [2] proposed an intelligent music classroom teaching system based on the Internet of Things. Using the theory of Internet of Things for reference, an intelligent music classroom teaching system is designed. The intelligent music classroom teaching system can analyze the characteristics of students and teaching content, and then push the appropriate content to students. Teachers can develop more flexible teaching strategies and more accurately evaluate students' performance. Reference [3] proposed a music classroom aided teaching system based on intelligent speech recognition. The auxiliary teaching system of music classroom supported by intelligent speech recognition technology is constructed, and the audio classification technology of music classroom is studied. The support vector machine is used to divide the audio into five types: mute, background, music, voice and noisy voice. At the same time, a smoothing method based on the classification result sequence is proposed to obtain audio segmentation points. According to the actual needs of music classroom teaching, the system model is constructed, and speech feature recognition is carried out with the support of intelligent speech recognition.

The two existing systems mentioned above have certain effectiveness, but the music teaching effect is not satisfactory and cannot meet the development needs of music teaching. Therefore, the research on the construction of music intelligent interactive teaching system based on J2EE platform is proposed. The concept of "interaction" first appeared in the computer field, which was extended from scholars to the field of education and teaching in the 1970s. The starting point of "interactive" teaching method is to let teachers and students enjoy the learning process of teaching and learning more, and attach great importance to interactive communication and reflection in the classroom. This paper introduces the concept of "interaction" in order to improve the quality of music teaching. The construction of a music intelligent interactive teaching system based on J2EE platform proposed in this article has innovative points in the following aspects:

(1) By using ASP and ADO technology to achieve intelligent interaction of teaching data, the efficiency of data interaction has been effectively improved.
(2) By reasonably allocating the short addresses of each device and designing system network communication, the response time of the system has been successfully shortened.
(3) By utilizing genetic algorithms to intelligently generate test papers and designing music teaching exam modules, the quality of music teaching has been improved.

## 2 Design of Music Intelligent Interactive Teaching System

### 2.1 System Development Platform Design Module

According to the design system requirements, J2EE is selected as the system development platform, and its structure is shown in Fig. 1.

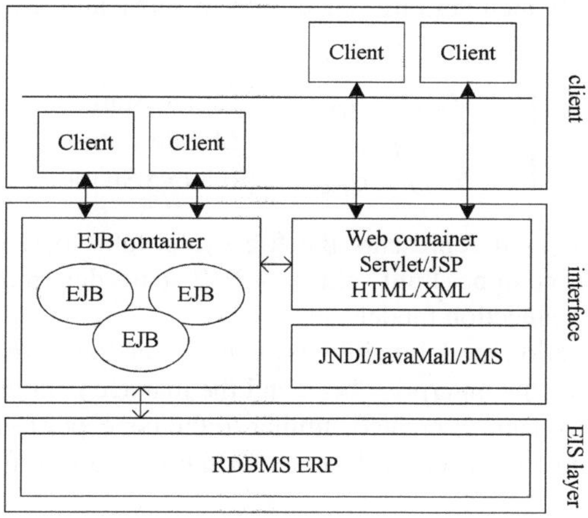


**Fig. 1.** J2EE Platform Structure

As shown in Fig. 1, J2EE is a technical architecture (application development direction) composed of various components and the standards and technical guidelines that standardize these components. Its main features can standardize and simplify the system deployment and development, and improve the reusability, security and cross platform of the system. The core of J2EE is to promote the compatibility between different architecture platforms using J2EE, and to standardize and standard various components, technical levels and architecture services. J2EE is essentially an architecture. Its core is the standard version of the Java 2 platform or the Java platform. It can simplify the management, deployment and development of solutions at the enterprise level. While inheriting the characteristics of the standard version of "write once, run across platforms", J2EE can fully support XML technology, JSP technology, Servlet technology and EJB technology. At the same time, it can apply security mode to protect the data in the Internet, and illustrate the convenience of database access through CORBA and

JDBC application interfaces. J2EE makes the development platform unified, and can support adding directory, deploying and packaging applications and EJB while supporting the integration of existing applications. It can reduce the complexity of the system and reduce the development cost of the whole system while improving the performance and security.

The core of J2EE is component, and the application using J2EE structure can simplify the development of programs. Reusable business logic is encapsulated in the form of components, and background services are provided by J2EE servers, which can be regarded as a container at this time. Developers can get rid of the heavy service development and only need to focus on the development of business logic.

Important services such as remote connection, JNDI addressing, transaction management and security management can be customized in the form of containers in the J2EE server. The main services are as follows:

(1) Life cycle model

The creation and removal of EJBs can be managed through the life cycle model. The life cycle of EJB mainly includes three states: create, move and remove. The expression is:

$$\begin{cases} T_{EJB} < \alpha_{\min} & \text{Create Status} \\ \alpha_{\min} \le T_{EJB} \le \alpha_{\max} & \text{Mobile status} \\ T_{EJB} > \alpha_{\max} & \text{Remove Status} \end{cases} \tag{1}$$

In formula (1), $T_{EJB}$ It represents the life cycle value of EJB; $\alpha_{\min}$ And $\alpha_{\max}$ Represents the lower and upper limit values for EJB status determination.

(2) J2EE remote connection model

The remote connection model mainly implements the low-level interaction, that is, the interaction between the enterprise bean and the management client. The client can call after the enterprise bean is created, similar to the concept of virtual machine. The success of J2EE remote connection depends on the network traffic, as shown in the following formula:

$$\begin{cases} Q_t \ge Q^* & \text{J2EE Remote connection successful} \\ Q_t < Q^* & \text{J2EE Remote connection failed} \end{cases} \tag{2}$$

In formula (2), $Q_t$ Represents the J2EE remote connection network traffic; $Q^*$ It represents the standard value of network traffic.

(3) J2EE Transaction Management Model

The transaction management model can complete the establishment of the relationship between transaction methods and divide the transaction methods into separate units. By configuring the transaction attributes of enterprise class beans in the configuration file, you can achieve relevant transaction processing. It does not need to write and debug the transaction code separately in each bean, and the container manages the transaction uniformly, reducing the complexity of the code and improving the readability of the system[4]. The calculation formula of J2EE code complexity is:

$$A = \frac{q_d}{\beta \times t_d} \times 100\% \tag{3}$$

In Eq. (3), $A$ It represents the complexity of J2EE code; $q_d$ Represents the number of J2EE codes; $\beta$ It represents auxiliary calculation parameters; $t_d$ It represents the running time of J2EE code.

(4) J2EE security model

The configuration of web components can be completed using the J2EE security model. Access to system resources is determined by the relationship between roles, customers, and permissions. Roles have activated permissions, customers belong to roles, and authorization can access resources. J2EE security is mainly determined by permissions, and the expression is:

$$B = \{B_1, B_2, B_3, B_4, B_5, B_\varepsilon\} \tag{4}$$

In Eq. (4), $B$ Represents the J2EE security permission set; $B_1$ Represents J2EE role security permissions; $B_2$ Represents J2EE client security permissions; $B_3$ Represents J2EE activation security permission; $B_4$ Represents J2EE authorized security permissions; $B_5$ Represents J2EE access security permissions; $B_\varepsilon$ It represents other J2EE security permissions.

(5) Database connection pool model

Due to connection restrictions, the database connection is time-consuming and limited. Through the use of the database connection pool, this problem can be solved through the management of the connection pool. Due to the limitation of research space, it is not necessary to repeat it too much.

J2EE server can run containers and Web components in containers; The execution of servlet components and ordinary JSP pages can be managed through the Web container. The management of client components is uniformly completed by the client container.

The above process completes the design of the system development platform, laying a solid foundation for the functional design and implementation of the subsequent music intelligent interactive teaching system.

## 2.2 System Network Communication Design Module

The network address mentioned in this study refers to the short address, which contains 16 bits in total. Before network communication, the music intelligent interactive teaching system needs to allocate the short address of each device[5]. After system initialization, the 16 bit network address will be dynamically allocated. The 16 bit network address includes 0 to 65535. All 0 addresses are used by the coordinator. Other addresses will be allocated using the following mechanism:

(1) Step 1: Determine the maximum number of all child nodes that can be connected to each parent node $N_m$, the system gives a reference parameter $N_m = 20$;
(2) Step 2: Determine the maximum number of all child routing nodes that can be connected to each parent node $R_m$, where $R_m \leq N_m$, the reference parameters given by the system $R_m = 6$;
(3) Step 3: Determine the maximum depth of the network node as $S_m$, the reference parameters given by the system $S_m = 6$;
(4) Step 4: Determine the network depth of the node's parent node $D_m$, where $D_m < S_m$, the reference parameters given by the system $D_m = 0, 1, 2, 3, 4, 5$;

(5) Step 5: Calculate the offset of the network address allocated by the parent node to the child node at a certain depth. The calculation formula is:

$$\chi(D_m) = \begin{cases} 1 + N_m * (S_m - D_m - 1) & R_m = 1 \\ \frac{1+N_m-R_m-N_m*R_m^{(S_m-D_m-1)}}{1-R_m} & otherwise \end{cases} \tag{5}$$

In formula (5),$\chi(D_m)$ It represents the offset corresponding to the network address allocated by the parent node to the child node at a certain depth.

(6) Step 6 starts to calculate the network addresses of router nodes and terminal nodes.

There are mainly two types of node network access, namely non router node network access and router node network access [6]. The address of the parent node is $C_k$, depth is $D_m$, and has $N$ Non routing child nodes, of which the $n$ When non routing sub nodes join the network,$n \leq N$, the short address calculation formula of this sub node is:

$$C_n = C_k + \chi(D_m) * R_m + n \tag{6}$$

In formula (6),$C_n$ Indicates the short address of the child node.

When the router node is connected to the network, the address of the parent node is $C_k$, depth is $D_m$, and has $N$ Routing child nodes, of which the $n$ When routing sub nodes join the network,$n \leq N$, the short address calculation formula of this sub node is:

$$C_n = C_k + \chi(D_m) * (n - 1) + 1 \tag{7}$$

In the process of network address allocation, the system will have a variety of problems, especially when the number of nodes in the network increases slowly, the network address limit will be highlighted. In general, the network address has 16 bits, which can accommodate up to 65535 nodes. During the allocation process, set the parameters of using network address allocation, and each parent node can accommodate at most $N_m$ Child nodes,$R_m$ Sub routing node, the maximum depth is $S_m$;Then there is a mathematical relationship between these parameters and the maximum value. At the same time, the reference value used is the parameter set by the system, and the relationship between these parameters and the maximum value is shown in Table 1.

As shown in Table 1, the formula for calculating the number of summary points is:

$$Z_n = \frac{R_m^{S_m} - 1}{R_m - 1} * N_m + 1 \tag{8}$$

In Eq. (8),$Z_n$ It represents the amount of summary points.

When deploying network nodes, the actual total number of nodes cannot exceed 65535. If the set parameters are used, when the set parameter value is greater than 65535 nodes, the nodes in the network can not form a full tree, but can only form part of the network. At this time, the address is not enough and new nodes cannot be added to the network; When the set parameter value is less than 65535 nodes, even if all nodes in the network reach the set value and join the network, 65535 addresses are not used up. At this time, all network nodes are assigned to network addresses, and the network forms a full tree, and the remaining network addresses cannot be used[7]. To avoid wasting

**Table 1.** Relation between set value and maximum value

| parameter | $Rm$ | $Sm$ | $Nm$ | Number of summary points |
|---|---|---|---|---|
| Initial parameters | 6 | 5 | 20 | 31101 |
| $Rm + 1$ | 7 | 5 | 20 | 56021 |
| $Rm + 2$ | 8 | 5 | 20 | 93621 |
| $Nm + 1$ | 67 | 5 | 21 | 32656 |
| $Nm + 1, Rm + 1$ | 7 | 5 | 21 | 58822 |
| $Nm + 1, Rm + 2$ | 7 | 5 | 22 | 61623 |
| $Nm + 1, Rm + 3$ | 7 | 5 | 23 | 64424 |
| $Nm + 1, Rm + 4$ | 7 | 5 | 24 | 67225 |
| $Sm + 1$ | 6 | 6 | 20 | 186621 |
| ... | ... | ... | ... | ... |

network addresses, the set value can be slightly greater than 65535, so the parameters selected in this paper are $N_m = 20$, $R_m = 6$, $S_m = 6$.

The above process completes the design of system network communication, reasonably distributes the short address of each device, and provides support for the stable operation of the design system.

### 2.3 Intelligent Interactive Module of Teaching Data

The design system mainly uses ASP and ADO technology to realize the intelligent interaction of teaching data, which provides the basis for the realization of music intelligent interactive teaching.

ASP is the abbreviation of Active Server Page. It is an open application environment without compilation. It provides flexibility of CGI programs and scripts while ensuring performance. Unlike CGI, ASP runs in the process of the server and is multi-threaded. It can be optimized to handle a large number of users. It combines the simple scripting of HTML with Active Server components and other tools to create a dynamic website with strong interactivity. The essence of ASP technology is the server side ActiveX technology, which is the object-oriented network data service technology[8]launched by Microsoft. ASP commands are first interpreted and executed on the server side, and then the execution results are downloaded to the web browser running on the client side or the local application system of the office web browser. It runs on the server side. Users can't see the ASP source code and can't interfere with the normal operation of the program, thus ensuring the security of the server side program.The teaching data interaction program is shown in Fig. 2.

As shown in Fig. 2, the teaching data is transmitted in the network based on the execution results, which improves the transmission speed. The page encapsulated with ASP instructions must submit an access request to the server program in HTTP mode, otherwise the server will refuse to provide the client copy and operation results because

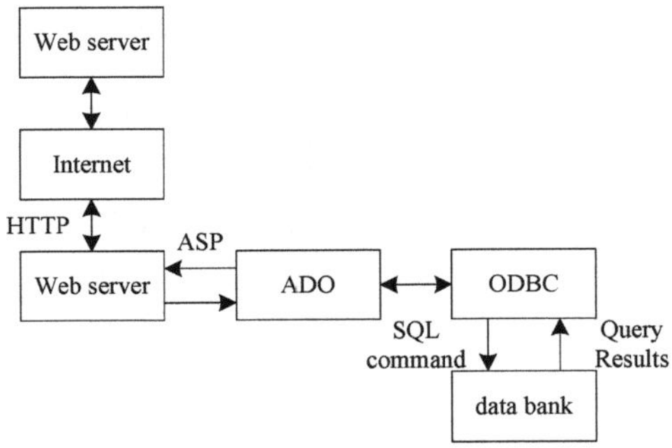


**Fig. 2.** Schematic diagram of teaching data interaction program

it is unable to determine the specific logical location of the client that is applying. As an object-oriented network application technology, ASP has 7 objects to complete the operation of remote database.

ADO technology can be combined with ASP to execute SQL in HTML pages and query, update and delete the data information of the site server in the browser.ADO uses the RecordSet object as the main interface for data access, and uses VbScript and Jscript languages to control database access and output display of query results. ADO can connect to SQL Server, Oracle, Sybase and other databases that support ODBC. Its advantages lie in its simplicity, high speed, low memory usage and low disk usage. The ActiveX Object based on ADO structure optimization is called ADODB. The execution environment required by ADO on the server side is Windows Server and IIS 5.0, and the execution environment on the client side only requires a general browser[9]. The specific steps of ADO data access are shown below.

Step 1: Set the database source.Generally, ODBC can be used to select the database name, and specify the drivers and database files for books and periodicals, or use OLE DB to access directly;

Step 2: Use "Sewer. CreateObj ect" to establish the connected object, and use the "Open" command to open the database to be accessed and queried;

Step 3: Set the SQL command, and use the "Execute" command to start the action of accessing the database. For example, Set rs = conn. Execute (SQL command), where corm is the name of the object to be connected;

Step 4: Use the RecordSet object command to display the results of the query operation.Where rs.fields.count represents the number of fields in the record; Rs. Eof indicates whether the specified last line has been reached.

The above process completes the development of intelligent interactive program for teaching data, providing a certain means of support for interactive teaching.

### 2.4 Music Intelligent Interactive Teaching Assessment Module

Music intelligent interactive teaching assessment is also a key component of music intelligent interactive teaching system. This research uses genetic algorithm intelligence to form music intelligent interactive teaching assessment papers. The specific process is as follows:

Genetic algorithm is a computer algorithm based on the principles of natural selection and genetic genetics, which is usually used to solve optimization problems.The design of music intelligent interactive teaching examination paper can be realized by using genetic algorithm through the following steps:

1. Determine optimization objectives and evaluation indicators: consider the knowledge points to be examined in the examination paper and their importance, and determine appropriate evaluation indicators, such as the difficulty, quality and coverage of the examination paper.
2. Design test paper generation rules: according to the assessment requirements and evaluation indicators, design a set of test paper generation rules, such as random selection of knowledge points, question type proportion control, etc.
3. Generate initial test paper library: use the above generation rules to generate a certain number of initial test paper libraries.
4. Define the chromosome coding mode of genetic algorithm: convert the components of different test papers (such as the number of questions, the combination of knowledge points, etc.) into chromosome coding mode to facilitate the comparison and selection of different test papers by genetic algorithm.
5. Determine the fitness function: convert the evaluation index of the examination paper into the fitness function, which is used to compare the advantages and disadvantages of different examination papers, and determine the selection and crossing mode of the parent chromosome.
6. Iterative optimization of genetic algorithm: select, cross and mutate the parent chromosomes to generate new offspring chromosomes, and evaluate and sort the offspring chromosomes according to the fitness function. Continue to iterate until the preset stop condition is reached.
7. Generate the final test paper: generate the final music intelligence interactive teaching examination paper according to the optimal solution obtained by genetic algorithm optimization.

It should be noted that the design of music intelligent interactive teaching examination paper using genetic algorithm is a relatively complex process, which requires reasonable details design and adjustment according to the actual situation.

Establish a state space to control the indicators of automatic test paper generation $E$. $E$ Each row of is composed of the control indicators of a test question, such as question number, question type, chapter, difficulty, etc., and these attribute indicators are coded and expressed in binary form, while each column is all the values of an indicator in the question bank. The following describes the definition of genetic algorithm in combination with the test paper generation system.

In genetic algorithm, the so-called $L$ individual $X$, that is, the length is $L$ 0 and 1 strings of, referred to as individuals;$L$ It is called individual chain length,$L$ All records of individuals $f = \{0, 1\}^L$, called individual space, and the expression is:

$$E = \begin{bmatrix} e_{11} & e_{12} & \cdots & e_{1,m+n} \\ e_{21} & e_{22} & \cdots & e_{2.m+n} \\ \vdots & \vdots & \ddots & \vdots \\ e_{m+n,1} & e_{m+n,2} & \cdots & e_{m+n,m+n} \end{bmatrix} \tag{9}$$

In the test paper generation system, the individual is each test question, and the number of control indicators of each test question is its chain length. The so-called population is $N$ A collection of individuals (individuals are allowed to repeat), referred to as a population.$N$ It is called the population size, and the expression is:

$$N = \left\{\overline{X} = (X_1, X_2, \cdots, X_N), X_i \in (E)\right\} \tag{10}$$

When genetic algorithm is applied, the quantity to be controlled must be coded first. In order to facilitate calculation, binary encoding is adopted here, that is, the character set is composed of 0 and 1. For the convenience of description, we only select a part of the control quantity: chapter, question type and difficulty of the test question for coding, such as 1001011100. After coding, determine the fitness function of the test question. In genetic algorithm, external information is basically not needed, and only the fitness function is used as the basis for optimization. The only requirement of genetic algorithm for fitness function is that the function cannot be negative. In the theory of evolution, the survival of the fittest is the principle of natural evolution. There should be criteria for excellence and inferiority, and the fitness function is used to describe the fitness of each individual. For optimization problems, the fitness function is the objective function. The purpose of introducing fitness function is to evaluate and compare individuals according to their fitness and determine the degree of superiority and inferiority. The fitness function expression is:

$$F : f \rightarrow g^+ \tag{11}$$

In Eq. (11),$F$ It represents the fitness function;$g^+$ It represents the space of positive real numbers.

Suppose that the difficulty distribution of each question in a question type follows normal distribution $\lambda \sim N\left(\eta, \delta^2\right)$, where $\eta$ Is the average difficulty,$\delta^2$ Is the variance, which falls in the interval $[\eta - 3\delta, \eta + 3\delta]$ The probability sum within the range is approximately 1. We have identified five levels of difficulty in this system.Set the total number of test questions as *sum*, the number of each difficulty question is $M_1$, $M_2$, $M_3$, $M_4$ and $M_5$, there are:

$$sum = M_1 + M_2 + M_3 + M_4 + M_5 \tag{12}$$

Among them, $M_1 = \int_{-\infty}^{-2\delta} F(x)dx$, $M_2 = \int_{-2\delta}^{-\delta} F(x)dx$, $M_3 = \int_{-\delta}^{\delta} F(x)dx$, $M_4 = \int_{\delta}^{2\delta} F(x)dx$, $M_5 = \int_{2\delta}^{+\infty} F(x)dx$.

After determining the number of each question, the fitness function of difficulty can be determined.Let the difficulty coefficient of each question be $P_f$, the expected difficulty coefficient is $e_f$, the reciprocal of the square difference between the difficulty coefficient of each question and the expected difficulty coefficient is the fitness function $F$, there are:

$$F = \frac{1}{\psi^o * \left[P_f - e_f\right]^2} \tag{13}$$

In Eq. (13), $\psi^o$ It represents the auxiliary factor of fitness function, which determines the performance of genetic algorithm.

According to the characteristics of this database and test paper generation method, we choose standard genetic algorithm to generate test papers.The process of generating test paper is as follows:

Step 1: According to the user's initial settings, randomly select a group of questions from the database and number each question. The function to generate the initial population is initpop(). Each chromosome coding bit in the population is selected from 0,1 with equal probability. After the chromosome coding is generated, the individual is decoded and fitness is calculated.

Step 2: Combine the calculation results with the state space library $E$ Indicators in $E(n)$ For comparison, if it matches, there are:$F(k) \leftarrow F(k)+1$;If not, there are:$F(k) \leftarrow F(k)+0$.

Step 3: Conduct elimination selection, namely $F(k)$ Remove the test questions that are 0 to generate a new test question model.

Step 4: Design genetic operation: use the roulette wheel to select the designed function select() and return the selected individual number in the population. First generate a random number between $(0,1)U$, if $U < sum$, the first individual is selected.

Step 5: Design the function crossover () for the single point crossing operation. The parent parent 1 and parent 2 generate child individuals child 1 and child 2. If the crossing occurs, process the code assignment and return the crossing point arrow cross; Otherwise, no processing is done and 0 is returned.

Step 6: Design the mutation () function for the mutation operation, and determine whether the individual child's code bit is operated according to the mutation probability Pmq. If a code bit is mutated, the code will be reversed.

Step 7: After the above steps of selection, crossover and variation are completed, a new test question model is generated, and its convergence is judged according to the set error precision. If it meets the requirements of the appropriate degree, the test paper is successfully formed, and it is transferred to the next step;Otherwise, go to step 3 and repeat the above process.

Step 8: Output the results and complete the test paper generation. When initializing the test questions, we choose the mode of parent selection, that is, random sampling without return, so that each test question can be selected. In the selection process, the probability of each question being selected is a non-uniform random event, and its probability depends on the last selection result [10].

Through the design of the above modules, the design and operation of the music intelligent interactive teaching system are realized, which helps to improve the quality of music intelligent interactive teaching.

# 3 Design System Performance Test

## 3.1 Experiment Preparation Stage

To verify the effectiveness of building a music intelligent interactive teaching system based on J2EE platform, a simulation experiment is designed. The experimental environment is as follows: Using Linux operating system and Eclipse development tools to develop a music intelligent interactive teaching system.

The preparation stage is the key to the smooth progress of the experiment. The design system adopts genetic algorithm in the music intelligent interactive teaching assessment module, which involves fitness function auxiliary factors $\psi^o$, which determines the advantages and disadvantages of the function of genetic algorithm, and is also the key to the stable operation of the design system. Therefore, before the experiment, it is necessary to add auxiliary factors to the fitness function $\psi^o$ Determine the best value.

Get fitness function auxiliary factors through testing $\psi^o$ The relationship with the running efficiency of genetic algorithm is shown in Fig. 3.

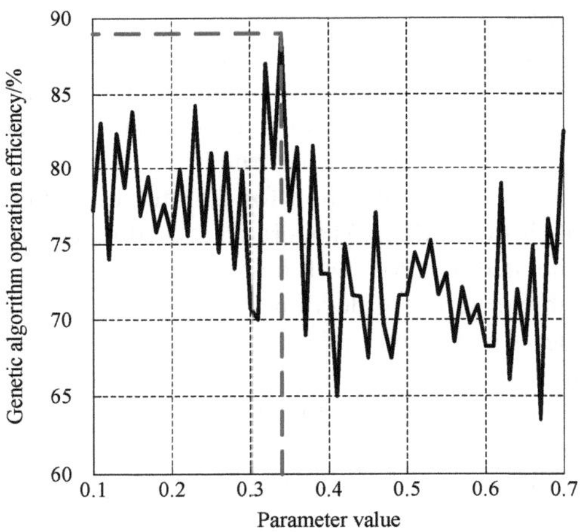


**Fig. 3.** Fitness function auxiliary factors $\psi^o$ Relation diagram with running efficiency of genetic algorithm

As shown in Fig. 3, when the fitness function auxiliary factor $\psi^o$ When the value is 0.34, the running efficiency of genetic algorithm reaches the maximum of 89%. Therefore, determine the fitness function auxiliary factor $\psi^o$ The optimal value is 0.34.

The above process has completed the preparation of the experiment and provided convenience for the subsequent experiments.

## 3.2 Analysis of Experimental Results

Set the intelligent music classroom teaching system based on the Internet of Things (Reference [2] method) and the music classroom auxiliary teaching system based on intelligent speech recognition (Reference [3] method) as comparison systems 1 and 2, and select teaching data interaction efficiency, system response time and music teaching results as evaluation indicators. The specific experimental results analysis process is shown below.

The efficiency of teaching data interaction obtained through experiments is shown in Fig. 4.

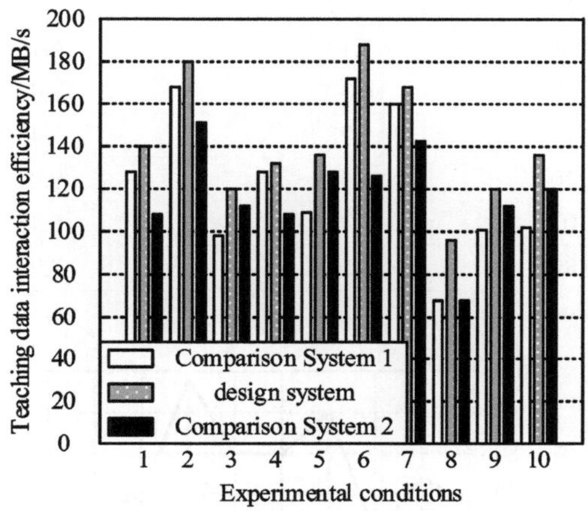


**Fig. 4.** Schematic diagram of teaching data interaction efficiency

As shown in Fig. 4, after the application of the designed system, the interaction efficiency of the teaching data obtained is higher than that of the two comparison systems, with the maximum value of 188 MB/s, while the maximum value of the interaction efficiency of the teaching data of System 1 is 172 MB/s, and the maximum value of the interaction efficiency of the teaching data of System 2 is 152 MB/s. It can be seen that the teaching data interaction efficiency of the designed system is high. This is because the proposed method in this study utilizes ASP and ADO technologies to achieve intelligent interaction of teaching data, which significantly improves the efficiency of data interaction compared to traditional teaching systems.

The system response time obtained through experiments is shown in Table 2.

As shown in the data in Table 2, the system response time obtained after the application of the designed system is shorter than that of the two comparison systems, with the minimum value of 0.45 s, while the minimum value of the system response time of System 1 is 3.56 s, and the minimum value of the system response time of System 2 is 4.15 s. The proposed method in this study significantly reduces waiting time for students and improves teaching efficiency by appropriately allocating short addresses to each device and designing system network communication.

The music teaching results obtained through the experiment are shown in Fig. 5.

**Table 2.** System Response Schedule/s

| Test conditions | design system | Comparison system 1 | Comparison system 2 |
|---|---|---|---|
| 1 | 2.03 | 3.56 | 5.02 |
| 2 | 1.56 | 4.23 | 4.15 |
| 3 | 1.02 | 5.02 | 5.02 |
| 4 | 0.56 | 6.12 | 5.23 |
| 5 | 0.45 | 5.18 | 6.45 |
| 6 | 0.89 | 6.32 | 7.02 |
| 7 | 1.10 | 5.78 | 7.45 |
| 8 | 1.20 | 6.59 | 8.02 |
| 9 | 1.02 | 7.70 | 5.45 |
| 10 | 0.89 | 6.59 | 7.25 |

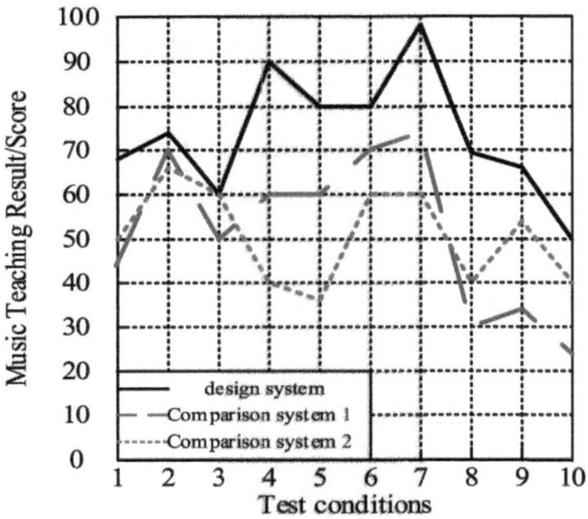


**Fig. 5.** Schematic diagram of music teaching results

As shown in the data in Fig. 5, after the application of the designed system, the music teaching results obtained are higher than those of the two comparison systems, with the maximum score of 98 points, while the maximum score of the music teaching results obtained by System 1 is 75 points, and the maximum score of the music teaching results obtained by System 2 is 67 points. It can be seen that the designed system can improve the efficiency of teaching data interaction, shorten the system response time, and effectively improve the music teaching performance of students. The proposed method in this study effectively enhances music teaching performance by utilizing genetic algorithm for intelligent paper composition and designing a music teaching examination module, thus demonstrating the effectiveness of the system in improving music teaching quality.

## 4 Conclusion

In the process of music teaching, through teachers' experience accumulation and summary, it can be found that the problems encountered by students in learning to a certain extent have their similarities. Through problem consultation, students can conduct real-time problem consultation, and understand and master the problems encountered by other students, so as to reduce unnecessary detours. Common problems can be solved by querying historical records; At the same time, teachers can summarize and summarize the original, typical and universal questions from the history question and answer records, and summarize them into the question database for unified processing, so as to facilitate later queries. By analyzing and summarizing the problem library irregularly, it is helpful for teachers to timely summarize and summarize the problems encountered in the teaching process, adjust teaching methods and teaching methods, improve teaching quality and increase feedback. Assisted teaching in the form of multimedia can stimulate students' interest, improve memory and understanding. The design system effectively improves the efficiency of teaching data interaction, shortens the system response time, improves the results of music teaching, and can provide more effective system support for music teaching.

**Aknowledgement.** Jiangxi College Humanities Social Science 2020 Project----The Infiltration of Chinese Ritual Thought in College Ethnic Music Teaching (YS20105).

## References

1. Gibson, S.J.: Shifting from offline to online collaborative music-making, teaching and learning: perceptions of Ethno artistic mentors. Music. Educ. Res. **23**(2), 1–16 (2021)
2. Lyu, D., Wang, Z.: Design and implementation of an intelligent classroom teaching system for music class based on internet of things. Int. J. Emerg. Technol. Learn. (iJET) **16**(18), 171–184 (2021)
3. Long, C., Wang, S.: Music classroom assistant teaching system based on intelligent speech recognition. J. Intell. Fuzzy Syst. **14**, 1–10 (2021)
4. Fitzgerald, M., Costello, R.: Book review. Irish J. Med. Sci. **175**(3), 79–80 (2006). https://doi.org/10.1007/BF03169180
5. Cain, T., Mariguddi, A.: Research-informed teaching: the case of musical futures. Br. Edu. Res. J. **48**(3), 519–535 (2022)
6. Hawkes, M.E.: Experiences of developing pre-performance routines with recreational pianists. Psychol. Music **49**(6), 1721–1736 (2021)
7. Yoku, T.: The effect of metacognitive strategies-based teaching practice in guitar education on performance achievement. Psychol. Music **49**(6), 1605–1619 (2021)
8. Shin, J.: Preservice music teachers in Korea and their collaborative reflection with peers. Int. J. Music. Educ. **39**(4), 371–382 (2021)
9. Zhao, H., Guo, L.: Design of intelligent computer aided network teaching system based on web. Comput. Aid. Des. App. **19**(S1), 12–23 (2021)
10. Yong, Y., Minsi, Z., Bo, W., et al.: Design of simulation system for discontinuity network in rock mass and its application in teaching. Comput. Simul. **39**(9), 268–272 (2022)

# Interactive Design Method of Mobile Art Education APP Interface Based on Virtual Reality Technology

Yan Zhao(✉) and Ya Xu

Modern College of Northwest University, Xi'an 710130, China
freyaxu8@gmail.com

**Abstract.** In view of the shortcomings of low fit and long conversion time of the mobile art education APP interface generated by traditional methods, this paper proposes an interactive design method of the mobile art education APP interface based on virtual reality technology. Through the adjustment of brightness and hue, the mobile art education APP interface is preprocessed. By adjusting brightness and tone, filtering and processing the mobile art education APP interface, the contrast and detail information in the interface are improved. Detect mutation points in the interface image of the art education APP by solving the first and second derivatives of the image. Extract the edges of the interface image of the mobile art education app using the local maximum of the gradient vector model. Combining the functional interface layout and 3D model construction, the visual information of the art education APP interface was designed. By using Non-local Means to denoise the image of the interactive interface of the mobile art education APP, an optimized interactive interface of the mobile art education APP was generated. The experimental results show that the method in this paper can generate the interactive interface of the mobile art education APP, provide users with an immersive roaming experience, and improve the fit and transition smoothness of the mobile art education APP interface.

**Keywords:** Virtual reality technology · Mobile terminal · Art education · APP interface · Interaction design

## 1 Introduction

Since the National Education Commission formally put forward the concept of distance education in 1994, online education has gradually come into everyone's vision. In 1995, the China Education and Research Network was launched. In 2001, the "school to school connection" project for primary and secondary schools was implemented in an all-round way to drive the modernization of education with informatization and strive to realize the leap forward development of basic education. Encourage school education to build an open platform with network curriculum system and the application and management of education network open curriculum, and support the construction of education system


G. Gui et al. (Eds.): eLEOT 2023, LNICST 543, pp. 350–364, 2024.
https://doi.org/10.1007/978-3-031-51465-4_23

with Chinese characteristics. For the various problems faced by mobile art education and the increasingly fierce competition of art education mobile applications, the school, as a group with a large number of professional courses, professional textbooks, scientific research content resources, can provide educational resources different from the content produced by some educational software in the current application market. Through the integration of its own educational resources. A large number of online courses [1] will be produced. Moreover, as an educational entity, the school can better and more actively promote the exchange and interaction of offline learning by using the network platform; Through the development of art education software applications, it provides students with massive learning content information resources, facilitates students to use their spare time more freely and efficiently, and also strengthens the interaction between teachers and students; Open online courses mainly benefit student user groups. At the same time, for those who do not have enough conditions to enter the offline classroom, they can obtain basic cultural level quality education through the mobile art education APP. The development of online education platform has great positive significance. Therefore, the demand for mobile art education APP is growing. As a platform that can provide online education, the mobile art education APP can meet the national strategic needs for the development of art education.

In the domestic research, Zhu Jihong et al. [2]. by summarizing the interaction design theory of preschool children's APP interface at home and abroad and comparing excellent APP cases, using the cognitive development of preschool children's vision, hearing, touch and motion, and combining Piaget's cognitive theory and the related theoretical research of children's cognitive development psychology, five aspects of excellent preschool children's APP design strategies are summarized. And apply it to project practice. Through the design practice of specific cases, the applicability of the research on the cognitive development of preschool children was preliminarily verified in the interactive design of APP interface, and the design strategy in line with the characteristics of children's cognitive development was proposed to meet the children's sense of honor and achievement in online learning, thus boosting the enthusiasm and attention of preschool children in online learning. Li Yang et al. [3] proposed a design idea of digital media mobile terminal interface based on human-computer interaction technology in order to design and meet the requirements of diversified and comprehensive functions of user interface. Through the introduction and research of human-computer interaction interface, the usability of human-computer interaction interface evaluation and testing is emphatically analyzed, and the model is optimized and improved by combining with GOMS model, and a new optimized GOMS layered quantitative model is proposed. Detailed analysis of the digital media interface information display mode of multi screen interactive human-computer interaction, as well as the television, mobile phone multi screen human-computer interaction digital media system interface, including system information architecture, grid system, drawing interface block diagram, multi screen interactive interaction model, as well as ensuring consistency of visual style, detailed interface design, charts and focus state. Applying the design system to the actual test, it is found that the design idea of the system can be based on human-computer interaction technology to achieve the effective combination of multi screen interaction and digital media, and also create a better scene interaction experience for the future development of digital media mobile terminals.

In foreign research, Chen Y et al. [4] realized the art design of real-time image interactive interface of advertising screen under the augmented reality technology and visual communication technology, digitalization enhanced the real situation, enriched the visual experience of advertising audience, and turned advertising into an interactive form. This paper analyzes the specific contents of composition, graphics, color, proportion, brightness and design principles in advertisements. We conducted a questionnaire survey and combined the above six indicators. Query a large number of documents for analysis, and conduct theoretical analysis on the design of real-time interactive image interface of advertising screen based on augmented reality technology. According to the experimental results obtained in this study, the data shows that the P-value of six age groups' scores on advertising texts is less than 0.05. There are significant differences; At the same time, the P value of each indicator in the advertisement is also less than 0.05. This significant difference indicates that text readability is an important factor in text interaction in interactive interfaces.

In the era of mobile Internet, online learning has formed a trend. The mobile art education APP on the market has been loved, recognized and used by many parents and students because it has broken through the restrictions of time and space. Therefore, this paper applies virtual reality technology to the interface interaction design of the mobile art education APP, so as to improve users' experience of using the mobile art education APP interface. The main content and innovative content of this study are as follows:

(1) By preprocessing the interface of the mobile art education app, key information is extracted to reduce redundant content and improve user experience.
(2) Utilize image processing technology to extract image edges from the interface of mobile art education apps, highlight important elements, and enhance visual effects.
(3) By optimizing the user interaction process through a reasonable functional interface layout, it improves the convenience and efficiency of user operations.
(4) Introducing 3D model design technology to make the art education app interface more three-dimensional, enhancing users' immersion and visual appeal.
(5) Based on the design and processing results in the previous steps, generate a mobile art education APP interface with innovative interactive methods and interface effects, providing a richer and more intuitive user experience.

## 2 Interface Interaction Design Method of Mobile Art Education APP

### 2.1 Pretreatment of Mobile Art Education APP Interface

In the process of preprocessing the mobile art education APP interface, the adaptive Gaussian filter is used to filter the art education APP interface, and the gradient direction of the interface image is converted into the derivative of the horizontal and vertical directions through the Guassian function to determine the gradient direction of the interface, and then the corrected interactive interface image is obtained. The Drago logarithm operator is used to adjust the corrected interactive interface hue [5]. According to the mapping relationship between the interactive interface brightness and the scene brightness, the brightness value compression of the interface pixel value and the visible detail level are obtained, and the art education APP interface image after the hue and brightness are improved is obtained.

When using adaptive Gaussian filter to process the art education APP interface, it is necessary to determine the gradient direction $\beta$ size. Convert $\beta$ into the derivatives of Vertical and horizontal directions through the Guassian function, and convolved with the art education APP interface at the same time to get the vertical gradient angle $\beta^*$ of the interface at $(x, y)$. To sum up, there are:

$$E_x = \frac{G(x, y, \beta)}{\partial x} \cdot M(x, y) \tag{1}$$

$$E_y = \frac{G(x, y, \beta)}{\partial y} \cdot M(x, y) \tag{2}$$

$$\beta^*(x, y) = \arctan\left[\frac{E_y(x, y)}{E_x(x, y)}\right] \tag{3}$$

Among them, $E_x$ represents the horizontal derivative of $\beta$, $E_y$ represents the vertical derivative of $\beta$, and $M(x, y)$ represents the Prehistoric art education APP interface.

The relationship between direction angle $\beta$ and vertical angle $\beta^*$ is as follows:

$$\beta = \beta^* + 90^\circ \tag{4}$$

Combining the above processes, the art education APP interface filtered by the adaptive Gaussian filter can be obtained:

$$L(x, y) = \frac{M(x, y) - G(x, y)}{1 - G(x, y)\beta} \tag{5}$$

Among them, $L(x, y)$ represent the filtered clear art education APP interface, $G(x, y)$ represents noise.

After the definition of the art education APP interface is corrected, the Drago logarithm operator is used to adjust the interface hue, so that the evaluation result of the interface saliency is more accurate.

Drago logarithm operator can adjust the brightness, detail preservation and contrast of the art education APP interface well, and the mapping relationship between the interface brightness and the scene brightness is as follows:

$$\lambda_d = \frac{\lambda_d^{\max} \cdot 0.01}{\lg\left(\lambda_d^{\max} + 1\right)} \times \frac{\ln(\lambda_w + 1)}{\ln\left\{2 + \left[\xi \lambda_w / \lambda_d^{\max}\right]\right\}} \tag{6}$$

Among them, $\lambda_w$ represents the brightness adjustment threshold in the dark of the art education APP interface, $\lambda_d$ represents the brightness of the art education APP interface, $\lambda_d^{\max}$ represents the maximum brightness of the art education APP interface, where $\lambda_d^{\max} = 100$. $\xi$ represents the degree of compression and visible detail of the brightness value of the art education APP interface. The higher the $\xi$ value, the more serious the brightness value is compressed.

The interface of the art education APP cleared by the adaptive Gaussian filter is dark, and the details will be affected to some extent. Therefore, by improving the brightness and contrast of the dark area of the interface, the interface details can be effectively maintained. According to experience. The value of $\xi$ can be defined as [1.3,1.6].

By using formula (6) and analyzing the $\xi$ value, we can get the interface image of the mobile art education APP after the brightness and hue are improved, which is expressed as:

$$H(x, y) = \lambda_d \times \lambda_w \times \xi \tag{7}$$

In the above formula, $H(x, y)$ represents the mobile end art education APP interface after color tone and brightness adjustment.

Through the adjustment of brightness and hue, the mobile art education APP interface was preprocessed.

## 2.2 Extract the Image Edge of the Mobile Art Education APP Interface

After the mobile art education APP interface has been preprocessed, the first and second derivatives of the art education APP interface image are solved, and the mutation points of the art education APP interface image are detected according to the characteristics of the derivatives, assuming $\gamma(x)$ meet:

$$\int_{-\infty}^{+\infty} \gamma(x)dx = 1, \lim_{x \to \infty} \gamma(x) = 0 \tag{8}$$

Then $\gamma(x)$ represents the smoothing function. Generally, Gaussian function is selected. Generally, the Gaussian function is selected. The smoothing function has a high low-frequency weight and functions as a low-pass filter. When the high-frequency components of the original signal and the smoothing function in the APP interface image are suppressed during convolution, the APP interface image signal is smoothed. If present:

$$\begin{cases} \varepsilon^1 = \dfrac{d\gamma(x)}{dx} \\ \varepsilon^2 = \dfrac{d\gamma^2(x)}{dx^2} \end{cases} \tag{9}$$

Then order:

$$\begin{cases} \sigma^1 = f(s, x) = f * \varepsilon_s^1(x) \\ \sigma^2 = f(s, x) = f * \varepsilon_s^2(x) \end{cases} \tag{10}$$

The first derivative of $f(x)$ smoothed by $\gamma(x)$ is proportional to the Non-local Means function $\sigma^1 f(s, x)$, and the second derivative of function $f(x)$ smoothed by $\gamma_s(x)$ is proportional to $\sigma^2 f(s, x)$. In order to detect signals in the APP interface image, large-scale $s$ is selected, and $f(x)$ and $\gamma(x)$ are convolved to eliminate signal waves in the APP interface image. By detecting the maximum value of the APP interface image after the

Non-local Means, the edge points of the APP interface image can be obtained. After the wavelet function is applied [6], the first-order derivative of the smoothing function is taken, and the edge points of the APP interface image are determined based on the information after the Non-local Means, achieving edge detection of the APP interface image.

Assuming that the pixel of the APP interface image is $N \times N$, then there is $I = \{d_{m,n}\}_{1 \in m,n \in N}$, decompose the APP interface image in $J = \log_2 N + 1$ scales, select scales $s = 2^j$, $1, \cdots j, \cdots, J$, and select $\gamma(x, y)$ as Gaussian function, then $\gamma(x, y)$ is second order derivable, with the following expression:

$$\begin{cases} \varphi^1(x, y) = \dfrac{\gamma(x, y)}{\partial x} \\ \varphi^2(x, y) = \dfrac{\gamma(x, y)}{\partial y} \end{cases} \tag{11}$$

where, $\varphi^1(x, y)$ and $\varphi^2(x, y)$ represent two-dimensional wavelet functions, and $2^j$ Discretization of $\varphi^1(x, y)$ and $\varphi^2(x, y)$ can obtain binary wavelet functions:

$$\begin{cases} \varepsilon^1_{2^j}(x, y) = \dfrac{1}{2^j}\varphi^1\left(\dfrac{x}{2^j}, \dfrac{y}{2^j}\right) \\ \varepsilon^2_{2^j}(x, y) = \dfrac{1}{2^j}\varphi^2\left(\dfrac{x}{2^j}, \dfrac{y}{2^j}\right) \end{cases} \tag{12}$$

The scale is $2^j$, and discrete dyadic Non-local Means function can be obtained. According to the two-dimensional discrete Non-local Means transform, the following can be obtained:

$$\begin{cases} \sigma^1_{2^j} = f * \varepsilon^1_{2^j}(x, y) \\ \sigma^2_{2^j} = f * \varepsilon^2_{2^j}(x, y) \end{cases} \tag{13}$$

The gradient vector can be expressed as:

$$\begin{bmatrix} \sigma^1_{2^j} f(x, y) \\ \sigma^2_{2^j} f(x, y) \end{bmatrix} = s\vec{\nabla}(f * \gamma)(x, y) \tag{14}$$

Among them, $\sigma^1_{2^j} f(x, y)$ and $\sigma^2_{2^j} f(x, y)$ represent the partial derivatives in the $x$ and $y$ directions of the page image, respectively. The modulus of Non-local Means in $2^j$ can be expressed as:

$$M_{2^j} f(x, y) = \sqrt{\left|\sigma^1_{2^j} f(x, y)\right|^2 \left|\sigma^2_{2^j} f(x, y)\right|^2} \tag{15}$$

Argument:

$$A_{2^j} f(x, y) = \arctan \frac{\sigma^1_{2^j} f(x, y)}{\sigma^2_{2^j} f(x, y)} \tag{16}$$

The gradient vector $s\vec{\nabla}(f * \gamma)(x, y)$ and $M_{2^j} f(x, y)$ are proportional, and the argument $A_{2^j} f(x, y)$ is the angle between the gradient vector and the horizontal direction of the APP interface image. The edge direction and argument direction of the APP interface image are the same. The local maximum of the gradient vector model can be used to determine the edge of the APP interface image.

### 2.3 Visual Information of Design Art Education APP Interface

The visual information design of the art education APP interface is the main part of the interaction design of the mobile art education APP interface based on virtual reality. The visual information design consists of three parts: functional interface layout, three-dimensional object model construction and scene space model construction.

#### 2.3.1 Function Interface Layout

The functional interface design is completed by the interactive interface layout optimization model, which is based on the interface visual attention division model and the function criticality analysis results, and sets the optimization objective function as the optimal visual attention division of the final layout of the interactive interface, so as to build the functional interface layout optimization model based on visual attention division.

The following definitions are implemented for the functional interface layout optimization model based on visual attention division:

$\cdot A = \{a_{ij}\}$ represents the visual attention level of the units occupied by a certain functional module in the visual area with different levels, where $a_{ij}$ represents the visual attention level of the units occupied by functional module $i$ in the visual area $j$;

$\cdot B = \{b_{ij}\}$ represents the visual attention level of the visual area where the central coordinate of a certain functional module is located, where $b_{ij}$ represents the visual attention level of the central coordinate of functional module $i$ in the visual distance region $j$;

$\cdot C = \{c_{ij}\}$ represents the number of units occupied by a certain functional module in the visual expectation with different levels, where $c_{ij}$ represents the number of units occupied by functional module $i$ in the visual area $j$.

In the above definition, $i = 1, 2, \cdots, n$ and $n$ represent the number of functional modules, while $j = 1, 2, 3$ respectively describe the three visual areas of the functional interface in the art education APP interface.

Select the $K_1$ method to determine the criticality of different functional modules in the functional interface [7], compare the criticality of all functional modules in pairs, and describe the relative criticality of functional modules with the following formula, namely:

$$g_k = \frac{\partial_{k-1}}{\partial_k} \tag{17}$$

Among them, $\partial_k$ represents the criticality of functional module $\ell_k$.

The criticality of functional module $\ell_k$ can be determined using the following formula:

$$\partial_i = \left(1 + \sum_{k=2}^{n} \prod_{i=k}^{n} g_i\right)^{-1} \tag{18}$$

In the process of functional interface design, there is a positive correlation with $g_k$, A, B and C, that is, the more critical the application direction of the art education APP interface, the larger the area of the function module in the interface, and the closer to the visual center.The intensity of visual attention division is described by formula (19):

$$Z = \sum_{i=1}^{n} \sum_{j=1}^{3} g_i a_{ij} b_{ij} c_{ij} \tag{19}$$

The upper limit value of visual attention division intensity represented by $Y$, which is $Y = \max Z$, is obtained as follows:

$$Y = \max \sum_{i=1}^{n} \sum_{j=1}^{3} g_i a_{ij} b_{ij} c_{ij} \tag{20}$$

The higher the $Z$ value, the more critical functional modules are divided by the visual attention of the user in the art education APP interface. The ppaper swarm optimization algorithm is selected to solve the functional interface layout optimization model based on visual attention division. The inertia weight is introduced to ensure the global and local search and optimization ability of the ppaper swarm, and the functional interface layout is completed[8]. For different areas in the functional interface, the image information of the art education APP interface needed in different areas is generated through 3D model construction.

### 2.3.2 Building 3D Model

The image information in the art education APP interface includes 3D objects and scene space, both of which are generated by 3D model building method. The main process of building a 3D model is shown in Fig. 1:

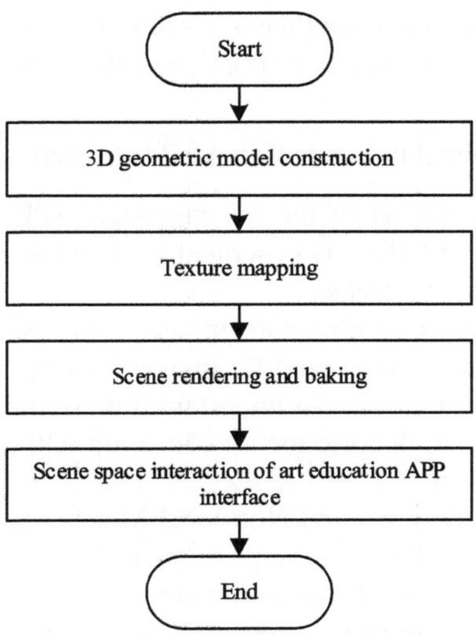


**Fig. 1.** 3D model construction process

Step 1: 3D geometric model construction.

Import the plan[9]obtained in the data collection process into the 3DS MAX software, and stretch the art education APP interface scene space according to the relevant information of the obtained art education APP interface scene space; For the complex art education APP interface scene space, several art education APP interface scene space units can be obtained by difference, and the art education APP interface scene space units can be synthesized as a whole using different modeling methods to build a 3D model of the art education APP interface scene space.

Step 2: Texture mapping.

In order to improve the authenticity of the scene space of the art education APP interface, texture mapping is applied to the scene space of the art education APP interface using the material editor. In general, different surfaces of the scene space of an art education APP interface need to map different textures. Under this condition, it is necessary to use multi-dimensional/sub object materials to load several maps on different sub materials with the same material.

Step 3: Scene rendering and baking.

After setting reasonable lights to simulate sunlight in the scene space, render the scene space of the art education APP interface. In order to obtain the optimal rendering effect, continuously adjust the brightness and position of the lights. Bake in a reasonable way after rendering, and store the scene space rendering results of the art education APP interface to a file in tga format.

Step 4: Scene space interaction of art education APP interface.

Import a tga format file into the VR Platform editor, optimize the scene space of the art education APP interface, and create a walking camera (simulating the height and walking speed of objects under human walking conditions) and a flying camera (simulating the overlooking scene above the scene space of the art education APP interface) in the scene space. Determine whether collision detection is required according to the actual application needs, and determine the balance between the scene space of the virtual art education APP interface and the smoothness of roaming interaction by compressing the texture to reduce the video memory consumption of the texture map.

## 2.4 Generation of Mobile Art Education APP Interactive Interface

Based on the visual information of the art education APP interface, the mobile art education APP interactive interface is generated by denoising the image of the mobile art education APP interactive interface.

There are many methods to eliminate image noise. Non-local Means threshold denoising is an efficient denoising method. Images that are not smooth or have sudden changes in grayscale are noise. An important link to improve the clarity of the art education APP interface is to denoise the art education APP interface image [10]. The steps of Non-local Means are:

Step 1: Compare the modulus and Non-local Means coefficients of each layer of coefficients after Non-local Means decomposition, and process the coefficients;

Step 2: After the Non-local Means coefficients are processed, the denoised image of the art education APP interface is restored. According to the principle of Non-local Means analysis, after the Non-local Means changes the Gaussian noise, it will be evenly distributed in the phase space. For the art education APP interface, it has its own limitations and is localized by layout.

The key and core of Non-local Means is to select and adjust the threshold, and select the appropriate threshold in the Non-local Means domain. In the process of denoising, the selection of threshold directly affects the quality of the art education APP interface image after denoising. The threshold estimation expression is as follows:

$$th = \sqrt{2\zeta \log n} \tag{21}$$

Among them, $\zeta$ and $n$ represent the variance of noise and the number of pixels in the interface image of the art education APP, respectively, while $th$ represents the threshold. According to relevant regulations, when $\zeta = 2$ is close to 2, the denoising effect of the art education APP interface image is better, and the denoising of the art education APP interface image is completed while retaining the edge details of the art education APP interface.

After the image of the art education APP interface is denoised, the virtual reality technology is used to generate the mobile art education APP interactive interface. The specific process can be divided into two links, namely, the design content link and the visual experience link. The interaction between the two links is shown in Fig. 2.

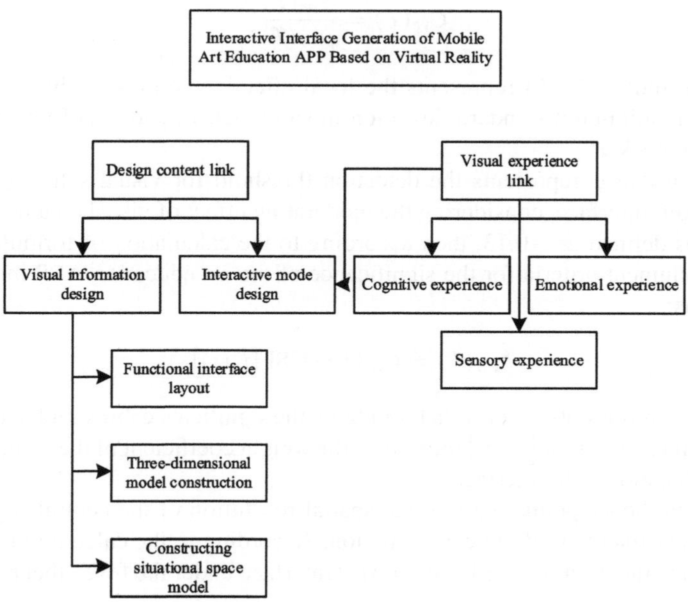


**Fig. 2.** Generation process of interactive interface of mobile art education APP based on virtual reality

The design content link can be divided into two parts, namely, visual information design and interaction mode design. The interactive interface layout design and interface content design are completed through the design content. The visual experience link can be divided into three parts: cognitive experience, emotional experience and sensory experience. On the basis of interactive interface layout design and interface content design, combined with the interaction mode design in the design content link, users can improve their visual experience of the mobile art education APP interface.

## 3 Experimental Analysis

In order to verify the application performance of the method in this paper in the interface interaction design of the mobile art education APP, an art education APP is taken as the application object, and the method in this paper is used to generate the interaction interface of the art education APP.

### 3.1 Evaluate the Visual Significance of the Mobile Art Education APP Interface

Before the experiment, the visual saliency of the generated APP interface is evaluated, assuming $V_{r_{s,o}}(x)$ represents the visual salient features of the reference interface image, it is divided into several image blocks, and the local effective contrast of the $T$-th block is defined as:

$$C_{vr}(T) = \frac{\chi_{vr}(T)}{\mu_{vr}(T)} \tag{22}$$

In the formula, $C_{vr}(T)$ represents the local effective contrast of block $T$, $\chi_{vr}(T)$ represents the minimum standard deviation in sub block $T$, and $\mu_{vr}(T)$ represents the mean of sub block $T$.

Assuming that $\varphi$ represents the detection threshold for visual saliency of the art education APP interface, considering the moderating effect of visual channel $(s, o)$, the value of $\varphi$ is defined as $-0.13$, then according to the calculation of formula (22), the threshold judgment criteria for the significance of the art education APP interface can be defined as:

$$\xi_{s,o}(T) = C_{vr}(T) \cdot \mathrm{CSF}\big[f_o(s)\big] \tag{23}$$

where, $\xi_{s,o}(T)$ represents the criteria for judging the significance threshold of the art education APP interface, $\mathrm{CSF}\big[f_o(s)\big]$ represents the weight coefficient of the visual direction of the art education APP interface.

The fovea theory points out that the spatial resolution of the central region of the fovea is higher than that of the central region. According to the calculation of formula (23), the space function of art education APP interface under the fovea theory is defined as:

$$K(T) = \frac{d_t}{d_t + d(T)/d_0} \tag{24}$$

Among them, $d(T)$ represents the distance from the center of the sub block $T$ to the center of the art education APP interface, $d_0$ represents the distance from the edge of the art education APP interface to the center, and $d_t$ is taken as 4.1.

According to the foveal visual effect, the Root-mean-square deviation value of visual channel $(s, o)$ can be deduced:

$$M(s, o) = \frac{1}{T}\sum_{T} \xi_{s,o}(T) \cdot \frac{D_{(s,o)}(T)}{K(T)} \tag{25}$$

where, $D_{(s,o)}(T)$ represents the significance of channel $(s, o)$ in the art education APP interface.

Overlay the saliency of all channels to get the evaluation results of visual saliency of art education APP interface:

$$VT = \sum_{s=1}^{M}\sum_{o=1}^{N} \left(F_{(s,o)}(T) - \mathrm{MSE}(s, o)\right) \tag{26}$$

where, $VT$ represents the evaluation results of visual saliency of art education APP interface, $N$ represents the number of channels in the visual direction of the art education APP interface, $M$ represents the quantity of $V_{r_{s,o}}(x)$, $F_{(s,o)}(T)$ represents the significance of all channels of the art education APP interface.

## 3.2 Results Generated from the Art Education APP Interface

After the visual saliency evaluation of the art education APP interface is completed, the interactive interface of the art education APP is generated using the method in the text, as shown in Fig. 3.

**Fig. 3.** The result of the mobile art education APP interactive interface

According to the results in Fig. 3, in the art education APP interface generated by the method in the paper, the immersive roaming experience is provided for users through virtual reality technology, and the user's experience is improved through different senses such as vision and hearing.

### 3.3 Comparative Analysis

The fit of the APP interface refers to the degree to which the design and layout of the application interface match user needs and usage habits. A well fitted interface can meet users' operational needs and provide an intuitive and consistent user experience. Conversion fluency refers to the smoothness of switching, transitioning, and animation effects between various elements in the application interface. An interface with high conversion smoothness can make users feel that the switching between interface elements is natural and without stuttering, providing a smooth and comfortable user interaction experience. Therefore, fit mainly focuses on the matching of interface design, while transition smoothness emphasizes the transition effect and animation performance between interface elements, which are important indicators for evaluating and optimizing application interface design. Therefore, based on the above two indicators as the judgment content, a comparative test is designed.

In order to avoid the oneness of the experimental results, the interaction design method based on children's cognitive development, the interaction design method based on human-computer interaction technology and the interaction design method based on augmented reality and visual communication were introduced for comparison, and the fit and transition smoothness of the art education APP interface were tested. The results are as follows.

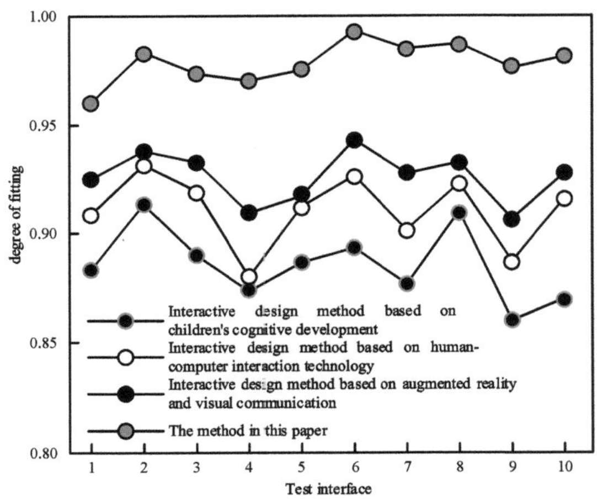


**Fig. 4.** Fit of art education APP interface

It can be seen from the results in Fig. 4 that the fitting degree of the art education APP interface is above 0.95 when using the method in the paper. However, when using the interaction design method based on children's cognitive development, the interaction design method based on human-computer interaction technology, and the interaction design method based on augmented reality and visual communication, the fitting degree of the art education APP interface is lower than 0.95, which indicates that the interaction interface generated by this method has a high fitting degree, which can provide users with a more realistic sensory experience.

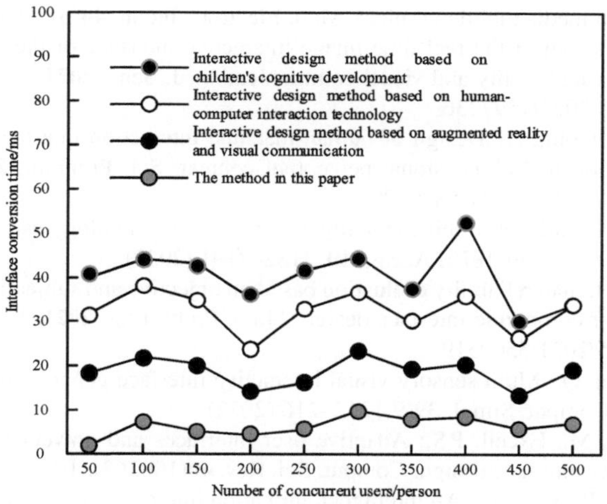


**Fig. 5.** Conversion fluency of art education APP interface

The results in Fig. 5 show that compared with the interaction design method based on children's cognitive development, the interaction design method based on human-computer interaction technology, and the interaction design method based on augmented reality and visual communication, the art education APP interface generated by the method in the text has a high transition fluency.

# 4 Conclusion

This paper proposes an interactive design method of mobile art education APP interface based on virtual reality technology. Through experimental testing, it is found that this method can generate the interactive interface of mobile art education APP, and provide users with immersive roaming experience. However, there are still many shortcomings in this research. In the future research, we hope to take into account the impact of color factors on user operation vision, so as to enhance the user experience. Meanwhile, with the continuous development and diversification of mobile devices, future research will be conducted on how to design art education APP interfaces that adapt to different screen sizes, resolutions, and operating systems, ensuring a good user experience on various devices.

## References

1. Chen, W., Haque, A., Sedig, K.: Design of interactive visualizations for next-generation ultra-large communication networks. IEEE Access **9**, 26968–26982 (2021). https://doi.org/10.1109/ACCESS.2021.3057803
2. Zhu, J., Zhao, Y.: APP interface design for preschool children based on children's cognitive development. Packag. Eng. **41**(10), 42–48 (2020)
3. Li, Y., Xie, J., Liu, B.: Application of human-computer interaction technology in interface design of digital media mobile terminal. Mod. Electron. Techn. **44**(6), 155–158 (2021)
4. Chen, Y.: Art design of the real-time image interactive interface of the advertising screen based on augmented reality and visual communication. J. Sens. **2021**, 1–12 (2021). https://doi.org/10.1155/2021/1597236
5. Jin, L., Ma, J., Gong, Z.: Design of human-machine interaction interface for autonomous vehicles based on multidimensional perceptual context. Sci. Program. **2021**, 1–8 (2021). https://doi.org/10.1155/2021/5859800
6. Zhou, Y., Hu, X.: Internet of things intelligent interaction technology using deep learning in public interaction design. IEEE Access **10**, 3182–3191 (2022)
7. Liu, X., et al.: Human reliability evaluation based on objective and subjective comprehensive method used for ergonomic interface design. Math. Probl. Eng. **2021**, 1–16 (2021). https://doi.org/10.1155/2021/5560519
8. Mei, J.Q., Chen, Q.: Multi sensory visual interactive interface generation method based on virtual reality. Comput. Simul. **39**(9), 212–216 (2022)
9. Miraz, D., Ali, M., Excell, P.S.: Adaptive user interfaces and universal usability through plasticity of user interface design. Comput. Sci. Rev. **40**(100363), 1–26 (2021)
10. Wang, Y., Han, P., Yang, B.: An intelligent animation interaction design algorithm based on example and parameterization. Comput. Intell. Neurosci. **2022**, 6017254 (2022)

# Author Index





G. Gui et al. (Eds.): eLEOT 2023, LNICST 543, p. 365, 2024.
https://doi.org/10.1007/978-3-031-51465-4

# Author Index

MIX
Papier aus verantwortungsvollen Quellen
Paper from responsible sources
FSC® C105338

If you have any concerns about our products,
you can contact us on
**ProductSafety@springernature.com**

In case Publisher is established outside the EU,
the EU authorized representative is:
**Springer Nature Customer Service Center GmbH**
**Europaplatz 3, 69115 Heidelberg, Germany**

Printed by Libri Plureos GmbH
in Hamburg, Germany